Optimality Theory

Optimality Theory
Constraint Interaction in Generative Grammar

Alan Prince

Rutgers University

Paul Smolensky

Johns Hopkins University

BLACKWELL PUBLISHING
350 Main Street, Malden, MA 02148-5020, USA
108 Cowley Road, Oxford OX4 1JF, UK
550 Swanston Street, Carlton, Victoria 3053, Australia

First published 2004 by Blackwell Publishing Ltd

Library of Congress Cataloging-in-Publication Data

Prince, Alan.
   Optimality theory : Constraint interaction in generative grammar / Alan Prince and
Paul Smolensky.
      p. cm.
   Includes bibliographical references and index.
   ISBN 1–4051–1932–2 (hardcover : alk. paper) — ISBN 1–4051–1933–0 (pbk. : alk. paper)
   1. Optimality theory (Linguistics)   2. Constraints (Linguistics)   3. Grammar,
Comparative and general—Phonology.   I. Smolensky, Paul, 1955–   II. Title.

P158.42.P75 2004
415—dc22

2004000723

A catalogue record for this title is available from the British Library.

Set in 10/12.5 pt Palatino
by Graphicraft Limited, Hong Kong
Printed and bound in the United Kingdom
by MPG Books Ltd, Bodmin, Cornwall

The publisher's policy is to use permanent paper from mills that operate a sustainable
forestry policy, and which has been manufactured from pulp processed using acid-free
and elementary chlorine-free practices. Furthermore, the publisher ensures that the text
paper and cover board used have met acceptable environmental accreditation standards.

For further information on
Blackwell Publishing, visit our website:
http://www.blackwellpublishing.com

Contents

Prefatory Note

This book derives from an informally circulated manuscript which was issued as a Technical Report by the University of Colorado Computer Science Department (CU-CS-696-95) and the Rutgers Center for Cognitive Science (RuCCS-TR-2), eventually coming to repose on the Rutgers Optimality Archive as ROA-537 (http://roa.rutgers.edu).

The current text is content-wise identical to its predecessors, with correction of as many typos, oversights, inconsistencies, and outright errors as we could track down. Footnote and example numbering has been retained. In revising the bibliography, we have tried to reconcile the twin goals of reference: to identify our sources and to provide the reader with usable modes of access to them. Those familiar with an earlier version of the text will not find new notions or notations here, but in various places a certain amount of local rewording has been attempted in the name of clarity.

The authors' names are arranged in lexicographic order.

Alan Prince
Paul Smolensky
January, 2004

Acknowledgments

Special thanks to John McCarthy for detailed discussion of virtually every issue raised here and for a fine-grained skepsis of the entire first draft; special thanks also to Junko Itô, Armin Mester, and Jaye Padgett for a valuable fine-grained review of the completed manuscript. These have resulted in innumerable improvements and would have resulted in innumerably more, were this a better world.

We wish to thank Robert Kirchner, Armin Mester, and Junko Itô for specific remarks that have had significant impact on the development of this work; John McCarthy for his comments and suggestions *in rē* chapters 7 and 9; Jane Grimshaw, Géraldine Legendre, and Bruce Tesar for much valuable discussion; as well as Vieri Samek-Lodovici, Cheryl Zoll, Henrietta Hung, Mark Hewitt, Ad Neeleman, Diana Archangeli, Henry Churchyard, Doug Pulleyblank, Moira Yip, Tom Bever, Larry Hyman, Andy Black, Mike Jordan, David Perlmutter, Lauri Karttunen, René Kager, Paul Kiparsky, Mike Kenstowicz, Ellis Visch, András Kornai, Akin Akinlabi, Clayton Lewis, Merrill Garrett, Jim Martin, Clara Levelt, Mike Mozer, Maria Bittner, Alison Prince, Dave Rumelhart, Mark Liberman, Jacques Mehler, Steve Pinker, Daniel Büring, Katharina Hartmann, Joshua Legendre Smolensky, Ray Jackendoff, Bruce Hayes, Geoff Pullum, Gyanam Mahajan, Harry van der Hulst, William Labov, Brian McHugh, Gene Buckley, Will Leben, Jaye Padgett, Loren Billings, and Fuad Isabegovic. None of these individuals can be sensibly charged with responsibility for any errors that may have crept into this work.

To Merrill Garrett (Cognitive Science, University of Arizona, Tucson) and to the organizers of the Arizona Phonology Conference we are grateful for providing in April 1991 the first public forums for the presentation of the theory, which proved a significant stimulus to the cohering thereof. We would also like to thank audiences at our 1991 LSA Summer Institute course and at the Feature Workshop there, at WCCFL 1992, at the OTS (Utrecht), the University of California at Berkeley (Phonology Laboratory), the University of Colorado at Boulder and the Boulder Connectionist Research Group, Rutgers University (New Brunswick and Piscataway), Brandeis University, the University of Pennsylvania (the

Linguistics Department and the Institute for Research in Cognitive Science), Princeton University Cognitive Science Center, Stanford University (Phonology Workshop and Parallel Distributed Processing Seminar), the University of Rochester Cognitive Science Program, and the International Computer Science Institute of Berkeley CA.

Tami Kaplan played an indispensable role in forwarding the publication arrangements with Blackwell; her energy, directness, and excellent advice have shaped the process. Ba mhaith linn buíochas ar leith a ghlacadh le Margaret Aherne, argus-eyed and Minerva-minded, whose sharpness has led to innumerable improvements in the text. And many thanks to Slavica Kochovska and Adam Cooper for their labors on the indexes and the index-text mapping.

Financial support was provided by a University of Colorado Faculty Fellowship, by research funds from Rutgers University and from the Rutgers Center for Cognitive Science, and, most crucially, by NSF SGER BNS-90 16806 without which the rigors of long-distance collaboration would have proved daunting indeed.

We remember Robert Jeffers with special appreciation for constructing the Rutgers environment that so greatly facilitated the progress of this work.

Everything is possible but not
everything is permitted . . .

– Richard Howard, "The Victor Vanquished"

"It is demonstrated," he said, "that things cannot be otherwise: for,
since everything was made for a purpose, everything is necessarily
made for the best purpose."

– Candide ou l'Optimisme, ch. I

Chapter 1

Preliminaries

1.1 Background and Overview

As originally conceived, the *RULE* of grammar was to be built from a Structural Description delimiting a class of inputs and a Structural Change specifying the operations that altered the input (e.g. Chomsky 1961). The central thrust of linguistic investigation would therefore be to explicate the system of predicates used to analyze inputs – the possible Structural Descriptions of rules – and to define the operations available for transforming inputs – the possible Structural Changes of rules. This conception has been jolted repeatedly by the discovery that the significant regularities were to be found not in input configurations, nor in the formal details of structure-deforming operations, but rather in the character of the *output* structures, which ought by rights to be nothing more than epiphenomenal. We can trace a path by which "conditions" on well-formedness start out as peripheral annotations guiding the interpretation of re-write rules, and, metamorphosing by stages into constraints on output structure, end up as the central object of linguistic study.

As the theory of representations in syntax ramified, the theory of operations dwindled in content, even to triviality and, for some, nonexistence. The parallel development in phonology and morphology has been underway for a number of years, but the outcome is perhaps less clear – both in the sense that one view has failed to predominate, and in the sense that much work is itself imperfectly articulate on crucial points. What is clear is that any serious theory of phonology must rely heavily on well-formedness constraints; where by 'serious' we mean 'committed to Universal Grammar'. What remains in dispute, or in subformal obscurity, is the character of the interaction among the posited well-formedness constraints, and, equally, the relation between such constraints and whatever derivational rules they are meant to influence. Given the pervasiveness of this unclarity, and the extent to which it impedes understanding even the most basic functioning of the grammar, it is not excessively dramatic to speak of the issues surrounding the role of well-formedness constraints as involving a kind of conceptual crisis at the center of phonological thought.

Our goal is to develop and explore a theory of the way that representational well-formedness determines the assignment of grammatical structure. We aim therefore to ratify and to extend the results of modern research on the role of constraints in phonological grammar. This body of work is so large and various as to defy concise citation, but we would like to point to such important pieces as Kisseberth 1972, Haiman 1972, Pyle 1972, Hale 1973, Sommerstein 1974, where the basic issues are recognized and addressed; to Wheeler 1981, 1988, Bach and Wheeler 1981, Broselow 1982, Dressler 1985, Singh 1987, Paradis 1988ab, Paradis & Prunet 1991, Noske 1982, Hulst 1984, Kaye & Lowenstamm 1984, Kaye, Lowenstamm, & Vergnaud 1985, Calabrese 1988, Myers 1991, Goldsmith 1991, 1993, Bird 1990, Coleman 1991, Scobbie 1991, which all represent important strands in recent work; as well as to Vennemann 1972, Hooper [Bybee] 1972, 1985, Liberman 1975, Goldsmith 1976, Liberman & Prince 1977, McCarthy 1979, McCarthy & Prince 1986, Selkirk 1980ab, 1981, Kiparsky 1981, 1982, Kaye & Lowenstamm 1981, McCarthy 1981, 1986, Lapointe & Feinstein 1982, Cairns & Feinstein 1982, Steriade 1982, Prince 1983, 1990, Kager & Visch 1984ab, Hayes 1984, Hyman 1985, Wurzel 1985, Borowsky 1986ab, Itô 1986, 1989, Mester 1986, 1992, Halle & Vergnaud 1987, Lakoff 1988, 1993, Yip 1988, Cairns 1988, Kager 1989, Visch 1989, Clements 1990, Legendre, Miyata, & Smolensky 1990bc, Mohanan 1991, 1993, Archangeli & Pulleyblank 1992, Burzio 1992ab, Itô, Kitagawa, & Mester 1992, Itô & Mester 1992 – a sample of work which offers an array of perspectives on the kinds of problems we will be concerned with – some close to, others more distant from our own, and some contributory of fundamental representational notions that will put in appearances throughout this work (for which, see the local references in the text below). Illuminating discussion of fundamental issues and an interesting interpretation of the historical development is found in Goldsmith 1990; Scobbie 1992 reviews further relevant background.

The work of Stampe 1973/79, though framed in a very different way, shares central abstract commitments with our own, particularly in its then-radical conception of substantive universality, which we will assume in a form that makes sense within our proposals. Perhaps more distantly related are chapter 9 of Chomsky & Halle 1968 and Kean 1974. The work of Wertheimer 1923, Lerdahl & Jackendoff 1983 (chs 3 and 12), Jackendoff 1983 (chs 7 and 8), 1987, 1991, though not concerned with phonology at all, provide significant conceptual antecedents in their focus on the role of preference; similarly, the proposals of Chomsky 1986, and especially 1989, 1992, though very different in implementation, have fundamental similarities with our own. Perlmutter 1971, Rizzi 1990, Bittner 1993, Legendre, Raymond, & Smolensky 1993, and Grimshaw 1993, are among works in syntax and semantics that resonate with our particular concerns.

The basic idea we will explore is that Universal Grammar (UG) consists largely of a set of constraints on representational well-formedness, out of which individual grammars are constructed. The representational system we employ, using ideas introduced into generative phonology in the 1970s and 1980s, will be rich enough to support two fundamental classes of constraints: those that assess output configurations *per se* and those responsible for maintaining the faithful preservation of underlying structures in the output. Departing from the usual view, we do not assume that the constraints in a grammar are mutually consistent, each true of the observable surface or of some level of representation or of the relation between levels of representation. On the contrary: we assert that the constraints operating in a particular language are highly conflicting and make sharply contrary claims about the well-formedness of most representations. The grammar consists of the constraints together with a general means of resolving their conflicts. We argue further that this conception is an essential prerequisite for a substantive theory of UG.

It follows that many of the conditions which define a particular grammar are, of necessity, frequently violated in the actual forms of the language. The licit analyses are those which satisfy the conflicting constraint set *as well as possible*; they constitute the optimal analyses of underlying forms. This, then, is a theory of optimality with respect to a grammatical system rather than of well-formedness with respect to isolated individual constraints.

The heart of the proposal is a means for precisely determining which analysis of an input *best satisfies* – or least violates – a set of conflicting conditions. For most inputs, it will be the case that every possible analysis violates many constraints. The grammar rates all these analyses according to how well they satisfy the whole constraint set and declares any analysis at the top of this list to be *optimal*. Such an analysis is assigned by the grammar as output to that input. The grammatically well-formed structures are exactly those that are optimal in this sense.

How does a grammar determine which analysis of a given input best satisfies a set of inconsistent well-formedness conditions? Optimality Theory relies on a conceptually simple but surprisingly rich notion of constraint interaction whereby the satisfaction of one constraint can be designated to take absolute priority over the satisfaction of another. The means that a grammar uses to resolve conflicts is to rank constraints in a *strict domination hierarchy*. Each constraint has absolute priority over all the constraints lower in the hierarchy.

Such prioritizing is in fact found with surprising frequency in the literature, typically as a subsidiary remark in the presentation of complex constraints.[1] We will show that once the notion of constraint-precedence is brought in from the periphery and foregrounded, it reveals itself to be of remarkably wide generality, the formal engine driving many grammatical interactions. It will follow that much that has been attributed to narrowly specific constructional rules or to highly particularized conditions is actually the responsibility of very general well-formedness constraints. In addition, a diversity of effects, previously understood in terms of the triggering or blocking of rules by constraints (or merely by special conditions), will be seen to emerge from constraint interaction.

---

[1] One work that uses ranking as a systematic part of the analysis is Cole 1992; thanks to Robert Kirchner for bringing this to our attention.

Although we do not draw on the formal tools of connectionism in constructing Optimality Theory, we will establish a high-level conceptual rapport between the mode of functioning of grammars and that of certain kinds of connectionist networks: what Smolensky (1983, 1986) has called 'Harmony maximization', the passage to an output state with the maximal attainable consistency between constraints bearing on a given input, where the level of consistency is determined exactly by a measure derived from statistical physics. The degree to which a possible analysis of an input satisfies a set of conflicting well-formedness constraints will be referred to as the *Harmony* of that analysis. We thereby respect the absoluteness of the term 'well-formed', avoiding terminological confusion and at the same time emphasizing the abstract relation between Optimality Theory and Harmony-theoretic network analysis. In these terms, a grammar is precisely a means of determining which of a pair of structural descriptions is more *harmonic*. Via pair-wise comparison of alternative analyses, the grammar imposes a harmonic order on the entire set of possible analyses of a given underlying form. The actual output is the most harmonic analysis of all, the optimal one. A structural description is well-formed if and only if the grammar determines it to be an optimal analysis of the corresponding underlying form.

With an improved understanding of constraint interaction, a far more ambitious goal becomes accessible: to build individual grammars directly from universal principles of well-formedness, much as Stampe 1973/79 and Bach 1965 envisioned, in the context of rule theories, building grammars from a universal vocabulary of rules. (This is clearly impossible if we imagine that constraints or rules must be surface- or level-true and hence non-interactive.) The goal is to attain a significant increase in the predictiveness and explanatory force of grammatical theory. The conception we pursue can be stated, in its purest form, as follows: Universal Grammar provides a set of highly general constraints. These often conflicting constraints are *all* operative in individual languages. Languages differ primarily in the way they resolve the conflicts: in how they rank these universal constraints in strict domination hierarchies that determine the circumstances under which constraints are violated. A language-particular grammar *is* a means of resolving the conflicts among universal constraints.

On this view, Universal Grammar provides not only the formal mechanisms for constructing particular grammars, but also the very substance that grammars are built from. Although we shall be entirely concerned in this work with phonology and morphology, we note the implications for syntax and semantics.

1.2 Optimality

The standard phonological rule aims to encode grammatical generalizations in this format:

(1)   A → B / C—D

The rule scans potential inputs for structures CAD and performs the change on them that is explicitly spelled out in the rule: the unit denoted by A takes on property B. For this format to be worth pursuing, there must be an interesting theory which defines the class of possible predicates CAD (Structural Descriptions) and another theory which defines the class of possible operations A → B (Structural Changes). If these theories are loose and uninformative, as indeed they have proved to be in reality, we must entertain one of two conclusions:

(i) phonology itself simply doesn't have much content, is mostly 'periphery' rather than 'core', is just a technique for data-compression, with aspirations to depth subverted by the inevitable idiosyncrasies of history and lexicon; or

(ii) the locus of explanatory action is elsewhere.

We suspect the latter.

The explanatory burden can of course be distributed quite differently than in the re-write rule theory. Suppose that the input–output relation is governed by conditions on the well-formedness of the *output*, 'markedness constraints', and by conditions asking for the *exact preservation of the input* in the output along various dimensions, 'faithfulness constraints'. In this case, the inputs falling under the influence of a constraint need share no input-specifiable structure (CAD), nor need there be a single determinate transformation (A→B) that affects them. Rather, we generate (or admit) a set of candidate outputs, perhaps by very general conditions indeed, and then we assess the candidates, seeking the one that best satisfies the relevant constraints. Many possibilities are open to contemplation, but some well-defined measure of value excludes all but the best.[2] The process can be schematically represented like this:

(2) **Structure of Optimality-Theoretic Grammar**
    (a) Gen (In_k) → $\{Out_1, Out_2, \ldots\}$
    (b) H-eval $(Out_i, 1 \leq i \leq \infty)$ → Out_{real}

The grammar must define a pairing of underlying and surface forms, ($input_i$, $output_j$). Each input is associated with a candidate set of possible analyses by the function Gen (short for 'generator'), a fixed part of Universal Grammar. In the rich representational system employed below, an output form retains its input as a subrepresentation, so that departures from faithfulness may be detected by scrutiny of output forms alone. A 'candidate' is an input–output pair, here formally encoded in what is called 'Out_i' in (2). Gen contains information about the representational primitives and their universally irrevocable relations: for example, that the node σ may dominate a node *Onset* or a node μ (implementing some

---

[2] This kind of reasoning is familiar at the level of grammar selection in the form of the Evaluation Metric (Chomsky 1951, 1965). On this view, the resources of UG define many grammars that generate the same language; the members of that set are evaluated, and the optimal grammar is the real one.

theory of syllable structure), but never vice versa. Gen will also determine such matters as whether every segment must be syllabified – we assume not, below, following McCarthy 1979 *et seq.* – and whether every node of syllable structure must dominate segmental material – again, we will assume not, following Itô 1986, 1989. The function H-eval evaluates the relative Harmony of the candidates, imposing an order on the entire set. An optimal output is at the top of the harmonic order on the candidate set; by definition, it best satisfies the constraint system. Though Gen has a role to play, the burden of explanation falls principally on the function H-eval, a construction built from well-formedness constraints, and the account of interlinguistic differences is entirely tied to the different ways the constraint-system H-eval can be put together, given UG.

H-eval must be constructible in a general way if the theory is to be worth pursuing. There are really two notions of generality involved here: general with respect to UG, and therefore cross-linguistically; and general with respect to the language at hand, and therefore across constructions, categories, descriptive generalizations, etc. These are logically independent, and success along either dimension of generality would count as an argument in favor of the optimality approach. But the strongest argument, the one that is most consonant with the work in the area, and the one that will be pursued here, breaches the distinction, seeking a formulation of H-eval that is built from maximally universal constraints which apply with maximal breadth over an entire language. It is in this set of constraints, Con, that the substantive universals revealed by the theory lie.

Optimality Theory, in common with much previous work, shifts the burden from the theory of operations (Gen) to the theory of well-formedness (H-eval). To the degree that the theory of well-formedness can be put generally, the theory will fulfill the basic goals of generative grammar. To the extent that operation-based theories cannot be so put, they must be rejected.

Among possible developments of the optimality idea, it is useful to distinguish some basic architectural variants. Perhaps nearest to the familiar derivational conceptions of grammar is what we might call 'harmonic serialism', by which Gen provides a set of candidate analyses for an input, which are harmonically evaluated; the optimal form is then fed back into Gen, which produces another set of analyses, which are then evaluated; and so on until no further improvement in representational Harmony is possible. Here Gen might mean: 'do any *one* thing: advance all candidates which differ in one respect from the input.' The Gen ⇄ H-eval loop would iterate until there was nothing left to be done or, better, until nothing that could be done would result in increased Harmony. A significant proposal of roughly this character is the *Theory of Constraints and Repair Strategies* of Paradis 1988ab, with a couple of caveats: the *constraints* involved are a set of parochial level-true phonotactic statements, rather than being universal and violable, as we insist; and the *repair strategies* are quite narrowly specifiable in terms of structural description and structural change rather than being of the general 'do-something-to-α' variety. Paradis confronts the central complexity implicit in the notion 'repair': what to do when applying a repair strategy to satisfy one constraint results in violation of another constraint (i.e. at an intermediate level of derivation). Paradis refers to such situations as 'constraint conflicts' and although these are not conflicts in our sense of the term – they cannot be, as Robert Kirchner has pointed out to us, since all of her constraints are surface- or level-true and therefore never disagree among themselves in the assessment of output well-formedness – her work is of unique importance in addressing and shedding light on fundamental complexities in the idea of well-formedness-driven rule-application. The 'persistent rule' theory of Myers 1991 can similarly be related to the notion of Harmony-governed serialism. The program for *Harmonic Phonology* in Goldsmith 1991, 1993, is even more strongly of this character; within its lexical levels, all rules are constrained to apply harmonically. Here again, however, the rules are conceived of as being pretty much of the familiar sort, *triggered* if they increase Harmony, and Harmony itself is to be defined in specifically phonotactic terms. A subtheory which is very much in the mold of harmonic serialism, using a general procedure to produce candidates, is the 'Move-x' theory of rhythmic adjustment (Prince 1983, Hayes 1991/95).[3]

A contrasting view would hold that the *Input → Output* map has no internal structure: all possible variants are produced by Gen in one step and evaluated in parallel. In the course of this work, we will see instances of both kinds of analysis, though we will focus predominantly on developing the parallel idea, finding strong support for it, as do McCarthy & Prince 1993a. Definitive adjudication between parallel and serial conceptions, not to mention hybrids of various kinds, is a challenge of considerable subtlety, as indeed the debate over the necessity of serial Move-α illustrates plentifully (e.g. Aoun 1986, Browning 1991, Chomsky 1981), and the matter can be sensibly addressed only after much well-founded analytical work and theoretical exploration.

Optimality Theory abandons two key presuppositions of earlier work. First, that grammatical theory allows individual grammars to narrowly and parochially specify the Structural Description and Structural Change of rules. In place of this is Gen, which defines for any given input a large space of candidate analyses by freely exercising the basic structural resources of the representational theory. The idea is that the desired output lies somewhere in this space, and the constraint system is strong enough to single it out. Second, Optimality Theory abandons the widely held view that constraints are language-particular statements of phonotactic truth. In its place is the assertion that the constraints of Con are universal and of very general formulation, with great potential for disagreement over the well-formedness of analyses; an individual grammar consists of a ranking of these constraints, which resolves any conflict in favor of the higher-ranked constraint. The constraints provided by Universal Grammar must be simple and general; interlinguistic differences arise from the permutations of constraint-ranking; typology is the study of the range of systems that re-ranking permits.

---

[3] An interesting variant is what we might call 'anharmonic serialism', in which Gen produces the candidate set by a nondeterministic sequence of constrained procedures ('do one thing; do another one') which are themselves not subject to harmonic evaluation. The candidate set is derived by running through every possible sequence of such actions; harmonic evaluation looks at this candidate set. To a large extent, classical Move-α theories (Chomsky 1981) work like this.

Because they are ranked, constraints are regularly violated in the grammatical forms of a language. Violability has significant consequences not only for the mechanics of description, but also for the process of theory construction: a new class of predicates becomes usable in the formal theory, with a concomitant shift in what we can think the actual generalizations are. We cannot expect the world to stay the same when we change our way of describing it.

1.3 Overall Structure of the Argument

This work falls into three parts. Part I develops the basic groundwork, theoretical and empirical, and illustrates the characteristic kinds of analytical results that can be gotten from the theory. Part II propounds a theory of universal syllable typology at two levels of idealization, drawing on and then advancing beyond various constraints introduced in Part I. The syllable structure typology provides the basis for a full-scale analysis of the rich system of prosodically conditioned alternations in the Lardil nominal paradigm. Part III begins with an investigation of the way that inventories are delimited both in UG and in particular grammars. A variety of issues are then explored which have to do with the conceptual structure of the theory and with its relation to other work along the same general lines. We conclude with an Appendix containing proofs of some theorems stated in the text proper and other material of interest.

The argument ranges over a variety of issues, problems, generalizations, and theoretical constructions. Some are treated rapidly, with the aim of extracting a general point, others are pursued in detail; sometimes the treatment is informal, at other times it is necessary to formalize carefully so that nonobvious results can be established by explicit proof. We have tried to segregate and modularize as much as possible, but the reader should feel free on first reading to tunnel through bits that do not appeal: the formalist can surely find another formal patch up ahead, the connoisseur of generalizations another generalization. We have tried to sign-post the way in the text.

If the reader's interest is piqued by the present contents, the following works, which make use of Optimality Theory in various ways and are roughly contemporary with its first inklings and exposures, may be of interest (full citations may be found in the References):

Archangeli, Diana and Douglas Pulleyblank. 1992. Grounded phonology. Ms. University of Arizona, Tucson and University of British Columbia, Vancouver.

Black, H. Andrew. 1993. Constraint-ranked derivation: truncation and stem binarity in Southeastern Tepehuan. Ms. University of California, Santa Cruz.

Churchyard, Henry. 1991. Biblical Hebrew prosodic structure as the result of preference-ranked constraints. Ms. University of Texas, Austin.

Goodman, Beverley. 1993. *The integration of hierarchical features into a phonological system.* Doctoral dissertation, Cornell University, Ithaca.

Hung, Henrietta. 1992. Relativized suffixation in Choctaw: a constraint-based analysis of the verb grade system. Ms. Brandeis University.

Hung, Henrietta. 1994. *The rhythmic and prosodic organization of edge constituents*. Doctoral dissertation, Brandeis University.

Itô, Junko, Yoshihisa Kitagawa, and R. Armin Mester. 1992. Prosodic type preservation in Japanese: evidence from *zuuja-go*. SRC-92-05. Syntax Research Center, University of California, Santa Cruz.

Itô, Junko and R. Armin Mester. 1992. Weak layering and word binarity. LRC-92-09, Linguistics Research Center, University of California, Santa Cruz.

Itô, Junko and R. Armin Mester. 1993. Licensed segments and safe paths. In Carole Paradis et al., eds., *Constraint-based theories in multilinear phonology*, a special issue of *Canadian Journal of Linguistics*.

Kirchner, Robert. 1992b. *Harmonic Phonology within One Language: an analysis of Yidin^y*. MA thesis, University of Maryland, College Park.

Kirchner, Robert. 1992c. Yidin^y prosody in Harmony Theoretic Phonology. Ms. UCLA.

Legendre, Géraldine, William Raymond, and Paul Smolensky. 1993. An Optimality-Theoretic typology of case marking and grammatical voice. Berkeley Linguistics Society.

McCarthy, John. 1993. A case of surface constraint violation. In Carole Paradis et al., eds., *Constraint-based theories in multilinear phonology*, a special issue of *Canadian Journal of Linguistics*.

McCarthy, John and Alan Prince. 1993a. *Prosodic Morphology I: constraint interaction and satisfaction*. University of Massachusetts, Amherst, and Rutgers University, New Brunswick.

Mester, R. Armin. 1992. The quantitative trochee in Latin. SRC-92-06, Syntax Research Center, University of California, Santa Cruz. [1994, *Natural Language & Linguistic Theory*.]

Prince, Alan. 1990. Quantitative consequences of rhythmic organization. In Michael Ziolkowski et al., eds., *Papers from the 26th Regional Meeting of the Chicago Linguistics Society*.

Rosenthall, Sam. 1994. *The phonology of vowels and glides*. Doctoral dissertation, University of Massachusetts, Amherst.

Samek-Lodovici, Vieri. 1992a. Universal constraints and morphological gemination: a crosslinguistic study. Ms. Brandeis University.

Samek-Lodovici, Vieri. 1992b. A unified analysis of crosslinguistic morphological gemination. In *Proceedings of CONSOLE-1*.

Selkirk, Elisabeth. 1993. The prosodic structure of functional elements: affixes, clitics, and words. Handout of talk presented at Signal to Syntax Conference, Brown University.

Sherer, Tim. 1994. *Prosodic phonotactics*. Doctoral dissertation, University of Massachusetts, Amherst.

Yip, Moira. 1993a. Cantonese loanword phonology and Optimality Theory. *Journal of East Asian Linguistics*.

Yip, Moira. 1993b. Phonological constraints, optimality, and phonetic realization in Cantonese. Colloquium, University of Pennsylvania.

Zec, Draga. In preparation 1993. Coda constraints and conditions on syllable weight. Ms. Cornell University.

Zoll, Cheryl. 1992a. When syllables collide: a theory of alternating quantity. Ms. Brandeis University.

Zoll, Cheryl. 1993. Ghost consonants and optimality. In *Proceedings of the Twelfth West Coast Conference on Formal Linguistics*.

The full range of research is well represented in the extensive bibliography of McCarthy 2002. Many contributors have made their work universally available at the Rutgers Optimality Archive, http://roa.rutgers.edu. Its search facilities provide a convenient route to the main avenues of development, analysis, and controversy that Optimality Theory has led to.

Part I

Optimality and Constraint Interaction

Overview of Part I

Our first goal will be to establish that the notion of optimality is, as claimed, indispensable to grammar. In chapter 2 we will argue this point from the results of Dell and Elmedlaoui in their landmark study of syllabification in Imdlawn Tashlhiyt Berber. In the course of this argument, we will introduce the notion of constraint domination and the fundamental mechanism for computing optimality with respect to a set of constraints that have been prioritized with this notion. We then move on in chapters 3 and 4 to analyze fundamental recurrent patterns of grammatical generalization, showing that constraint domination explicates and improves on the notions of *triggering* and *blocking* that figure prominently in current linguistic discussion. We examine a number of phenomena central to prosodic theory, including (aspects of) the relation between foot structure and syllable structure; the interactions of prominence, minimality, and extrametricality; and the relation between syllable structure and the prosodic-morphological processes of edge-oriented infixation, arguing that proper understanding of constraint domination sheds new light on these phenomena. The formal theory of extrametricality is dissolved into interaction effects between independently required constraints. We conclude chapter 4 with an analysis of prosodic structure in Latin which brings together the various empirical and theoretical themes pursued in the discussion. Part I draws to a close in chapter 5 with a formal characterization of the notion 'evaluation with respect to a constraint hierarchy' and the study of some properties of constraint ranking.

Chapter 2

Optimality in Grammar: Core Syllabification in Imdlawn Tashlhiyt Berber

Here we argue that certain grammatical processes can only be properly understood as selecting the *optimal output* from among a set of possibilities, where the notion *optimal* is defined in terms of the constraints bearing on the grammatical domain at issue.

2.1 The Heart of Dell and Elmedlaoui

The Imdlawn Tashlhiyt dialect of Berber (ITB) has been the object of a series of remarkable studies by François Dell and Mohamed Elmedlaoui (Dell & Elmedlaoui 1985, 1988, 1989, 2003). Perhaps their most surprising empirical finding is that in this language any segment – consonant or vowel, obstruent or sonorant – can form the nucleus of a syllable. One regularly encounters syllables of the shape *tK, rB, xZ, wL*, for example. (Capitalization represents nucleus-hood of consonants.) The table below provides illustrative examples, with periods used to mark syllable edges.[4] The relevant instances of each nucleus type are bolded.

Dell and Elmedlaoui marshall a compelling range of evidence in support of the claimed patterns of syllabification. In addition to native speaker intuition, they adduce effects from segmental phonology (emphasis spread), intonation, versification practice, and prosodic morphology, all of which agree in respecting their syllabic analysis.

The domain of syllabification is the phonological phrase. All syllables must have onsets except when they occur in absolute phrase-initial position. There, syllables may begin with vowels, either with or without glottal striction (Dell &

---

[4] Glosses are *ratkti* 'she will remember'; *bddl* 'exchange!'; *maratgt* 'what will happen to you?'; *tftkt* 'you (2psg) suffered (pf.) a strain'; *txznt* 'you stored'; *txznakkʷ* 'she even stockpiled'; *tzmt* 'it (f.) is stifling'; *tmzḥ* 'she jested'; *trglt* 'you locked'; *ildi* 'he pulled'; *ratlult* 'you will be born'; *trba* 'she carried-on-her-back'.

Nucleus type	Example	Morphology	Reference
voiceless stop	.ra.t**K**.ti.	ra-t-kti	1985: 113
voiced stop	.b**D**.d**L**.	bddl	1988: 1
	.ma.ra.t**G**t.	ma=ra-t-g-t	1985: 113
voiceless fricative	.t**F**.t**K**t.	t-ftk-t	1985: 113
	.t**X**.z**N**t.	t-xzn-t	1985: 106
voiced fricative	.tx**Z**.nakk^{w}.	t-xzn#nakk^{w}	1985: 113
nasal	.tz**M**t.	t-zmt	1985: 112
	.t**M**.zħ.	t-mzħ	1985: 112
liquid	.t**R**.g**L**t.	t-rgl-t	1985: 106
high vowel	.il.di.	i-ldi	1985: 106
	.rat.lult.	ra-t-lul-t	1985: 108
low vowel	.t**R**.b**a**.	t-rba	1985: 106

Elmedlaoui 1985: 127 fn. 20), evidently a matter of phonetic implementation. Since any segment at all can form the nucleus of a syllable, there is massive potential ambiguity in syllabification, and even when the onset requirement is satisfied, a number of distinct syllabifications will often be potentially available. But the actual syllabification of any given string is almost always unique. Dell & Elmedlaoui discovered that assignment of nuclear status is determined by the relative sonority of the elements in the string. Thus we find the following typical contrasts:

(3)   **Sonority Effects on Nuclear Status**
    (a)   .tz**M**t. – *.t**Z**mt.   '*m* beats *z* as a nucleus'
    (b)   .rat.lult. – *.ra.t**L**.w**L**t.   '*u* beats *l* as a nucleus'

Orthography: we write *u* for the nuclear version, *w* for the marginal version of the high back vocoid, and similarly for *i* and *y*: as with every other margin/nucleus pair, we assume featural identity.

    All the structures in (3), including the ill-formed ones, are locally well-formed, composed of licit substructures. In particular, there is nothing wrong with syllables *tZ*, *tL*, or *wLt*, nor with the word-final sequence *mt* – but the more sonorous nucleus is chosen in each case. By examining the full range of such contrasts, Dell and Elmedlaoui establish the relevance of the following familiar kind of 8-point hierarchy:

(4)   **Sonority Scale**
    |Low V| > |High V| > |Liquid| > |Nasal| > |Voiced Fric.| > |Voiceless Fric.| >
    |Voiced Stop| > |Voiceless Stop|

We write |α| for the sonority or intrinsic prominence of α.

With the sonority scale in hand, Dell and Elmedlaoui then propose an iterative syllable-construction procedure that is designed to select the correct nuclei. Their algorithm can be stated in the following way, modified slightly from Dell & Elmedlaoui 1985: 111(15):

(5)   **Dell–Elmedlaoui Algorithm for Core Syllabification** (DEA)
       Build a core syllable ("CV") over each substring of the form XY, where
           X is any segment (except [*a*]), and
           Y is a matrix of features describing a step of the sonority scale.
       Start Y at the top of the sonority scale and replace it successively with the matrix of features appropriate to the next lower step of the scale.
       (Iterate from Left to Right for each fixing of the nuclear variable Y.)

Like all such procedures, the DEA is subject to the Free Element Condition (FEC: Prince 1985), which holds that rules establishing a level of prosodic structure apply only to elements that are not already supplied with the relevant structure. By the FEC, the positions analyzed by the terms X,Y must be free of syllabic affiliation. Effectively, this means that any element seized as an onset is no longer eligible to be a nucleus, and that a segment recruited to nucleate a syllable is not then available to serve as an onset.

There are other syllabification phenomena in ITB that require additional rules beyond the DEA; we will abstract away from these and focus on the sense of DEA itself.[5] We will also put aside some wrinkles in the DEA which are related to parenthesized expressions in (5) – the lack of a glide counterpart for /a/, the phrase-initial loosening of the onset requirement, and the claimed left-to-rightness of the procedure.[6]

---

[5] Not the least of these is that syllables can have codas; the DEA serves essentially to locate syllable nuclei, which requires that onsets be taken into consideration. But it is not difficult to imagine plausible extensions which lead to adjunction of codas. More subtle, perhaps, are these phenomena:

   (a)   obstruents are always nonsyllabic in the envs. #— and —#.
   (b)   sonorant C's are optionally nonsyllabic —# under certain conditions.
   (c)   the first element of a tautomorphemic geminate is never an onset.

In addition, the DEA does not completely resolve sequences /~aa~/ which, according to other sources, surface as ~*aya*~ (Guerssel 1986). The appropriate approach to epenthetic structure within Optimality Theory involves the constraint FILL, which makes its appearance below in §3.1 and receives full discussion in ch. 6.

[6] We deal with the fact that [a] cannot occupy syllable margins in §8.1.1. The commonly encountered relaxation of the onset requirement in initial position is resolved in McCarthy & Prince 1993a in terms of constraint interaction, preserving the generality of the onset-requiring constraint ONS. Dell & Elmedlaoui are themselves somewhat ambivalent about the need for directionality (Dell & Elmedlaoui 1985: 108); they suggest that "the requirement [of directionality] is not concerned with left to right ordering *per se*, but rather with favoring applications of [the DEA] that maximize the sonority differences between [onset and nucleus]" (Dell & Elmedlaoui 1985: 127, fn. 22). In addition, they note that directionality falsely predicts ***.*i.tBd.rin.* from

The DEA is a rule, or rather a schema for rules, of exactly the classical type A → B / C—D. Each rule generated by the schema has a Structural Description specified in featural terms and a Structural Change ('construct a core syllable'). To see how it works, consider the following derivations:

(6) **DEA in Action**

Steps of the DEA		/ratlult/ 'you will be born'
Seek [X][+low,−cns]	*& Build*	(**ra**)tlult
Seek [X][−low,−cns]	*& Build*	(ra)t(**lu**)lt
Seek [X][+cns,+son,−nas]		*– blocked by FEC –*
Seek [X][+cns,+son,+nas]		—
Seek [X][−son, +cnt,+voi]		—
Seek [X][−son, +cnt,−voi]		—
Seek [X][−son,−cnt,+voi]		—
Seek [X][−son,−cnt,−voi]	*& Build*	(ra)t(lu)(**lT**)[7]

(7) **DEA in Action**

Steps of the DEA		/txznt/ 'you sg. stored'
Seek [X][+low,−cns]		—
Seek [X][−low,−cns]		—
Seek [X][+cns,+son,−nas]		—
Seek [X][+cns,+son,+nas]	*& Build*	tx(**zN**)t
Seek [X][−son,+cnt,+voi]		*– blocked by FEC –*
Seek [X][−son,+cnt,−voi]	*& Build*	(**tX**)(zN)t
Seek [X][−son,−cnt,+voi]		—
Seek [X][−son,−cnt,−voi]		*– blocked by FEC –*

/i=t-!bdri-n/ 'for the cockroaches', whereas the only licit syllabification is *.it.bD.rin*. The reason for this syllabification is not understood. A directionless theory leaves such cases open for further principles to decide.

[7] We show the form predicted by the DEA. The form is actually pronounced .rat.**lu**lt. because obstruents cannot be nuclear next to phrase boundaries, as mentioned in fn. 5.

(8)   **DEA in Action**

Steps of the DEA	/txznas/ 'she stored for him'
Seek [X][+low,−cns] *& Build*	txz(**na**)s
Seek [X][−low,−cns]	—
Seek [X][+cns,+son,−nas]	—
Seek [X][+cns,+son,+nas]	*– blocked by FEC –*
Seek [X][−son,+cnt,+voi] *& Build*	t(**xZ**)(na)s
Seek [X][−son,+cnt,−voi]	*– blocked by FEC –*
Seek [X][−son,−cnt,+voi]	—
Seek [X][−son,−cnt,−voi]	—

The DEA provides an elegant and straightforward account of the selection of syllable nuclei in the language. But it suffers from the formal arbitrariness characteristic of re-writing rules when they are put to the task of dealing locally with problems that fall under general principles, particularly principles of output shape. (By 'formal arbitrariness', we mean that a formal system rich enough to allow expression of the desired rule will also allow expression of many undesired variations of the rule, so that the rule itself appears to be an arbitrary random choice among the universe of possibilities.) The key to the success of the DEA is the way that the variable Y scans the input, starting at the top of the sonority scale and descending it step by step as the iterative process unfolds. We must ask, why start at the top? why *descend* the scale? why not use it in some more elaborate or context-dependent fashion? why apply the scale to the nucleus rather than the onset?[8]

The answers are to be found in the theory of syllable structure markedness, which is part of Universal Grammar. The more sonorous a segment is, the more satisfactory it is as a nucleus. Conversely, a nucleus is more satisfactory to the degree that it contains a more sonorous segment. It is clear that the DEA is designed to produce syllables with optimal nuclei; to ensure that the syllables it forms are the most *harmonic* that are available, to use the term introduced in chapter 1. Dell and Elmedlaoui clearly understand the role of sonority in choosing between competing analyses of a given input string; they write:

> When a string ...PQ... could conceivably be syllabified as ...Pq... or as ...pQ... (i.e. when either syllabification would involve only syllable types which, when taken

---

[8] These are exactly the sort of questions that were fruitfully asked, for example, of the Transformational Grammar rule of Passive that moved subject and object, inserted auxiliaries, and formed a PP: why does the post-verbal NP move *up* not *down*? why does the subject NP move at all? why is *by*+NP a PP located in a PP position? and so on.

individually, are possible in ITB), the only syllabification allowed by ITB is the one that takes as a syllabic peak the more sonorous of the two segments. (Dell & Elmedlaoui 1985: 109)

But if phonology is couched in re-writing rules, this insight cannot be cashed in as part of the function that assigns structural analyses. It remains formally inert. Dell and Elmedlaoui refer to it as an "empirical observation," emphasizing its extra-grammatical status.

The DEA itself makes no contact with any principles of well-formedness; it merely scans the input for certain specific configurations, and acts when it finds them. That it descends the sonority scale, for example, can have no formal explanation. But the insight behind the DEA can be made active if we re-conceive the process of syllabification as one of choosing the optimal output from among the possible analyses rather than algorithmic structure-building. Let us first suppose, with Dell and Elmedlaoui, that the process of syllabification is serial, affecting one syllable at a time (thus, that it operates like Move-α, or more exactly, Move-x of grid theory). At each stage of the process, let all possible single syllabic augmentations of the input be presented for evaluation. This set of candidates is evaluated by principles of syllable well-formedness and the most harmonic structure in the set is selected as the output. We can state the process informally as follows:

(9)   **Serial Harmonic Syllabification (informal)**
Form the optimal syllable in the domain.
Iterate until nothing more can be done.

This approach depends directly on the principles of well-formedness which define the notion 'optimal'. No instructions are issued to the construction process to contemplate only one featurally specified niche of the sonority scale. The Harmonic Syllabification algorithm has no access to any information at all about absolute sonority level or the specific featural composition of vowels, which are essential to the DEA. It needs to know only whether segment α is *more* sonorous than segment β, not what their sonorities or features actually are. All possibilities are entertained simultaneously and the choice among them is made on grounds of general principle. That you start at the top of the scale, that you descend the scale rather than ascending it or touring it in some more interesting fashion, all this follows from the universal principles that define the relative Harmony of nucleus-segment pairings. The formal arbitrariness of the DEA syllable-constructing procedure disappears because the procedure itself ('make a syllable') has been stripped of intricacies.[9]

This is an instance of Harmony-increasing processing (Smolensky 1983, 1986; Goldsmith 1991, 1993). The general rubric is this:

---

[9] Further development of this idea could eliminate complications at the level of the general theory; in particular, the appearance of obeying the Free Element Condition during serial building of structure could be seen to follow from the fact that disobeying it inevitably decrements the Harmony of the representation.

(10)   **Harmonic Processing**
Go to the most harmonic available state.

We speak not of 'relative well-formedness' but rather of *relative Harmony*: Harmony is a well-formedness scale along which a maximal-Harmony structure is well-formed and all other structures are ill-formed.

We conclude that the Dell–Elmedlaoui results establish clearly that harmonic processing is a grammatical mechanism, and that optimality-based analysis gives results in complex cases. Let us now establish a formal platform that can support this finding.

2.2   Optimality Theory

What, then, is the *optimal* syllable that Harmonic Syllabification seeks? In the core process that we are focusing on, two constraints are at play, one ensuring onsets, the other evaluating nuclei. The onset constraint can be stated like this (Itô 1986, 1989):

(11)   **The Onset Constraint (Ons)**
Syllables must have onsets (except phrase-initially).

As promised, we are not going to explicate the parenthesized caveat, which is an interaction effect, not part of the actual UG constraint (see McCarthy & Prince 1993a: §4).

The constraint on nuclei looks like this:[10]

(12)   **The Nuclear Harmony Constraint (Hnuc)**
A higher sonority nucleus is more harmonic than one of lower sonority.
I.e. If $|x| > |y|$ then $\text{Nuc}/x > \text{Nuc}/y$.

The formalizing restatement appended to the constraint uses some notation that will prove useful.

For *x is more harmonic than y* we write $x > y$.
For *the intrinsic prominence of x* we write $|x|$.
A/x means *x belongs to category A, x is the constituent-structure child of A*.

---

[10] It is also possible to conceive of the operative constraint in a kind of 'contrapositive' manner. Because all underlying segments of ITB are parsed, a segment is a nucleus iff it is not a member of the syllable margin. Consequently, negative constraints identifying the badness of syllable margins can have the same effect as positive constraints identifying the goodness of nuclei. We investigate this approach below in §8.1.1, §8.3.3, §4.4.2. This gives fresh content to the question raised above (p. 18) as to why (now, whether) the determinative sonority constraint applies to the onset or the nucleus.

are distinguished notationally to emphasize their
ants of high sonority are not intrinsically more har-
rity. It is only when sonority is contemplated in a
e of well-formedness arises.

t only the relevant constraints, but also the set of
do this we need to spell out the function Gen that
range of structurings or parses of the input. In the
ing roughly like this:

(partial) syllabifications of *input*ᵢ which differ from
one syllabic adjunction.

go Serial Harmonic Syllabification, the candidate set
with respect to the constraints Ons and Hnuc. There
lation were simply a matter of choosing the candid-
aints. Crucially, and typically, this straightforward
approach cannot work. conflict between the constraints Ons and Hnuc is unavoidable; there are candidate sets in which no candidate satisfies both constraints.

Consider, for example, the syllabification of the form /ħaul-tn/ 'make them
(m.) plentiful' (Dell & Elmedlaoui 1985: 110). Both Ons and Hnuc agree that the
core syllable *ħa* should be formed: it has an onset as well as the best possible
nucleus. Similarly, we must have a final syllable *tN*. But what of the rest of the
string? In the ultimate output, we have two monosyllabic choices for the sequence
/ul/: a superior nucleus lacking an onset, as in $(ul)_\sigma$; or an onetted syllable with
an inferior nucleus, as in $(wL)_\sigma$. This contrast shows up in the course of serial
syllabification at the point where the disposition of input /u/ first comes into
question: shall it be a nucleus or an onset? At this intermediate stage of derivation,
in which syllabification is as yet incomplete, the choice will be between open syllables involving /u/ – either $(wL)_\sigma$ or $(u)_\sigma$. Any such situation can be perspicuously
displayed in tabular form:[11]

(14)   **Constraint Conflict**

Candidates /ħaul-tn/	Ons	Hnuc
~ $(w\mathbf{L})_\sigma$~		|l|
~ $(\mathbf{u})_\sigma$l~	*	|u|

We write '~' to abbreviate portions of the candidates which are irrelevant to the
comparison in virtue of being identical in the two alternatives under consideration.

---

[11] The second candidate would surface as .ħa.ul.tN., the stray *l* being adjoined as a coda to the
preceding nucleus in a further round of syllabic adjunction. Observe that the bisyllabic analysis
of /ul/ as .u.L. will not be optimal since it incurs the same Ons violation as .ul. at *u*, plus one
more at .L. Further details of the serial conception of syllabification are taken up in fn. 47, ch. 5.

The cells contain information about how each candidate fares on the relevant constraint. A blank cell indicates that the constraint is satisfied; a star indicates violation. In the case of a scalar constraint like Hnuc we mention the contents of the evaluated element. The first form succeeds on Ons, while the second form violates the constraint. The relative performance is exactly the opposite on Hnuc: because |u| > |l|, the second, onsetless form has the better nucleus. The final output is, of course, .ħa.wL.tN. The onset requirement, in short, takes priority.

Such conflict is ubiquitous, and to deal with it, we propose that a relation of *domination*, or priority-ranking, can be specified to hold between constraints. When we say that one constraint *dominates* another, we mean that when they disagree on the relative status of a pair of candidates, the dominating constraint makes the decision. If the dominating constraint does not decide between the candidates – as when both satisfy or both violate the constraint equally – then the comparison is passed to the subordinate constraint. (In the case of a more extensive hierarchy, the same method of evaluation can be applied repeatedly.)

In the case at hand, it is clear that Ons must dominate Hnuc. The top priority is to provide syllables with onsets; the relative Harmony of nuclei is a subordinate concern whose force is felt only when the Ons issue is out of the way. We will write this relation as Ons ≫ Hnuc. Given such a hierarchy, an optimality calculation can be usefully presented in an augmented version of display (14) that we will call a *constraint tableau*:

(15) **Constraint Tableau** for partial comparison of candidates from /ħaultn/

Candidates	Ons	Hnuc
☞ ~ (wL)$_\sigma$~		|l|
~ (u)$_\sigma$l~	* !	|u|

Constraints are arrayed across the top of the tableau in domination order. As above, constraint violations are recorded with the *mark* *, and blankness indicates total success on the constraint. These are the theoretically important conventions; in addition, there is some clarificatory typography. The symbol ☞ draws the eye to the optimal candidate; the sign ! marks the *crucial* failure for each suboptimal candidate, the exact point where it loses out to other candidates. In each row, cells are shaded below the point of decision on the fate of the candidate. For the case at hand, the contest is decided by the dominant constraint Ons; Hnuc plays no role in the comparison of .u.l and .wL. Hnuc is literally irrelevant to this particular evaluation, as a consequence of its dominated position – and to emphasize this, we shade its cells. Of course, Hnuc is not irrelevant to the analysis of *every* input; but a precondition for relevance is that there be a set of candidates that tie on Ons, all violating it to the same extent.

If we were to reverse the domination ranking of the two constraints, the predicted outcome would change: now .u.l would be superior to .wL. by virtue of its relative success on Hnuc, and the Ons criterion would be submerged. Because of this, the ranking O_{NS} ≫ H_{NUC} is *crucial*; it must obtain in the grammar of Berber if the actual language is to be generated.

The notion of domination shows up from time to time in one form or another in the literature, sometimes informally, sometimes as a clause clarifying how a set of constraints is to be interpreted. For example, Dell and Elmedlaoui write, "The prohibition of hiatus . . . *overrides*" the nuclear sonority comparison (Dell & Elmedlaoui 1985: 109, emphasis added). For them, this is an extra-grammatical observation, with the real work done by the Structural Descriptions provided by the DEA and the ordering of application of the subrules. Obviously, though, the insight is clearly present. Our claim is that the notion of domination, or 'over-riding', is the truly fundamental one. What deserves extra-grammatical status is the machinery for constructing elaborately specific Structural Descriptions and modes of rule application.

To see how Serial Harmonic Syllabification (9) proceeds, let us examine the first stage of syllabifying the input /txznt/ 'you (sg.) stored (pf.)'. It is evident that the first syllable constructed must be .zN. – it has an onset, and has the highest sonority nucleus available, so no competing candidate can surpass or even equal it. A more discursive examination of possibilities might be valuable; the larger-scale comparisons are laid out in the constraint tableau below.

Here are some leading candidates that illustrate the first round of the process:

(16)   **Constraint Tableau for Serial Syllabification** of /txznt/ (partial, first step)

Candidates	O_{NS}	H_{NUC}	Comments
☞ tx(z**N**)t		n	optimal: onsetted, best available nucleus
txz(**N**)t	* !	n	no onset, H_{NUC} irrelevant
t(x**Z**)nt		z !	|z| < |n|
(t**X**)znt		x !	|x| < |n|
txz(n**T**)		t !	|t| < |n|

Syllabic parsing is conceived here as a step-by-step serial process, just as in the DEA. A candidate set is generated, each produced by what is defined to be a single licit change from the input; the relative status of the candidates is evaluated, yielding an optimal candidate (the output of the first step); and that output will then be subject to a variety of further single changes, generating a new candidate set to be evaluated; and so on, until there are no bettering changes to be made: the final output has then been determined.

This step-by-step Harmony evaluation is not intrinsic to the method of evaluation, though, and, in the more general context, when we discard the restricted notion of Gen in (13), it proves necessary to extend the procedure so that it is capable of evaluating entire parsed strings, and not just single (new) units of analysis. To do this, we apply the same sort of reasoning used to define domination, but *within* the constraint categories. To proceed by example, consider the analysis of /txznt/ taking for candidates all syllabified strings. We present a sampling of the candidate space.

(17)   **Parallel Analysis of Complete Syllabification** of /txznt/

Candidates	Ons	Hnuc		Comments
☞ .tX.zNt.		n	x	optimal
.Tx.zNt.		n	t !	$|n| = |n|, |t| < |x|$
.tXz.nT.		x !	t	$|x| < |n|$, t irrelevant
.txZ.Nt.	* !	n	z	Hnuc irrelevant
.T.X.Z.N.T.	* ! ***	n z x t t		Hnuc irrelevant

In evaluating the candidates we have kept to the specific assumptions mentioned above: the onset requirement is suspended phrase-initially, and the nonnuclear status of peripheral obstruents is, as in the DEA itself, put aside (see fn. 5).

In this tableau, all the relevant information for harmonic evaluation of the parse of the whole string is present. We start by examining the first column, corresponding to the dominant constraint Ons. Only the candidates which fare best on this constraint survive for further consideration. The first three candidates all have syllables with onsets; the last two do not (to varying degrees). Lack of onset in even a single non-initial syllable is immediately fatal, because of the existence of competing candidates that satisfy Ons.

The remaining three parses are not distinguished by Ons, and so Hnuc, the next constraint down the hierarchy, becomes relevant. These three parses are compared by Hnuc as follows. The most sonorous nucleus of each parse is examined: these are the most harmonic nuclei according to Hnuc. For each of the first two candidates the most sonorous nucleus is *n*. For the last candidate, the most sonorous nucleus is *x*, and it drops out of the competition since *n* is more sonorous than *x*. We are left with the first two candidates, so far tied on all comparisons. The Hnuc evaluation continues now to the next-most-harmonic nuclei, where the competition is finally settled in favor of the first candidate *.tX.zNt.* It should be clear that this candidate is truly optimal over the entire candidate set, and not just over the sampling displayed: all syllables in it have onsets, and its nuclei are the best possible, given onset priority (only *.txZ.Nt.* has better nuclei, but the onsetlessness of its second syllable is fatal).

What we have done, in essence, is to replace the iterative procedure (act/ evaluate, act/evaluate, . . .) with a recursive scheme: collect the results of all possible actions, then sort recursively. Rather than producing and pruning a candidate set at each step of sequential processing, striving to select at each step the action which will take us eventually to the correct output, the whole set of possible parses is defined and harmonically evaluated. The correct output is the candidate whose complete structure best satisfies the constraint hierarchy. And 'best satisfies' can be recursively defined by descending the hierarchy, discarding all but the best possibilities according to each constraint before moving on to consider lower-ranked constraints.

The great majority of analyses presented here will use the parallel method of evaluation. A distinctive prediction of the parallel approach is that there can be significant interactions of the top-down variety between aspects of structure that are present in the final parse. In chapters 3, 4, and 7 we will see a number of cases where this is borne out, so that parallelism is demonstrably crucial; further evidence is presented in McCarthy & Prince 1993a. 'Harmonic serialism' is worthy of exploration as well, and many hybrid theories can and should be imagined; but we will have little more to say about it. (But see fn. 49 below on Berber syllabification.)

The notion of parallel analysis of complete parses in the discussion of constraint tableau (17) is the crucial technical idea on which many of our arguments will rest. It is a means for determining the relative harmonies of entire candidate parses from a set of conflicting constraints. This technique has some subtleties, and is subject to a number of variant developments, so it is worth setting out with some formal precision exactly what we have in mind. A certain level of complexity arises because there are two dimensions of structure to keep track of. On the one hand, each individual constraint typically applies to several substructures in any complete parse, generating a *set* of evaluations. (ONS, for example, examines every syllable, and there are often several of them to examine.) On the other hand, every grammar has multiple constraints, generating multiple sets of evaluations. Regulating the way these two dimensions of multiplicity interact is a key theoretical commitment.

Our proposal is that evaluation proceeds by constraint. In the case of the mini-grammar of ONS and HNUC, entire syllabifications are first compared via ONS alone, which examines each syllable for an onset; should this fail to decide the matter, the entire syllabifications are compared via HNUC alone, which examines each syllable's nucleus.

Another way to use the two constraints would be to examine each (completely parsed) candidate syllable-by-syllable, assessing each syllable on the basis of the syllabic mini-grammar. The fact that ONS dominates HNUC would then manifest itself in the Harmony assessment of each individual syllable. This is also the approach most closely tied to continuous Harmony evaluation during a step-by-step constructive derivation. Here again, we do not wish to dismiss this conception, which is surely worthy of development. Crucially, however, this is not how Harmony evaluation works in the theory we will develop and pursue (see §5.2.3.1 for further discussion).

In order to characterize harmonic comparison of candidate parses with full generality and clarity, we need to specify two things: first, a means of comparing entire candidates on the basis of a single constraint; then, a means of combining the evaluation of these constraints. The result is a general definition of *Harmonic Ordering of Forms*; this is, in its formal essence, our theory of constraint inter- action in generative grammar. It is the main topic of chapter 5.

2.3   Summary of Discussion to Date

The core syllabification of Imdlawn Tashlhiyt Berber provides a particularly clear case where the function assigning structural analyses must be based on the optimality of the output if it is to be properly founded on principle. Once the relevant principles have been moved into grammatical theory, it becomes pos- sible to undertake a radical simplification of the generative procedure that admits candidate syllable structures. The focus shifts away from the effort to construct an algorithm that assembles the correct structure piece-by-piece, an effort that we believe is doomed to severe explanatory shortcomings. Linguistic theory, prop- erly conceived, simply has little to say about such constructional algorithms, which (we claim) are no more than implementations of grammatical results in a particular computational-like framework. The main explanatory burden falls on the constraints themselves, and on the apparatus that governs their interactions.

The Berber situation is particularly interesting in that core syllabification simply cannot proceed without the intervention of *two* distinct constraints. As with other forms of prosodic organization, the most common picture is one in which the structure is built (more-or-less) bottom-up, step-by-single-step, with each step falling under the constraints appropriate to it. Taking this seriously in the syllable structure domain, this would mean, following Levin [Blevins] 1985 and ulti- mately Kahn 1976, that you first locate the nuclei – the heads of syllables; then project higher-order structure that includes the onsets; then project the structure that includes postnuclear consonantism. In ITB, however, as in many other lan- guages, the availability of nuclei depends on the choice of onsets: an early step in the derivational constructive procedure, working on a low level in the structural hierarchy, depends on later steps that deal with the higher levels. Indeed, the higher-level constraint is very much the more forceful. Technical solutions to this conundrum can be found in individual cases – Dell and Elmedlaoui's being a particularly clever one; but the theme will re-appear persistently in every domain of prosody, defying a uniform treatment in constructionist terms.

In the theory advocated here, where outputs are evaluated, we expect exactly this kind of interaction. The whole output is open to inspection; how we choose to inspect it, or how we are forced by UG to inspect it, is not determined by the course that would be taken in bottom-up construction. The potential force of a constraint is not indexed to the level of structure that it pertains to, and under certain circumstances (UG permitting or demanding), constraint domination will be invoked to give higher-level constraints absolute priority over those relevant to the design of lower structural levels.

Chapter 3

Generalization-Forms in Domination Hierarchies I
Do Something Only When: Triggering, or The Theory of Economy

Blocking and Triggering: Profuseness and Economy

Two patterns of constraint interaction appear repeatedly in modern grammatical work. The first can be informally characterized as *Do Something Only When Necessary*. Under this rubric, a process of wide formal generality, say ø →V, nevertheless applies only in special circumstances, namely those in which it is necessary for well-formedness. The default is *not to do*; the process is *triggered* by the constraint or constraints that it subserves. In operational phonology, a 'repair strategy' is exactly a process which applies only when it leads to satisfaction of otherwise-violated constraints (Singh 1987, Paradis 1988ab). Epenthesis is a typical example; it is so closely tied to syllable-structure and word-structure constraints that the process itself can be given an entirely general formulation (e.g. ø →V), with no limiting environmental restrictions, so long as it is understood to apply *only when needed*. (This notion appears in Sommerstein 1974 and is closely related to the proposals of Kisseberth 1970ab, 1972.) There is a considerable body of work on the idea, including Singh, Paradis, Prunet, Myers, McCarthy, Itô, Mester, Yip, Goldsmith, though we believe it is fair to say that no consensus emerged on how the rule–constraint interaction was to be understood; that is, how and when the rule will be triggered by the constraint(s). In syntax the notion *Do Something Only When Necessary* appears under the heading of 'movement as a last resort' or, more generally, 'Economy of Derivation' (Chomsky 1989).

The second common pattern can be characterized as *Do Something Except When Banned*. This is the original Rossian and Kisseberthian style of rule–constraint interaction, in which the constraint *blocks* the rule: front a *wh*-phrase *except when* such-and-such conditions prevail. Here the default is *to do*; the process is inhibited under narrowly specifiable conditions. In operational phonology, deletion rules are often stated this way: delete a certain vowel everywhere, *except when* it leads to ill-formed syllable-structure, stress-clash, or violations of the OCP (Obligatory Contour Principle: Kisseberth 1970ab, 1972; Hammond 1984; McCarthy 1986). This phenomenon we might call 'Profuseness of Derivation'.

Both patterns emerge from strict domination, where the basic fact of life is that a higher-ranked constraint forces violations of a lower-ranked constraint. How this looks to the operational describer depends on the character of the lower-ranked constraint. The economy or triggering class (*Do Something Only When*) emerges when the lower-ranked constraint bans some structural option; when the dominating constraint is at stake, the banned option will be taken – and only then. The profuseness or blocking class (*Do Something Except When*) emerges when the lower-ranked constraint *favors* some option – perhaps by blocking its blocking by a yet-lower-ranked constraint; now the high-ranked constraint can force rejection of the otherwise-favored option.

We now turn to the analysis of a range of interactions exhibiting the descriptive characters of Economy and Profuseness. We will see that constraint-domination theory exposes the common conceptual core of a number of different-seeming phenomena, leading to a deeper understanding of some poorly resolved issues in phonological theory and practice.

3.1   Epenthetic Structure

> Nothing ain't worth nothing, but it's free.
> – Common Misconception

To illustrate the characteristic form of the economic interaction, let us consider a pattern of epenthesis in the phonology of (Classical) Arabic. Simplifying for purposes of exposition, let us focus entirely on C-epenthesis, which supplies a glottal stop in certain environments. From an input /al-qalam+u/ 'the-pen (+nom.)', we get an output ʔalqalamu. Arabic syllables must be of the form CV(X); epenthesis ensures that the obligatory onset is present, whatever the input configuration. However, if the rule is stated with maximal generality, context-free, as ø →C, we must ask why we don't get such forms as these, which are all in fine accord with the Arabic syllable canon:

(18)   **Free Epenthesis into /al-qalamu/** (all ungrammatical)
    (a)   ʔalqaʔlamu
    (b)   ʔalqalʔamu
    (c)   ʔalqalamʔu
    (d)   ʔalqaʔlaʔmu
    (e)   ʔalqaʔlamuʔ
    (f)   ʔalqalʔamuʔ
    (g)   ʔalqalʔaʔmu

(h)   ʔalqaʔlaʔmuʔ
(i)   ʔalqalʔaʔmuʔ

Let us suppose, following Selkirk 1981, Broselow 1982, Piggott & Singh 1985, and Itô 1986, 1989 quite closely, that the site of epenthesis is an empty syllabic position that arises during the course of syllabification. The phonetic value of the epenthetic item is filled in by interpretive principles that read the output of the level of structure we are concerned with. On this view, the basic principles of syllable structure assignment already have within them all that is required to produce the correct output forms. An epenthetic structure is simply a licit syllable form that contains a substructure not motivated by the presence of a segment that it dominates. There are no additional specialized operations of repair recapitulating aspects of parsing itself; no rule "insert Onset" or the like, since that is part of what syllabification does in the first place. The candidate set of possible analyses already contains the correct output; the constraint system will locate it. We believe this is a major insight into the way grammar works.

What is called *epenthesis*, then, is a by-product of the syllable parse, which must therefore contemplate candidates that have empty structure in them. Empty structure is avoided, obviously, as indeed is anything that would lead to structural complexity in the relationship between base and surface forms. We therefore hypothesize that there is a system of constraints that deals with sources of such complexity; call these the 'faithfulness' constraints. Itô's *Prosodic Licensing*, which requires that realized segments belong to syllables, is clearly among these (Itô 1986, 1989; Goldsmith 1990; Itô & Mester 1993), as is the *Melody Integrity* of Borowsky 1986ab. Prosodic Licensing looks up from the segment, and more generally up from any node, to check that it has a parent, and an appropriate one. We will call this family of constraints by the name PARSE; several members of the family will be encountered below. (Unparsed elements are denied phonetic realization, in accord with the notion of 'Stray Erasure' familiar from McCarthy 1979, Steriade 1982, Itô 1986, 1989.) We also need the counterpart of Prosodic Licensing that looks *down* from a given node to be sure that its immediate contents are appropriate. Let's call this family of constraints FILL, the idea being that every node must be filled properly; the idea dates back to Emonds 1970.[12] In the case at hand, we are interested in syllable structure, and the constraint can be stated like this:

(19)   FILL
     Syllable positions are filled with segmental material.

---

[12] PARSE and FILL are conceived here in simple constituent structure terms. This suits the straightforwardly monotonic relation we assume throughout this work between input and output, and allows clean technical development of the leading ideas. The ideas themselves, of course, admit extension to the "feature-changing" arena, which shows other kinds of breaches of faithfulness to input forms. Generally conceived, the PARSE family militates against any kind of failure of underlying material to be structurally analyzed ('loss') and the FILL family against any kind of structure that is not strictly based on underlying material ('gain').

Arabic unmistakably exhibits the ONS constraint, which we state as follows:

(20)   **ONS**
       Every syllable has an Onset.

For concreteness, let us assume that Onset is an actual node in the syllable tree; the ONS constraint looks at structure to see whether the node σ dominates the node Onset. This provides us with the simplest formal interpretation of FILL as banning empty nodes.[13]

The function Gen produces candidates that meet these requirements:

(21)   **Assumed Syllable Structures**
       (a)   σ → (Ons) Nuc (Coda)
             'If an analysis contains a node σ, it must dominate Nuc and may dominate Ons and Coda.'
       (b)   Ons, Coda → (consonant)
             'If an analysis contains a node Ons or Coda, it may dominate a consonant.'
       (c)   Nuc → (vowel)
             'If an analysis contains a node Nuc, it may dominate a vowel.'

Any parse at all of the input string is admitted by Gen, so long as any structure in it accords with the prescriptions of (21).[14]

The constraint ONS is never violated in Arabic. FILL is violated, but only to provide onsets. This establishes the domination relation ONS ≫ FILL.

---

[13] A more general view of the matter would see FILL as a specialized member of a broad family of constraints that ban structure altogether: *STRUC. See Zoll 1992b for discussion of this notion. Constraints of the *STRUC family ensure that structure is constructed minimally: a notion useful in syntax as well as phonology, where undesirable options (move-α; nonbranching nonterminal nodes) typically involve extra structure. For example, the suggestion in Chomsky 1986: 4 that nonbranching N' (no adjunct) is disallowed, with NP directly dominating N in such cases, would be a reflex of *STRUC, as would Grimshaw's proposal that extended projections are minimal in extent (Grimshaw 1993). X'-theory then reduces entirely to the principle that a syntactic category has a head of the same category, [X] → ... [X] .... Pointless nonbranching recursion is ruled out by *STRUC, and bar-level can be projected entirely from functional information (argument, adjunct, specifier). In economy of derivation arguments, there is frequently a confound between shortness of derivation and structural complexity, since each step of the derivation typically contributes something to the structure. In the original case discussed in Chomsky 1989, we have for example a contrast between *isn't* and *doesn't be*; the presence of *DO* is a kind of FILL violation.

[14] We do not urge this as the ultimate theory of syllable structure; what is important for the argument is that the distinctions that it makes will be inevitably reflected in other theories. Other assumptions, for example those in McCarthy & Prince 1986 or Itô 1986, require technical re-formulation of FILL. See Hung 1992, Kirchner 1992bc, Samek-Lodovici 1992ab, McCarthy & Prince 1993a.

The Gen function for syllable structure should admit every conceivable structure, with every conceivable array of affiliations and empty and filled nodes. In order to retain focus on the issue at hand, let's admit every structure that allows empty onsets and empty codas, deferring till chapters 6–8 a more ambitious investigation of syllable theory.

To establish that ʔalqalamu is the optimal outcome, we offer here a sampling of the candidate set, as a basis for discussion. All forms are fully parsed syllabically.

(22) **Syllabification under Ons ≫ Fill**, fully parsed forms

	Candidates	Ons	Fill
a. ☞	.□al.qa.la.mu.		*
b.	.□al.qa□.la.mu.		** !
c.	.□al.qal.□a.mu.		** !
d.	.□al.qa□.la□.mu.		** ! *
e.	.□al.qa□.la□.mu□.		** ! **
f.	.al.qa.la.mu.	*!	

The symbol □ notates an empty position, a nonterminal node Ons, child of σ.

It is evident that any form violating Ons – e.g. candidate (f) – cannot be optimal, since there will always be competitors that meet the constraint by virtue of empty Onset nodes. Violations of Fill are therefore compelled. What then of the competition among the Fill violators? To see how this works out, and why it exactly parallels the Ons competition, it is useful to be more precise about the nature of candidate comparison, previewing the treatment of chapter 5.

The evaluation of candidates with respect to a constraint hierarchy is to be handled by a principle of Harmonic Ordering of Forms (HOF). With respect to a single constraint such as Fill, HOF works to compare two candidates by examining the *list of marks* *Fill that each incurs. The Fill-cell marked '* *' for candidate (b) denotes the mark list (*Fill, *Fill). By the very sense of constraint violation, we must have ø > (*C, . . .), meaning that it is better to satisfy a constraint C, earning the empty mark list ø, than to fail it to any degree.

When each has an empty mark list for a constraint, two competitors tie on that constraint. Comparison among candidates (a)–(e) on Ons shows this effect directly: these tie with respect to Ons, all having null Ons-mark lists. Comparing any one of them to (f) involves a comparison of an empty Ons-mark list with (f)'s non-empty mark list, (*Ons). When only one of two compared mark lists is empty, the better form has been found – the one with an empty list. This is exemplified under Ons in the relation between the failed faithful candidate (f) and each of its competitors.

When both mark lists are non-empty, as in comparisons among candidates (a)–(e) on the constraint Fill, a further calculation must be performed. We throw away the first mark – the 'First Member' – of each list. If one of the lists is thereby emptied, we are done: the candidate with the null list is superior, as always. This is what happens in comparison between (a) and any of (b)–(e) over FILL. If both lists should still contain marks after deleting the First Member of each, as in the comparison of (c) and (d), we simply repeat the discarding procedure until it empties one or both of the mark lists. (The very same process of matching and elimination also defines the relation between constraints in a hierarchy; at this level, the 'First Member' corresponds to the highest-ranked constraint. See chapter 5 for development.)

It follows that a competitor with the fewest violations will win the comparison over a single constraint. In the case at hand, victory on FILL will be awarded to *ʔalqalamu* and only *ʔalqalamu*, among all possible well-onsetted candidates.

At this point, it might be objected that we have introduced *counting* into the reckoning of optimality, contrary to our explicit assertion above. HOF does not count, however – *not even to one*. To see this, observe that no effect can ever be arranged to occur if and only if there is exactly one violation of a certain constraint. (Why? Suppose that we altered the constraint so as to add one additional violation to every candidate it assesses. The HOF is completely unaffected, and the theory operates exactly as before, even though the candidates with exactly one violation have all changed.) HOF merely distinguishes more from less, presence from absence, something from nothing, the empty set from all others. In particular, HOF can never determine the absolute number of violations; that is, *count* them.[15] HOF deals not in quantities but in comparisons, and establishes only relative rankings, not positions on any fixed absolute scale.[16]

This method of evaluation leads to an important result, worthy of separate statement.

(23)   **Economy Property of Optimality Theory**
       Banned options are available only to avoid violations of higher-ranked constraints and can only be used *minimally*.

In constraint-domination grammars, the 'economy of derivation' pattern emerges because violations are always minimized.

Since we have ranked ONS above FILL for one particular language, it is reasonable to ask what happens when the ranking is reversed, with FILL ≫ ONS. In this situation, any violation of FILL will rule a candidate out; so the ONS constraint must simply give way when there is no consonant around to fill the Onset node. We will have, for example, .a.>.□a., the onsetless syllable rated as better than one

---

[15] There is a parallel here to the analysis of Imdlawn Tashlhiyt Berber nucleus choice in the conception of ch. 2, where evaluation never knows what features are involved, just whether a candidate nucleus is more or less harmonic than its competitors. In §§8.1.1, 8.3.3, 8.4.2 below we show how to treat the ITB system in a strictly mark-sensitive way, in full accord with the HOF as described here.

[16] The same is of course true of the misnamed 'feature-counting' evaluation metric, which was hypothesized to select the optimal *grammar* from among a candidate set of grammars.

that is onset-containing by virtue of empty structure. This gives us a different type of language, but still a natural language, and shows that re-ranking of constraints yields a typology of admissible systems. The set of all possible rankings generates what we can call a *factorial typology* of the domain to which the constraints are relevant. Below in chapter 6 we explore a factorial typology of syllable structure, based on the interaction of FILL, PARSE, ONS, and other relevant constraints.[17]

3.2   The Failure of Bottom-Up Constructionism

> . . . piled buildung supra buildung pon the banks for the livers
> by the Soangso.
> – Finnegans Wake, 4

Tongan, a language of the Pacific, shows an interaction between stress and syllable structure which raises interesting issues for prosodic theory. Poser 1985, following Churchward 1953, provides the original generative discussion. Mester 1991, improving on Poser, proposes a line of analysis that can be illuminatingly pursued within constraint domination theory.

Syllables in Tongan are always open, and all heavy syllables are stressed. Since there are no syllable-closing consonants, the weight contrast is necessarily based on the distinction between short vowels (V) and long vowels or diphthongs (VV). Main-stress falls on the penultimate mora (V) of the word. This suggests that the pattern is established by bimoraic trochees, with a right-to-left directionality.

Prosodic systems of this sort inevitably face a conflict between the demands of syllabification and the demands of foot structure. Unless other constraints impinge, any sequence CVV is optimally syllabified as .CVV., avoiding a violation

---

[17] To complete the argument about epenthesis, we must consider a larger range of candidates than we have examined so far. In particular, Gen freely admits analyses in which segments are left out of syllable structure, and these analyses must be disposed of. Such 'underparsing' analyses violate the constraint PARSE. As will be shown in ch. 6, the domination relation PARSE≫FILL eliminates them. To preview, observe that underparsing can lead to satisfaction of ONS, as in output ⟨V⟩.CV. from input /VCV/. (We write ⟨X⟩ for stray X with no parent node.) With ONS out of the way, PARSE and FILL are brought into direct conflict, resolved in Arabic in favor of PARSE (nothing left out), as the following tableau illustrates:

Candidates	ONS	PARSE	FILL
☞ .□V.CV.			*
⟨V⟩.CV.		* !	

(The dotted vertical line indicates that ONS and PARSE are not crucially ranked with respect to each other.) The investigation in ch. 6 of the ONS–PARSE–FILL ranking typology resolves issues of exactly this character.

of ONs. But if footing is to start immediately at the right edge of the word, forms /~CVVCV/ would have to suffer splitting of the VV sequence in two, yielding .CV.(V.CV)#. In many familiar languages, e.g. Latin (Hayes 1987), the foot-parse begins one mora over in such forms, yielding ~(.CVV).CV., where the last foot does not sit at the right edge of the word. Stress settles on the penultimate *syllable* and therefore (prominence falling on the peak thereof) on the *ante*penultimate mora. This effect has been charged to a Principle of Syllabic Integrity (Prince 1976), which holds that foot-parsing may not dissect syllables.

Tongan, however, requires strict penultimacy of main-stress, and syllabification is not allowed to stand in its way. The word /maːma/ 'world' is parsed *ma.á.ma* not **máː.ma*. Churchward provides the useful contrast *húː* 'go in' (monosyllabic) versus *hu.ú.fi* 'open officially' (trisyllabic), both involving the stem /huː/. Mester observes that the *last* foot must be strictly final, with exact coincidence of foot-edge and word-edge. He proposes a rule he calls Edge-Foot which builds a foot at the right edge, disturbing syllable structure if necessary. Mester notes that although the *rule* of Edge-Foot violates Syllabic Integrity in one sense, the actual output (with resyllabification) ultimately meets the constraint, since no foot edge falls in the middle of a syllable.

This apparent conundrum vanishes when the interaction is understood in terms of constraint domination. Mester's insight into strict edgemostness can be brought into direct confrontation with the principles of syllabification. Both syllabic and stress-pattern considerations will bear simultaneously on establishing the optimal prosodic parse. Two constraints are centrally involved: ONs, and something that does the work of Mester's Edge-Foot. Note that along with Edge-Foot, the system requires a statement to the effect that the last foot bears main stress: Mester calls on the End-Rule (Right) to accomplish this. We suggest that the most promising line of attack on the whole problem is to generalize the notion of *End-Rule* so that it can carry the entire burden, forcing penultimate 'breaking' as well as final prominence. Instead of demanding that prominence fall on an element in absolute edgemost position, suppose we pursue the scalar logic made usable by the present theory and demand instead that the prominence fall on the position *nearest* to the edge, comparing across candidates. In the more familiar parsing mode of #(CVV)CV#, the foot is as near to the edge as it can be while upholding the canons of syllable form, ONs in particular. In Tongan, by contrast, the heterosyllabic parse of the vowel sequence in ~CVVCV# words successfully puts the main-stress foot as far right as can be – in absolute edge position. The actual statement of the revised End-Rule is the same as before:

(24)   EDGEMOST position of head foot in word
       The most prominent foot in the word is at the right edge.

The difference is one of interpretation. We now have the means to deal with gradient or multiple violations of the constraint, in terms of a measure of distance from the edge, say syllables. Each element that intervenes between the last foot and the edge counts as a separate violation; the economy property of the theory ensures that any such violations will be minimal in all optimal forms.

For the candidate set, let us consider only those parses that are properly brack-eted. In this way Gen encodes those aspects of the Principle of Syllabic Integrity that are empirically supportable. Because syllable well-formedness gives way to the edgemostness requirement, we must have EDGEMOST ≫ ONS. Since EDGEMOST is the only foot constraint that dominates any syllabic criteria, it follows that VV sequences elsewhere in the word will never split, regardless of their position.

The comparison of alternatives runs like this:

(25) **Tongan Penultimacy**, from /huu+fi/ 'open officially'

Candidates	EDGEMOST	ONS
☞ hu.(ú.fi)	ø	*
(húu).fi	σ !	

The cells in the EDGEMOST column of the tableau indicate the degree of concord-ance with the constraint by mentioning the string intervening between the main foot and word-edge. If the order of domination is reversed, the second candidate becomes optimal and we get the more familiar pattern of stressing.

As for the observed stressing of heavy syllables throughout the word, there are a number of descriptive options. One could assume that feet are distributed throughout the word, but that (aside from main-stress) only heavy syllable foot-heads are interpreted as especially prominent, or 'stressed'. Or one could assume with Mester that feet are not assigned generally but only to heavy syllables. Or one could assume that it's not footing at all, but merely the intrinsic prominence of heavy syllables that observers of the language are reporting (Prince 1983, Hayes 1991/95). Such issues can only be decided at the level of general prosodic theory, and we leave the matter open.

It is instructive to compare the constraint-domination solution with that offered by Poser 1985 in the spirit of what we might call *Bottom-Up Constructionism*: the view that structures are literally *built by re-write rules* in a strictly bottom-up fashion, constructing layer upon layer. Poser distinguishes an initial round of syllabification, the first step of construction, from a later re-adjustment stage. At first, all VV sequences throughout the entire word are parsed as bisyllabic V.V., the idea being that moras are independent of syllables. Feet are then built on the syllables thus obtained, and main-stress is determined from the feet. When all prosodic structure has been built, there is a final round of syllabic processing (post-lexical?) in which the sequence V.V coalesces everywhere except when the second mora bears main-stress.

The analytical strategy is to build structure bottom-up and then to do such repairs as are necessary. Under this approach, the unusual word-final situation (V.V before CV#) must be extended to the entire word. This is no quirk of Poser's particular proposal; Bottom-Up Constructionism leaves little choice in the matter. If syllabification is to be done with more-or-less familiar and uniform mechan-isms, then there is no way to anticipate the specific demands of main-stressing when the syllable level is being constructed. Consequently, there will be levels of derivation in which the syllabification of words is highly marked, perhaps even impossible, with heterosyllabic sequences of identical vowels. No known phenomena of Tongan, however, are sensitive to the postulated V.V syllables.

Poser's analysis shows that Bottom-Up Constructionism is empirically inconsistent with the appealing and often-assumed idea that initial syllabification is governed by markedness considerations. By this, only the least marked options are initially available to syllabify underlying forms. Indeed, we might argue that Bottom-Up Constructionism is *antithetical* to the idea. Since the burden of establishing well-formedness falls on the later rules that function as repair strategies, it is always possible to allow great divergences from well-formedness at earlier stages. It becomes *necessary* to do so in cases like Tongan, where the generality of early rules of construction can be maintained only by letting them ignore basic markedness principles.

In the present theory, divergences from the locally unmarked state of affairs are allowed at any level of structure, but only when compelled. The Tongan ranking of EDGEMOST above syllabic Harmony promotes an alternative (V.V) that is usually suppressed, but promotes it only in those circumstances where it makes a difference. Bottom-Up Constructionism has no way to express this kind of dependency. The only relevant model of interaction is one in which two general rules happen to overlap in territory, with one re-doing part of what the other has done. Here, general coalescence corrects general syllabification. Consequently, the V.V syllabification must be portrayed as general in Tongan, and UG must be accordingly distorted to allow it as a real option that is independent of coalescence – an intolerable conclusion.

Bottom-Up Constructionism is suited to a state of affairs in which the package of constraints relevant to syllable structure completely and universally dominates the constraint-package pertaining to foot structure: SYLL-FORM ≫ FOOT-FORM. Tongan shows that this hierarchy is not, in fact, rigidly adhered to. Bimoraic trochaic footing at the end of a word necessarily entails a conflict between syllable and foot constraints in words ending Heavy-Light. Some languages resolve the conflict in favor of the syllabic constraints, using the bottom-up domination pattern; others, like Tongan, place one of the foot constraints in dominant position.[18]

We have classified the Tongan situation as an example of the 'do something only when' or triggering pattern. In the operational analysis of Mester 1991, which works bottom-up, the breaking of long penultimate vowels occurs at the level of foot-formation, "as a structure-changing imposition of the foot, violating

---

[18] This conflict can also be dealt with by unfaithful treatment of the segmental input, as in 'Trochaic Shortening', whereby underlying HL is realized as LL (Prince 1990; Hayes 1991/95). Fijian provides a clear example (Dixon 1988; Hayes 1991/95), as does the phenomenon of trisyllabic shortening in English and other languages (Prince 1990). Here a PARSE-type constraint (PARSE-μ) occupies a position inferior to FOOT-FORM in the hierarchy, so that a mora in the input will be left unparsed in order to get ~(LL)# out of /~HL/. Similar phenomena are discussed in §4.5 below and in Mester 1992.

syllable integrity" (p. 2). Local resyllabification is *triggered* by the requirement of utmost finality on the main foot; breaking is therefore a last resort.[19] We take from Mester the idea that foot-form is what's at stake, but we recognize no operation of breaking as a necessary part of the history of the optimal form. The broken parse is among the many alternatives that are always available to construe any string with a long vowel or VV sequence in it. (There is no 'violation of syllable integrity' since there is never a syllable .CVV. whose integrity could be violated.) Furthermore, we recognize no special relationship of *triggering*: there is only constraint domination. Because of the constraint Ons, which it violates, any "broken" parse is going to be suboptimal unless Ons itself is appropriately dominated. In Tongan, the dominance of EDGEMOST entails that Ons will be violated (once) in the optimal parse of certain words: those ending ~CVVCV.

Tongan provides us with our first case where it is important to have the entire structural analysis present at the time of evaluation. The imposition of prosodic requirements top-down is not an isolated peculiarity of one language, however. In prosodic systems, the main stress of a domain is often required to meet its edge-location requirements at the expense of other characteristics of the pattern. In Finnish, for example, the sequence LH – stressed light syllable followed by a heavy syllable – is generally avoided (Carlson 1978, Kiparsky 1991), but every polysyllable nevertheless begins with a bisyllabic foot, the strongest in the word, no matter what the composition of the first two syllables is. The constraint EDGEMOST is crucially involved. Anticipating the formulation of §4.1, p. 41, ex. (31), we identify it as EDGEMOST(Hd-F;Left;Wd), the member of the EDGEMOST family which requires the head foot of the prosodic word to be placed in initial position. EDGEMOST(Hd-F;Left;Wd) evidently dominates whatever prominential or foot-shape constraint is responsible for the LH effect. Among the Yupik languages, it is typically the case that the quantity sensitivity of the basic pattern is restricted to the contrast V vs. VV; but in the first foot, arguably the prosodic head, CVC will count as heavy. (On this, see Hewitt 1992: §2 for extensive discussion, though from a somewhat different point of view; and Hayes 1991/95, §6.3.8 for another perspective.) Here EDGEMOST(Hd-F;Left;Wd) dominates the constraint that limits moras to vocality; this is not unlike Tongan, in that the higher-level foot-placement constraint influences the basic interpretation of syllable structure. Similarly, it is often the case that the location of the main-stressed foot has a different directional sense from the rest of the foot pattern, a fact whose importance is emphasized in the work of Hulst 1984, 1992, which advocates top-down analysis of stress patterns in an operational framework. In Garawa, for example, the rhythmic pattern is built from bisyllabic trochees and every word begins with the main-stressed foot; but the rest of the word is organized with reference to the far end, right-to-left in iterative terms (Hayes 1980 working from Furby 1974). In Polish, also syllabic-trochaic, the principal foot lies at the end, but otherwise the pattern has a left-to-right orientation (Rubach & Booij 1985). Here again the

---

[19] Poser's analysis is configured so that coalescence is *blocked* when the second vowel of a sequence bears main-stress. Triggering and blocking are often interconvertible in this way; it all depends on what you think the ameliorative process is.

constraint EDGEMOST(Hd-F;Right;Wd), which governs main-stress distribution, dominates the constraint checking the directional uniformity of the pattern, call it SENSE(F), which is concerned with the lower hierarchical level of mere feet.[20] As we expect in the current context, reversing domination to SENSE(F) ≫ EDGEMOST(Hd-F;Right;Wd) is entirely sensible, and defines the class of languages which is in accord with the spirit of Bottom-up Constructionism.

[20] Exact formulation of the directionality-sensitive principle is a matter of interest. One tack, noted by Green 1992 *inter alia*, is to have the constraint sensitive to the location of *unfooted* material; thus a left-to-right operational iteration leaves the stray bits on the right side of the run; sometimes internally, in the case of bimoraic feet. It is also possible to deal directly with the matter and define a recursive checking procedure which is similar in spirit to the original iterative constructional conception (Howard 1973, Johnson 1972). Let there be a constraint EDGEMOST* which is just like EDGEMOST except that it operates along these lines: string α is more harmonic than string β under EDGEMOST*(F,E,D) if α is more harmonic than β under simple EDGEMOST(F,E,D); but if α and β are not distinguished by simple EDGEMOST, because the edgemost foot of α, F_α, is as well-located as the edgemost foot of β, F_β, then resume the evaluation with respect to EDGEMOST* – note recursive reference – on $\alpha\backslash F_\alpha$ and $\beta\backslash F_\beta$, where $x\backslash y$ means 'x with y removed'. This method of evaluation, which is like the Lexicographic Order on Composite Structures (LOCS) of Prince & Smolensky 1991ab, 1992, has been independently suggested by Itô, Mester, and McCarthy. Zoll 1992a offers yet another approach to directionality, in which an entire subhierarchy works across the word, in the spirit of Prince 1990. Further research is required to distinguish among these possibilities. McCarthy & Prince 1993b, generalizing EDGEMOST, obtain directionality effects parallelistically, pursuing a suggestion by Robert Kirchner.

Chapter 4

Generalization-Forms in Domination Hierarchies II
Do Something Except When: Blocking, or The Theory of Profuseness

When specific conditions limit the scope of an otherwise broadly applicable generalization, we have the second major form of constraint interaction. The operational imperative is to do something *except when* an adverse condition prevails or an adverse outcome would result. The default is to do; but there may be reasons not to do. In the literature, this is often understood as the *blocking* of a rule by a constraint; though the effect is also achieved when a later rule undoes part of what an earlier rule has accomplished, or when the Elsewhere Condition preserves the specific in the face of the general. This generalization structure emerges when a constraint that functions to encourage some easily identifiable state-of-affairs is dominated by another that can force a violation, ruling out the otherwise desired state-of-affairs in certain circumstances.

Clearly, this pattern of generalization is central to linguistic theory and appears in every branch of it. We will focus our discussion on basic elements of prosodic theory. Here are some examples of phenomena that earn the 'do something except when' interpretation:

(26) **Blocking of the Generally Applicable**
  (a) A final syllable is extrametrical *except when* it is the only syllable in the word.
  (b) A certain affix is a prefix *except when* the base is C-initial/V-initial (in which case, it is an infix).
  (c) Stress is nonfinal *except when* the final syllable is the heaviest in the word.
  (d) Rhythmic units are iambic *except when* there are only two syllables in the word.

(e)   Rhythmic units are trochaic, and never of the form LH *except when* those are the only two syllables in the word.

Explicating such patterns via constraint domination will significantly advance the understanding of such fundamentalia as prosodic minimality, extrametricality, foot-typology, as well as the sometimes subtle interactions between them.

4.1   Edge-Oriented Infixation

Infixation comes in two varieties, each a mild variant of ordinary suffixation/ prefixation, according to the typology of McCarthy & Prince 1990a. In both cases, the infix is a suffix/prefix which takes as its base not some morphological cat- egory (stem, root, etc.) but instead a phonologically defined subdomain within the morphological category.

In one type, the affix attaches to a minimal word (foot-sized unit) that lies at the edge of the morphological base. For McCarthy & Prince 1990a, the internal minimal word that forms the actual base of affixation is specified by positive Prosodic Circumscription. Thus, we find in the Nicaraguan language Ulwa that the personal possessive affixes are suffixed to the first foot, as in /kuhbil+ka/ → kuh*ka*bil 'his knife' (Hale & Lacayo Blanco 1988). Reduplicative infixation may also follow this pattern. Samoan 'partial reduplication', for example, prefixes a syllable to the last foot, giving /σ+faːgota/ → faː*go*(góta) 'fish_V pl.' (Broselow & McCarthy 1983, McCarthy & Prince 1990a, Levelt 1991).

In the other type, the affix lies near an edge; its location can be determined by subtracting something (often a consonant or vowel) from the edge and prefixing or suffixing to the remainder. Characteristic instances are displayed below:

(27)   **Tagalog Prefixal Infixation** (Schachter & Otanes 1972)
um+tawag	→ t-*um*-awag	'call (pf., actor trigger)'
um+abot	→ *um*-abot	'reach for (pf., actor trigger)'

(28)   **Pangasinán Prefixal Reduplicative Infixation** (Benton 1971)
σ+amigo	→ a-*mi*-migo	'friend/friends'
σ+libro	→ *li*-libro	'book/books'

(29)   **Chamorro Suffixal Reduplicative Infixation** (Topping 1973)
métgot+σ	→ métgo-*go*-t	'strong/very strong'
buníta+σ	→ buníta-*ta*	'pretty/very pretty'

In each of these examples, exactly one peripheral element is bypassed. For McCarthy & Prince 1990a, Prosodic Circumscription identifies the unit that is subtracted from consideration, and the morphological operation applies to the residue of the form as though to an ordinary base. Ignoring a single peripheral element is extrametricality, and Prosodic Circumscription successfully formalizes extrametricality within a generalized theory of the prosodic conditioning of rules.

This approach is beset by a serious shortcoming: it cannot explain the relation between the *shape* of the affix and the manner of its placement. Infixes that go after initial C– are common throughout Austronesian, and they always have the form VC, never CV or V or CVC. Anderson (1972) observes that just when the affix is VC, infixation after a word-initial C results in a considerably more satisfactory syllable structure than prefixation would. The VC.CV entailed by simple prefixation (*um.tawag) is abandoned in favor of CV.CV. (tu.mawag). Of course, in the theory of Anderson's day, such an observation – concerned with the relative markedness of different possible outputs – had to remain grammatically inert, and Anderson offered a 6-term transformational rule to describe the facts. Similarly, the observation plays no role in the Prosodic Circumscription account developed by McCarthy & Prince, which accordingly suffers from the same kind of formal arbitrariness diagnosed in the Dell–Elmedlaoui Algorithm. Optimality Theory, by contrast, allows us to make this insight the keystone of a significantly improved theory of edge-oriented infixation.

The relevant syllabic constraint is the one that discriminates against closed syllables: let us call it –COD and formulate it as follows:

(30)   **–COD**
    Syllables do not have codas.

Any closed syllable will violate this constraint, which (as always) we assume to be universally present in every grammar. It is often, though not always, in subordinate position in constraint rankings, dominated by faithfulness, so that a coda is forced when input like /CVC/ is faithfully parsed. (See chapter 6 below.)

We need to generalize the notion *prefix* so that it can refer to items that are only approximately in first position in the string. The standard hard-line assumption is that a *prefix* always falls completely to the left of its base. Scalar evaluation allows us to relativize the demand, using the now-familiar pattern of competition between alternatives that vary in degree of adherence to the ideal. Consider all possible affix placements: the nearer an affix lies to the left edge of the affix-base collocation, the more *prefixal* its status. The observed location of any particular affix will be that which best satisfies the entire set of constraints bearing on it, among them the requirement that it be a prefix or suffix.

The constraint needed to implement this idea is already at hand: it is EDGEMOST, familiar from the discussion of Tongan above, which we now formulate more precisely. Like the End Rule that it supplants, the predicate EDGEMOST takes several arguments. The relevant domain must be specified, as must the choice of edge (*Right*, *Left*), as must the item whose position is being evaluated. The schema for the constraint family, then, looks like this:

(31)   **EDGEMOST** (φ; E; D)
    The item φ is situated at the edge E of domain D.

Crucially, violation of EDGEMOST is reckoned in designated units of measure from the edge E, where each intervening unit counts as a separate violation. In Tongan, the constraint comes out as EDGEMOST(F';R;Wd), which asserts that the main foot (F′) must be Rightmost in the Word. For conciseness, the Domain argument will be suppressed when its content is obvious. With this in hand, we can define the two affixal categories:

(32) Dfn. **Prefix**

A *prefix* is a morpheme $\mathfrak{M}$ subject to the constraint EDGEMOST($\mathfrak{M}$; L).

(33) Dfn. **Suffix**

A *suffix* is a morpheme $\mathfrak{M}$ subject to the constraint EDGEMOST($\mathfrak{M}$; R).

Traditional prefixes or suffixes, which always appear strictly at their corresponding edges, are morphemes $\mathfrak{M}$ for which EDGEMOST($\mathfrak{M}$;L|R) dominates other conflicting constraints and thus always prevails. In the case of edge-oriented infixation, prosodic well-formedness constraints dominate EDGEMOST, forcing violations, which are minimal as always. For the Austronesian VC prefixes, the important interaction is −COD ≫ EDGEMOST(*af*;L). Consider the effects on the Tagalog prefix /um/, characterized in Schachter 1987, Schachter & Otanes 1972 as signaling 'Actor Trigger' on the verb.

Let us examine first the case of a vowel-initial base, say /abot/ 'reach for'. For purposes of this discussion, we assume that the candidate set produced by Gen will consist of all forms in which (1) the linear order of tautomorphemic segments is preserved, and (2) the segments of the affix are contiguous. We will also assume, following the view of much (though by no means all) scholarship in the area, that there are vowel-initial syllables at the level of analysis we are concerned with, even though all surface syllables have onsets, glottal stop being the default filler. The following constraint tableau lays out the results.

(34) **Analyses of /um/ + /abot/**

Candidates		−COD	EDGEMOST(*um*;L)
a. ☞	.**u**.**m**a.bot.	*	
b.	.a.**um**.bot.	* * !	#a
c.	.a.b**u**.**m**ot.	*	#ab !
d.	.a.bo.**um**t.	*	#abo !
e.	.a.bo.t**um**.	*	#abot !

The degree of violation of EDGEMOST is indicated informally by listing the string that separates *um* from the beginning of the word. The sign '#' is included merely as a visual clue. The syllabically illicit form *aboumt* would of course be defeated on other grounds as well: it is included to emphasize the generality of the candidate set.

The form *umabot* is more harmonic than any competitor. Like all the best candidates, it has one −COD violation. (It is a fact of the language that this one violation cannot be circumvented by deletion or by epenthesis; this shows that –COD is dominated by both FILL and PARSE, as detailed in chapter 6 below.) All ties on –COD are adjudicated by EDGEMOST. In the optimal form, the affix lies nearest to the beginning of the word: in this case, right *at* the beginning.

Consonant-initial bases provide the more interesting challenge. Consider the richest possible case, with an initial C-sequence, as in /um+gradwet/. (This datum is from French 1988.)

(35)   **Analyses of /um + gradwet/**

	Candidates	–COD	EDGEMOST(*um*;L)
a.	.**um**.grad.wet.	* * * !	
b.	.g**um**.rad.wet.	* * * !	#g
c. ☞	.gr**u**.**m**ad.wet.	* *	#gr
d.	.gra.**um**.dwet.	* *	#gra !
e.	.gra.d**um**.wet.	* *	#gra ! d
f.	.grad.w . . . **um** . . .	* *	#gra ! dw . . .

Again, for completeness, we include *graumdwet* as a representative of the horde of syllabically disastrous candidates – including still more hopeless contenders such as *.u.mgra.dwet.* and *.u.m.gra.dwet.* – which are all rendered suboptimal by constraints dominating –COD but of no relevance to the present discussion.

Here all the best competitors tie at two –COD violations each; these violations are due to intrinsic stem structure and cannot be evaded. Prefixing *um* to the whole base, as in (35a), or after the initial C, as in (35b), induces a third, fatal violation. Among the surviving forms, *grumadwet* wins on the grounds of superior affix position.

We have shown that certain prefixes are minimally infixed when prosodic constraints dominate the basic morphological principle of affix placement. McCarthy & Prince 1991b, 1993a, extending the present account, observe that the same explanation holds for edge-oriented *reduplicative* infixation. As an instance of suffixal σ, Chamorro *met.go-go-t.* is prosodically superior to **met.got.-got.* in that it more successfully avoids closed syllables; exactly the same reason that *t-**u**.**m**-a.wag* bests **um**.-ta.wag.

(36)   **Suffixal Reduplication under Prosodic Domination**

Candidates	–COD	EDGEMOST(σ_{aff};R)
☞ .met.go.**got**.	* *	t#
.met.got.**got**.	* * * !	

The widely attested Pangasinán type *lilibro* / *amimigo*, in which the reduplicat-ive prefix skips over an onsetless initial syllable, falls under the prosodic compul-sion account as well. Here infixation – *a.**mi**.migo* vs. **.a.amigo* – avoids the V-V hiatus which straightforward prefixation would entail (cf. McCarthy & Prince 1993a: ch. 7). The active constraint is ONS, which discriminates against onsetless syllables.

The theory has a subtle and important range of consequences, whose existence was brought to our attention by John McCarthy: *certain types of infixation can only be reduplicative*. Under prosodic forcing, no phonemically specified prefix can ever be placed after an initial onsetless syllable; the advantage of avoiding abso-lute initial position only accrues when reduplication is involved. To get a sense of this, note that under reduplication the failed candidate *aa.migo*, with pure prefixation, incurs two ONS violations, and the successful candidate *$a.mi.migo* but one. (The *ad hoc* siglum $ marks a missing Onset.) Reduplication has the unique pathology of copying an onset violation. By contrast, a fixed-content affix like (fictive) /ta/ leads to just one ONS violation wherever it is placed: pseudo-Pangasinán *ta$amigo* is not ONS-distinct from *$a.ta.migo*. Since ONS is indifferent, EDGEMOST will demand full left-placement. Since all the known cases of post-onsetless syllable infixation are in fact reduplicative, we have a striking argument in favor of the present approach. The argument applies in a kind of mirror-image or dual form to suffixal infixation as well. The Chamorro *metgogot* type can only be reduplicative. Consider, for example, the effects of placing an imaginary affix /ta/ in and around a form like *metgot*: *met.got.**ta**.*, *metgo.**tat***. All such candidates agree on the extent of –COD violation, as the reader may verify; therefore EDGEMOST(*ta*;R) compels exterior suffixation.[21] To firmly establish the claim that fixed-content morphemes cannot be forced into infixation after initial onsetless syllables or before final C, more must be done: one needs to run through all relevant affix patterns, checking the effects of contact between the edges of the affix with the base. In addition, the reduplicative pattern must be nailed down. Detailed analysis is undertaken in McCarthy & Prince 1993a: §7, to which the reader is referred.

We have, then, the beginnings of a substantive theory of infixability, a theory in which prosodic shape modulates the placement of morphemes. Edge-oriented infixation arises from the interaction of prosodic and morphological constraints. The principal effect – interior placement – comes about because Edgemostness is a gradient property, not an absolute one, and violations can be forced. It follows from the principles of the harmonic ordering of forms that violations in the output are minimal. Consequently, such infixes fall *near* the edge, as near as pos-sible given the dominant constraints. Edge-oriented infixation can be construed

---

[21] Observe that in all the cases discussed we can assume that the entire package of syllabic constraints, including both ONS and –COD, dominates the morphological conditions on affixation; one or the other member of the package turns out to be relevant depending on what the content of the affix is and whether it is a prefix or suffix. This idea figures centrally in McCarthy & Prince 1993a, where the Optimality-theoretic scheme "prosody dominates morphology" is pro-posed as the account of what makes morphology prosodic.

in the 'Do-Something-Except-When' style of descriptive language, should that prove illuminating: the affix falls at the edge *except when* a prosodic constraint can be better met inside. The theory, of course, recognizes no distinction between 'except when' and 'only when' – blocking and triggering – but deals only in the single notion of constraint domination.

The internalizing effects attributed to extrametricality follow, on this view, from constraint interaction and from the way that constraints are defined. There is no formal mechanism called Extrametricality or (negative) Prosodic Circumscription to which the analysis appeals. This suggests the general hypothesis, natural within the context of Optimality Theory, that what we call Extrametricality is no more than the name for a family of effects in which Edgemostness interacts with other prosodic constraints. We pursue this line in the following two sections as we explore more instances of the *except when* configuration, showing that key properties of extrametricality, thought to be axiomatic, follow from this re-conception.

4.2   Interaction of Weight Effects with Extrametricality

Certain varieties of Hindi/Urdu show an interaction between weight and nonfinal placement of stress which sheds further light on the interaction of gradient edgemostness and other factors operative in prosodic patterning. First, we provide some background on "unbounded" "stress" systems; then we turn to the revelatory twists of Hindi/Urdu prosody.

4.2.1   Background: Prominence-Driven Stress Systems

Stress systems typically reckon main-stress from a domain edge, often enhancing an edgemost or near-edgemost syllable or foot. There are also stress systems that call on EDGEMOST but make no use of binary structure to define the position of main word-stress: instead the additional determining factor is *syllable weight*. In the canonical cases, main-stress falls on the leftmost/rightmost heavy syllable (pick one); elsewise, lacking heavies in the word, on the leftmost/rightmost syllable (pick one). Systems like these have been called "unbounded" because the distance between the edge and the main-stress knows no principled limits and because metrical analysis has occasionally reified these unbounded spans as feet (Prince 1976, 1980; Halle & Vergnaud 1987; Hayes 1980, 1991/95). The best current understanding, however, is that what's involved is not a foot of unbounded magnitude (presumed nonexistent), but a kind of prominential enhancement that calls directly on contrasts in the intrinsic prominence of syllables. These then are prominence-driven systems, in which a word's binary rhythmic structure is decoupled from the location of main word-stress. (For discussion, see Prince 1983, 1990; Hayes 1991/95.)

Two basic constraints are involved. First, it is necessary to establish the relation between the intrinsic prominence of syllables and the kind of elevated prominence known as stress. There are a number of ideas in the literature as to how this is to be done (Prince 1983, 1990, McCarthy & Prince 1986, Davis 1988ab, Everett 1988, Zec 1988, Goldsmith & Larson 1990, Hayes 1991/95), none perhaps entirely satisfactory. Generalizing over particular representational assumptions, we can write, following essentially the 'Quantity/Prominence Homology' of McCarthy & Prince 1986 (as 1996: 11):

(37)   **Peak-Prominence** (Pk-Prom)
       Peak(x) > Peak(y) if $|x| > |y|$.

By Pk-Prom, the element x is a better peak than y if the intrinsic prominence of x is greater than that of y. This is the same as the nuclear-Harmony constraint Hnuc formulated above, which holds that higher-sonority elements make better syllable peaks.

The second relevant constraint determines the favored position of the prominence-peak or main-stress of the word. It is nothing other than the familiar Edgemostness.

(38)   **Edgemost**(pk;L|R;Word)
       A peak of prominence lies at the L|R edge of the Word.

We use 'Word' loosely to refer to any stress domain; as before, Edgemost is subject to gradient violation, determined by the distance of the designated item from the designated edge.

To see how these constraints play out, let us consider a simple prominence-driven system such as "stress the rightmost heavy syllable, else the rightmost syllable." Here we have

(39)   Pk-Prom ≫ Edgemost(pk;R)

If there are no heavy syllables in the word, the rightmost syllable faces no competition and gains the peak. The results are portrayed in the following tableau:

(40)   **Right-Oriented Prominence System**, no heavy syllables

Candidates	Pk-Prom	Edgemost(pk;R)
☞ L L L Ĺ		
L L Ĺ L		σ# !
L Ĺ L L		σσ# !
Ĺ L L L		σσσ# !

Here Pκ-Prom plays no role in the decision, since all candidates fare equally on the constraint. This kind of data provides no argument for ranking the constraints; either ranking will do. With heavy syllables in the string, the force of constraint Pκ-Prom becomes evident:

(41) **Right-Oriented Prominence System**, with heavy syllables

Candidates	Pκ-Prom	Edgemost(pk;R)
L H H Ĺ	Ĺ	
☞ L H H́ L	H́	σ#
L H́ H L	H́	σσ# !
Ĺ H H L	Ĺ !	σσσ#

With the other domination order, a strictly final main-stress location would always win. With Pκ-Prom dominant, candidates in which a heavy syllable is peak-stressed will eclipse all those where a light syllable is the peak. When several potential peaks are equivalent in weight, or in intrinsic prominence construed more generally, the decision is passed to Edgemost, and the surviving candidate containing the peak nearest the relevant edge is evaluated as optimal; exactly the generalization at hand.

4.2.2 The Interaction of Weight and Extrametricality: Kelkar's Hindi/Urdu

Certain dialects of Hindi/Urdu display an interesting variant of the prominence-driven pattern of edgemostness.[22] From the work of Kelkar 1968, Hayes (1991/95: 276–8) has constructed the following generalization:

(42) **Kelkar's Hindi/Urdu**
      "Stress falls on the heaviest available syllable, and in the event of a tie, the rightmost nonfinal candidate wins." (Hayes 1991/95: 276)

The first complication is that this variety of Hindi/Urdu recognizes three degrees of syllable weight or intrinsic prominence; hence Hayes's 'heaviest' holding the place of the usual 'heavy'. The ordering of weight classes is as follows:

[22] Judgments of stress in Hindi and Urdu are notoriously delicate and unstable, a consequence of dialectal variation and the nonobviousness of whatever events and contrasts the term 'stress' actually refers to in the language. Therefore it is essential to distinguish the observations of distinct individuals and to seek non-impressionistic support for the claims involved. Hayes (1991, as 1995: 162–3) cites work along these lines.

(43)   **Heaviness Scale**
       |CVVC, CVCC| > |CVV, CVC| > |CV|

Hayes suggests that the superheavy syllables are trimoraic, yielding the scale |μμμ| > |μμ| > |μ|. Whatever the proper interpretation may be, the heaviness scale fits directly into the constraint PK-PROM.

The effects of PK-PROM may be seen directly in forms which contain one syllable that is heavier than all others:

(44)   **Heaviest Wins**
       (a)   .ki.**d^{h}ár**.   .μ̆μ. > .μ̆.   'which way'
       (b)   .ja.**náab**.   .μ̆μμ. > .μ̆.   'sir'
       (c)   .as.**báab**.   .μ̆μμ. > .μ̆μ.   'goods'
       (d)   .ru.pi.**áa**.   .μ̆μ. > .μ̆.   'rupee'
       (e)   .**réez**.ga.rii.   .μ̆μμ. > .μ̆μ.   'small change'

(All examples here and below are from Hayes 1991/95.)

The second complication in the pattern is the avoidance of stress on final syllables. This is a very commonly encountered phenomenon in stress systems of all kinds, typically attributed to various forms of extrametricality, stress-shift, and de-stressing. We formulate the basic constraint, NONFINALITY, as follows:

(45)   **NONFINALITY**
       The prosodic head of the word does not fall on the word-final syllable.

By 'prosodic head' we mean the prosodically most prominent element, here the main-stress. NONFINALITY is quite different in character from extrametricality; it focuses on the well-formedness of the stress peak, not on the parsability of the final syllable.[23] Furthermore, it is a substantive stress-specific constraint, not a general mechanism for achieving descriptive 'invisibility' (Poser 1986).

When heaviness alone does not decide between candidates, the position of the peak is determined by the relation NONFINALITY ≫ EDGEMOST. By this, it is more important for the peak to be nonfinal than for it to be maximally near the edge. Exactly as in the simple prominence-driven systems, however, the package of positional constraints is completely dominated by the weight-measuring PK-PROM. Here are some examples illustrating the positional effects (syllables of the heaviest weight class in a word are in bold type):

---

[23] NONFINALITY does not even imply by itself that the literally last syllable is unstressed. Representational nonfinality can be achieved in the manner of Kiparsky 1992 by positing an empty metrical node or grid position (analogous to the 'silent demi-beat' of Selkirk 1984) after the final syllable within the stress domain. Use of empty structure is proposed in Giegerich 1985 and Burzio 1987 for various purposes, and is explored in Kiparsky 1992 under the name of 'catalexis', in connection with preserving Foot Binarity (q.v. inf., §§4.3.1, 4.3.2). Here we want empty metrical positions to be unavailable; clearly, they are proscribed by a constraint of the FILL family, and we will tacitly assume that this constraint is undominated in the grammars under discussion.

(46)   **Positional Adjudication among Equals**
    (a)   μ   .sa.**mí**.ti.   'committee'
    (b)   μμ   .*ru*.**káa**.yaa.   'stopped (trans.)'
                 .**pús**.*ta*.kee.   'books'
                  .roo.**záa**.naa.   'daily'
    (c)   μμμ   .**áas**.*māā*.jaah.   'highly placed'
                  .aas.**máan**.jaah.   'highly placed (var.)'

The full constraint hierarchy runs Pk-Prom ≫ Nonfinality ≫ Edgemost. The following tableaux show how evaluation proceeds over some typical examples.

(47)   **Light vs. Light**: /samiti/

Candidates	Pk-Prom	Position	
		Nonfinality	Edgemost
.sa.mi.**tí**.	.μ̗.	* !	
☞ .sa.**mí**.ti.	.μ̗.		σ#
.**sá**.mi.ti.	.μ̗.		σσ# !

The form .*sa.mí.ti.* is optimal because it has a nonfinal peak that is nearest the end of the word.

(48)   **Heavy vs. Light**: /kidʰar/

Candidates	Pk-Prom	Position	
		Nonfinality	Edgemost
☞ .ki.**dʰár**.	.μμ.	*	
.**kí**.dʰar.	.μ̗. !		σ#

The optimal form .*ki.dʰár.* violates Nonfinality, but it wins on Pk-Prom, which is superordinate.

(49)   **Heavy vs. Heavy vs. Light**: /pustakee/

Candidates	Pk-Prom	Position	
		Nonfinality	Edgemost
.pus.ta.**kée**.	.μμ.	* !	
.pus.**tá**.kee.	.μ̗. !		σ#
☞ .**pús**.ta.kee.	.μμ.		σσ#

The form *.pús.ta.kee.* is the worst violator of EDGEMOSTness among the candidates, but it bests each rival on a higher-ranked constraint.

(50) **Contest of the Superheavies**: /aasmããjaah/

Candidates	Pᴋ-Pʀᴏᴍ	Position	
		Nᴏɴғɪɴᴀʟɪᴛʏ	Eᴅɢᴇᴍᴏsᴛ
.aas.mãã.**jáah**.	΄µµµ	* !	
.aas.**mã́ã**.jaah.	΄µµ !		σ#
☞ .**áas**.mãã.jaah.	΄µµµ		σσ#

Here again, the optimal candidate is the worst violator of EDGEMOSTness, but its status is assured by success in the more important confrontations over weight and nonfinality.

The stress pattern of Kelkar's Hindi/Urdu shows that extrametricality can be 'canceled' when it interferes with other prosodic constraints. It is rarely if ever the case that final syllables are categorically extrametrical in a language; rather, prominence is nonfinal *except when* being so entails fatal violation of higher-ranked constraints. This behavior is exactly what we expect under Optimality Theory. In the familiar view, of course, such behavior is a total mystery and the source of numerous condundra, each to be resolved by special stipulation; for if extrametricality is truly a rule assigning a certain feature, there can be no explanation for why it fails to apply when its structural description is met.

4.3 Nonfinality and Nonexhaustiveness

The exclusion of *word-final syllables* from prosodic structure is the prototypical extrametricality effect. Latin provides the touchstone example, and parallels can be multiplied easily.[24] Writing the extrametricality rule to apply word-finally leads immediately to the basic quirk of the theory: *monosyllabic* content words receive stress without apparent difficulty. Since the unique syllable of the mono-syllable is indubitably final, it should by all rights be extrametrical. Why is this syllable different from all others? The following examples illustrate the situation, where ⟨ . . . ⟩ encloses the extrametrical material:

---

[24] In words of length two syllables or longer, Latin places main word-stress on the penult if it is heavy or if it is the first syllable in the word, otherwise on the antepenult. This array of facts is standardly interpreted to mean that final syllables are completely extrametrical – outside foot structure. Bimoraic trochees are applied from left to right on the residue of extrametricality; the last foot is the strongest (as in Hayes 1987).

(51) **Extrametricality in Latin**
    (a) cór⟨pus⟩   *corpús
    (b) méns   *⟨mens⟩

This state of affairs arises from an interaction exactly parallel to the one that 'revokes extrametricality' in Hindi/Urdu. NONFINALITY is simply not the *ne plus ultra* of the system; it can be violated.

The dominant, violation-forcing constraint is not far to seek. Relations must be established between the categories of morphology and those of phonology. These take the form of requirements that any member of a certain morphological category (root, stem, word) must be, or correspond to, a phonological category, typically the prosodic word *PrWd*. (See Liberman & Prince 1977; Prince 1983; McCarthy & Prince 1986, 1990a, 1991ab, 1993ab; Nespor & Vogel 1986; Inkelas 1989.) The PrWd is composed of feet and syllables; it is the domain in which "main-stress" is defined, since every PrWd contains precisely one syllable bearing main-stress. As in many languages, Latin requires that the lexical word be a prosodic word as well. Following McCarthy & Prince 1991ab, we can put the morphology–phonology interface constraint like this, with one parameter:

(52) **Lx≈Pr** (*MCAT*)
    A member of the morphological category *MCat* corresponds to a PrWd.

Another line of approach is to demand that the left or right *edge* of a morphological category match to the corresponding edge of the relevant phonological category (Selkirk 1986, Chen 1987, McCarthy & Prince 1993ab). For present purposes it is not necessary to pursue such refinements of formulation, although we return in chapter 7, §7.1, to the virtues of edge-reference.

All words of Latin satisfy Lx≈Pr; not all final syllables are stressless. (On the standard view of Latin prosody, a final syllable is included in stress structure only in monosyllables.) NONFINALITY is violated exactly when Lx≈Pr is at stake. We deduce that Lx≈Pr ≫ NONFINALITY. It remains to formulate a satisfactory version of the constraint from the NONFINALITY family that is visibly active in Latin. For present purposes, the following will suffice:

(53) **NONFINALITY**
    The head *foot* of the PrWd must not be final.

This is related to NONFINALITY (45) §4.2.2, p. 48, which deals with peaks of stress – syllabic heads of PrWd – but not identical with it. We will bring the two versions together shortly (§4.5), in order to deal with the subtler interactions between nonfinality and foot-form restrictions.

The effect of the constraint hierarchy on monosyllables is illustrated in this tableau:

(54)   **The Parsed Monosyllable of Latin**

Candidates	Lx≈Pr	Nonfinality
☞ [(méns)$_F$]$_{PrWd}$		*
⟨mens⟩	* !	

The constraint Lx≈Pr thus 'revokes extrametricality' when content-word mono-syllables are involved.

It is instructive to compare the present approach with the standard conception, due to Hayes, which holds that extrametricality is a feature assigned by rule as part of the bottom-up process of building prosodic structure. Under Bottom-Up Constructionism, there must be a strict serial order of operations:

1   Extrametricality marking must take place: this prepares the syllabified but footless input for further processing.
2   Feet are then formed, determining the location of stressed and unstressed syllables.
3   Higher-order structure is then built on the feet – i.e., the Prosodic Word is formed – and the location of main-stress is determined.

Under this plan of action, it is essential that extrametricality be assigned *correctly* at the very first step. If monosyllabic input is rendered entirely extrametrical at Step 1, then Prosodic Word Formation (Step 3) will have no feet to work with, and will fail. To avoid this disastrous outcome, a caveat must be attached to the theory of extrametricality to ensure that the fatal misstep is never taken. Hayes formulates the condition in this way:

(55)   **Nonexhaustivity**
"An extrametricality rule is blocked if it would render the entire domain of the stress rules extrametrical." (Hayes 1991/95: 58)

It is an unavoidable consequence of Bottom-Up Constructionism that condition (55) must be stated as an independent axiom of theory, unrelated to any other constraints that bear on prosodic well-formedness. Its existence is entirely due to the theory's inability to recognize that Lx≈Pr is a constraint on the *output* of the system, a condition that must be met, and not the result of scanning input for suitable configurations and performing Structural Changes on them. The putative rule assigning PrWd status cannot be allowed to fail due to lack of appropriate input.[25] The Axiom of Nonexhaustivity is not motivated by restrictiveness or any

---

[25] Compare, in this regard, the discussion of relative clause formation in Chomsky 1965: 137–8, where it is noted that it is insufficient to say that the rule of relative clause formation is *obligatory*, because nothing guarantees that it will be able to apply at all (*the man that the house looks nice). Compare also the notion of "positive absolute exception" in Lakoff 1965, a

other such higher explanatory motive. Its motivation is strictly empirical; remove it and you have an equally restrictive theory, but one which predicts the opposite treatment of monosyllables.

Nonexhaustiveness appears not to be part of any *general* theory of extrametricality. Hewitt & Prince (1989), for example, argue that extrametricality with respect to tonal association may indeed exclude entire monosyllabic domains. Hayes is careful to refer to the notion *"stress* domain" in his statement of the condition. The proposal offered here makes sense of this: the integrity of the stress domain is guaranteed by the theory of the morphology–phonology interface, as encoded in Lx≈Pr. When that particular theory is not involved, as in certain tonal associations, there is no reason to expect nonexhaustiveness, and we do not find it. Similarly, the end-of-the-word bias of stress-pattern extrametricality is not mirrored in other phenomena which ought to fall under the theory of extrametricality (were there to be one). For example, tonal extrametricality (Prince 1983, Pulleyblank 1983) is not restricted to final position; nor is edge-oriented infixation (McCarthy & Prince 1986, 1990a). We expect this: 'extrametricality' is not a unified entity, but rather a diverse family of consequences of the gradience of Edgemostness. In the subtheory pertaining to stress, Edgemost interacts with Nonfinality. In other phenomenal domains besides stress, other constraints are at play, shown above in the case of edge-oriented infixation, §4.1, yielding a rather different typology of edge-avoidance.

Nonexhaustiveness, then, emerges from constraint interaction. What of the other properties that have been ascribed to formal extrametricality? There are four, and in each case, we would argue, what is correct about them follows from the constraint interaction analysis. Let's take them in turn.

(56) Property 1: *Constituency*
      "Only constituents (e.g. segment, mora, syllable, foot, phonological word) may be marked as extrametrical." (Hayes 1991/95: 57)

We suggest that this property has nothing to do with extrametricality *per se* but rather with the substantive constraint that pushes the relevant item off an edge. Constraints on stress, for example, deal in syllables quite independently of extrametricality. When the relevant constraint is from a different domain, it may well be that constituency is irrelevant. In edge-oriented infixation, for example, as analyzed above in §4.1, the constraint −Cod can force prefixes away from the initial edge of the word, over consonant sequences that needn't be interpreted as unitary constituents ("onsets").

---

rule whose structural description *must be met*. These phenomena are diagnostic of deep failure in the simple re-write rule conception of grammar, since remedied. In the case of relative clauses, it is clear that the syntax is entirely free to create structures in which no *wh*-movement can apply, because independent principles of interpretation, defined over the *output* of the syntax, will fail in all such forms, ruling them out. Interestingly, Chomsky does not follow this line, but instead posits the presence of a formal symbol '#' in Deep Structure, which is disallowed in well-formed Surface Structures, and must therefore be deleted by a successful application of the relative clause transformation.

(57)   Property 2: *Peripherality*
"A constituent may be extrametrical only if it is at a designated edge (left or right) of its domain." (Hayes, ibid.)

This is because the phenomena gathered under the name of extrametricality have to do with items that are positioned by the constraint EDGEMOST – prominences, feet, tones, affixes. If by extrametrical, we mean "unparsed into the relevant structure," then there are many other situations where constraints force non-parsing. Hayes's "weak local parsing," for example, compels unparsed syllables to separate binary feet (the similarity to extrametricality is recognized in Hammond 1992). Syllables may be left unparsed internally as well as peripherally because of restrictions on the quantitative shape of feet (the "prosodic trapping" of Mester 1992/94). Similar observations may be made about segmental parsing. Many kinds of constraints can lead to nonparsing; we assert that there is no reason to collect together a subset of them under the name of extrametricality.

(58)   Property 3: *Edge Markedness*
"The unmarked edge for extrametricality is the right edge." (Hayes, ibid.)

As noted, this is true only for stress, not for tone or affixation. The explanation must lie in the properties of stress, not in a theory of the treatment of edges.

(59)   Property 4: *Uniqueness*
Only *one* constituent of any type may be extrametrical.

This is a classic case of constraint interaction as we treat it. Extrametricality arises, for example, when NONFINALITY ≫ EDGEMOSTness. It follows that EDGEMOSTness is violated when extrametrical material is present. Because of the way Harmony is evaluated (HOF: chapter 5), such violations must be minimal. Under NONFINALITY, this will commonly mean that only one element is skipped over or left unparsed, the minimal violation of EDGEMOSTness. Thus, in many cases – enough to inspire belief that a parochial principle is involved – the unparsed sequence will be a constituent.

We conclude that there are strong reasons to believe that extrametricality should be retired as a formal device. Since its basic properties submit to explanation in the substantive domain under scrutiny here, it is worthwhile to pursue the argument into the other areas where it has proved to be such a useful tool of analysis. (For further exploration of nonfinality and related edge effects, see Hung 1994.)

Demoting nonexhaustivity from clause-of-UG to epiphenomenon of inter-action raises an important issue, however: the universality (or at least generality) of the effect is not directly accounted for. What ensures that Lx≈PR outranks NONFINALITY? Why not have it the other way around in the next language over? It may be that some further condition is required, restricting the place of Lx≈PR in constraint hierarchies. Have we therefore exchanged one stipulation for another, failing to net an overall gain at the bottom line?

Reviewing the spectrum of possible responses, it's clear that we're not in a simple tit-for-tat situation. Suppose we straightforwardly call on some principle relevant only to Lx≈Pr; for example, that it must sit at the top of all hierarchies, undominated. Any such condition fixes the range of relations between Lx≈Pr and many other constraints, not just NONFINALITY, so the cost of the stipulation is amortized over a broad range of consequences having to do with the prosodic status of lexical items. Thus, even with the most direct response, we put ourselves in a better position than the adherent of pure axiomatic status for non-exhaustiveness as a property local to extrametricality.[26]

It is useful to compare the kind of ranking argument just given with a familiar form of argument for rule ordering in operational theories. One often notes that if Rule A and Rule B were to apply simultaneously, then the conditions of Rule A must be written into Rule B; whereas if Rule A strictly precedes Rule B, the two can be disentangled, allowing the development of an appropriately restrictive theory of type A and type B rules.[27]

Here we have seen that the empirical generalization about extrametricality (that it holds *except when* it would obliterate a monosyllable) emerges properly from the ranking of independent constraints. The rule-ordering theory of extra-metricality, by contrast, exhibits a pathological quirk similar to the one that affects simple non-ordering operational theories. Information proper to one rule must be written into another, solely to get the right outcome: the Nonexhaustivity axiom embodies a covert reference to PrWd-formation. A grammar of re-write rules is simply not suited to the situation where a rule *must apply*, where its structural description *must be met* by all inputs so that all outputs conform to its structural change (see fn. 25 above). Inserting special conditions into rules so that this happens to happen is no answer. Rule ordering must therefore be abandoned in favor of constraint ranking, for the same reason that simultaneity was previously abandoned in favor of rule ordering.

---

[26] More optimistically, we might expect to find principles of universal ranking that deal with whole *classes* of constraints; in which desirable case, the nonexhaustiveness effect would fully follow from independent considerations. Also worth considering is the idea that there are no principles involved at all and the predominance of the cited ranking is due to functional factors extrinsic to grammar, e.g. the utility of short words. (This comports as well with the fact that conditions on word minimality can differ in detail from language to language, including or excluding various categories from the 'lexical word': see the discussion of Latin which immediately follows; implying a family of related constraints, rather than a single one.) Grammar allows the ranking to be easily learnable from the abundant data that justifies it. On this view, nothing says that NONFINALITY must be dominated; but it is easy to observe that it is; and there are extra-grammatical, functional reasons why it is useful for it to be. Note too that even in stipulating the ranking of Lx≈Pr, we would construct the needed restriction from UG-building tools already needed; as opposed to tacking on nonexhaustiveness as a *sui generis* codicil to some mechanism.

[27] Notice that the argument has nothing to do with 'redundancy', which (here as elsewhere) is nothing more than a diagnostic indication that greater independence could be achieved; and with that, explanation.

4.3.1   Nonfinality and the Laws of Foot Form: Raw Minimality

Latin displays a typical minimality effect of the type made familiar by work in Prosodic Morphology: the language lacks monomoraic words. Here is a list of typical monosyllabic forms (Mester 1992, as 1994: 20–1):

(60)   **Latin Monosyllables**

	Category	Exempla	Glosses
(a)	N	mens, cor, mel, rē, spē, vī	'mind, heart, honey (nom.), thing, hope, force (abl.)'
(b)	V	dō, stā, sum, stat	'I give, stand, am; he stands'
(c)	Pron.	mē, sē, tū, is, id, quis	'1sg.-acc., 3-refl.-acc.; you-sg.-nom.; he, it, who-nom.'
(d)	Conj.	nē, sī, cum, sed	'lest, if, when, but also'
(e)	P	ā, ē, prō, sub, in, ab	'from, out of, in front of, under, in, from'

We have then *cum, mens, re:* and *rem* (acc.), all bimoraic, but no *rĕ* (Mester 1992, citing Kuryłowicz 1968, Allen 1973: 51). A morpheme like -*quĕ* 'and' can only be enclitic. The standard account points to the prosody–morphology interface constraint Lx≈Pr as the source of the restriction (Prince 1980; McCarthy & Prince 1986 *et seq.*). The PrWd must contain at least one foot; a foot will contain at least two moras; hence, lexical words are minimally bimoraic. The deduction rests on the principle *Foot Binarity*, which we state in (61), following the formulation of McCarthy & Prince 1986:[28]

(61)   **Foot Binarity** (FᴛBɪɴ)
       Feet are binary at some level of analysis (μ, σ).

Foot Binarity is not itself a direct restriction on minimal foot size; it defines a general property of structure. (Indeed the obvious virtue of the prosodic theory of minimality is that it obviates the need for such a thing as a 'minimal word constraint'; but see Itô & Mester 1992.) Because syllables *contain* moras, Foot Binarity entails that the smallest foot is bimoraic.

---

[28] Foot Binarity is generalized from the account of Estonian foot structure in Prince 1980. The foot of Estonian is there defined as F = uu, where u is a variable ranging uniformly over μ and σ. It is shown that this definition holds of the stress system, and the entailed minimality result – all monosyllables are bimoraic, hence overlong – is shown to hold as well. With such a foot, there are parsing ambiguities in certain circumstances – Hσ may be (H)σ or (Hσ) – and it is proposed that the maximal (bisyllabic) analysis is the one taken. The Estonian type of foot has been dubbed the "Generalized Trochee" in Hayes 1991/95, and new applications of it are reported; cf. Kager 1992ab, 1993 for further exploration. Since iambic feet also meet the description 'bimoraic or bisyllabic', we go beyond the realm of the trochaic and, with McCarthy & Prince 1986 and Prince 1990, demand that FᴛBɪɴ hold of all feet, regardless of headedness. Of course, FᴛBɪɴ excludes the 'unbounded' feet of early metrical theory.

One then argues that the lexicon of Latin cannot contain e.g. a noun /re/ because any such item wouldn't be assigned foot-structure (assuming FTBIN), and therefore wouldn't be assigned PrWd status. Since (on this view, not ours) a version of the constraint Lx≈PR holds categorically of the output of the lexicon, rejecting all violators, it happens that a potential lexical form like /re/ would underlie no well-formed output and is therefore impossible, or at least pointless as a lexical entry. On this view, the constraint Lx≈PR assigns absolute ill-formedness to the output; in consequence, an input form /re/ yields no output at all.

In the present theory, failure to satisfy a constraint does not entail ill-formedness, and every input is always paired with an output: whichever analysis best satisfies the constraint hierarchy under HOF. We must therefore delve deeper to see how *absolute* ill-formedness – lack of an effective output – could emerge from a system of interacting constraints which always selects at least one analysis as optimal; this (or these) being by definition the output of the system.

The key, we suggest, is that among the analyses to be evaluated is one which assigns no structure at all to the input: the *Null Parse*, identical to the input. The Null Parse will certainly be superior to some other possibilities, because it vacuously satisfies any constraint pertaining to structures that it lacks. For example, FTBIN says *if* there is a foot in the representation, *then* it must be binary; violations are incurred by the *presence* of non-binary feet. The Null Parse therefore satisfies FTBIN, since it contains no feet of any kind. Similar remarks hold for syllable structure constraints such as ONS, because the Null Parse contains no syllables; for structural constraints such as FILL, which demands that empty nodes be absent (they are). Of course, the Null Parse grossly fails such constraints as PARSE, which demands that segments be prosodically licensed, to use Itô's term, because the input will always contain segments. The Null Parse will fail Lx≈PR when the input string *is a* lexical category, because the constraint applies to all items in the category; it says that all such items must be parsed as prosodic words.

A direct phonological assault on the Latin type of minimality would run like this: suppose that FTBIN ≫ Lx≈PR, with PARSE the lowest-ranked relevant faithfulness constraint. We have then the following:

(62)   **Optimality of the Null Parse**

Candidates	FTBIN	Lx≈PR	. . .	PARSE
☞ re	*vacuous*	*	. . .	*
[(ré)$_F$]$_{PrWd}$	* !		. . .	

In the language of actions and exceptions, it would be said that a lexical word becomes a prosodic word *except when* it is monomoraic; the "assignment" of PrWd status to subminimals is *blocked* by FTBIN.[29]

---

[29] One looseness of formulation here is the exact category to which 'Lx' in the constraint refers. John McCarthy reminds us that there are no alternations of the form ø (nom.) ~ *rem* (acc.) from /re+m/, even though the inflected form is legitimately bimoraic. One could argue that the

Clearly, then, there exist constraint hierarchies under which the Null Parse is optimal for certain inputs. The Null Parse, however, is uniquely unsuited to life in the outside world. In the phonological realm alone, the principle that unlicensed material is phonetically unrealized (our take on the "Stray Erasure" of McCarthy 1979, Steriade 1982, Itô 1986, 1989) entails that any item receiving the Null Parse will be entirely silent. In a broad range of circumstances, this would render an item useless, and therefore provide the basis for an explanation for its absence from the lexicon. (Observe that some similar account is required under any theory, since nothing in the formal nature of a lexical entry prevents it from being entirely empty of phonetic content in the first place.)

A more bracing line of attack on the general problem is disclosed if we broaden our attention to include morphology. As with phonology, morphological structure can be understood as something that the input lacks and the output has, the product of parsing. In the simple case of affixation, a structure like [Root Af]$_{Stem}$ is an output possibility, sometimes the best one, related to a hierarchically unstructured input {$root_i$, $affix_j$} which merely collects together the consistuent morphemes. Here too, though, the Null Parse must be among the options, and will be superior to some others, often to *all* others. For example, if $affix_j$ is restricted to combining with a certain subset of the vocabulary, and $root_i$ is not in this set, then the **non**combination of the morphological Null Parse $\langle root_i, affix_j \rangle$ is going to be superior to the parsed *mis*combination [$root_i$ $affix_j$]$_{Stem}$. A real-life example is provided by English comparative–superlative morphology, which attaches only to (one-foot) Minimal Words: thus [violet-er], parsed, is inferior to $\langle$violet, er$\rangle$, which evades the one-foot constraint by evading attachment. Similarly, the input {write, ation} is best left untouched, but the analysis of {cite, ation} is optimally a parsable word. (For discussion of related cases, see McCarthy & Prince 1990a, 1993a).

Failure to achieve morphological parsing is fatal. An unparsed item has no morphological category, and cannot be interpreted, either semantically or in terms of higher morphological structure. This parallels the phonetic uninterpretability of unparsed segmental material. The requirements of higher-order prosody will parallel those of higher-order morphology and syntax: a phonological Null Parse, which assigns no Prosodic Word node, renders a word unusable as an element in a Phonological Phrase (Selkirk 1980ab, Nespor & Vogel 1986, Inkelas 1989), which is built on prosodic words. This is the structural correlate of phonetic invisibility. Members of the 'PARSE' family of constraints demand that the links in the prosodic hierarchy be established; let us use 'M-PARSE' for the constraint which requires the structural realization of morphological properties.

Applying this reasoning to the Latin case changes the game in certain crucial respects. Above we assumed that a lexical form /re/ inevitably had membership in a lexical category; consequently failure of phonological parsing led inevitably

---

absence of such alternations is not properly grammatical, but functional in origin, considering the serious communicative problems entailed by lack of a nominative form. One might also argue that this shows that the Latin constraint must actually apply to the category (noun) *root*. There are, however, a number of further issues concerning how minimality plays out over the various morphological categories; see Mester 1992, especially §2.2, for analysis.

to violation of Lx≈Pr. Now we assume that a form "has" a lexical category in the relevant sense only when the morphological parse is accomplished. A morphologically unassembled item *cannot* violate Lx≈Pr, since the phonological string is not in the "is a" relation with a morphological category.

Under this assumption, it is not possible to rank FtBin and Lx≈Pr with respect to each other except arbitrarily, since they are both satisfied in optimal output. With M-Parse ranked below them, the optimal output for subminimal input will lack morphological structure. To see how this plays out, examine the following tableau.

(63)   **Effect of Morphological Null Parse** on {re, N}

	Candidates	FtBin	Lx≈Pr	M-Parse	(Ph)-Parse
a.	[(ré)$_{F,PrWd}$]$_N$	* !			
b.	[re]$_N$	*vac*	* !		*
c.	(ré)$_{F,PrWd}$, N	* !	*vac*	*	
d. ☞	re, N	*vac*	*vac*	*	*

Hierarchical morphological structure, when present, is indicated by labeled brackets; phonological structure by labeled parentheses. The *ad hoc* indication *vac* marks vacuous satisfaction. Constraints which are not crucially ranked with respect to each other are separated in the tableau by dotted rather than solid lines. We assume that faithfulness constraints like Fill, which would be violated when the input is augmented to minimality, are ranked above M- and Ph-Parse, and we do not display augmented candidates; we consider the reverse ranking below.

Under these assumptions, any attempt to give /re, N/ a prosodic analysis violates FtBin, as in (a) and (c). Morphological analysis without phonological analyis violates Lx≈Pr, as in (b). This leaves only the Null Parse, phonological and morphological, which satisfies, vacuously, both FtBin and Lx≈Pr. Since the Null Parse ⟨re, N⟩ violates M-Parse, we want M-Parse subordinated in the hierarchy so that the issue can be decided by FtBin and Lx≈Pr.

On this view, then, the underlying form of an item will consist of a very incompletely structured set of specifications which constrain but do not themselves fully determine even the morphological character of the output form. These specifications must be put in relation, parsed into structure, in order to be interpretable. In mild cases of Parse violation, bits of underlying form will not correspond to anything in the output: underlying consonants will not be realized, underlying long vowels will appear as short due to unparsed moras, and so on. But in the face of a battery of high-ranking structural constraints which the input is not suited to meet when faithfully mapped to the output, an entire Null Parse can be optimal. In this case, there is no interpretable output from the input form, and we have what amounts to absolute ill-formedness.[30]

---

[30] The notion of absolute ill-formedness is taken up again in ch. 9 below.

It is worth taking a look at another line of attack, developed further in chapter 9, that bears on the analysis of certain kinds of ill-formedness. The Null Parse is a kind of neutralization with ø. We can also have neutralization with something tangible. Suppose that we have /A/,/B/ → Ω for two distinct inputs A and B. Suppose further that the input–output pairing (A,Ω) incurs more serious violations than (B,Ω) does. Then, under the natural assumption that the lexicon is chosen to minimize violations in the input–output mapping, and assuming that there is no other (e.g. morphological) reason to choose violation-prone A, one would be compelled to say that what underlies visible Ω is actually B and not A. For example, in the Latin case, suppose (contrary to the assumptions just explored) that putative /re/ must always parsed be as [reː], as in Mester 1992. Then, if there are no other relevant repercussions of underlying vowel quantity, the surface form [reː] will be identified as /reː/ underlyingly.

To implement this approach, assume moraic structure and a correlated structural constraint FILL-μ. With FILL-μ appropriately subordinated in the hierarchy, unfilled moras can be posited in optimal forms under the compulsion of higher-ranked constraints. Assume further that unfilled moras are interpreted in the output as continuations of a tautosyllabic vowel, phonetically interpreted as length. For input /re/, the analysis r[e]$_μ$[]$_μ$ ≡ [reː] now becomes superior to the Null Parse. The output [reː] satisfies FtBin and Lx≈Pr, just like the Null Parse, but has the additional virtue of satisfying both the phonological and the morphological versions of the PARSE constraint. This state of affairs is portrayed in the following tableau:

(64)   **Besting the Null Parse** when FILL-μ is low

Candidates	FTBIN, LX≈PR	M-PARSE	(Ph-)PARSE	FILL-μ
☞ [[(r[e]$_μ$[ ]$_μ$)$_F$]$_{PrWd}$]$_N$				*
re, N	*vac*	* !	* !	

We now ask why, given [reː] in the observed world, the abstract learner would bother to posit underlying /re/ in the first place. If there is no adequate response, we can never have /re/ in the lexicon. Monomoraic forms are absent from the lexicon on this analysis not because they lead to uninterpretable output, but because the output they lead to is better analyzed as coming from something else. We might call this effect 'occultation', since the possible input /re/ is hidden, as it were, behind /reː/, and therefore inaccessible.

Mester (1992, as 1994: 20–3) provides evidence that this analysis is appropriate for actual Latin. The form of argument is due originally, we believe, to Stampe (1969, 1973, 1973/79) and has been reasserted independently by Dell (1973), Hudson (1974), Myers (1991) and probably others we are unaware of. We deal with related matters in the discussion of inventory theory below in chapter 9.

Stampean occultation cannot always be appropriate. One common worry should perhaps be set aside: how do we determine what the occulting body actually *is* in cases with inadequate surface clues? For example, in the case at hand, in the absence of further, typically morphophonemic evidence, all that's required is that /re/ come out as bimoraic; many epenthetic pathways are open. This issue can in principle be resolved by markedness theory or perhaps even left unresolved: anything, after all, will do. But there are still many circumstances, particularly in morphology, where it appears that there is simply no well-formed output from many kinds of input. (See McCarthy & Prince 1993a: §7 for discussion.) The output from {violet, er} cannot be 'bluer' nor can the output from {write, ation} be 'inscription': these combinations simply yield nothing at all. For such cases, the Null Parse is superior to all alternatives.

4.3.2   Nonfinality and the Laws of Foot Form: Extended Minimality Effects

Like so many languages, Latin bars monomoraic items because it respects both Lx≈Pr, which *demands* feet, and FtBin, which bans *monomoraic* feet. Like many other languages, Latin also keeps stress off word-final syllables, by imposing Nonfinality on its prosodic structure. Parsing of bimoraic monosyllables, in outright violation of Nonfinality, is forced by the dominance of Lx≈Pr, as we have seen. In a less obvious class of cases, Nonfinality also conflicts with FtBin.

Consider bisyllabic words shaped LL and LH like *áqua* and *ámoɪ*. Under the standard view of extrametricality, these must be analyzed as L⟨L⟩ and L⟨H⟩, that is, as the exact equivalent of #L#. The naive expectation, then, is that such words should be impossible rather than plentiful. Hayes (1991/95) terms this state of affairs "the unstressable word syndrome."

The solution to the #LL# case is already at hand, given what has been established above. We know from monosyllable behavior that Lx≈Pr ≫ Nonfinality. Bisyllable behavior will follow when we impose the additional ranking FtBin ≫ Nonfinality on the constraint set.[31] With these rankings in place, an input /LL/ must be parsed $[(LL)_F]_{PrWd}$. The following tableau should make this clear:

---

[31] In terms of the empirically necessary domination order, we have Lx≈Pr ≫ Nonfinality from (c) vs. (a), and FtBin ≫ Nonfinality, from (c) vs. (b) in ex. (65). Either ranking between Lx≈Pr and FtBin will produce the same outcome, since there is a solution, namely (c), that satisfies *both* of them at the expense of Nonfinality. With a grammar defined as a total ranking of the constraint set, the underlying hypothesis is that there is *some* total ranking which works; there could be (and typically will be) several, because a total ranking will often impose noncrucial domination relations (noncrucial in the sense that either order will work). It is entirely conceivable that the grammar should recognize nonranking of pairs of constraints, but this opens up the possibility of *crucial* nonranking between conflicting constraints (neither can dominate the other; both rankings are allowed), a far richer theory to which we should not move without strong motivation. In this work, we assume the hypothesis that there is a total order of domination on the constraint set; that is, that all nonrankings are noncrucial.

(65)   **Best Parse for /LL/ in Latin: FᴛBɪɴ, Lx≈Pʀ ≫ Nᴏɴғɪɴᴀʟɪᴛʏ**

	Candidates	Lx≈Pʀ	FᴛBɪɴ	Nᴏɴғɪɴᴀʟɪᴛʏ
a.	.a.qua.	* !		
b.	(á.)_F qua		* !	
c. ☞	(á.qua)_F			*

In short, FᴛBɪɴ and Lx≈Pʀ jointly force *all* bimoraic words to have a complete metrical analysis,[32] eliminating extrametricality from both #H# and #LL#.

The behavior of words shaped LH is more intriguing. If Nᴏɴғɪɴᴀʟɪᴛʏ could be completely ignored, as above, we'd expect L(Ĥ), and thus e.g. *amóː with final stress. The candidate parse (á)moː fails FᴛBɪɴ, while incorrect *a(móː) satisfies both FᴛBɪɴ and Lx≈Pʀ, running afoul only of low-ranked Nᴏɴғɪɴᴀʟɪᴛʏ.

Forms like *ámoː* have two virtues which will allow us to rescue them from the oblivion in which forms like *á repose. First, such words are *bisyllabic*: unlike true subminimals, they have enough substance to support a binary foot. The foot may not be beautifully formed, because (ĹH) makes a poor trochee; but it satisfies FᴛBɪɴ nonetheless. Second, the exhaustively monopodic (ámoː) nonetheless displays a kind of nonfinality: the stress peak is indeed off the final syllable. With the notion of relative Harmony securely in hand, we can take advantage of these partial successes. The trochaic parse (ĹH) is equipped to succeed modestly on the constraints FᴛBɪɴ and Nᴏɴғɪɴᴀʟɪᴛʏ, besting other analyses which fail them entirely. To implement this program of explanation, we need to refine our analyses of nonfinality and foot form.

The desired version of nonfinality simply puts together its forms from above in (45) and (53):

(66)   **Nᴏɴғɪɴᴀʟɪᴛʏ**
    No head of PrWd is final in PrWd.

The head of the PrWd is, immediately, the strongest foot F′ dominated by the node PrWd. By transitivity of headship (the head of X′ counting also as the head of X″), the PrWd will also be headed by the strongest syllable in F′. In Latin, then, the PrWd has two heads, one inside the other. Nᴏɴғɪɴᴀʟɪᴛʏ is violated when *either* abuts the trailing edge of the PrWd; we assume that each violation counts separately. The candidate *a(móː) manages to violate Nᴏɴғɪɴᴀʟɪᴛʏ at both levels: the head foot is final, as is the head syllable. The form (ámoː) is more successful: only the head foot is in final position. This is the result we want: the form #(ĹH)#

---

[32] This contradicts the theory of Steriade 1988, in which the word-final accent that appears in pre-enclitic position is attributed to extrametricality of the final syllable. But Mester 1992 offers good reasons to doubt the Steriade proposal.

achieves a modest degree of success, since it keeps the main-stress – the head of the head foot – out of final position.[33]

Foot form is already known to be determined by a composite of various principles. There must be a constraint which sets the rhythmic type at either iambic or trochaic; call this RʜTʏᴘᴇ=I/T. Other factors regulate the well-formedness of various syllable groups, qua feet and qua bearers of iambic and trochaic rhythm (Hayes 1985, 1991/95; McCarthy & Prince 1986; Prince 1990; Kager 1992ab, 1993; Mester 1992). For present purposes, we focus only on candidate principles that are relevant to the badness of (LH) as a trochee. One such is the Weight-to-Stress Principle of Prince 1990 (cf. "w-nodes do not branch" of Hayes 1980).

(67) **Weight-to-Stress Principle** (WSP)
      Heavy syllables are prominent in foot structure and on the grid.

By the WSP, the trochaic group (ĹH) is subpar because it puts a heavy syllable in a weak position.[34]

Since the trochee (ĹH) is inferior with respect to the WSP, it will be avoided in parses of syllable strings in favor of other structures that meet the constraint – *ceteris paribus*.

In Latin, Nᴏɴꜰɪɴᴀʟɪᴛʏ (66) renders the ceteris *im*paribus, as it were. We must have Nᴏɴꜰɪɴᴀʟɪᴛʏ ≫ WSP to force all final syllables to be foot-loose and nonprominent, regardless of their weight. With all the parts of the argument put together, the best parse [ámoː] emerges as in the following:

---

[33] The contrast with Kelkar's Hindi/Urdu, which has #LĤ# and #LĹL#, admits of several interpretations. The relation Pᴋ-Pʀᴏᴍ ≫ Nᴏɴꜰɪɴᴀʟɪᴛʏ yields the first of these forms without elaboration, but when Pᴋ-Pʀᴏᴍ is not at issue, we'd expect the Latin pattern of antepenultimacy. The direct approach would redivide Nᴏɴꜰɪɴᴀʟɪᴛʏ into Nᴏɴꜰɪɴ(σ′) (45) and Nᴏɴꜰɪɴ(F′) (53), each specifying whether the head syllable or the head foot was being regulated. The argument also depends on the kind of feet which are present in Hindi/Urdu; if they are fundamentally iambic, then nothing need be said. If they are moraic trochees, we must split Nᴏɴꜰɪɴᴀʟɪᴛʏ and subordinate to Eᴅɢᴇᴍᴏsᴛ the version that refers to the head foot. Otherwise, we incorrectly predict antepenultimate rather than penultimate stress in light-syllabled words. The foot structure of languages like Hindi/Urdu is, to say the least, incompletely understood.

[34] A different line of attack is also available for exploration, since the WSP is effectively the converse, at the foot level, of a principle that we have seen active above in Berber and Hindi/Urdu: Pᴋ-Pʀᴏᴍ.

(i) Peak-Prominence (Pᴋ-Pʀᴏᴍ). Peak(x) > Peak(y) if |x| > |y|.

Pᴋ-Pʀᴏᴍ favors analyses in which positions of prominence are occupied by the heaviest syllables. By Pᴋ-Pʀᴏᴍ, the (ĹH) trochee is relatively bad because the counter-analysis L(Ĥ) has a better (heavier) peak. Pᴋ-Pʀᴏᴍ, in contrast to the WSP, says nothing directly about the occurrence of H in nonhead position. Complications arise in analyses where L(Ĥ) is ruled out by higher-ranking constraints, for example Nᴏɴꜰɪɴᴀʟɪᴛʏ, and we will not pursue this alternative here.

(68)   **Treatment of #LH#** (Classical Latin): FtBin, Lx≈Pr ≫ Nonfinality ≫ WSP

Candidates		Lx≈Pr	FtBin	Nonfinality	WSP
a. ☞	[(ámoː)]			*	*
b.	[a (móː)]			* * !	
c.	[(á) moː]		* !		*
d.	amoː	* !			*

The feet considered here are trochaic; it is fatal to advance an iambic parse in violation of the top-ranking but unmentioned constraint RhType=T, since a better alternative, trochaic not iambic, always exists.

The ranking of Nonfinality above WSP is part of the grammar of Latin. When the ranking is permuted, we get a language that looks more like Kelkar's Hindi/Urdu, for example English. It is well known, due to the work of Oehrle (1971), that English bisyllabic nouns of the form LH are mostly end-stressed (*políce*) while all others are mostly initially stressed (HH: *árgyle*; HL: *bándit*; LL: *édda*). (For some discussion, see Halle 1973; Zonneveld 1976; Liberman & Prince 1977; Hayes 1982, 1991/95.) When WSP ≫ Nonfinality, we get the effect of 'extrametricality revocation'. The analysis runs exactly parallel to that of *ámoː* just presented in tableau (68). Observe that *amóː* is the local winner within WSP and the local loser within Nonfinality; were it the case that WSP dominated Nonfinality, **amóː* would defeat *ámoː*. The *amóː*-like form *políce* [pʰəlíːs] is therefore optimal in the English-like system, as shown in the following tableau:

(69)   **Treatment of LH** in an English-like system: . . . WSP ≫ Nonfinality

Candidates		Lx≈Pr	FtBin	WSP	Nonfinality
a.	[(póliːce)]			* !	*
b. ☞	[po(líːce)]				* *
c.	[(pó) liːce]		* !	*	
d.	poliːce	* !		*	

The Latin-style ranking of Nonfinality above constraints relevant to foot form can have even more radical consequences. In many otherwise iambic languages, Nonfinality forces bisyllables to be *trochaic*. Familiar examples include Choctaw, Munsee, Southern Paiute, Ulwa, Axininca Campa.[35] In such cases, we have

---

[35] Relevant references include: for Choctaw (Muskogean), Lombardi & McCarthy 1991; for Munsee (Algonkian), Hayes 1985; for Southern Paiute (Uto-Aztecan), Sapir 1930; for Ulwa (Misumalpan), Hale & Lacayo Blanco 1988; for Axininca (Arawakan), Payne 1981, Payne, Payne, & Sánchez 1982.

NONFINALITY ≫ RHTYPE. In Southern Paiute we find, for example, qaɣíni 'my necklace' but kúna 'fire'. Final syllables are voiceless, as indicated by the font; examples from Hale (undated). Southern Paiute phonology is such as to make it clear that the effect occurs in all forms: NONFINALITY is therefore not restricted to a single head-foot of the prosodic word but applies to all feet and to their heads.

(70)   **Rhythmic Reversal** due to NONFINALITY: Southern Paiute
/puNpuNkuŋwɨtaŋwa/ 'our (incl.) horses owned severally'

Candidates	NONFINALITY	RHTYPE=I
☞ (pumpúŋ) (kuŋwɨ̀) (tàŋwa)		*
(pumpúŋ) (kuŋwɨ̀) (taŋwà)	* !	

The consequences are most dramatic in bisyllables, where the placement of the only stress in the word is affected:

(71)   **Rhythmic Reversal** due to NONFINALITY: Southern Paiute /kuna/ 'fire'

Candidates	NONFINALITY	RHTYPE=I
☞ (kúna)		*
(kuná)	* !	

We have only sketched the core of the phenomenon here. For further discussion, see McCarthy & Prince 1993a: §7;[36] detailed further exploration is found in Hung 1994.

4.4   Summary of Discussion of the *Except When* Effect

Explicating the 'except when' or blocking pattern in terms of constraint domination leads to new understanding of a variety of prosodic phenomena. We have been able to put edge-oriented infixation on a principled basis, leading to predictions

---

[36] McCarthy & Prince 1993a: 162–3 note that in an iambic system operating under the compulsion of exhaustive parsing (PARSE-σ, i.e. parse syllables into feet), the appearance of left-to-right parsing is a consequence of NONFINALITY. In odd parity strings, NONFINALITY puts the free syllable at the very end, no matter where it is in the ranking, above or below RHTYPE. (In even parity strings, the domination relationship determines whether the iambic foot will be inverted at word-end.) This result holds whether the iamb is sensitive to quantity or not. It may be relevant that almost all iambic systems are left-to-right in directional sense (see Kager 1993 for discussion from a different perspective).

about the kind of affixes liable to such treatment. The properties previously attributed to a formal theory of extrametricality follow from construing extrametricality as an interaction effect which arises when items placed by the gradient constraint EDGEMOST are subject to higher-ranking substantive constraints such as NONFINALITY or ONS which force violations of EDGEMOST, minimal of course. Effects of 'extrametricality revocation', rather than being due to quirks in the formal theory or special re-write rules applying in arbitrary environments, are seen instead to follow from the dominance of constraints such as FTBIN, PK-PROM, and LX≈PR, easily recognizable as authentic, independently required principles of prosody and of the prosody–morphology interface.

The interaction that 'revokes extrametricality' is exactly of the same sort as that which introduces it in the first place – constraint domination. Just as NONFINALITY overrules EDGEMOST producing the appearance of extrametricality, so does FTBIN (for example) overrule NONFINALITY, taking extrametricality away. We have examined a number of such cases, embodying the *except when* or *blocking* form of descriptive generalization.

- Syllables are descriptively extrametrical everywhere in a language like Latin *except when* nonparsing would leave nothing (monosyllables) or a single mora (bisyllables /Lσ/).
- Feet take on their independently favored forms – obeying the WSP and the language's RHTYPE – everywhere *except when* in bisyllables, where FTBIN is at stake due to the force of NONFINALITY.
- Stress falls on an edgemost syllable *except when* there is a heavy syllable in the word (in which case it falls on the edgemost such syllable).
- Stress falls on a nonfinal syllable *except when* it is the heaviest syllable in the word.
- Affixes are situated at the edge of the {affix, stem} collocation *except when* stem-internal positioning results in more harmonic syllable structure (and even then, given satisfaction of the syllabic requirements, they are positioned at minimal distance from the target edge.)

The sometimes intricate patterns of dependency that lie behind descriptive notions like *minimality* and *extrametricality* thus emerge from the interaction of principles of prosodic form. The success of the theory in rationalizing this domain and opening up the way to new forms of explanation stands as a significant argument in its favor.

4.5   Except Meets Only: Triggering and Blocking in a Single Grammar

To conclude our overview of generalization patterns, we take on some empirical issues made accessible by the results of the preceding discussion.[37] We show how

---

[37] Thanks to Armin Mester for discussing various points with us. Errors are ours, of course.

nonfaithful parsing interacts with the kind of minimality, extrametricality, and prominence effects just examined. The empirical focus will be on Latin, viewed with finer resolution of detail, and we will show how a renovated conception of the language's prosody is mandated. By its nature, the analysis must reach a fair level of complexity, and the reader who wishes to focus on the main line of the argument may wish to return after examining chapter 6.

Words ending in difficult-to-foot sequences like LH pose a challenge that is sometimes met quite aggressively. In the Pre-classical Latin of Terence and Plautus – presumably reflecting a less normative interpretation of the actual spoken language – bisyllabic words /LH/ may come out optionally as LL, whence *ámo* instead of *ámoː*, yielding a far more satisfactory trochee, one that does not violate WSP. This phenomenon goes by the name of 'iambic shortening', in reference to the quantitative shape of the input, and has recently been examined in a number of studies, especially Mester 1992, whose results have inspired these remarks, but also including Allen 1973; Devine & Stephens 1980; Kager 1989; Prince 1990; Hayes 1991/95. Mester 1992 emphasizes, with Devine & Stephens, that words shaped /…HLH/ suffer an entirely parallel reduction to …HLL – also optionally, and at the same historical period. Here are some examples involving the first person singular present ending -ōː[38]

(72)   /HLH/   /LLH/   /HH/
       dēsinŏ   studeō   laudō
       nescĭ   habitō   mandō

This is called 'cretic shortening' after the cretic foot of Greek lyric meters (HLH). Mester produces a wide variety of phenomena of Latin phonology and morphology, including these shortening effects, which are responsive to constraints demanding exhaustive footing with high-quality trochees. The structure (H)(LL) puts all syllables into bimoraic trochees, where (H)L(H) traps a syllable between two feet, (H)LH leaves the final two syllables dangling, and (H)(LH) involves a poor final trochee, the very same (LH) that is forced on bisyllables like *ámoː* in the classical language. Common to both iambic and cretic shortening is the interpretation of underlying …LH# as surface …LL#, which results in notably improved prosodic organization.

Taking this explanation seriously will push our understanding of Latin prosodic organization well beyond what can be deduced from the simple facts of main-stress placement. For one thing, words HLL must be structured (H)(LL) not (H)LL, as has been assumed in previous scholarship, and words HH must be structured (H)(H), not (H)H. Mester sees a two-step process: standard foot-assignment and main-stressing, followed by a stage of repair in the direction of well-formedness, which incorporates loose syllables into foot structure when

---

[38] Glosses are *dēsinŏ* 'cease', *studeō* 'strive', *laudō* 'praise', *nescĭ* 'don't-know', *habitō* 'reside', *mandō* 'entrust', all 1psg. We have normalized Mester's example *mandā* 'entrust (2sg. imp.)' to the 1psg. Note that in later Latin there is a phenomenon whereby word-final o is often short, regardless of preceding context (Mester 1992, as 1994: 32n). This phenomenon is irrelevant to the Pre-classical situation, but could mislead the casual observer.

possible, with the assistance of a rule 'Remove μ'. By contrast, and in line with the general thrust of our argument throughout, we wish to explore the idea that iambo-cretic shortening is a direct by-product of the one prosodic parse, in the same way that epenthesis and deletion are by-products of the one syllabic parse (Selkirk 1981, Itô 1986, 1989). On this view, iambo-cretically shortened forms are among the many candidate analyses that forms ~HLH# and #LH# are subject to in any language. The constraint system of Pre-classical Latin, at least at its collo-quial level, picks them out as optimal.

Before grappling with the details of iambo-cretic shortness, it is useful to map the structure of the basic rhythmic system of the language. This involves three components:

1   Positional theory: nonfinality and edgemostness.
2   Parsing theory: to compel footing of syllables, and syllabification of segments and moras.
3   Foot theory: of trochees, their shape and proclivities.

First, the positional constraints. Iambo-cretic shortening indicates that Latin final syllables are not to be excluded in principle from foot structure; quite the contrary. The doctrine of total extraprosodicity is a superficial conclusion drawn from focusing on examples like (*spátu*)*la*, where there is simply nothing to be done. We know that /dēsin-ō/ will be parsed (dē)(sino) in the colloquial lan-guage, and from this we can infer that *blandula* is parsed (blan)(dula) and that *mandō* is (man)(dō). Maximality of prosodic organization is not abandoned whole-sale just to place the main-stress in the right position. (It is abandoned minimally, as we expect.) There is no law banning feet from final position; rather it is the prosodic heads of the word – main-stress and main foot – that are banned. This is exactly what was claimed above in the statement of NONFINALITY for Latin (66), which we repeat here:

(73)   **NONFINALITY**
   No prosodic head of PrWd is final in PrWd.

The constraint applies to the main-stressed syllable itself and to the foot in which it is housed. Descriptively, one would say that main-stress falls not on the *last* foot, as in previous analyses, but on the last *nonfinal* foot, rather like Palestinian Arabic, Cairene Radio Arabic, and Munsee, among others (Hayes 1991/95).

The constraint of NONFINALITY pushes the main-stress off the final syllable, often leaving open a number of possibilities for its location. As usual, the major positioning constraint is EDGEMOST: the prosodic heads fall as far to the right as possible. We must have, of course, NONFINALITY ≫ EDGEMOST, otherwise no nonfinality effects would be observable.[39] The constraint EDGEMOST(φ;E) penalizes

---

[39] This is related to Pāṇini's Theorem, ch. 5 below, whereby with relations between constraints A and B, the ranking B ≫ A entails that A has no effect on the grammar. Notice that we are not saying that they are 'ranked by the Elsewhere Condition': they are ranked by the facts; either ranking is possible.

forms according to the extent that item φ is removed from edge E. In Latin φ = prosodic head, E = right edge. For purposes of reckoning distance from the edge, we will take the relevant prosodic head to be the main-stressed syllable itself, and the distance from the edge will be measured in syllables.

To see the effects of this scheme, consider first forms LLL, which have two reasonable parses (ĹL)L and L(ĹL). For head foot, we write F′, for head syllable of head foot we write σ′.

(74)   **Nonfinality Effect** in trisyllables

Candidates	Nonfinality(F′;σ′)	Edgemost(σ′;R)
☞ (spátu)la		tula#
spa(túla)	*F′ !	la#

Assumed is the dominance of FtBin and of Lx≈Pr, which entails that a form must have at least one foot and a binary one at that. In the more general context, the effects of a principle of exhaustive metrical analysis, familiar from the earliest work in the area (Liberman 1975), is visibly at work. This principle is part of the parsing theory, and we will call it Parse-σ, omitting from the name the information that σ is parsed into F. It ensures, for example, that forms shaped HH will be parsed [(H́)(H)]₍ᵣWd rather than [(H́)H]₍ᵣWd. Both candidates have perfect nonfinality of F′ and σ′ and both agree in edgemostness of the main-stressed syllable; only Parse-σ dictates that the second foot must be posited. Similarly, forms LLH must be parsed (ĹL)(H). Note that the appearance of Parse-σ on the scene does not affect the argument (74) just given, since the competitors are perfectly matched for Parse-σ violations, at one each.

That Parse-σ is relegated to a subordinate role becomes apparent when we examine forms LLLL. Examination of the natural candidates for analysis of LLLL shows that Edgemost must dominate Parse-σ:

(75)   **Edgemost ≫ Parse-σ**, from LLLL

Candidates	Nonfinality(F′;σ′)	Edgemost(σ′;R)	Parse-σ
a. ☞ pa(tríci)a		i.a#	**
b. (pátri)(ci.a)		tri.ci.a# !	
c. (patri)(cí.a)	*F′ !		

The correct output *patrícia* (a) is poorly σ-parsed, while both of its competitors are perfect on that score. Edgemost, however, rules in its favor in the competition with (b), and so must dominate Parse-σ. Note that the pre-antepenultimate form (b) is correct for systems like that of Palestinian Arabic, indicating a different ranking of the constraints in such languages.

These considerations give us the core of the system of both Classical and Preclassical Latin. We have *Position* ≫ *Parsing*, or, in detail:

(76)   **Antepenultimacy**
NONFINALITY(F';σ') ≫ EDGEMOST(σ';R) ≫ PARSE-σ

The fundamental constraints Lx≈Pr and FTBIN are of course superordinate.

On this account, a word LLL is analyzed (ĹL)L not because the final syllable is marked extrametrical, but rather because the main *foot* stands in a nonfinal position, a pure nonfinality effect. The fate of words LLLL is decided by a combination of NONFINALITY, which winnows the candidate set down to L(ĹL)L and (ĹL)(LL), and EDGEMOST, which decides the matter in favor of the antepenult-stressed form, in which the prosodic head σ' stands nearest to the end of the word.

This kind of argument, in its use of constraint violation to compare distances, parallels the one given above about prefixing infixation (§4.1), and can only be made in a theory that evaluates over the set of possible structures. Under Bottom-Up Constructionism, which builds structure by deterministic rule, the feet must first be fixed correctly in place, and you can only choose the head-foot from among the ones you have before you, in the input to the rule of main-stress placement.

Exactly a *single* syllable ends up extrametrical here. But this follows from the very interaction of EDGEMOST and NONFINALITY which is necessary to generate the extrametricality effect in the first place. There is no special notion [+extrametrical], distinct from 'unparsed' or 'occupying weak position in prosodic structure', conditions which befall many an element, for many reasons. Consequently, as argued above in §4.3, there is no theory of extrametricality as a formal device, which requires among its axioms a principle limiting the scope of the feature [+extrametrical] to a single constituent. Because violations are always minimal, only the minimal amount of non-edgemostness will be tolerated. This minimum will often turn out to be a single constituent. (But not necessarily so, unless other factors conspire: cf. Tagalog *gr-um-adwet*, §4.1, where *gr* need not be regarded as constituent for the explanation to go through.)

The remaining component of the system is the foot theory. The bedrock constraints are FTBIN and RHTYPE = Trochaic. These are unviolated in the optimal forms of the language: every foot is binary on syllables or moras, and every foot is trochaic. In addition, universal prosody recognizes the Weight-to-Stress Principle WSP, which urges that the intrinsic prominence of heavy syllables be registered as prosodic prominence; this discriminates against the quantity–prominence mismatch of trochees (ĹH). Feet (ĤL) satisfy all these constraints but are known to be marked or even absent in trochaic systems (Hayes 1987, Prince 1990, Mester 1992); we wish to ban these on grounds of *rhythmic* structure, which favors length at the end of constituents. Let us call the relevant constraint 'Rhythmic Harmony' (RHHRM); for present purposes we can simplify its formulation to *(HL).

Of these constraints, only the WSP shows any mobility in the dialects (or register levels) of Latin under discussion. In Classical Latin, as shown above in (68), we must have NONFINALITY ≫ WSP, to obtain (*ámoː*) rather than **a*(*móː*). Both candidates contain a foot, satisfying the morphology–prosody interface constraint Lx≈Pr; both contain binary feet, satisfying FTBIN; but only (*ámoː*) succeeds in getting the main-stress off the last syllable. The cost is violation of the WSP. In the iambo-cretic shortening register of Pre-classical Latin, by contrast, we have (*ámo*) and no violation of the WSP at all. All four foot-relevant constraints are unviolated, and are therefore not dominated crucially by any other constraints in the grammar. These observations are summarized in the following table.

(77)   **Foot Form Constraints**

Constraint	Effect	Status
FTBIN	F = μμ, σσ	unviolated
RHTYPE=T	(σσ) = (σ́σ)	unviolated
RHHRM	*(HL)	unviolated
WSP	* H̆	violated in Classical Latin unviolated in Pre-classical shortening register

Having secured the proper infrastructure, we can approach the issue of iambo-cretic shortening. Mester proposes a special rule of repair, 'Remove μ', which works in concert with his second round of footing. Optimality Theory does not recognize repair strategies as distinct from the ordinary resources available for assigning structure in the first place. Structure is posited freely, though always subject to evaluation. Empty nodes are violations (of the constraint we have called FILL), but violation can be forced. Similarly, elements present in the input can remain structurally unanalyzed, violating PARSE. Such violations are tolerated in an optimal candidate only when they lead to better performance on higher-ranked constraints. In the case at hand, an underlying mora (as in the second syllable of /amoː/) is left unparsed – unattached to syllable structure – and hence uninterpreted, giving rise to a phonetic short vowel. The resulting structure looks something like this:

(78)   **Syllabically Unparsed Mora**

This is a monomoraic syllable. Failure to construe the second mora is a violation of Parse, specifically of the constraint Parse-μ, which must be distinguished from the other members of the Parse-*element* family. In Classical Latin, quantity is quite stable under prosodic analysis; Parse-μ is widely observed and no constraint discussed here forces it to be violated. Therefore, Parse-μ in Classical Latin is undominated by the constraints at hand.[40] But in the shortening register of Pre-classical Latin, Parse-μ is subordinated in the ranking, leading to the appearance of phonetic short vowels as the globally optimal but locally unfaithful renditions of lexical long vowels.

Following Mester 1992 (as 1994: 33), we want /HLH/ words like /diːcitoː/ 'say (imp. fut.)' to be parsed (diː)(cito)⟨ː⟩. Similarly, we want /LH/ words like /amoː/ to be parsed (amo)⟨ː⟩. With the *ad hoc* notation H⁻ used to indicate a potentially heavy syllable parsed as light, as for example in diagram (78), the relevant lexical–surface associations can be written as follows:

(79)   **Pre-classical Latin Parsing of Interesting Strings**

	Base	Faithful	*Parse-μ
a.	HH	(H)(H)	
b.	LH		(LH⁻)
c.	HLL	(H)(LL)	
d.	HLH		(H)(LH⁻)

What forces the Parse-μ violations? For bisyllabic words, it is clear that the parse (ĹH⁻) successfully avoids the wretched trochee (ĹH), which violates the WSP. Therefore we have WSP ≫ Parse-μ, meaning that it is more important to ensure that all heavy syllables are stressed than to retain underlying vowel length. One way to satisfy the WSP is to omit potential heaviness from syllables that stand in unstressable positions.

A second constraint that crucially dominates Parse-μ is Parse-σ, which compels exhaustive footing. This relation is manifest in the treatment of forms ending in HLH, which show cretic shortening.

(80)   **Parse-σ ≫ Parse-μ** from /HLH/

	Candidates	Parse-σ	Parse-μ
☞	(H́)(LH⁻)		*
	(H́)L(H)	* !	

The suboptimal parse *(H́)L(H) has nothing wrong with it, given the constraint set entertained here, but the 'trapping', as Mester puts it, of the middle syllable:

---

[40] By contrast, numerous violations of Parse-*segment* are forced by syllable structure conditions, as in /mell/ → *mel*, /cord/ → *cor*, /ment+s/ → *mens* (Steriade 1982). See below chs 6–8 for further discussion.

it is unaffiliated with F. The counter-analysis (H́)(LH⁻) is fully σ-parsed, but the price is leaving the final μ out of syllable structure. This shows that Parse-σ is dominant, forcing the Parse-μ violation. This ranking recognizes Mester's basic claim: that exhaustive parsing is the motive force behind the shortness effect.

With Parse-μ subordinated in the ranking, feet (H⁻ L) also become significant contenders. They also resolve the parsing problem presented by HLH, leading to *(dési)(noː), for example, in place of actual (déː)(sino). Both candidates are fully σ-parsed; both have nonfinal prosodic heads; and they agree on the rightmostness of the main-stress. The only difference is the location of the H that is incompletely parsed as H⁻. The outcome (H⁻L)H is witnessed in various languages, famously English (Myers 1987b, Prince 1990) and Boumaa Fijian (Dixon 1988, Hayes 1991/95), but not Latin. What makes the difference in Latin? The plausible candidate is Pk-Prom, repeated from (37):

(81)   **Peak-Prominence** (Pk-Prom).
       Peak(x) > Peak(y) if $|x| > |y|$

In terms of a two-way H/L contrast, this means that H́ is a better peak than Ĺ. Because of the unparsed mora, H⁻ is a light syllable, and the foot (H́⁻ L) has inferior peak-prominence compared with (H́). The contrast becomes important in the analysis of HLH, as this tableau demonstrates:

(82)   **Pk-Prom and Parse-μ**

Candidates		Pk-Prom	Parse-μ
☞	(H́)(LH⁻)	|H|	*
	(H́⁻L)(H)	|H⁻| = |L| !	*

This is not a ranking argument: Parse-μ does not discriminate between these candidates, so the constraints are not in diametric conflict. Pk-Prom will decide the issue no matter where it is located in the hierarchy.[41] In Latin Pk-Prom cannot be allowed to play the same role that it does in Hindi/Urdu, singling out a heavy syllable anywhere among a string of light syllables; the positional constraints must dominate it, Edgemost in particular. The following comparison, in which the competitors are matched for their performance on all other constraints considered here except for Edgemost and Pk-Prom, demonstrates the necessity of the ranking relation.

---

[41] Observe that Pk-Prom as stated deals only with the main-stress, the peak of the PrWd. Feet (H⁻L) are banned everywhere in the word, and so the explanation must be extended to these cases. The issue does not arise to the right of the main-stress, and we will return to it only after the basic argument is laid out.

(83) EDGEMOST ≫ PK-PROM, from HLLL /incipere/ 'to begin'

Candidates	EDGEMOST	PK-PROM
☞ (in)(cípe)re	pe.re#	|L|
(ín)(cipe)re	ci.pe.re# !	|H|

This relation also holds in the grammar of Classical Latin, where PK-PROM has no visible effects. It is worth emphasizing that PK-PROM is quite distinct notionally from the WSP, even putting aside the limitation of the WSP to the foot level. The WSP goes from weight to stress: 'if heavy then stressed' (equivalently, 'if unstressed then light'). PK-PROM essentially goes the other way: 'if stressed then heavy' (contrapositively and equivalently: 'if light then unstressed'). To see this, imagine PK-PROM playing out over a binary weight contrast; it says H́>Ĺ, or in the language of violations, *Ĺ. The WSP has nothing to say about the configuration Ĺ: it proscribes only weak H. These two halves of the purported biconditional 'heavy iff stressed' have very different status in stress systems, as Prince 1990 observes; the present case is a further demonstration of this fact.

We have now established the form of the constraint system. For convenience of reference, the rationale for the crucial rankings is summarized in the following table (84).

(84) **Support for Rankings**

Ranking	Because:	Remarks
NONFINALITY(F′;σ′) ≫ EDGEMOST(σ′;R)	(ĹL)L] > L(ĹL)]	*Shared, all Registers:* Position of main-stress
EDGEMOST(σ′;R) ≫ PARSE-σ	L(ĹL)L] > (ĹL)(LL)]	
EDGEMOST(σ′;R) ≫ PK-PROM	HĹLL] > H́LLL]	
WSP ≫ PARSE-μ	[(ĹH⁻)] > [(ĹH)] (H́)(LH⁻)] > (H́)(LH)]	*Shortening Register:* Iambo-cretic effect
PARSE-σ ≫ PARSE-μ	(H́)(LH⁻)] > (H́)L(H)]	

Observe that the three relations above the double line are shared in all dialects or speech-levels; those below it delimit the characteristics of iambo-cretic shortening.

To conclude this discussion, we assemble the constraint relations established for Latin and go on to demonstrate the efficacy of the constraint system in dealing with the key examples.

(85) **Constraint Structure of Pre-classical Latin Shortening Grammar**

  a. Undominated

  WSP, RhHrm, FtBin, RhType=T, Lx≈Pr

  b. Main Sequence

  Lx≈Pr, FtBin ≫ Nonfinality(F′;σ′) ≫ Edgemost(σ′;R) ≫ Parse-σ ≫ Parse-μ

  c. Weight Effect

  WSP ≫ Parse-μ

  d. Bounding

  Edgemost(σ′;R) ≫ Pk-Prom

Empirical considerations do not force a total order on the set of constraints. Any total order consistent with the partial order will yield equivalent results. Without violating the crucial rankings we can place all four of the foot-relevant constraints WSP, RhHrm, FtBin, and RhType=T in a single package at the top of the hierarchy, which we will label 'foot form'. More arbitrarily, under the compulsion of the planar format of the tableau, we will list Pk-Prom at the very bottom. This conveniently divides the constraint system into four blocks:

(86) **Block Structure of the Constraint System**, in domination order

  a. Foot Form

  b. Position

  c. Parsing

  d. Prominence

To simplify the presentation, all candidate parses that fail to satisfy Lx≈Pr, FtBin, and RhType=T will be omitted from consideration, since violation is obvious and inevitably fatal.

  First, let us contrast the treatment of bisyllables LH and HH.

(87) **Parsing of LH**: Iambic shortening

Candidates /LH/	Foot Form	Position		Parsing		
		Nonfinal	Edgem	Parse-σ	Parse-μ	Pk-Prom
a. ☞ (ĹH⁻)		*F′	σ#		*	|L|
b. L (Ĥ)		*F′ *σ′ !		*		|H|
c. (ĹH)	*WSP !	*F′	σ#			|L|

Here the parse (ĹH⁻) is optimal because (ĹH) is a poor foot violating the WSP, and because L(Ĥ) violates both requirements on the nonfinality of heads. This shows that we have 'iambic shortening'.

(88) **Parsing of HH**: No shortening

Candidates /HH/	Foot Form	Position		Parsing		Pk-Prom
		Nonfinal	Edgem	Parse-σ	Parse-μ	
a. ☞ (H́)(H)			σ#			|H|
b. (H́) H⁻			σ#	* !	*	|H|
c. (H́⁻H⁻)		*F'!	σ#		**	|L|
d. (H́⁻H)	*WSP !	*F' *σ'!	σ#		*	|L|
e. (H)(H́)		*F' *σ'!				|H|
f. (H́) H	*WSP !		σ#	*		|H|

The form (H́)(H) incurs only the violation of EDGEMOST(σ';R) that is necessitated by adherence to NONFINALITY(F';σ'). All other candidates do worse. Of particular interest are the shortening candidates (b), (c), (d). They enjoy no advantage whatsoever over the optimal candidate, showing that over this set of constraints none of them could win, regardless of ranking. (They are 'harmonically bounded' on these constraints by the optimal form; see §§6.2.3, 8.2.3, 9.1.1, A.2 for use of this notion, and Samek-Lodovici 1992a for independent development of it.)

(89) **Parsing of HLH**: Cretic shortening

Candidates /HLH/	Foot Form	Position		Parsing		Pk-Prom
		Nonfinal	Edgem	Parse-σ	Parse-μ	
a. ☞ (H́)(LH⁻)			σσ#		*	|H|
b. (H́⁻L)(H)			σσ#		*	|L| !
c. (H́)L(H)			σσ#	* !		|H|
d. (H́(LH)	*WSP !		σσ#			|H|
e. (H́L)(H)	*RhHrm!		σσ#			|H|

Among the most interesting comparisons are those between the shortened optimal form (H́)(LH⁻) and its faithful nonshortening competitors (c), (d), (e). These show how cretic shortening is forced by the dominance of the WSP, RHHRM, and PARSE-σ. Observe, for example, how competition with (H́)L(H), form (c), is decided by PARSE-σ, which forces the inclusion of syllables in foot structure, at the expense of an unfaithful rendering of the underlying moraic structure.

(90) **Parsing of HLL**

Candidates /HLL/	Foot Form	Position		Parsing		
		Nonfinal	Edgem	Parse-σ	Parse-μ	Pk-Prom
a. ☞ (Ĥ)(LL)				σσ#		|H|
b. (Ĥ̄L) L				σσ#	* !	*	|L|
c. (Ĥ)LL				σσ#	* ! *		|H|
d. (H)(L̇L)		*F′ !	σ#			|L|
e. (ĤL) L	*RhHrm !			σσ#	*		|H|

Like its moraic parallel HH, the wordform HLL has the near-perfect parse (Ĥ)(LL), with only Edgemost being violated, a necessary infraction. Its rivals must all incur more serious violations.

The form /LLH/ is similarly stable under the constraint system posited here. The most attractive rival to the actual (L̇L)(H) is perhaps (L̇L)H⁻, which would normalize /LLH/ to the /LLL/ pattern. But this competitor has literally nothing going for it, viewed in terms of the constraints under discussion: like (b) above, it pointlessly violates both Parse-μ and Parse-σ, while achieving no superiority on the other constraints. Crucially, the WSP is satisfiable with respect to the final syllable of /LLH/ either by footing it faithfully as (H) or by treating it unfaithfully as H⁻. But in this grammar there is no sufficiently high-ranked constraint – for example, no dominating nonfinality constraint demanding absolute stresslessness of the final syllable – that would compel the unfaithful rendering.

This completes our review of the basic patterns, those involving main-stress and shortening. A couple of further subtleties deserve mention. Iambo-cretic shortening not only affects long vowels, it also treats *closed syllables* as light, as evidenced by versification practice (Allen 1973, Kager 1989, Mester 1992). We have quantitative analyses like these:[42]

(91) **Light Closed Syllables**

	Base	Analysis	Pattern
a.	/kanis/	(.ka.nis.)$_{\mu.\mu}$	(LH⁻)
b.	/volupta:te:s/	(.vo.lup.)$_{\mu.\mu}$ (ta:)$_{\mu\mu}$ (te:s)$_{\mu\mu}$	(LH⁻) (H) (H)
c.	/ve:nerant/	(ve:)$_{\mu\mu}$ (.ne.rant.)$_{\mu.\mu}$	(H) (LH⁻)

In such cases, the syllable-closing consonant is analyzed as nonmoraic, merely adjoined to the syllable, so that .nis. = .n[i]$_\mu$s, for example (cf. Kager 1989). What is ineffective, here, is the parsing principle requiring that a syllable-final consonant (sequence) correspond to a heaviness-inducing weak mora. To ensure the parallelism with long-vowel shortening, we can assume that moraic parsing is

---

[42] Glosses: 'dog'; 'desires'; 'come (3pl.fut.pf.)'. Examples from Mester 1992 (as 1994: 12, 17, 31).

not itself violated, but rather that the mora it licenses remains unparsed syllabic-ally. The structure looks like this:

(92)   **Unparsed Syllable-Closing Mora**

If this kind of structure is admitted, both kinds of lightness effects of iambo-cretic shortening show up as PARSE-μ violations.[43]

Iambic shortening also shows up in nonfinal position, as example (91b) illus-trates.[44] We will offer only a few remarks here on this phenomenon and on the more general predictions of the constraint hierarchy for quantitative structure in the stretch preceding the main-stress. The following tableau gives a sense of how the constraint hierarchy parses examples shaped LHHH, like (91b):

(93)   **Internal Nonparsing of Moras**

Candidates LHHH	Foot Form	Position		Parsing		
		NONFINAL	EDGEM	PARSE-σ	PARSE-μ	PK-PROM
a. ☞ (LH⁻)(H́)(H)			σ#		*	|H|
b. L(H)(H́)(H)			σ#	* !		|H|

An interesting issue arises in longer words which have the potential for feet (H⁻L) before the main-stress, for example HLHH. As noted in fn. 41, p. 73 above,

---

[43] These phenomena can also be construed in metrical rather than syllabic terms, perhaps more interestingly. Suppose that the actual terminal nodes of metrical structure are the positions on the first grid row (Prince 1983, Halle & Vergnaud 1987). (Bracketing of syllable strings is derivative from this in the obvious way.) Mapping syllable structure to the grid is what's at issue. In general, $\mu \to x$. But we can also have $[\mu\mu]_\sigma \to x$, 'compression' in the manner of Yupik (Woodbury 1981, Hewitt 1992), somewhat like the 'mora sluicing' of Prince 1983. The constraint that's being violated is not PARSE-μ-to-σ but rather PARSE-μ-to-x. To make it perfectly parallel to discussion in the text, instead of $\mu_i\mu_j \to x_ix_j$, we get $\mu_i\mu_j \to x_i$, with μ_j unassociated. Thus both V: and VC violate PARSE-μ-to-x equally. Compressed V: is interpreted as equivalent to a short vowel; that is, quantity is read off the first layer of the grid. Evidence for this view comes from the fact that geminates may suffer iambic shortening, e.g. *supellectilis* 'utensils' without appar-ently being literally degeminated (Mester 1992, as 1994: 18n).

[44] Mester (1992, as 1994: 18n) points to a number of other subtleties, such as the fact that the vowel-shortening wing of the phenomenon applies only sporadically to internal long vowels. He suggests that preserving lexical (distinctive) quantity may drive this difference in behavior. We refer the reader to Mester's discussion.

if Pᴋ-Pʀᴏᴍ is stated so as to apply only to the peak or main-stress of the PrWd, it will have no consequences outside the head foot. Without further remark, we expect (H̄L)(H́)(H) from HLHH. This avoids the Foot Form violation (HL), which we know to be avoided in the parse of /HLH/, shown in (89); and it achieves complete foot-parsing at the expense of Pᴀʀsᴇ-μ, which is well-motivated in the grammar. We suggest that Pᴋ-Pʀᴏᴍ in fact applies to all 'peaks' or heads, both of PrWd and of F. But within this subsystem, there is also a ranking of priorities: evaluation of the head of PrWd takes priority over evaluation of foot-heads. To see this, consider the rival parses *(H́̄L)(H) and (H́)(LH̄). At the foot level each sports one heavy head and one light head, since |H̄| = |L|. It is only at the PrWd level that the decision can be made in favor of the correct form, which has a heavy main peak. In chapter 8, we provide a general mechanism for constructing complex constraints like Pᴋ-Pʀᴏᴍ from the coordination of two distinct scales of relative prominence, here (1) head of PrWd vs. foot-head and (2) heavy syllable vs. light syllable.

A final, fundamental question raised by the analysis concerns the relation between Classical Latin and Pre-classical Latin, or, more precisely, between the formal register and the informal shortening register of the Pre-classical language. The shortening register is derived by two re-rankings: Pᴀʀsᴇ-μ is made subordinate and the WSP rises to the top. It might be objected, on aesthetic grounds, that one should aim to get the difference out of a single re-ranking. This seems to us too superficial a judgment. The notion of colloquial register surely has a substantive characterization which is not even approximated by counting changes in a constraint or rule system; certain single re-rankings will massively alter the surface appearance of the system. In Latin, the effect of the re-ranking is to render the foot-defining block of constraints entirely transparent, at the cost of some failures to realize underlying quantity. This is consistent with the general sense that colloquial language simplifies prosodic structures, rendering them in closer accord with universal *structural markedness* constraints, while subordinating *Faithfulness*.

Chapter 5

The Construction of Grammar in Optimality Theory

Phonological theory contains two parts: a theory of substantive universals of phonological well-formedness and a theory of formal universals of constraint interaction. These two components are respectively the topics of §§5.1 and 5.2. Since much of this work concerns the first topic, the discussion here will be limited to a few brief remarks. In §5.3, we give Pāṇini's Theorem, a theorem about the priority of the specific which follows from the basic operation of Optimality Theory as set out in §5.2.

5.1 Construction of Harmonic Orderings from Phonetic and Structural Scales

To define grammars from hierarchies of well-formedness constraints, we need two distinct constructions: one that takes given constraints and defines their interactions, another that pertains to the constraints themselves. The first will be discussed at some length in §5.2; we now take up the second briefly.

Construction of constraints amounts in many ways to a theory of contextual markedness (Chomsky & Halle 1968: ch. 9, Kean 1974, Cairns & Feinstein 1982, Cairns 1988, Archangeli & Pulleyblank 1992). Linguistic phonetics gives a set of scales on phonetic dimensions; these are not well-formedness ratings, but simply the analyses of phonetic space that are primitive from the viewpoint of linguistic theory. (We use the term 'scale' in the loosest possible sense, to encompass everything from unary features to n-ary orderings.)

Issues of relative well-formedness, or markedness, arise principally when elements from the different dimensions are combined into interpretable representations. High sonority, for example, does not by itself entail high (or low) Harmony; but when a segment occurs in a structural position such as nucleus, onset, or coda, its intrinsic sonority in combination with the character of its position gives rise to markedness-evaluating constraints such as Hnuc above. Similarly, tongue-height in vowels is neither harmonic nor disharmonic in isolation, but when the dimension of tongue-root advancement/retraction is brought in, clear patterns of relative well-formedness or Harmony emerge, as has been emphasized in the work of Archangeli & Pulleyblank (1992). These *Harmony scales* are intimately tied to the repertory of constraints that grammars draw on. Inasmuch as there are principled harmonic concomitants of dimensional combination, we need ways of deriving Harmony scales from phonetic scales. Symbolically, we have

(94) **Harmony Scale from Interaction of Phonetic Scales**
    $\{a > b \ldots\} \otimes \{x > y > \ldots\} = ax > \ldots$

The goal of contextual markedness theory is to give content to the operator $\otimes$. Below in §8.2 we introduce a formal mechanism of *Prominence Alignment* which generates constraint rankings from paired phonetic scales, yielding a Harmony scale on their combination. In the syllable structure application of §8.2, the two phonetic scales which are aligned are segmental prominence (the sonority dimension) and syllable position prominence (Peak is a more prominent position than Margin). The result is a Harmony scale on associations of segments to syllable positions.

It is important to distinguish the three kinds of scales or hierarchies which figure in Optimality Theory. To minimize confusions, we have given each its own distinctive comparison symbol. Two of these figure in (94): elements are ordered on a phonetic scale by the relation '>', and on a Harmony scale according to '≻'. The third type of hierarchy in the theory is the domination hierarchy, along which constraints are ranked by the relation '≫'. These different types of scales are enumerated and exemplified in (95) below.

(95) **Three Different Scales in Optimality Theory**

Type of scale or hierarchy	Relates	Symbol	Example	Meaning
Phonetic scale	Points along elementary representational dimensions	>	a > l	*a* is more sonorous than *l*
Harmony scale	Well-formedness of structural configurations built from elementary dimensions	≻	á ≻ í	a nucleus filled by *a* is more harmonic than a nucleus filled by *l*
Domination hierarchy	Relative priority of well-formedness	≫	Ons ≫ Hnuc	the constraint Ons strictly dominates the constraint Hnuc

5.2   The Theory of Constraint Interaction

The criterion defining grammaticality in Optimality Theory is optimality among competitors: for a given input i, a grammatical structural description or output A is one that has the greatest Harmony among the set Gen(i) of all possible parses of i. That is, a parse A of i is grammatical if and only if there is no competing parse B in Gen(i) such that B has higher Harmony than A: no B such that B > A. The grammatical parses are thus by definition the maximal elements in the harmonic ordering of parses, so the central concept requiring formal definition is harmonic ordering itself: what exactly defines the relation A > B among competing parses A and B?

In order to define harmonic comparison of candidates consisting of entire parses, we will proceed in two steps. First, we get clear about comparing entire candidates on the basis of a single constraint, using Ons and Hnuc from the Berber analysis in chapter 2 as our examples. Then we show how to combine the evaluation of these constraints using a domination hierarchy.

5.2.1   Comparison of Entire Candidates by a Single Constraint

The first order of business is a precise definition of how a single constraint harmonically orders entire parses. We start with the simpler case of a single binary constraint, and then generalize the definition to non-binary constraints.

5.2.1.1   Ons: Binary constraints

It is useful to think of Ons as examining a syllable to see if it has an onset; if it does not, we think of Ons as assessing a **mark** of violation, *Ons. Ons is an example of a *binary constraint*: a given syllable either satisfies or violates the constraint entirely. The marks Ons generates are all of the same type: *Ons. For the moment, all the marks under consideration are identical. Later, when we consider the interaction of multiple binary constraints, there will be different types of marks to distinguish; each binary constraint $\mathbb{C}$ generates marks of its own characteristic type, *$\mathbb{C}$. Furthermore, some constraints will be non-binary, and will generate marks of different types representing different degrees of violation of the constraint: the next constraint we examine, Hnuc, will illustrate this.

When assessing the entire parse of a string, Ons examines each σ node in the parse and assesses one mark *Ons for each such node which lacks an onset. Introducing a bit of useful notation, let A be a prosodic parse of an input string, and let Ons(A) = (*Ons, *Ons, . . .) be a list containing one mark *Ons for each onsetless syllable in A. Thus for example Ons(.txź.ńt.) = (*Ons): the second, onsetless, syllable earns the parse .txź.ńt. its sole *Ons mark. (Here we use ź to indicate that z is parsed as a nucleus.)

Ons provides a criterion for comparing the Harmony of two parses A and B; we determine which of A or B is more harmonic ('less marked') by comparing $\text{Ons}(A)$ and $\text{Ons}(B)$ to see which contains fewer *Ons marks. We can notate this as follows:

$$A >_{\text{Ons}}^{\text{parse}} B \text{ iff } \text{Ons}(A) >^{(*)} \text{Ons}(B)$$

where '$>_{\text{Ons}}^{\text{parse}}$' denotes comparison of entire parses and '$\text{Ons}(A) >^{(*)} \text{Ons}(B)$' means 'the list $\text{Ons}(A)$ contains fewer marks *Ons than the list $\text{Ons}(B)$'. (We will use the notation '(*)' as a mnemonic for 'list of marks'.) If the lists are the same length, then we write[45]

$$A \approx_{\text{Ons}}^{\text{parse}} B \text{ iff } \text{Ons}(A) \approx^{(*)} \text{Ons}(B).$$

What is crucial to $>^{(*)}$ is not numerical counting, but simply comparisons of *more* and *less*. This becomes clear in the recursive definition of $>^{(*)}$, which provides the basis for the entire Optimality Theory formalism for Harmony evaluation. The idea behind this recursive definition is straightforward.

Suppose we are given two lists of identical marks *ℂ; we need to determine which list is shorter, and we can't count. Here's what we do: we toss away pairs of marks, one from each list, until one of the lists disappears. More precisely, we use the following procedure. First, we check to see if either list is empty. If both are, the conclusion is that neither list is shorter. If one list is empty and the other isn't, the empty one is shorter. If neither is empty, then we remove one mark *ℂ from each list, and start all over. The process will eventually terminate with a correct conclusion about which list is the shorter – but with no information at all about the original numerical lengths of the lists.

Formalizing this recursive definition is straightforward; it is also worthwhile, since the definition will be needed to characterize the full means of evaluating the relative harmonies of two candidate parses.

We assume two simple operations for manipulating lists. The operation we'll call **FM** extracts the First Member (or ForeMost element) of a list; this is what we use to extract the First Mark *ℂ from each list. The other operation **Rest** takes a list, throws away its First Member, and returns the rest of the list; we use this for

---

[45] In §5.1 we define several formally distinct orders in terms of one another. At the risk of overburdening the notation, we use superscripts like ^{parse} and $^{(*)}$ to keep all these orders distinct. We prefer to resist the temptation to sweep conceptual subtleties under the rug by using extremely concise notation in which many formally distinct relations are denoted by the same symbol. It is important to remember, however, that the symbols '>' and '≈' – no matter what their subscripts and superscripts – always mean 'more harmonic' and 'equally harmonic'. We need to compare the Harmonies of many different kinds of elements, and for clarity while setting up the fundamental definitions of the theory, we distinguish these different Harmony comparison operators. Once the definitions are grasped, however, there is no risk of confusion in dropping superscripts and subscripts, which we will indeed do. The superscripts and subscripts can always be inferred from context – once the whole system is understood.

the recursive step of 'starting over', asking which list is shorter after the first $*\mathbb{C}$ has been thrown out of each.

Since we keep throwing out marks until none are left, it's also important to deal with the case of empty lists. We let ( ) denote an empty list, and we define FM so that when it operates on ( ), its value is ø, the null element.

Now let α and β be two lists of marks. We write $\alpha >^{(*)} \beta$ for 'α is more harmonic than β', which in the current context means 'α is *shorter* than β', since marks are anti-harmonic. To express the fact that an empty list of marks is more harmonic than a non-empty list, or equivalently that a null first element indicates a more harmonic list than does a non-null first element $*\mathbb{C}$, we define the Harmony relation $>^*$ between single marks as follows:

(96)   **Marks are Anti-Harmonic**
    ø $>^*$ $*\mathbb{C}$

Remembering that $\approx$ denotes 'equally harmonic' (or 'equally marked'), we also note the obvious facts about identical single marks:

ø $\approx^*$ ø and $*\mathbb{C} \approx^* *\mathbb{C}$

Our recursive definition of $>^{(*)}$ can now be given as follows, where α and β denote two lists of identical marks:

(97)   **Harmonic Ordering – Lists of Identical Marks**
    $\alpha >^{(*)} \beta$ iff either:
        (i) $FM(\alpha) >^* FM(\beta)$
    or
        (ii) $FM(\alpha) \approx^* FM(\beta)$ and $Rest(\alpha) >^{(*)} Rest(\beta)$

Along with the definition (97) of $>^{(*)}$ come obvious corresponding definitions of $<^{(*)}$ and $\approx^{(*)}$. '$\beta <^{(*)} \alpha$' is equivalent to '$\alpha >^{(*)} \beta$'; '$\alpha \approx^{(*)} \beta$' is equivalent to 'neither $\alpha >^{(*)} \beta$ nor $\beta >^{(*)} \alpha$'. In subsequent definitions of various types of >-orders, the obvious definitions of the corresponding <- and $\approx$-relations will be assumed implicitly.

To repeat the basic idea of the definition one more time in English: α is shorter than β if and only if one of the following is true: (i) the first member of α is null and the first member of β is not (i.e., α is empty and β is not), or (ii) the list left over after removing the first member of α is shorter than the list left over after removing the first member of β.[46]

---

[46] A simple example of how this definition (97) works is the following demonstration that

($*\mathbb{C}$) $>^{(*)}$ ($*\mathbb{C}$, $*\mathbb{C}$).

Now we can say precisely how ONS assesses the relative Harmony of two candidate parses, say $.t\acute{x}.z\acute{n}t.$ and $.tx\acute{z}.\acute{n}t.$ ONS assesses the first as more harmonic than the second, because the second has an onsetless syllable and the first does not. We write this as follows:

$$.t\acute{x}.z\acute{n}t. >_{\text{ONS}}{}^{\text{parse}} .tx\acute{z}.\acute{n}t. \text{ because } \text{ONS}(.t\acute{x}.z\acute{n}t.) = (\ ) >^{(*)} (\ ^*\text{ONS}\ ) = \text{ONS}(.tx\acute{z}.\acute{n}t.)$$

where $>^{(*)}$ is defined in (97).

As another example:

$$.t\acute{x}.z\acute{n}t. \approx_{\text{ONS}}{}^{\text{parse}} .tx\acute{z}.n\acute{t}. \text{ because } \text{ONS}(.t\acute{x}.z\acute{n}t.) = (\ ) \approx^{(*)} (\ ) = \text{ONS}(.tx\acute{z}.n\acute{t}.)$$

In general, for any binary constraint $\mathbb{C}$, the harmonic ordering of entire parses which it determines, $>_{\mathbb{C}}{}^{\text{parse}}$, is defined as follows, where A and B are candidate parses:

(98) **Harmonic Ordering of Forms – Entire Parses, Single Constraint $\mathbb{C}$**
  $A >_{\mathbb{C}}{}^{\text{parse}} B$ iff $\mathbb{C}(A) >^{(*)} \mathbb{C}(B)$

with $>^{(*)}$ as defined in (97).

It turns out that these definitions of $>^{(*)}$ (97) and $>_{\mathbb{C}}{}^{\text{parse}}$ (98), which we have developed for binary constraints (like ONS), apply equally to non-binary constraints (like HNUC); in the general case, a constraint's definition includes a harmonic ordering of the various types of marks it generates. The importance of the definition justifies bringing it all together in self-contained form:

Define α and β as follows (we use '$\equiv$' for 'is defined to be'):

$$\alpha \equiv (\ ^*\mathbb{C}\ ) \qquad \beta \equiv (\ ^*\mathbb{C},\ ^*\mathbb{C}\ )\ .$$

Then

$\alpha >^{(*)} \beta$ because
  (97.ii) $\text{FM}(\alpha) = {}^*\mathbb{C} \approx^* {}^*\mathbb{C} = \text{FM}(\beta)$ and
       $\text{Rest}(\alpha) = (\ ) >^{(*)} (\ ^*\mathbb{C}\ ) = \text{Rest}(\beta);$

where the last line, $(\ ) > (\ ^*\mathbb{C}\ )$, is in turn demonstrated by letting

$$\alpha' \equiv (\ ) \qquad \beta' \equiv ({}^*\mathbb{C})$$

and noting that

$\alpha' >^{(*)} \beta'$ because
  (97.i) $\text{FM}(\alpha') = \varnothing >^* {}^*\mathbb{C} = \text{FM}(\beta')$

by (96).

(99)

> **Harmonic Ordering of Forms – Entire Parse, Single Constraint**
>
> Let $\mathbb{C}$ denote a constraint. Let A,B be two candidate parses, and let α,β be the lists of marks assigned them by $\mathbb{C}$:
>
> $\quad \alpha \equiv \mathbb{C}(A), \beta \equiv \mathbb{C}(B)$
>
> $\mathbb{C}$ by definition provides a Harmony order $>^*$ of the marks it generates. This order is extended to a Harmony order $>^{(*)}$ over lists of marks as follows:
>
> $\quad \alpha >^{(*)} \beta$ iff either:
>
> $\qquad$ (i) $\qquad FM(\alpha) >^* FM(\beta)$
>
> $\quad$ or
>
> $\qquad$ (ii) $\quad FM(\alpha) \approx^* FM(\beta)$ and $Rest(\alpha) >^{(*)} Rest(\beta)$
>
> This order $>^{(*)}$ is in turn extended to a Harmony order over candidate parses (with respect to $\mathbb{C}$), $>_{\mathbb{C}}^{parse}$, as follows:
>
> $\quad A >_{\mathbb{C}}^{parse} B$ iff $\mathbb{C}(A) \equiv \alpha >^{(*)} \beta \equiv \mathbb{C}(B)$

The case we have so far considered, when $\mathbb{C}$ is binary, is the simplest precisely because the Harmony order over marks which gets the whole definition going, $>^*$, is so trivial:

$$\o >^* {}^*\mathbb{C}$$

'a mark absent is more harmonic than one present' (96). In the case we consider next, however, the ordering of the marks provided by $\mathbb{C}$, $>^*$, is more interesting.

5.2.1.2   *HNUC: Non-binary constraints*

Turn now to HNUC. When it examines a single syllable, HNUC can usefully be thought of as generating a symbol designating the nucleus of that syllable; if the nucleus is *n*, then HNUC generates *ń*. HNUC arranges these nucleus symbols in a Harmony order, in which $\acute{x} >_{\text{HNUC}} \acute{y}$ if and only if x is more sonorous than y: $|x| > |y|$.

If A is an entire prosodic parse, HNUC generates a list of all the nuclei in A. For reasons soon to be apparent, it will be convenient to think of HNUC as generating a list of nuclei *sorted from most to least harmonic, according to HNUC* – i.e., from most to least sonorous. So, for example, HNUC(.txź.ńt.) = (ń, ź).

When HNUC evaluates the relative harmonies of two entire syllabifications A and B, it first compares the most harmonic nucleus of A with the most harmonic nucleus of B: if that of A is more sonorous, then A is the winner without further ado. Since the lists of nuclei HNUC(A) and HNUC(B) are assumed sorted from most to least harmonic, this process is simply to compare the First Member of HNUC(A) with the First Member of HNUC(B): if one is more harmonic than the other, according to HNUC, the more harmonic nucleus wins the competition for its entire parse. If, on the other hand, the two First Members of HNUC(A) and

Hnuc(B) are equally harmonic according to Hnuc (i.e., equally sonorous), then we eject these two First Members from their respective lists and start over, comparing the Rest of the nuclei in exactly the same fashion.

This procedure is exactly the one formalized above in (99). We illustrate the formal definition by examining how Hnuc determines the relative harmonies of

$$A \equiv .t\hat{x}.z\acute{n}t. \quad \text{and} \quad B \equiv .\acute{t}x.z\acute{n}t.$$

First, $\mathbb{C} \equiv$ Hnuc assigns the following:

$$\alpha \equiv \mathbb{C}(A) = (\acute{n}, \hat{x}) \qquad \beta \equiv \mathbb{C}(B) = (\acute{n}, \acute{t})$$

To order the parses A and B, i.e., to determine whether

$$A >_{\mathbb{C}}^{\text{parse}} B,$$

we must order their list of marks according to $\mathbb{C}$, i.e., determine whether

$$\mathbb{C}(A) \equiv \alpha >^{(*)} \beta \equiv \mathbb{C}(B).$$

To do this, we examine the First Member of each list of marks (its First Mark), and determine whether

$$\text{FM}(\alpha) >^* \text{FM}(\beta).$$

As it happens,

$$\text{FM}(\alpha) \approx \text{FM}(\beta),$$

since both First Marks are $\acute{n}$, so we must discard the First Marks and examine the Rest, to determine whether

$$\alpha' \equiv \text{Rest}(\alpha) >^{(*)} \text{Rest}(\beta) \equiv \beta'.$$

Here,

$$\alpha' = (\hat{x}); \beta' = (\acute{t}).$$

So again we consider First Marks, to determine whether

$$\text{FM}(\alpha') >^* \text{FM}(\beta').$$

Indeed this is the case:

$$\text{FM}(\alpha') = \hat{x} >^* \acute{t} = \text{FM}(\beta')$$

since $|x| > |t|$. Thus we finally conclude that

.tx̂.znt. $>_{\text{Hnuc}}^{\text{parse}}$.íx.znt.

Hnuc assesses nuclei from most to least harmonic, and that is how they are ordered in the lists Hnuc generates for Harmony evaluation. Hnuc is an unusual constraint in this regard; the other non-binary constraints we consider in this book will compare their *worst* marks first: the mark lists they generate are ordered from least to most harmonic (see *P and *M in §8.4.1). Both kinds of constraints are treated by the same definition (99). The issue of whether mark lists should be generated worst- or best-first will often not arise, for one of two reasons. First, if a constraint $\mathbb{C}$ is binary, the question is meaningless because all the marks it generates are identical: *$\mathbb{C}$. Alternatively, if a constraint applies only once to an entire parse, then it will generate only one mark per candidate, and the issue of ordering multiple marks does not even arise. (Several examples of such constraints, including edgemostness of main-stress, or edgemostness of an infix, are discussed in chapter 4.) But for constraints like Hnuc which are non-binary and which apply multiply in a candidate parse, part of the definition of the constraint must be whether it lists worst or best marks first.

5.2.2   Comparison of Entire Candidates by an Entire Constraint Hierarchy

We have now defined how a single constraint evaluates the relative Harmonies of entire candidate parses (99). It remains to show how a collection of such constraints, arranged in a strict domination hierarchy [$\mathbb{C}1 \gg \mathbb{C}2 \gg \cdots$], *together* perform such an evaluation: that is, how constraints interact.

Consider the part of the Berber constraint hierarchy we have so far developed: [Ons ≫ Hnuc]. The entire hierarchy can be regarded as assigning to a complete parse such as .txź.nt. the following list of lists of marks:

(100a)   [Ons ≫ Hnuc](.txź.nt.) = [Ons(.txź.nt.), Hnuc(.txź.nt.)] = [(*Ons), (ń, ź)]

The First Member here is the list of marks assigned by the dominant constraint: (*Ons). Following are the lists produced by successive constraints down the domination hierarchy; in this case, there is just the one other list assigned by Hnuc. As always, the nuclei are ordered from most to least harmonic by Hnuc.

We use square brackets to delimit this list of lists, but this is only to aid the eye, and to suggest the connection with constraint hierarchies, which we also enclose in square brackets. Square and round brackets are formally equivalent here, in the sense that they are treated identically by the list-manipulating operations FM and Rest.

The general definition of the list of lists of marks assigned by a constraint hierarchy is simply:

(101) **Marks Assigned by an Entire Constraint Hierarchy**
The marks assigned to an entire parse A by a constraint hierarchy
[C1 ≫ C2 ≫ ⋯] is the following list of lists of marks:
[C1 ≫ C2 ≫ ⋯](A) ≡ [C1(A), C2(A), ⋯]

Consider a second example, .tx̂.zńt.:

(100b) [Oɴs ≫ Hɴᴜᴄ](.tx̂.zńt.) = [Oɴs(.tx̂.zńt.), Hɴᴜᴄ(.tx̂.zńt.)] = [( ), (ń, x̂)]

Since there are no onsetless syllables in this parse, Oɴs(.tx̂.zńt.) = ( ), the empty
list. A third example is:

(100c) [Oɴs ≫ Hɴᴜᴄ](.tx̂.zńt.) = [( ), (ń, t́)]

As always in Berber, the Oɴs constraint is lifted phrase-initially, so this parse
incurs no marks *Oɴs.
Now we are ready to harmonically order these three parses. Corresponding
directly to the example tableau (17) of chapter 2, p. 24, repeated here:

(102) **Constraint Tableau** for three parses of /txznt/

Candidates	Oɴs	Hɴᴜᴄ
☞ .tx̂.zńt.		ń x̂
.tx̂.zńt.		ń t́ !
.txẑ.ńt.	* !	ń ẑ

we have, from (100a–c):

(103) **Marks Assessed by the Constraint Hierarchy** on three parses of /txznt/

A	[Oɴs ≫ Hɴᴜᴄ] (A)		
.tx̂.zńt.	[( ) ,	(ń x̂)	]
.tx̂.zńt.	[( ) ,	(ń t́)	]
.txẑ.ńt.	[(*Oɴs) ,	(ń ẑ)	]

To see how to define the Harmony order $>_{[Oɴs \gg Hɴᴜᴄ]}$ that the constraint hierarchy
imposes on the candidate parses, let's first review how Harmony comparisons
are performed with the tableau (102). We start by examining the marks in the

first column, ONS. Only the candidates which fare best by these marks survive for further consideration. In this case, one candidate, *.txź.ńt.*, is ruled out because it has a mark *ONS while the other two do not. That is, this candidate is less harmonic than the other two with respect to the hierarchy [ONS ≫ HNUC] because it is less harmonic than the other two with respect to the dominant individual constraint ONS. The remaining two parses *.tx̂.zńt.* and *.îx.zńt.* are equally harmonic with respect to ONS, and so to determine their relative Harmonies with respect to [ONS ≫ HNUC] we must continue by comparing them with respect to the next constraint down the hierarchy, HNUC. These two parses are compared by the individual constraint HNUC in just the way we have already defined: the most harmonic nuclei are compared first, and since this fails to determine a winner, the next-most harmonic nuclei are compared, yielding the final determination that *.tx̂.zńt.* $>_{[\text{ONS} \gg \text{HNUC}]}$ *.îx.zńt.*

For the case of [ONS ≫ HNUC], the definition should now be clear:

(104)   **Harmonic Ordering of Forms – Entire Parses by [ONS ≫ HNUC]**
   A $>_{[\text{ONS} \gg \text{HNUC}]}$ B iff either
      (i)   A $>_{\text{ONS}}$ B
  or
      (ii) A $\approx_{\text{ONS}}$ B and A $>_{\text{HNUC}}$ B

For a general constraint hierarchy, we have the following recursive definition:

(105)

Harmonic Ordering of Forms – Entire Parse, Entire Constraint Hierarchy

A $>_{[\text{C1} \gg \text{C2} \gg \ldots]}$ B iff either
    (i) A $>_{\text{C1}}$ B
  or
    (ii) A $\approx_{\text{C1}}$ B and A $>_{[\text{C2} \gg \ldots]}$ B

All the orderings in (104) and (105) are of complete parses, and we have therefore omitted the superscript ^{parse}. The Harmony order presupposed by this definition, $>_{\text{C1}}^{\text{parse}}$, the order on entire parses determined by the single constraint C1, is defined in (99).

It is worth showing that the definitions of whole-parse Harmony orderings by a single constraint $>_{\text{C}}$ (99) and by a constraint hierarchy $>_{[\text{C1} \gg \text{C2} \gg \ldots]}$ (105) are essentially identical. To see this, we need only bring in FM and Rest explicitly, and insert them into (105); the result is the following:

(106)   **Harmonic Ordering of Forms – Entire Parses, Entire Constraint Hierarchy**
   (opaque version)
   Let $\mathbb{CH} \equiv [\text{C1} \gg \text{C2} \gg \cdots]$ be a constraint hierarchy and let A,B be two candidate parses. Let ℵ,ℶ be the two lists of lists of marks assigned to these parses by the hierarchy:

א ≡ CH(A),   ב ≡ CH(B)

It follows that:

FM(א) = C1(A),   Rest(א) = [C2 ≫ ···](A);

FM(ב) = C1(B),   Rest(ב) = [C2 ≫ ···](B)

The hierarchy CH determines a harmonic ordering over lists of lists of marks as follows:

א >$^{[(*)]}$ ב iff either

   (i) FM(א) >$^{(*)}$ FM(ב) (i.e., C1(A) >$^{(*)}$ C1(B), i.e., A >$_{C1}$ B)

or

   (ii) FM(א) ≈$^{(*)}$ FM(ב) (i.e., A ≈$_{C1}$ B)

    and

      Rest(א) >$^{[(*)]}$ Rest(ב)

The harmonic ordering over candidate parses determined by CH is then defined by:

A >$_{CH}$^{parse} B iff CH(A) ≡ א >$^{[(*)]}$ ב ≡ CH(B)

This definition of >$_{CH}$^{parse} is identical to the definition of >$_C$^{parse} (99) except for the inevitable substitutions: the single constraint C of (99) has been replaced with a constraint hierarchy CH in (106), and, accordingly, one additional level has been added to the collections of marks.

The conclusion, then, is that whole-parse Harmony ordering by constraint hierarchies is defined just like whole-parse Harmony ordering by individual constraints. To compare parses, we compare the marks assigned them by the constraint hierarchy. This we do by first examining the First Marks – those assigned by the dominant constraint. If this fails to decide the matter, we discard the First Marks, take the Rest of the marks (those assigned by the remaining constraints in the hierarchy) and start over with them.

Thus, there is really only one definition for harmonic ordering in Optimality Theory; we can take it to be (99). The case of binary marks (§5.2.1.1) is a simple special case, where 'less marked' reduces to 'fewer (identical) marks'; the case of constraint hierarchies (106) is a mechanical generalization gotten by making obvious substitutions.

5.2.3   Discussion

5.2.3.1   Non-locality of interaction

The definition used in Optimality Theory to determine the Harmony ordering of entire parses is a central contribution to the theory of constraint interaction. In the Berber hierarchy [Ons ≫ Hnuc], for example, one might have imagined that the method for ordering two parses is to compare the parses syllable-by-syllable, assessing each syllable independently first on whether it meets Ons, and then on how well it fares with Hnuc. As it happens, this can be made to work for the special case of [Ons ≫ Hnuc] if we evaluate syllables in the correct order: from most to least harmonic. This procedure can be shown to determine essentially the same optimal parses as the different harmonic ordering procedure we have defined above, but only because some very special conditions obtain: first, there are only two constraints, and second, the dominant one is never violated in optimal parses.[47]

[47] The argument goes as follows. Suppose A is the optimal parse of an input I according to harmonic ordering, so that A > B for any other parse B of I. We need to show that A beats B in the following syllable-by-syllable comparison: compare the most harmonic syllable in A with the most harmonic syllable in B; if one is more harmonic than the other, its parse wins; if they are equally harmonic, discard these two best syllables and recursively evaluate the remaining ones. To determine which of two syllables is the more harmonic, evaluate them by [Ons ≫ Hnuc]; that is, compare them against each other on Ons and if that fails to pick a winner, compare them on Hnuc.

Here's the argument. Every input has parses which do not violate the dominant constraint Ons, so parses judged optimal by harmonic ordering never violate Ons. Since A is optimal, none of its syllables violates Ons. Thus, in comparing any syllable σ_A of A with a syllable σ_B of B, A will win if σ_B violates Ons. So the only competitors B which could possibly beat A are those with no onsetless syllables. But in that case, Ons is irrelevant to the comparison of A and B: the syllable-by-syllable comparison will compare syllables from most to least harmonic based solely on Hnuc. But this is exactly how the comparison goes according to harmonic ordering when both candidates have no violations of Ons. So the two methods must give the same result.

In short: Ons in either case serves to knock out all parses which violate it at all, and of the remaining parses the same one is picked out as optimal by the two methods because they both degenerate to the single remaining constraint Hnuc.

This argument is correct regarding the core of the matter, but fails on a subtle issue: comparisons of parses with different numbers of syllables. In this case it can happen that the comparison has not yet been settled when one parse runs out of syllables and the other still has some remaining (which may or may not violate Ons). A definite procedure is required to handle the comparison of the null syllable ø and a non-null syllable σ. And indeed here syllable-by-syllable comparison (but not harmonic ordering) fails: neither ø > σ nor σ > ø will work. To minimize distractions, consider the two hypothetical Berber inputs /tat/ and /tnmn/. The Dell–Elmedlaoui algorithm (and harmonic ordering) determine the corresponding outputs to be .tát. and .tń.mń. Now in order that .tát. beat .tá.t́. in the syllable-by-syllable comparison, we must assume ø > σ, because after the two best syllables (.tát. and .tá.) tie, the correct parse has no more syllables while the incorrect parse has the remaining (miserable) syllable .t́. On the other hand, in order that the correct parse .tń.mń. beat .tnmń., we must assume σ > ø; for now, after the two best syllables (say .tń. [which ≈ .mń.], and .tnmń.) tie, the competitor has no more syllables while the correct parse still has one left (.mń.).

The intuition evoked here is that really ø is better than a syllable which violates Ons but worse than one which satisfies Ons. What this intuition really amounts to, we claim, is that Ons-violating syllables should lose the competition for their parses, and that this should have priority over trying to maximize nuclear Harmony – exactly as formalized in harmonic ordering. It is precisely because the Ons-violating syllable .t́. in .tá.t́. is so *bad* that it ends up being considered too late to clearly lose against a proper syllable in the correct parse. That is, postponing consideration of Ons-violating syllables until after considering better Ons-satisfying ones is exactly backwards – yet this is what the syllable-by-syllable method requires. Our diagnosis is that correctly handling Ons requires considering first those syllables that violate it – the *worst* syllables, according to Ons; whereas correctly handling Hnuc requires considering first the syllables it rates the *best*. This is just what harmonic ordering does, by virtue of having separate passes over the parse for Ons and later for Hnuc. Syllable-by-syllable evaluation is fundamentally incorrect in forcing one pass through the parse, evaluating each syllable according to both constraints and then discarding it. It is fortuitous that in the case of [Ons ≫ Hnuc], in

Failing such special conditions, however, harmonic ordering as defined above and as used in the remainder of this book gives results which, as far as we know, cannot be duplicated or even approximated using a scheme of syllable-by-syllable evaluation. Indeed, when we extend our analysis of Berber even one step beyond the simple pair of constraints Ons and Hnuc (see chapter 8), harmonic ordering clearly becomes required to get the correct results.[48]

The Optimality Theory definition of harmonic ordering completely solves a difficult conceptual problem which faces any syllable-by-syllable approach as soon as we expand our horizons even slightly. For in general we need to order complex parses which contain much more structure than mere syllables. The 'syllable-by-syllable' approach is conceptually really a 'constituent-by-constituent' approach, and in the general case there are many kinds and levels of constituents in the parse. Harmonic ordering escapes the need to decide in the general case how to correctly break structures into parts for Harmony evaluation so that, in

---

the majority of cases, best-first syllable comparison gives the correct answer: as long as a competitor has the same number of syllables as the optimal parse, an Ons violation will eventually get caught – even though such violations should really be handled first rather than last. Such postponement is revealed for the mistake it really is when parses with different numbers of syllables are examined.

[48] Our more complete analysis of Berber will include, among others, a universal constraint −Cod which states that syllables must not have codas (this constraint was introduced in §4.1). This constraint is lower-ranked in the Berber hierarchy than Hnuc, so a slightly more complete Berber hierarchy is [Ons ≫ Hnuc ≫ −Cod]. Now consider the input /ratlult/; the Dell–Elmedlaoui algorithm (and harmonic ordering) parses this as .rát.lú.lí̩. Note that the most harmonic syllable in this correct parse, .rát., has a coda, violating −Cod. Note further that there is a competing parse without the coda (which also respects Ons): .rá.tl̩.wl̩t. Since Hnuc ≫ −Cod, the most harmonic syllable in this competing parse is also the one with the most sonorous nucleus, .rá. Now if we compare the most harmonic syllables of these two parses, we see that the correct parse *loses* because of its violation of −Cod. (In case it is unclear whether comparing *least* harmonic syllables first might work, note that this also gives the wrong result here, since of the two parses being compared here, the correct parse contains the worst syllable: .lí̩.)

Again, harmonic ordering gets the correct result in comparing these two parses. First, Ons is checked throughout the parses; both respect it so the next constraint is considered. Hnuc now declares the correct parse the winner, since its nuclei are more harmonic than those of its competitor: (á, ú, í̩) > (á, l̩, l̩). The competition is correctly resolved without ever consulting the lowest constraint −Cod, which in this case can only lead the evaluation astray.

This example illustrates a kind of non-local constraint interaction captured by harmonic ordering but missed in the syllable-by-syllable approach. In order for the second syllable of the correct parse .rát.lú.lí̩. to optimize its nucleus (ú), the first syllable pays with a coda. (The parse .rá.tlú.lí̩. is blocked by a high-ranking constraint which limits onsets to one segment; this is part of our fuller account of Berber in ch. 8.) Raising the Harmony of the second syllable with respect to Hnuc at the cost of lowering the Harmony of the first with respect to −Cod is in this case optimal because Hnuc ≫ −Cod. However, Hnuc and −Cod interact here *across syllables*; and, in fact, the best syllable must pay to improve the less-good syllable. The syllable-by-syllable theory cannot correctly handle this sort of non-local interaction, as we have seen; it wrongly rules against the correct parse because its best syllable has sacrificed Harmony (on a low-ranked constraint), never getting to the next-best syllable to see that it has improved Harmony (on a higher-ranked constraint).

part-by-part evaluation, all the relevant constraints have the proper domains for their evaluation. In harmonic ordering, each constraint $\mathbb{C}$ independently generates its own list of marks $\mathbb{C}(A)$ for evaluating a parse A, considering whatever domains within A are appropriate to that constraint. In comparing A with parse B, the marks $\mathbb{C}(A)$ are compared with the marks $\mathbb{C}(B)$; implicitly, this amounts to comparing A and B with respect to the domain structure peculiar to $\mathbb{C}$. This comparison is decoupled from that based on other constraints which may have quite different domain structure.

The interaction of constraints in a constituent-by-constituent approach is in a sense limited to interactions within a constituent: for ultimately the comparison of competing parses rests on the assessment of the Harmony of individual constituents as evaluated by the set of constraints. Optimality Theory is not limited to constraint interactions which are local in this sense, as a number of the subsequent analyses will illustrate (see also fn. 48).

5.2.3.2 Strictness of domination

The theory of constraint interaction embodied in harmonic ordering is remarkably strong. In determining the correct – optimal – parse of an input, as the constraint hierarchy is descended, each constraint acts to disqualify remaining competitors with absolute independence from all other constraints. A parse found wanting on one constraint has absolutely no hope of redeeming itself by faring well on any or even all lower-ranking constraints. It is striking that such an extremely severe theory of constraint interaction has the descriptive power it turns out to possess.

Such strict domination of constraints is less dramatic in the Berber hierarchy [ONS ≫ HNUC] than it will be in subsequent examples. This is because the dominant constraint is never violated in the forms of the language; it is hardly surprising then that it has strict priority over the lower constraint. In the general case, however, most of the constraints in the hierarchy will *not* be unviolated as ONS is in Berber. Nonetheless, *all* constraints in Optimality Theory, whether violated or not in the forms of the language, have the same absolute veto power over lower constraints that ONS has in Berber.

5.2.3.3 Serial vs. parallel Harmony evaluation and Gen

Universal Grammar must also provide a function Gen that admits the candidates to be evaluated. In the discussion in chapter 2 we have entertained two different conceptions of Gen. The first, closer to standard generative theory, is based on serial or derivational processing; some general procedure (Do-α) is allowed to make a certain single modification to the input, producing the candidate set of all possible outcomes of such modification. This is then evaluated; and the process continues with the output so determined. In this serial version of grammar, the theory of rules is narrowly circumscribed, but it is inaccurate to think of it as trivial. There are constraints inherent in the limitation to a single operation; and in the requirement that each individual operation in the sequence improve

Harmony. (An example that springs to mind is the Move-x theory of rhythmic adjustments in Prince 1983; it is argued for precisely on the basis of entailments that follow from these two conditions, pp. 31–43.)

In the second, parallel-processing conception of Gen, all possible ultimate outputs are contemplated at once. Here the theory of operations is indeed rendered trivial; all that matters is what structures are admitted – which operations may have been used to construct a final output can make no difference. Much of the analysis given in this book will be in the parallel mode, and some of the results will absolutely require it. But it is important to keep in mind that the serial/ parallel distinction pertains to Gen and not to the issue of harmonic evaluation *per se*. It is an empirical question of no little interest how Gen is to be construed, and one to which the answer will become clear only as the characteristics of harmonic evaluation emerge in the context of detailed, full-scale, depth-plumbing, scholarly, and responsible analyses.[49]

---

[49] A faithful reconstruction of the sequential parsing process of the Dell–Elmedlaoui algorithm seems to be possible within the harmonic serial approach. Here is a quick sketch; the analysis has not been well developed. Many ideas are imported which will later be developed in the text in the context of the parallel approach. It seems highly unlikely that the sequential approach presented here for Berber can be extended to a sequential account of syllabification more generally.

The process starts with an input. Gen then generates a set of alternatives which are 'one change away' from the input. We let Gen perform any one of the following 'changes':

- (a)   build a new syllable from free segments;
- (b)   adjoin a free element to an existing syllable;
- (c)   mark a segment x as surface-free: ⟨x⟩.

A surface-free segment is not phonetically realized in the surface form, as though deleted by Stray Erasure. Once a segment has been marked as surface-free it no longer counts as 'free'; it is no longer available to Gen for operations (a–c). Berber never chooses to exercise the surface-free option, but we will derive this as a result rather than assuming it. The syllables constructed in (a) may include empty syllable positions which denote epenthetic elements; again, an option we show Berber not to exercise.

Now initially all segments in the input are free. Gen produces a set of candidates each of which is generated from the input by applying one of the 'changes' (a–c). The most harmonic of these is chosen as the next representation in the derivation. At each step at least one segment which was free becomes no longer free. The process is repeated until no free elements remain; this is the output.

At each step of the derivation, the candidates generated by Gen each contain one 'changed' element; for (a), it is a newly constructed syllable; for (b), a syllable with a segment newly adjoined; for (c), a segment marked surface-free. To compare the Harmonies of two such candidates, we simply compare the one changed element of each candidate; the remaining parts of the two candidates are identical. If both candidates are generated by either (a) or (b), then we are comparing two syllables. This we can do using a constraint hierarchy, as previously explained in the text. The hierarchy we assume for Berber is as follows:

Nuc ≫ *Complex ≫ Parse ≫ Fill ≫ Ons ≫ –Cod ≫ Hnuc

This is virtually identical to the hierarchy of the parallel analysis we develop in §8.1.1 (ignoring exceptional epenthesis), except that –Cod is higher-ranked in this sequential analysis, for reasons

Many different theories of the structure of phonological outputs can be equally well accommodated in Gen, and the framework of Optimality Theory *per se* involves no commitment to any set of such assumptions. Of course, different

---

to be discussed. The constraints are more fully developed in the text; here is a quick summary. Nuc requires nuclei; *Complex forbids more than one segment in onset, nucleus, or coda; Parse forbids surface-free segments; Fill forbids empty (epenthetic) syllable positions; −Cod forbids codas.

At each step Gen generates via (a) candidates each with a new syllable. When these are compared using the constraint hierarchy, the most harmonic such new syllables will always have a single-segment onset and a single-segment nucleus, with no epenthetic positions and no coda. That is, they will always be core syllables. Gen generates all sorts of new syllables, but the most harmonic will always be those built as xy → {xY}, for only these satisfy all of the top six constraints. Of these, the most harmonic will be determined by the seventh constraint, Hnuc. As long as there is a free pair of adjacent segments xy, a candidate generated from xy → {xY} via (a) will be more harmonic than all candidates generated via adjunction (b) or surface-free marking (c); for adjunction to a core syllable already built (b) will violate *Complex unless the adjunction is to coda position, in which case it will violate −Cod; and a surface-free marking (c) violates Parse. No such violations occur with {xY}. Thus, as long as free pairs xy exist, the most harmonic candidate generated by Gen will always be the one which performs xy → {xY} where Y is the most sonorous available such segment. This is, of course, exactly the principal step of the Dell–Elmedlaoui algorithm.

The final part of the Dell–Elmedlaoui algorithm takes place when there are no longer any free pairs xy. Then free singleton segments are adjoined as codas to the preceding already built core syllable. This too is reconstructed by harmonic sequential parsing. For when there are no longer free pairs xy, any new syllables generated via (a) by Gen are no longer the most harmonic changes. Such a new syllable must be erected over a single underlying segment x (or be totally epenthetic), and this syllable must therefore violate at least one of the constraints Nuc, Fill, or Ons. These constraints are all higher ranked than −Cod, which is the only constraint violated by the changed element in candidates generated via (b) by adjoining x as the coda of an existing core syllable. The other candidates are generated via (c) by marking x as surface-free; the changed element in such candidates, ⟨x⟩, violates Parse, which dominates −Cod, so surface-free candidates (c) are less harmonic than coda-adjoined ones (b). At each step in this last phase of parsing, then, one free singleton segment will be coda-adjoined, until finally there are no free segments left and parsing is complete.

For this sequential approach to work, it is crucial that −Cod ≫ Hnuc – although in the parallel approach developed in the text, it is equally crucial that Hnuc ≫ −Cod. The sequential parsing algorithm must build all possible core syllables before creating any codas; the location of codas in the correct parse can only be determined after the nuclei have been taken in descending sonority order. −Cod ≫ Hnuc ensures that a newly closed syllable will be suboptimal as long as new core syllables exist in the candidate set. To see what would happen if Hnuc ≫ −Cod, consider the example input /ratlult/, considered in (6), p. 17, §2.1. The most harmonic first step is {ra}tlult. Now the next step should be to {ra}t{lu}lt, with changed element {lu}. But consider the adjunction (b) candidate {rat}lult, with changed element {rat}. On Hnuc, {rat} bests {lu}, while on −Cod, {lu} is preferred. Thus the right choice will only be made if −Cod ≫ Hnuc.

To most clearly see why the parallel approach requires Hnuc ≫ −Cod, consider the hypothetical input /tat/, which the Dell–Elmedlaoui algorithm parses as {tat}, a closed syllable. An alternative complete parse with only open syllables is {T}{aT}. In the parallel approach, we first scan the complete parse for violations of the top-ranked constraint; if this were −Cod, then the correct parse would lose immediately, and its redeeming qualities with respect to lower-ranked Hnuc would be irrelevant.

structural assumptions can suggest or force different formal approaches to the way that Optimality-theoretic constraints work. In this work, to implement Faithfulness straightforwardly, we entertain a nonobvious assumption about Gen which will be useful in implementing the parallel conception of the theory: we will assume, following the lead of McCarthy 1979 and Itô 1986, 1989, that every output for an input *In* – every member of Gen(*In*) – includes *In* as an identifiable substructure. In the theory of syllable structure developed in Part II, Gen(/txznt/) will be a set of possible syllabifications of /txznt/ all of which contain the input string /txznt/, with each underlying segment either associated to syllable structure or left unassociated. We will interpret unassociated underlying segments as phonetically unrealized (cf. 'Stray Erasure'); thus on this conception, input segments are never 'deleted' in the sense of disappearing from the structural description; rather, they may simply be left free – unparsed. Our discussion of Berber in this section has focused on a fairly restricted subset of the full candidate set we will subsequently consider; we have considered only syllabifications in which underlying segments are in one-to-one correspondence with syllable positions. In following chapters, we turn to languages which, unlike Berber, exhibit syllabifications manifesting deletion and/or epenthesis.

5.2.3.4   Binary vs. non-binary constraints

As might be suspected, it will turn out that the work done by a single non-binary constraint like HNUC can also be done by a *set* (indeed a subhierarchy) of binary constraints. This will prove fundamental for the construction of the Basic Segmental Syllable Theory in chapter 8, and we postpone treatment of the issue until then. For now it suffices simply to remark that the division of constraints into those which are binary and those which are not, a division which we have adopted earlier in this section, is not in fact as theoretically fundamental as it may at this point appear.

5.3   Pāṇini's Theorem on Constraint Ranking

One consequence of the definition of harmonic ordering is that there are conditions under which the presence of a more general constraint in a superordinate position in a hierarchy will eliminate all opportunities for a more specialized constraint in a subordinate position to have any effects in the grammar. The theorem states, roughly, that if one constraint is more general than another in the sense that the set of inputs to which one constraint applies non-vacuously includes the other's non-vacuous input set, and if the two constraints *conflict* on inputs to which the more specific applies non-vacuously, then the more specific constraint must dominate the more general one in the grammar in order for it to have any visible effects. (This is an oversimplified first cut at the true result; such claims must be stated carefully.) Intuitively, the idea is that if the more specific constraint were lower-ranked, then for any input to which it applies non-vacuously, its effects would be over-ruled by the higher-ranked constraint with which it conflicts. The utility of the result is that it allows the analyst to spot certain easy ranking arguments.

We call this Pāṇini's Theorem on Constraint Ranking, in honor of the first known investigator in the area; in §7.2.1, we discuss some relations to the Elsewhere Condition of Anderson 1969 and Kiparsky 1973c. In this section we introduce some concepts necessary to develop a result; the proof is relegated to the Appendix. The result we state is undoubtedly but one of a family of related theorems which cover cases in which one constraint hides another.

Due to the complexities surrounding this issue, we will formally state and prove the result only in the case of constraints which are Boolean at the whole-parse level: constraints which assign a single mark to an entire parse when they are violated, and no mark when they are satisfied.

(107)   Dfn. **Separation**. A constraint $\mathbb{C}$ *separates* a set of structures if it is satisfied by some members of the set and violated by others.

(108)   Dfn. **Non-vacuous Application**. A constraint $\mathbb{C}$ *applies non-vacuously* to an input i if it separates Gen(i), the set of candidate parses of i admitted by Universal Grammar.

A constraint may sometimes apply vacuously to an input, in that every possible parse of i satisfies the constraint. For example, in chapter 7 we will introduce a constraint FREE-V which requires that stem-final vowels *not* be parsed into syllable structure. Clearly, this constraint is vacuously satisfied for a stem which is not vowel-final; all the parses of such an input meet the constraint since none of them have a stem-final vowel which is parsed.

(109)   Dfn. **Accepts**. A constraint hierarchy $\mathbb{CH}$ *accepts* a parse P of an input i if P is an optimal parse of i.

When $\mathbb{CH}$ is the entire constraint hierarchy of a grammar, it is normally the case that only one parse P of an input i is optimal: the constraint set is sufficient to winnow the candidate set down to a single output. In this section we will need to consider, more generally, initial portions of the constraint hierarchy of a grammar, i.e., all the constraints from the highest-ranked down to some constraint which may not be the lowest-ranked. In these cases, $\mathbb{CH}$ will often consist of just a few constraints, insufficient to winnow the candidate set down to a single parse; in that case, $\mathbb{CH}$ will accept an entire set of parses, all equally harmonic, and all more harmonic than the competitors filtered out by $\mathbb{CH}$.

(110)   Dfn. **Active**. Let $\mathbb{C}$ be a constraint in a constraint hierarchy $\mathbb{CH}$ and let i be an input. $\mathbb{C}$ is *active on i in* $\mathbb{CH}$ if $\mathbb{C}$ separates the candidates in Gen(i) which are admitted by the portion of $\mathbb{CH}$ which dominates $\mathbb{C}$.

In other words, the portion of $\mathbb{CH}$ which dominates $\mathbb{C}$ filters the set of candidate parses of i to some degree, and then $\mathbb{C}$ filters it further. When $\mathbb{C}$ is not active for an input *i* in $\mathbb{CH}$, the result of parsing *i* is not at all affected by the presence of $\mathbb{C}$ in the hierarchy.

(111)   Dfn. **Pāṇinian Constraint Relation**

Let $\mathbb{S}$ and $\mathbb{G}$ be two constraints. $\mathbb{S}$ *stands to* $\mathbb{G}$ *as special to general in a Pāṇinian relation* if, for any input *i* to which $\mathbb{S}$ applies non-vacuously, any parse of *i* which satisfies $\mathbb{S}$ fails $\mathbb{G}$.

For example, the constraint FREE-V stands to PARSE as special to general in a Pāṇinian relation: for any input to which FREE-V applies non-vacuously (that is, to any input with a stem-final vowel V), any parse which satisfies FREE-V (that is, which leaves V unparsed) must violate PARSE (in virtue of leaving V unparsed). For inputs to which the more specialized constraint FREE-V does *not* apply non-vacuously (C-final stems), the more general constraint PARSE need not conflict with the more specific one (for C-final stems, FREE-V is vacuously satisfied, but PARSE is violated in some parses and satisfied in others).

Now we are finally set to state the theorem:

(112)   **Pāṇini's Theorem on Constraint Ranking**

Let constraints $\mathbb{S}$ and $\mathbb{G}$ stand as specific to general in a Pāṇinian relation. Suppose these constraints are part of a constraint hierarchy $\mathbb{CH}$, and that $\mathbb{G}$ is active in $\mathbb{CH}$ on some input *i*. Then if $\mathbb{G} \gg \mathbb{S}$, $\mathbb{S}$ is not active on *i*.

In chapter 7, we will use this theorem to conclude that in the grammar of Lardil, the more specific constraint FREE-V must dominate the more general constraint PARSE with which it conflicts.

Part II

Syllable Theory

Overview of Part II

The typology of syllable structure systems has been the object of a successful research effort over the last century and is fairly well understood empirically.[50] Basic theoretical questions remain open or undecided, of course, despite (or because of) the body of modern work in the area. Here we aim to show that the fundamental typological generalizations receive principled explication through the notion of *Factorial Typology*. The idea is that Universal Grammar provides a set of violable constraints on syllable structure, and individual grammars fix the relative ranking of these constraints. The typology of possible languages is then given by the set of all possible rankings.

Because of the considerable complexity that inheres in this domain, it is appropriate to approach it via the strategies of Galilean science, sometimes referred to as *Rational Inquiry* in the linguistic literature. Our discussion will therefore proceed through three degrees of decreasing idealization. First, in chapter 6, we examine a kind of C/V theory: the key simplifying assumption being that the terminal nodes (segments) are pre-sorted binarily as to their suitability for peak (V) and margin (C) positions (*cf.* McCarthy 1979, Clements & Keyser 1983). Further, we consider only syllables with at most *one* symbol C or V in any syllabic position. Under these restrictions, the basic structural constraints are introduced and the ranking-induced typology is explored. Then, still within CV theory, we examine the finer grain of interactions between the structural constraints and various methods of enforcing them upon recalcitrant inputs.

Next, in chapter 7, we show how the theory allows a rich set of alternations in Lardil to be explicated strictly in terms of the interactions of constraints on prosodic structure. In chapter 8, we extend the CV theory, taking up the more ambitious task of constructing syllables from segments classified into a multi-degree sonority scale. We show how simple assumptions in Universal Grammar

---

[50] We do not pretend to cite this veritably oceanic body of work. The interested reader should refer to such works as Bell & Hooper 1978 and, say, the references in the references of Goldsmith 1990.

explain a universal typology of inventories of onset, nucleus, and coda segments. A licensing asymmetry between onsets and codas is derived from the structural asymmetry in the basic theory: well-structured syllables *possess* onsets but *lack* codas. In the course of extracting these typological consequences, a number of general analytical techniques are developed.

Chapter 6

Syllable Structure Typology: The CV Theory

6.1 The Jakobson Typology

It is well known that every language admits consonant-initial syllables .CV~., and that some languages allow no others; that every language admits open syllables .~V., and that some admit only those. Jakobson puts it this way:

> There are languages lacking syllables with initial vowels and/or syllables with final consonants, but there are no languages devoid of syllables with initial consonants or of syllables with final vowels. (Jakobson 1962: 526: Clements & Keyser 1983: 29)

As noted in the fundamental work of Clements & Keyser 1983, whence the quotation was cadged, these observations yield exactly four possible inventories. With the notation Σ^{XYZ} to denote the language whose syllables fit the pattern XYZ, the Jakobson typology can be laid out as follows, in terms of whether onsets and codas are obligatory, forbidden, or neither:

(113) **CV Syllable Structure Typology**

		Onsets	
		required	not required
Codas	forbidden	Σ^{CV}	$\Sigma^{(C)V}$
	allowed	$\Sigma^{CV(C)}$	$\Sigma^{(C)V(C)}$

There are two independent dimensions of choice: whether onsets are required (first column) or not (second column); whether codas are forbidden (row one) or allowed (row two).

The **Basic Syllable Structure Constraints**, which generate this typology, divide notionally into two groups. First, the structural or 'markedness' constraints – those that enforce the universally unmarked characteristics of the structures involved:

(114)   **Ons**
   A syllable must have an onset.

(115)   **–Cod**
   A syllable must *not* have a coda.

Second, those that constrain the relation between output structure and input:

(116)   **Parse**
   Underlying segments must be parsed into syllable structure.

(117)   **Fill**
   Syllable positions must be filled with underlying segments.

Parse and Fill are Faithfulness constraints: they declare that perfectly well-formed syllable structures are those in which input segments are in one-to-one correspondence with syllable positions.[51] Given an interpretive phonetic component that omits unparsed material and supplies segmental values for empty nodes, the ultimate force of Parse is to forbid deletion; of Fill, to forbid insertion.

It is relatively straightforward to show that the Factorial Typology on the Basic Syllable Structure Constraints produces just the Jakobson Typology. Suppose Faithfulness dominates *both* structural constraints. Then the primacy of respecting the input will be able to force violations of both Ons and –Cod. The string /V/ will be parsed as an onsetless syllable, violating Ons; the string /CVC/ will be parsed as a closed syllable, violating –Cod: this gives the language $\Sigma^{(C)V(C)}$.

When a member of the Faithfulness family is dominated by one or the other or both of the structural constraints, a more aggressive parsing of the input will result. In those rankings where Ons dominates a Faithfulness constraint, every syllable must absolutely have an onset. Input /V/ cannot be given its faithful parse as an onsetless syllable; it can either remain completely unsyllabified, violating Parse, or it can be parsed as .□V., where '□' refers to an empty structural position, violating Fill.

---

[51] Both Fill and Parse are representative of families of constraints that govern the proper treatment of child nodes and mother nodes, given the representational assumptions made here. As the basic syllable theory develops, Fill will be articulated into a pair of constraints:

Fill^{Nuc}: Nucleus positions must be filled with underlying segments.
Fill^{Mar}: Margin positions (Ons and Cod) must be filled with underlying segments.

Since unfilled codas are never optimal under syllable theory alone, shown below in §6.2.3 (141), p. 116, Fill^{Mar} will often be replaced by Fill^{Ons} for perspicuity.

Those rankings in which $-$Cod dominates a Faithfulness constraint correspond to languages in which codas are forbidden. The imperative to avoid codas must be honored, even at the cost of expanding upon the input (*Fill) or leaving part of it outside of prosodic structure (*Parse).

In the next section, we will explore these observations in detail. The resulting Factorial construal of the Jakobson Typology looks like this (with '$\mathscr{F}$' denoting the Faithfulness set and 'F$_i$' a member of it):

(118)   **Factorial Jakobson Typology**

		Onsets	
		Ons $\gg$ F$_j$	$\mathscr{F} \gg$ Ons
Codas	$-$Cod $\gg$ F$_i$	Σ^{CV}	$\Sigma^{(C)V}$
	$\mathscr{F} \gg -$Cod	$\Sigma^{CV(C)}$	$\Sigma^{(C)V(C)}$

At this point, it is reasonable to ask whether there is any interesting difference between our claim that constraints like Ons and $-$Cod can be violated under domination and the more familiar claim that constraints can be *turned off* – simply omitted from consideration. The Factorial Jakobson Typology, as simple as it is, contains a clear case that highlights the distinction. Consider the language $\Sigma^{(C)V(C)}$. Since onsets are not required and codas are not forbidden, the Boolean temptation would be to hold that both Ons and $-$Cod are merely absent. Even in such a language, however, one can find certain circumstances in which the force of the supposedly nonexistent structural constraints is felt. The string CVCV, for example, would always be parsed .CV.CV. and never .CVC.V. Yet both parses consist of licit syllables; both are entirely faithful to the input. The difference is that .CV.CV. satisfies Ons and $-$Cod while .CVC.V. violates both of them. We are forced to conclude that (at least) one of them is still active in the language, even though roundly violated in many circumstances. This is the basic prediction of ranking theory: when all else is equal, a subordinate constraint can emerge decisively. In the end, summary global statements about *inventory*, like Jakobson's, emerge through the cumulative effects of the actual parsing of individual items.

6.2   The Faithfulness Interactions

Faithfulness involves more than one type of constraint. Ranking members of the Faithfulness family with respect to each other and with respect to the structural markedness constraints Ons and $-$Cod yields a typology of the ways that languages can enforce (and fail to enforce) those constraints. We will consider only the Faithfulness constraints Parse and Fill (the latter to be distinguished by sensitivity to Nucleus or Ons); these are the bare minimum required to obtain a contentful, usable theory, and we will accordingly abstract away from distinctions that they do not make, such as between deleting the first or second element of a cluster, or between forms involving metathesis, vocalization of consonants, de-vocalization of vowels, and so on, all of which involve further Faithfulness constraints, whose interactions with each other and with the markedness constraints will be entirely parallel to those discussed here.

6.2.1 Groundwork

To make clear the content of the Basic Syllable Structure Constraints ONS, –COD, PARSE, and FILL, it is useful to lay out the Galilean arena in which they play. The inputs we will be considering are CV sequences like CVVCC; that is, any and all strings of the language {C,V}*. The grammar must be able to contend with any input from this set: we do not assume an additional component of language-particular input-defining conditions; the universal constraints and their ranking must do all the work (see §9.3 for further discussion). The possible structures which may be assigned to an input are all those which parse it into syllables; more precisely, into zero or more syllables. There is no insertion or deletion of *segments* C, V.

What is a syllable? To avoid irrelevant distractions, we adopt the simple analysis that the syllable node σ must have a daughter *Nuc* and *may* have as leftmost and rightmost daughters respectively the nodes *Ons* and *Cod*.[52] The nodes Ons, Nuc, and Cod, in turn, may each dominate C's and V's, or they may be empty. Each Ons, Nuc, or Cod node may dominate at most one terminal element C or V.

These assumptions delimit the set of candidate analyses. Here we list and name some of the more salient of the mentioned constraints. By our simplifying assumptions, they will stand at the top of the hierarchy and will be therefore unviolated in every system under discussion:

Syllable form:

(119) NUC
Syllables must have nuclei.

(120) *COMPLEX
No more than one C or V may associate to any syllable position node.[53]

---

[52] For versions of the structural constraints within the perhaps more plausible moraic theory of syllable structure see Kirchner 1992bc, Hung 1992, Samek-Lodovici 1992ab, Zoll 1992a, 1993, McCarthy & Prince 1993a.

[53] On *complex* margins, see Bell 1971, a valuable typological study. Clements 1990 develops a promising quantitative theory of cross-linguistic margin-cluster generalizations in what can be seen as harmonic terms. The constraint *COMPLEX is intended as no more than a cover term for the interacting factors that determine the structure of syllable margins. For a demonstration of how a conceptually similar *complex* vs. *simple* distinction derives from constraint interaction, see §9.1–2 below.

Definition of C and V, using M(argin) for Ons and Cod and P(eak) for Nuc:

(121) *M/V

V may not associate to Margin nodes (Ons and Cod).

(122) *P/C

C may not associate to Peak (Nuc) nodes.

The theory we examine is this:

(123) **Basic CV Syllable Theory**
- Syllable structure is governed by the Basic Syllable Structure Constraints ONS, –COD, NUC; *COMPLEX, *M/V, *P/C; PARSE, and FILL.
- Of these, ONS, –COD, PARSE, and FILL may be relatively ranked in any domination order in a particular language, while the others are fixed in superordinate position.
- The Basic Syllable Structure Constraints, ranked in a language-particular hierarchy, will assign to each input its optimal structure, which is the output of the phonology.

The output of the phonology is subject to phonetic interpretation, about which we will here make two assumptions, following familiar proposals in the literature:

(124) **Underparsing Phonetically Realized as Deletion**

An input segment unassociated to a syllable position ('underparsing') is not phonetically realized.

This amounts to 'Stray Erasure' (McCarthy 1979, Steriade 1982, Itô 1986, 1989). Epenthesis is handled in the inverse fashion:

(125) **Overparsing Phonetically Realized as Epenthesis**

A syllable position node unassociated to an input segment ('overparsing') is phonetically realized through some process of filling in default featural values.

This is the treatment of epenthesis established in such works as Selkirk 1981, Lapointe & Feinstein 1982, Broselow 1982, Archangeli 1984, Kaye & Lowenstamm 1984, Piggott & Singh 1985, and Itô 1986, 1989; cf. also Anderson 1982 on empty syllabic positions in underlying forms.

The terms 'underparsing' and 'overparsing' are convenient for referring to parses that violate Faithfulness. If an input segment is not parsed in a given structure (not associated to any syllable position nodes), we will often describe this as 'underparsing' rather than 'deletion' to emphasize the character of our assumptions. For the same reason, if a structure contains an empty syllable structure node (one not associated to an input segment), we will usually speak of 'overparsing' the input rather than 'epenthesis'.

Suppose the phonology assigns to the input /CVVCC/ the following bisyllabic structure, which we write in three equivalent notations:

(126)   **Transcription of Syllabic Constituency Relations**, from /CVVCC/

a.

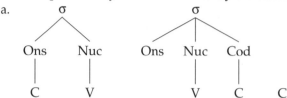

b. $[_\sigma [_{Ons} C] [_{Nuc} V]]$ $[_\sigma [_{Ons}] [_{Nuc} V] [_{Cod} C]]$ C

c.   .CV́.□V́C.⟨C⟩

Phonetic interpretation ignores the final C, and supplies featural structure for a consonant to fill the onset of the second syllable.

The dot notation (126c) is the most concise and readable; we will use it throughout. The interpretation is as follows:

(127)   **Notation**
a.   .X.   'the string X *is a* syllable'
b.   ⟨x⟩   'the element x has no parent node; is free (unparsed)'
c.   □   'a node *Ons, Nuc,* or *Cod* is empty'
d.   x́   'the element x is a Nuc'

In the CV theory, we will drop the redundant nucleus-marking accent on V́, writing only V. Observe that this is a 'notation' in the most inert and de-ontologized sense of the term: a set of typographical conventions used to refer to well-defined formal objects. The objects of linguistic theory – syllables here – are not to be confused with the literal characters that depict them. Linguistic operations and assessments apply to structure, not to typography.

We will say a syllable 'has an onset' if, like both syllables in the example (126), it has an Ons node, whether or not that node is associated to an underlying C; similarly with nuclei and codas.

The technical content of the Basic Syllable Structure Constraints (114–117) above can now be specified. The constraint ONS (114) requires that a syllable node σ have as its leftmost child an Ons node; the presence of the Ons node satisfies ONS whether empty or filled. The constraint –COD (115) requires that syllable nodes have no Cod child; the presence of a Cod node violates –COD whether or not that node is filled. Equivalently, any syllable which does not contain an onset in this sense earns its structure a mark of violation *ONS; a syllable which does contain a coda earns the mark *–COD.

The PARSE constraint (116) is met by structures in which all underlying segments are associated to syllable positions; *each* unassociated or free segment earns a mark *PARSE. This is the penalty for deletion. FILL (117) provides the penalty for epenthesis: each unfilled syllable position node earns a mark *FILL, penalizing insertion. Together, PARSE and FILL urge that the assigned syllable structure be faithful to the input string, in the sense of a one-to-one correspondence between syllable positions and segments. This is Faithfulness in the basic theory.

6.2.2   Basic CV Syllable Theory

We now pursue the consequences of our assumptions. One important aspect of the Jakobson Typology (113) follows immediately:

(128)   **THM. Universally Optimal Syllables**
          No language may prohibit the syllable .CV. Thus, no language prohibits onsets or requires codas.

To see this, consider the input /CV/. The obvious analysis .CV. (i.e., $[_\sigma [_{Ons} C]$ $[_{Nuc} V]]$) is *universally optimal* in that it violates *none* of the universal constraints of the Basic CV Syllable Theory (123). No alternative analysis, therefore, can be more harmonic. At worst, another analysis can be equally good, but inspection of the alternatives quickly rules out this possibility.

    For example, the analysis .CV□. violates −COD and FILL. The analysis .CÓ.V. violates ONS in the second syllable and FILL in the first. And so on, through the infinite set of possible analyses – [.⟨C⟩V.], [.CÓ.⟨V⟩.], [.□.C □.□V.], etc. *ad inf.* No matter what the ranking of constraints is, a form that violates even one of them can never be better than a form, like .CV., with no violations at all.

    Because every language has /CV/ input, according to our assumption that every language has the same set of possible inputs, it follows that .CV. can never be prohibited under the Basic Theory.

6.2.2.1   Onsets

Our major goal is to explicate the interaction of the structural constraints ONS and −COD with Faithfulness. We begin with onsets, studying the interaction of ONS with PARSE and FILL, ignoring −COD for the moment. The simplest interesting input is /V/. All analyses will contain violations; there are three possible one-mark analyses:

(129)   /V/ →
              a.   .V.   i.e., $[_\sigma [_{Nuc} V]]$
              b.   ⟨V⟩   i.e., no syllable structure
              c.   .□V.   i.e., $[_\sigma [_{Ons}] [_{Nuc} V]]$

Each of these alternatives violates exactly one of the Basic Syllable Structure Constraints (114–117):

(130)   **Best Analyses of /V/**

Analysis	Interpretation	Violation	Remarks
.V.	σ lacks Ons	*ONS	satisfies FILL, PARSE
⟨V⟩	null parse	*PARSE	satisfies ONS, FILL
.□V.	Ons is empty	*FILL	satisfies ONS, PARSE

Every language must evaluate all three analyses. Since the three candidates violate one constraint each, any comparison between them will involve weighing the importance of different violations. The optimal analysis for a given language is determined precisely by whichever of the constraints ONS, PARSE, and FILL is *lowest* in the constraint hierarchy of that language. The lowest constraint incurs the least important violation.

Suppose .V. is the optimal parse of /V/. We have the following tableau:

(131)   **Onset Not Required**

/V/	FILL	PARSE	ONS
☞ .V.			*
⟨V⟩		* !	
.□V.	* !		

The relative ranking of FILL and PARSE has no effect on the outcome. The violations of PARSE and FILL are fatal because the alternative candidate .V. satisfies both constraints.

Of interest here is the fact that the analysis .V. involves an onsetless syllable. When this analysis is optimal, then the language at hand, by this very fact, does not absolutely require onsets. The other two inferior analyses do succeed in satisfying ONS: ⟨V⟩ achieves this vacuously, creating no syllable at all; .□V. creates an onsetful syllable by positing an empty Ons node, leading to epenthesis. So if .V. is best, it is because ONS is the lowest of the three constraints, and we conclude that the language does not require onsets. We already know from the previous section, Thm. (128), that onsets can never be forbidden. This means the following condition holds:

(132)   If PARSE, FILL ≫ ONS, then onsets are not required.

(The comma'd grouping indicates that PARSE and FILL each dominate ONS, but that there is no implication about their own relative ranking.)

On the other hand, if ONS is not the lowest-ranking constraint – if either PARSE or FILL is lowest – then the structure assigned to /V/ will be consistent with the language requiring onsets. The following two tableaux lay this out:

(133) **Enforcement by Overparsing (Epenthesis)**

/V/	Ons	Parse	Fill
.V.	* !		
⟨V⟩		* !	
☞ .□V.			*

(134) **Enforcement by Underparsing (Deletion)**

/V/	Fill	Ons	Parse
.V.		* !	
☞ ⟨V⟩			*
.□V.	* !		

These lucubrations lead to the converse of (132):

(135)   If Ons dominates either Parse or Fill, then onsets are required.

There is an important difference in status between the two Ons-related implications. To prove that something is *optional*, in the sense of 'not forbidden' or 'not required' in the inventory, one need merely exhibit one case in which it is observed and one in which it isn't. To prove that something is *required*, one must show that everything in the universe observes it. Thus, formal proof of (135) requires considering not just one trial input, as we have done, but the whole (infinite) class of strings on {C,V}* which we are taking to define the universal set of possible inputs for the Basic Theory. We postpone this exercise until the Appendix; in chapter 8 we will develop general techniques which will enable us to extend the above analysis to arbitrary strings, showing that what is true of /V/ and /CV/ is true of all inputs.

The results of this discussion can be summarized as follows:

(136) **Onset Theorem**
Onsets are not required in a language if Ons is dominated by both Parse and Fill.
Otherwise, onsets are required in all syllables of optimal outputs.
In the latter case, Ons is enforced by underparsing (phonetic deletion) if Parse is the lowest-ranking of the three constraints; and by overparsing (phonetic epenthesis) if Fill is lowest.

If Fill is to be articulated into a family of node-specific constraints, then the version of Fill that is relevant here is Fill^{Ons}. With this in mind, the onset finding may be recorded as follows:

Lowest constraint	Onsets are . . .	Enforced by . . .
Ons	Not required	N/A
Parse	Required	V 'Deletion'
Fill^{Ons}	Required	C 'Epenthesis'

6.2.2.2   Codas

The analysis of onsets has a direct parallel for codas. We consider the input /CVC/ this time; the initial CV provides an onset and nucleus to meet the Ons and Nuc constraints, thereby avoiding any extraneous constraint violations. The final C induces the conflict between −Cod, which prohibits the Cod node, and Faithfulness, which has the effect of requiring just such a node. As in the corresponding onset situation (130), the parses which violate only one of the Basic Syllable Structure Constraints are three in number:

(137)   **Best Analyses of /CVC/**

Analysis	Interpretation	Violation	Remarks
.CVC.	σ has Cod	*−Cod	satisfies Fill, Parse
.CV⟨C⟩.	No parse of 2nd C	*Parse	satisfies −Cod, Fill
.CV.C□.	2nd Nuc is empty	*Fill	satisfies −Cod, Parse

The optimal analysis of /CVC/ in a given language depends on which of the three constraints is lowest in the domination hierarchy. If .CVC. wins, then the language must allow codas; −Cod ranks lowest and violation can be compelled. If .CVC. loses, the optimal analysis must involve open (codaless) syllables; in this case −Cod is enforced through empty nuclear structure (phonetic V-epenthesis) if Fill is lowest, and through nonparsing (phonetic deletion of C) if Parse is the lowest, most violable constraint. In either case, the result is that open syllables are *required*. This is a claim about the optimal parse in the language of every string, and not just about /CVC/, and formal proof is necessary; see the Appendix.

The conclusion, parallel to (136), is this:

(138)   **Coda Theorem**
>   Codas are allowed in a language if −Cod is dominated by both Parse and
>   Fill^{Nuc}.
>   Otherwise, codas are forbidden in all syllables of optimal outputs.
>   In the latter case, −Cod is enforced by underparsing (phonetic deletion) if
>   Parse is the lowest-ranking of the three constraints; and by overparsing
>   (epenthesis) if Fill^{Nuc} is the lowest.

The result can be tabulated like this:

Lowest constraint	Codas are . . .	Enforced by . . .
−Cod	Allowed	N/A
Parse	Forbidden	C 'Deletion'
Fill^{Nuc}	Forbidden	V 'Epenthesis'

Motivation for distinguishing the constraints Fill^{Ons} and Fill^{Nuc} is now available. Consider the languages Σ^{CV} in which only CV syllables are allowed. Here Ons and −Cod each dominate a member of the Faithfulness group. Enforcement of the dominant constraints will be required. Suppose there is only one Fill constraint, holding over all kinds of nodes. If Fill is the lowest-ranked of the three constraints, we have the following situation:

(139)   **Triumph of Epenthesis**

Input	Optimal analysis	Phonetic
/V/	.□V.	.CV.
/CVC/	.CV.C□̇.	.CV.CV.

The single uniform Fill constraint yokes together the methods of enforcing the onset requirement ('C-epenthesis') and the coda prohibition ('V-epenthesis'). There is no reason to believe that languages Σ^{CV} are obligated to behave in this way; nothing that we know of in the linguistic literature suggests that the appearance of epenthetic onsets requires the appearance of epenthetic nuclei in other circumstances. This infelicitous yoking is avoided by the natural assumption that Fill takes individual node-classes as an argument, yielding Fill^{Nuc} and Fill^{Ons} as the actual constraints. In this way, the priority assigned to filling Ons nodes may be different from that for filling Nuc nodes.[54]

It is important to note that onset and coda distributions are completely independent in this theory. Any ranking of the onset-governing constraints {Ons, Fill^{Ons}, Parse} may coexist with any ranking of coda-governing constraints {−Cod, Fill^{Nuc}, Parse}, because they have only one constraint, Parse, in common. The universal factorial typology allows all nine combinations of the three onset patterns given in (136) and the three coda patterns in (138). The full typology of interactions is portrayed in table (140). We use subscripted *del* and *ep* to indicate the phonetic

---

[54] It would also be possible to break this yoke by having two separate Parse constraints, one that applies to C and another to V. Basic syllable structure constraints that presuppose a C/V distinction, however, would not support the further development of the theory in ch. 8, where the segment classes are derived from constraint interactions.

consequences of enforcement; when both are involved, the onset-relevant mode comes first.

(140) **Extended CV Syllable Structure Typology**

Codas			Onsets		
			required		not required
			Ons, Fill^{Ons} $\gg$ Parse	Ons, Parse $\gg$ Fill^{Ons}	Parse, Fill^{Ons} $\gg$ Ons
Codas	forbidden	$-$Cod, Fill^{Nuc} $\gg$ Parse	$\Sigma^{\text{CV}}_{\text{del,del}}$	$\Sigma^{\text{CV}}_{\text{ep,del}}$	$\Sigma^{\text{(C)V}}_{\text{del}}$
		$-$Cod, Parse $\gg$ Fill^{Nuc}	$\Sigma^{\text{CV}}_{\text{del,ep}}$	$\Sigma^{\text{CV}}_{\text{ep,ep}}$	$\Sigma^{\text{(C)V}}_{\text{ep}}$
	allowed	Parse, Fill^{Nuc} $\gg -$Cod	$\Sigma^{\text{CV(C)}}_{\text{del}}$	$\Sigma^{\text{CV(C)}}_{\text{ep}}$	$\Sigma^{\text{(C)V(C)}}$

If we decline to distinguish between the Faithfulness constraint rankings, this simplifies to the Jakobson Typology of (118).

6.2.3 The Theory of Epenthesis Sites

The chief goal of syllabification-driven theories of epenthesis is to provide a principled account of the location of epenthetic elements (Selkirk 1981, Broselow 1982, Lapointe and Feinstein 1982, Itô 1986, 1989). Theories based on manipulation of the segmental string are capable of little more than summary stipulation on this point (e.g. Levin 1985: 331; see Itô 1986: 159, 1989 for discussion). The theory developed here entails tight restrictions on the distribution of empty nodes in optimal syllabic parses, and therefore meets this goal. We confine attention to the premises of the Basic CV Syllable Structure Theory, which serves as the foundation for investigation of the theory of epenthesis, which ultimately involves segmental and prosodic factors as well.

There are a few fundamental observations to make, from which a full positive characterization of syllabically motivated epenthesis emerges straightaway.

(141) **Prop. 1.** *[ ]$_{\text{Cod}}$
Coda nodes are never empty in any optimal parse.

Structures with unfilled Cod can never be optimal; there is always something better. To see this, take a candidate with an unfilled Cod and simply remove that one node. This gives another candidate which has one less violation of $-$Cod and one less violation of Fill. Since removing the node has no other effects on the evaluation, the second candidate must be superior to the first. (To show that something is *non*-optimal, we need merely find something better: we don't have to display the best.) This method of demonstration is *Harmonic Bounding*: the structure with unfilled Cod is *harmonically bounded* by the Cod-less competitor. (See §9.1.1 for general discussion.)

We know from the earlier discussion that Ons and Nuc must be optimally unfilled in certain parses under certain grammars. So the remaining task is to determine the conditions under which these nodes must be posited and left empty.

(142) **Prop. 2**. *.($\square$)$\acute{\square}$.
    A whole syllable is never empty in any optimal parse.

The same style of argument applies. Consider a parse that has an entirely empty syllable. Remove that syllable. The alternative candidate thereby generated is superior to the original because it has (at least) one less Fill^{Nuc} violation and no new marks. The empty syllable parse can always be bested and is therefore never optimal.

Of course, in the larger scheme of things, whole syllables can be epenthesized, the canonical examples being Lardil and Axininca Campa (Hale 1973, Klokeid 1976, Itô 1986, Wilkinson 1988, Kirchner 1992a; Payne 1981, Payne et al. 1982, Spring 1990, Black 1991, McCarthy & Prince 1993a). In all such cases, it is the impact of additional constraints that forces whole-syllable epenthesis. In particular, when the prosody–morphology interface constraints like Lx≈Pr are taken into account, prosodic minimality requirements can force syllabic epenthesis, as we will see for Lardil in chapter 7 below.

(143) **Prop. 3**. *.($\square$)$\acute{\square}$C.
    No syllable can have *Cod* as its only filled position.

Any analysis containing such a syllable is bested by the alternative in which the content of this one syllable (namely 'C') is parsed instead as .C$\acute{\square}$. . This alternative incurs only the single mark *Fill^{Nuc}, but the closed-syllable parse .($\square$)$\acute{\square}$C. shares this mark and violates −Cod as well. (In addition, the closed-syllable parse must also violate either Ons or Fill^{Ons}.)

Such epentheses are not unknown: think of Spanish /slavo/ → *e*slavo and Arabic /ħmarar/ → ʔi*ħ*marar. We must argue, as indeed must all syllable theorists, that other constraints are involved (for Arabic, see McCarthy & Prince 1990b).

(144) **Prop. 4**. *[ ][ ]
    Adjacent empty nodes cannot occur in an optimal parse.

Propositions 1, 2, and 3 entail that [ ][ ] cannot occur inside a syllable. This leaves only the intersyllabic environment .C$\acute{\square}$.$\square$V~. This bisyllabic string incurs two marks, *Fill^{Nuc} and *Fill^{Ons}. Consider the alternative parse in which the substring

/CV/ is analyzed as tautosyllabic .CV~. This eliminates both marks and incurs no others. It follows that two adjacent epentheses are impossible.

We now pull these results together into an omnibus characterization of where empty nodes can be found in optimal parses.

(145)   **FILL Violation THM. Location of Possible Epenthesis Sites**
        Under the Basic Syllable Structure Constraints, epenthesis is limited to the following environments:
        (a)   Onset, when Nucleus is filled:
              .□V.
              .□VC.
        (b)   Nucleus, when Onset is filled:
              .CŪ.
              .CŪC.
        Furthermore, two adjacent epentheses are impossible, even across syllable boundaries.

We note that this result will carry through in the more complex theory developed below in chapter 8, in which the primitive C/V distinction is replaced by a graded sonority-dependent scale.

Chapter 7

Constraint Interaction in Lardil Phonology

The nominal paradigm of LARDIL, a Pama-Nyungan language of Australia,[55] displays a set of sometimes dramatic alternations that are responsive to constraints on syllable structure and word form. Detailed study and analysis of the language has established not only the facts of the matter, but also uncovered the essential structural factors that drive the phonology (Hale 1973; Klokeid 1976; Itô 1986; Wilkinson 1988; Kirchner 1992a). Of principal interest, from our point of view, is the coexistence of prosodically governed augmentation and truncation patterns, competing for the same territory at the end of the word. Short stems are augmented; long stems can be truncated; and nothing happens to stems that are just the right size.

According to a current operational conception, the phonology would have rules of deletion and epenthesis that are blocked and triggered by various constraints: deletion of a final vowel *except when* the resulting output would be too short (blocking); addition of a vowel (or even consonant and vowel) *only when* the stem is not long enough (triggering); deletion of a final consonant sequence when unsyllabifiable (deletion triggered when syllabification is blocked). The major problem is to make sure that the right rule is controlled by the right constraint: although vowel-epenthesis is in the grammar, it is not used to save unsyllabified consonants; they delete. A second problem is keeping the rules at bay: excessive application of final V- and C-deletion (both in evidence) would result in very short words indeed.

It is important to see through such mechanical challenges to the fundamental insight behind the account: the role of prosodic output constraints in defining the system. Surely the key advance in the understanding of Lardil and similar systems

---

[55] According to Hale, Lardil is "rather distantly related to the other Pama-Nyungan languages." The language is spoken on Mornington Island, one of the Wellesley group at the bottom of the Gulf of Carpentaria. Hale notes that it "is closely related to the other language spoken in the Wellesley group and adjacent mainland, . . . [which has] at least three dialects, Yanggal, Yukulta, Gayardilt" (Hale 1973: 421).

was the introduction of analytical techniques that allowed many mutations of this sort to be rendered as consequences of syllabification and foot-formation, as in the work of Selkirk 1981, Broselow 1982, Steriade 1982, Itô 1986, 1989, McCarthy & Prince 1986, and for Lardil, Itô 1986 and Wilkinson 1988. The basic idea here is that the assignment of prosodic structure is *directly responsible* for a range of phenomena which early generative phonology attributed to a battery of structure-modifying re-write rules. Our program is to pursue this line of analysis with full vigor; we will argue that the major paradigmatic alternations in the Lardil noun are entirely consequent upon the prosodic parse.

7.1   The Constraints

We begin in this section by identifying the principal prosodic constraints operative in the language; in the next, we proceed to determine their relative ranking. The data are taken from Hale 1973, Klokeid 1976, Wilkinson 1988, and Kirchner 1992a. (After glosses we provide page number references, which are to Hale, except where otherwise noted.)

The phonological action we seek is found in the nominative case.[56] To make clear the character of the inflections we show some simple, alternation-free forms here:

(146)   **Lardil Inflections**

	Stem	Nominative	Nonfuture acc.	Future acc.	Gloss
a.	/kentapal/	kentapal	kentapal-in	kentapal-uɽ	'dugong' 423
b.	/piɳen/	piɳen	piɳen-in	piɳen-uɽ	'woman' 423

The nominative ending is null; the nonfuture accusative is *-in*; the future accusative is *-uɽ*.

Most of Lardil syllable structure falls comfortably within the purview of the Basic Theory of chapter 6. Lardil admits only syllables CV(C). Onsets are required, and underparsing is evidently used to enforce the Ons constraint when morphology puts V against V, as in the following example, showing the nonfuture accusative of /yukařpa/ 'husband':

---

[56] There are a number of segmental and allomorphic alternations which will not be treated here, including the lowering of final vowels *u,i→a,e* and the process of sonorization t,ʈ→ř,ɻ/—#, of which the latter may be relevant to a later level of phonology than we discuss (see Hale 1973: 426 fn. 32, Klokeid 1976 for details). These can be safely abstracted away from inasmuch as they do not interact with basic syllabification, which lies at the center of our concerns. For a different view of the system, the reader is referred to Kirchner 1992a, where the nominative form is analyzed not as uninflected but as bearing an abstract consonantal affix, one whose featural specification (though ill-formed at the surface) plays into the segmental alternations and which provides material for the cases that we regard as full syllable augmentation. In our formulations we note, but do not dwell on, Kirchner's conclusion that truncation is limited to nominals.

(147) **Resolution of V + V**

Input	Phonological analysis	Phonetic
/yukařpa+in/	.yu.kař.pa⟨i⟩n.	yukařpan
	*.yu.kař.pa.□in.	*yukařpatin

(We will not be concerned with the details of the V + V phenomenon, however.) Lardil thus exemplifies the typological family $\Sigma^{CV(C)}_{del}$ in the terminology of the Basic CV Syllable Structure Theory of chapter 6, ex. (140). This means that the Faithfulness constraints dominate –COD, allowing codas when there is segmental motive for them in the input; and the constraint ONS dominates at least one of the Basic Theory's Faithfulness constraints, disallowing onsetless syllables.

Both Onsets and Codas are limited to a single segment, and nuclei consist of a single either short or long vowel. The relevant constraint from the Basic Theory is *COMPLEX (120), which says that syllable positions are limited to single segments. Long vowels, being monosegmental, satisfy this constraint. The constraint *COMPLEX is unviolated in Lardil, and will be seen to play an important role in the system.

For explicitness, we recall a few other characteristics of the Basic Theory. The constraint NUC (119) requiring syllables to have nuclei is assumed without comment to be undominated; similarly for the constraints *M/V (121) and *P/C (122) which prohibit vowels from being parsed as syllable margins and consonants from being parsed as syllable peaks. These are unviolated in Lardil and therefore cannot be crucially subordinated. (A domination relation will be said to be 'crucial' if the output changes when it is reversed. When clear from context, 'crucial' will be omitted and, in particular, we will feel free to use 'undominated' to mean 'not crucially dominated'.) The division of segments in Lardil into vowels and consonants is uncomplicated: there is, evidently, no need to posit segments which alternate between peak and margin positions.

Looking beyond purely structural concerns, we find that codas in Lardil are subject to further strong limitations of the familiar kind (Steriade 1982, Itô 1986). Adopting Itô's term, we refer to the relevant constraint as the Coda Condition, CODACOND for short. The generalization offered by Wilkinson is that Codas may be occupied only by 'nonback coronals' and by nasals homorganic with a following (onset) consonant. The consonant inventory of Lardil looks like this, with the 'nonback' coronals boxed:

(148) **Lardil Consonants** (Hale 1973)

	labial	lamino-dental	apico-alveolar	lamino-alveolar	apico-domal	dorso-velar
obstruent	p	t̪	t	t^y	ṭ	k
nasal	m	n̪	n	n^y	ṇ	ŋ
lateral			l			
flap			ř			
approximant	w			y	ɻ	

Caveat lector: the Lardil coronals referred to by Wilkinson as *back* are the farthest forward: the lamino-dentals [t̪ n̪]. The feature assignment is due to Stevens, Keyser,

& Kawasaki 1986; evidently the lamino-dentals are velarized, so that they have a Dorsal as well as a Coronal articulation. Excluded from syllable-final position, then, is any consonant with a noncoronal specification (Labial or Dorsal), even secondarily. (On the unmarked status of coronals, see Paradis & Prunet 1991, McCarthy & Taub 1992). When a consonant has no place of its own, such as a linked nasal, it is of course also allowed in Coda position. Here we will do little more than summarize the effects of the condition, making no serious attempt to provide it or its variants with a proper analysis (for recent approaches, see Goldsmith 1990, Itô & Mester 1993, and within the present theory, Kirchner 1992bc, Zec 1994, and chapter 8 and chapter 9.1.2 below).

(149) CODACOND

A coda consonant can have only Coronal place or place shared with another consonant.

The Coda Condition has serious consequences at the end of words, as can be seen in table (150) in the *Nominative* column.

(150) **Lardil Paradigms with Truncation**

Underlying stem	Nominative	Nonfut. acc.	Fut. acc.	Gloss
a. **C** Loss from stem				
/ŋaluk/	ŋalu	ŋaluk-in	ŋaluk-uɽ	'story' 438
/wuŋkunuŋ/	wuŋkunu	wuŋkunuŋ-in	wuŋkunuŋ-kuɽ	'queen-fish' 438
/waŋalk/	waŋal	waŋalk-in	waŋalk-uɽ	'boomerang' 438
b. **V** Loss from stem				
/yiliyili/	yiliyil	yiliyili-n	yiliyili-wuɽ	'oyster sp.' 424
/mayaɽa/	mayaɽ	mayaɽa-n	mayaɽa-ɽ	'rainbow' 424
c. **CV** Loss from stem				
/yukaɽpa/	yukaɽ	yukaɽpa-n	yukaɽpa-ɽ	'husband' 424
/wuṭaltʸi/	wuṭal	wuṭaltʸi-n	wuṭaltʸi-wuɽ	'meat' 424
/ŋawuŋawu/	ŋawuŋa	ŋawuŋawu-n	ŋawuŋawu-ɽ	'termite' 425
/muɽkunima/	muɽkuni	muɽkunima-n	muɽkinima-ɽ	'nullah' 425
d. **CCV** Loss from stem				
/muŋkumuŋku/	muŋkumu	muŋkumuŋku-n	muŋkumuŋku-ɽ	'wooden axe' 425
/tʸumputʸumpu/	tʸumputʸu	tʸumputʸumpu-n	tʸumputʸumpu-ɽ	'dragonfly' 425

These underlying stems show up intact only when suffixed, here by the endings -in and -uɽ.[57] In the Nominative, with null affixation, a considerable amount of word-final material can be left behind. In the simplest case, a single consonant is

---

[57] In addition to regular V-loss from /uɽ/, the fut. acc. ending shows a couple of allomorphs (-wuɽ and -kuɽ) under conditions of limited or unclear generality (Klokeid 1976: 42–3), which will not be dealt with here. See Mester 1992 for discussion of allomorphy within an Optimality-theoretic conception of phonology.

lost, always one that cannot be syllabified because of the narrowness of the Coda Condition. Violations of CODACOND are avoided by failure to parse segments, as in the following typical example /ŋaluk/ 'story (nom.)' (150a):

(151)   **Enforcement of CODACOND through underparsing**

Stem	Parse	Phonetic
/ŋaluk/	.ŋa.lu.⟨k⟩	ŋalu
	*.ŋa.lu.k□.	*ŋaluka

Unparsed segments occur in Lardil, as in many other languages, in situations where violations of ONS and CODACOND are at risk. In addition, word-final vowels are generally left unparsed in the nominative. The stem /yiliyili/ is analyzed as *.yi.li.yil.⟨i⟩* when uninflected (150b). There are immediate further consequences: preceding consonants must also be left unparsed if syllabifying them would violate CODACOND. The resulting heavy losses are illustrated in (150c–d).

Since nonparsing violates the prosodic licensing constraint PARSE, it will be avoided unless there is another, higher-ranked constraint that compels it. Wilkinson (1986: 10) makes the interesting proposal that extrametricality is what's involved. Following this general line, we formulate the relevant constraint so as to require that word-final vowels not be parsed. By 'word-final' we mean specifically a vowel that is not separated by other segmental material from the end of the word.

(152)   **FREE-V**
Word-final vowels must not be parsed (in the nominative).

The codicil 'in the nominative' is no more than a conveniently explicit stand-in for a more principled understanding of the restrictions on the constraint. Observing that nominal affixes are all consonant-final, we could generalize the limitation to the entire class of nouns. In his detailed study of the language, Klokeid 1976: 81 goes further, arguing that "the phonological rules motivated for nouns apply in identical fashion to verb forms." He argues (p. 85) that the verb stem suffix /t̪/ is uniformly present in all verbs (three exceptions only), and that its presence inevitably blocks truncation. If Klokeid is right, the codicil can simply be erased: there would be no need for any categorial information at all in the constraint itself, beyond the reference to the general morphological notion 'word'.

As for the core content of FREE-V, it appears to be a grammaticized reflex of the prosodic weakness of final open syllables, which are liable to de-stressing, de-voicing, shortening, truncation, and so on, under purely phonological conditions. (Estonian morphology has virtually the same constraint, including limitation to the nominative, the null-affixed case.) It may also have connection with the commonly encountered constraint to the effect that stems or words must end in a consonant (McCarthy & Prince 1990ab, Prince 1990).

There is an important class of cases where, despite phonetic appearances, FREE-V is *not* violated. Since the constraint is phonological and pertains to phonological structure, it is vacuously satisfied in forms like *.ŋa.lu.⟨k⟩*, because the form *has no word-final vowel* in the relevant sense, its last vowel being separated from the word-edge by *k*. And the constraint is actively satisfied in *.muŋ.ku.mu.⟨ŋku⟩*, where the word-final vowel is unparsed, even though the phonetic interpretation *.muŋ.ku.mu.* ends, irrelevantly, in a syllabified vowel. Our analysis crucially rests, then, on the parallel satisfaction of constraints, as opposed to serial application of structure-deforming rules, and on the assumption of 'monotonicity' in the input–output relation – that the input is literally contained in the output, with no losses (cf. Wheeler 1981, 1988). Under our assumptions about Gen, then, word-finality of segment is an immutable property of the input morphological structure which is transparently preserved in every output, however it is parsed.

By contrast, the constraint FREE-V is flagrantly violated in bisyllabic stems, as illustrated in (153) by /wiṭe/, which is parsed simply as *.wi.ṭe*.

(153)   **No Truncation in Minimal Words**

	Stem	Nominative	Nonfut. acc.	Fut. acc.	Gloss	
a.	/wiṭe/	wiṭe	wiṭe-n	wiṭe-ṛ	'inside'	W326
b.	/mela/	mela	mela-n	mela-ṛ	'sea'	433

Construing these as monosyllables to satisfy FREE-V would lead to violation of the strong universal prosody–morphology interface constraint discussed above in §4.3:

(154)   **Lx≈Pr**
Every Lexical Word must correspond to a Prosodic Word.

Since the phonological category PrWd must dominate a foot, and since Lardil feet are binary by Foot Binarity (FTBIN, §4.3.1), adherence to Lx≈Pr entails bimoraic minimality. As shown in Wilkinson 1988, the resulting minimal word-size limitation correctly blocks stem-final vowel loss. The actual foot in Lardil may be the bimoraic trochee, with a syllable having one or two moras depending on whether its vowel is short or long, regardless of whether it has a coda. Details of foot form, of course, do not affect the minimality argument, since moraic binarity is the universal lower limit.

Not only does Lx≈Pr, in consort with FTBIN, prevent nonparsing of word-final vowels; it also forces the appearance of syllables with empty positions. The monomoraic stems illustrated in (155) all receive syllabic augmentation in the nominative:[58]

---

[58] In addition to the well-populated stem-shape categories exemplified in the table, there are two known CV stems: /ṛu/ 'body fat, grease', /tʸa/ 'foot' (Hale 1973: 428, Klokeid 1976: 55). These have the following forms: ṛuwa, ṛuyin, ṛuuṛ; tʸaː, tʸayin, tʸawuṛ. These are of interest for several reasons. Note the blocking of truncation of the affixal vowel, obviously due to the word minimality requirement; note also the use of a spreading structure rather than featural epenthesis to fill the Onset. The form ṛuuṛ (unattested: constructed from Klokeid's description) raises an issue about VV sequences; perhaps it is really *uwu*, with the *w* of low perceptibility in the *u–u* environment. The most serious problem for the analysis we give is the *tʸaː* nominative from /tʸa/. We point out the exact problem below, fn. 64, p. 142.

(155)   **Lardil Augmentation of Short Stems**

Underlying stem	Nominative	Nonfut. acc.	Fut. acc.	Gloss	
a. **V** Augmentation					
/yak/	yak**a**	yak-in	yak-uɽ	'fish'	438
/ɽelk/	ɽelk**a**	ɽelk-in	ɽelk-uɽ	'head'	438
b. **CV** Augmentation					
/maɽ/	maɽ**ʈa**	maɽ-in	maɽ-uɽ	'hand'	427
/ɽil/	ɽil**ta**	ɽil-in	ɽil-uɽ	'neck'	427
c. **CV** Augmentation					
/kaŋ/	kaŋ**ka**	kaŋ-in	kaŋ-kuɽ	'speech'	438
/tʸaŋ/	tʸaŋ**ka**	tʸaŋ-in	tʸaŋ-kuɽ	'some'	438

These stems cannot end underlyingly in the *-a* that shows up in the phonetics. The accusative markers are *-n* and *-ɽ* after true vowel-final stems, *-in* and *-uɽ* after consonant finals, as seen in (146) and (150) above. Nor can the underlying stems in (155b,c) be analyzed as ending in *-ta* or *-ka*, or even in *-t* and *-k*. Were the nominatives taken to reflect underlying consonantism, there would be no explanation for the putative disappearance of the additional consonants *t* and *k* in the oblique cases.

All subminimal stems are augmented. Not only are Lx≈Pr and FtBin unviolated in the language, but the Null Parse output is inferior to the augmented forms, even though they violate Fill, which is therefore well down in the hierarchy.

Augmentation violates Fill, but it does not always do so minimally, contrary to *ceteris paribus* expectation. Although a single empty position – a Nucleus – is sufficient to rescue excessively short stems CVC from Foot Binarity violations, the fact is that the accessory syllable may be entirely empty, with an unfilled Onset as well, as in .maɽ.□◌́. and .kaŋ.□◌́. (155b,c). Since all consonants of Lardil may stand in onset position, there is no phonological need for this extra Fill violation; the last consonant of the stem could easily fill the required Onset. Whence the supererogatory empty Onset? What's crucial, as Wilkinson points out (1986: 7), is whether or not the stem-final consonant can be parsed as a Coda: when it can be, it is.[59]

The generalization is clear in table (155). Supererogation is manifest in forms like (a) and (b) below:

---

[59] Two patterns have been observed that indicate the need for refinement: /bit/→*bita*, *bitta; and /teř/ →*teřa*, *teřta (Hale 1973, Wilkinson 1988, Kirchner 1992a). In these cases, it appears that an onset [t] cannot be epenthesized because of constraints against geminate consonants and against the sequence [řt] (Hale 1973: 427; recall the untreated alternation t~ ř, fn. 56, p. 120). These constraints are sensitive to the phonetic content of the epenthetic onset, and not merely to its presence, yet they bear on syllabification, contrary to the hypothesis that epenthetic structure is nothing more than an empty syllabic node. For a further discussion of this phenomenon, see immediately below, fn. 60.

(156) **FILL Patterns** depending on syllabifiability of stem

	Stem	Analysis	Phonetic
a.	/maɻ/	.maɻ.□□́.	maɻʈa
		*.ma.ɻ□́.	*maɻa
b.	/kaŋ/	.kaŋ.□□́.	kaŋka
		*.ka.ŋ□́.	*kaŋa
c.	/yak/	.ya.k□́.	yaka
		*.yak.□□́.	*yakta

Where CODACOND can be met, as in (a) and (b), the stem-final consonant closes the stem syllable. Where it can't be met, as in (c), augmentation is minimal.[60] We propose that this pattern of generalization reflects another type of constraint on the morphology–phonology interface, one that requires edges of morphological constituents to match up with edges of phonological constituents. In the examples of (156), we see that the end of the stem is made to coincide with a syllable edge, if that state of affairs can be achieved by epenthesis while still deferring to the general syllable structure restrictions of the language.

Although the phonological integrity of the stem is protected in forms like *maɻ.□□́*, no such effect is observed internally at stem + affix junctures. We do not find, for example, *maɻ.□in* from /maɻ + in/ or *ken.ta.pal.□in* from /kentapal + in/. The morphological category at issue can therefore be determined quite precisely: the phenomenon involves only the final edge of the entire underlying collocation of stem + affixes. Let us call this entity the 'Morphological Word', or MWord. We may then state the relevant constraint:

---

[60] The fact that the Coda Condition *is* met in forms like *.kaŋ.□□́.* (phonetic *kaŋka*) requires explication. Coda nasals must be homorganic to a following C; here there is no following C, only a syllabic position (under the current construal) lacking segmental content. This is of course a typical conundrum encountered in underspecification theories, in which the phonetic properties of the to-be-phonetically-filled-in material enter into the phonological constraint system of the language (Kiparsky 1973a, Mohanan 1991, McCarthy & Taub 1992, McCarthy 1994). Such phenomena provide compelling evidence that the empty structure technology used here needs amplification: perhaps, for example, the set of candidates issued by Gen should include actual featural and segmental insertions, as well as new association lines. In such a theory, the cognate of FILL would militate against the presence of material not in the input, an obvious kind of unfaithfulness. We postpone consideration of such refinements for future research (see Yip 1993ab for some suggestions). For present purposes, let us imagine that a syllable node bears the index of the segments associated with it (Aoun 1979), specifically of the *place* node of that segment, its head (Itô & Mester 1993); assume also that empty nodes can be introduced with indices. A form like *.kaŋᵢ.□ᵢ□́.* is regarded as legitimate by CODACOND because the nasal is indexed to a non-coda node. It appears that in Lardil only sonorants may be coindexed in this way. The phonetic interpretation process that fills in values for empty nodes would derive place information from coindexation. For deeper exploration of CODACOND-type issues, see Prince 1984, Goldsmith 1990, Kaye 1990, Itô & Mester 1993 and the references cited therein.

(157)   **ALIGN**
The final edge of a Morphological Word corresponds to the final edge of a syllable.

ALIGN belongs to the family of constraints which govern the relation between prosody and grammatical structure. Considerable further development and investigation of the ALIGN idea is found in McCarthy & Prince 1993a, which posits a general format for alignment constraints: ALIGN(GCat-edge(L|R), PCat-edge(L|R)), where GCat denotes a morphological or syntactic category; PCat denotes a prosodic category; L,R denote 'left' and 'right'. McCarthy & Prince demonstrate the central role of such constraints in a wide range of prosodic–morphological phenomena and explore the variety of effects that can be obtained by using them. Of particular interest in the present context is their finding that Axininca Campa right-aligns the Stem itself and not the MWord. (McCarthy & Prince 1993b show that the Alignment family is instrumental in much prosodic phonology as well, incorporating and generalizing the EDGEMOST constraints posited above.) The ALIGN pattern is closely analogous to that proposed for the domain of phrasal phonology by Chen 1987 and further explored in Selkirk 1986, 1993. Observe that Lx≈PR really falls into the same family: a lexical word edge is to be aligned with the edge of a Prosodic Word.

In the case at hand, the constraint ALIGN is violated unless the MWord's final segment stands as the final segment in a syllable. A consonant-final MWord satisfies ALIGN only if its final C is a Coda. A vowel-final MWord satisfies ALIGN only if its final V is parsed as the Nucleus of an open syllable. MWords in which the final segment is not parsed at all will violate ALIGN because the morphological-category edge does not fall at a syllable edge.

Like Axininca Campa, Lardil evidences both left and right morphology/prosody alignment. Truncation and Augmentation lead to frequent violations of final ALIGN (157), which looks at the end of the domain. By contrast, ALIGN-L, aimed at the leading edge of the Stem or MWord, is never violated: prosodic structure begins crisply at the beginning of the word, and empty structure never appears there. Word minimality considerations alone are insufficient to determine the placement of empty material, and languages differ on its location. Shona, Mohawk, and Choctaw, to cite three genetically separated examples, all use prothetic vowels to attain minimality (Myers 1987a, Hewitt 1992; Michelson 1988; Lombardi & McCarthy 1991). In Lardil, as in Axininca Campa, augmentation is always final, being ruled out initially by ALIGN-L (McCarthy & Prince 1993a: §4). Note that if Lx≈PR actually works along Chen–Selkirk lines, as suggested above, then we can identify ALIGN-L with Lx≈PR. The constraint would be that the initial edge of the lexical word must align with the initial edge of the prosodic word. Let's tentatively assume this formulation, and speak no more of ALIGN-L.

We have now surveyed the principal constraints involved in the alternations. The following list summarizes and categorizes the constraint set:

(158)   **Principal Lardil Constraints** (not yet ranked)
   a.   Basic Syllable Structure
        ONS, –COD, FILL^{Ons}, FILL^{Nuc}, PARSE, *COMPLEX

b. Segmental Association
   CodaCond
c. Foot Structure
   FtBin
d. Morphology–Phonology Interface
   Lx≈Pr, Align, Free-V

Of these constraints, only Free-V involves a significant degree of language-particular idiosyncrasy. The others are strictly universal; and some, like Align (i.e. Align-R) and Lx≈Pr (qua Align-L), point to the existence of a universal family of constraints whose other members are presumably available but subordinated out of sight in Lardil.

For the reader's convenience, the table in (159) lays out the alternation system that the constraint set, when ranked, will generate.

Inputs are distinguished first according to whether they are consonant- or vowel-final, and then according to whether they are subminimal (one mora), minimal (two moras), or supraminimal (more than two moras). On stems CV, see fn. 58, p. 124 above.

The table uses the following code:

T pure coronal, a *possible* coda
$\mathbb{K}$ C with dorsal or labial articulation, *impossible* coda
$\mathbb{M}$ a nasal not pure coronal (a *possible coda only when* followed by a homorganic onset)
$\mathbb{Q}$ C that is an *impossible coda* for any reason. $\{\mathbb{Q}\} = \{\mathbb{M}\} \cup \{\mathbb{K}\}$
X^+ sequence of one or more elements of type X

(159) **Summary of Lardil Nominative Forms**
Consonant-Final Stems

Stem ≥ μμ

a.	~T	→ ~T.	kentapal	→ .ken.ta.pal.
b.	~$\mathbb{Q}^+$	→ ~.⟨$\mathbb{Q}^+$⟩	waŋalk	→ .wa.ŋal.⟨k⟩
			ŋaluk	→ .ŋa.lu.⟨k⟩

Stem < μμ

c.	~T	→ ~T.□Ó.	maṛ	→ .maṛ.□Ó.
d.	~$\mathbb{K}$	→ ~.$\mathbb{K}$Ó.	ṛelk	→ .ṛel.kÓ.
			yak	→ .ya.kÓ.
e.	~$\mathbb{M}$	→ ~$\mathbb{M}$.□Ó.	kaŋ	→ .kaŋ.□Ó.

Vowel-Final Stems

Stem > μμ

f.	~TV	→ ~T.⟨V⟩	yiliyili	→ .yi.li.yil.⟨i⟩
g.	~$\mathbb{Q}^+$V	→ ~.⟨$\mathbb{Q}^+$V⟩	yukařpa	→ .yu.kař.⟨pa⟩
			ŋawuŋawu	→ .ŋa.wu.ŋa.⟨wu⟩
			muŋkumuŋku	→ .muŋ.ku.mu.⟨ŋku⟩

Stem = μμ

h.	~V	→ ~V.	wiṭe	→ .wi.ṭe.

7.2   The Ranking

To construct a grammar of Lardil from the assembled constraints, it is necessary to fix their ranking. Our basic analytical strategy will be to examine competitions between pairs of candidates, one of which is desired to be optimal, the other of which provides a serious challenge, because it is favored by some constraint or constraints (§7.2.2). Each such competition will turn out to bear on the ranking relations between a small number of conflicting constraints. The end result will be a collection of ranking conditions, which must hold of any grammar that is successful in generating the desired forms. These conditions are combined into an overall ranking (more precisely: class of rankings) for the whole set of constraints.

We then go on to show in §7.3 that the posited rankings are not only necessary, but sufficient to produce the desired outputs: that a grammar of constraints so ranked will dismiss not just the small set of losing competitors considered in §7.2.2, but will indeed dismiss *every* nonattested output candidate as suboptimal.

Before we plunge into this task, we offer two remarks on the logic of constraint-ranking arguments. The first is fundamental to the project of advancing from empirical observations to sound conclusions about necessary rankings. The second offers a refinement useful for deducing rankings under the particular conditions comprehended by Pāṇini's Theorem (§5.3).

7.2.1   Some Ranking Logic

There are risks involved in focusing on only two constraints in a situation where a number of constraints are swarming about, their interactions unresolved. When is it safe to conclude that an argument about two constraints can't be invalidated by the introduction of a third into the discussion? Fortunately, the issue submits to a simple resolution.

Consider the basic situation in which two constraints, call them C_1 and C_2, are directly rankable. For a ranking argument to exist at all, the constraints must *conflict*. This means that they disagree on the relative Harmony of competing candidate forms arising from a given input, where one of the candidates is the true output. Let's denote the forms on which C_1 and C_2 conflict by the names ω and z. Suppose ω is the empirically correct output, which must be optimal under the constraint hierarchy, if the grammar is to be successful. Suppose further that C_1 favors ω over z, but that the conflicting C_2 favors z over ω.

In this situation, it is clear that C_2 must be subordinated in the ranking to *some* constraint favoring ω over z – otherwise ω will not win against z. If the choice between ω and z is relevant to the ranking of C_1 and C_2, then the constraint that grants relative superiority to ω – here, C_1 – must be dominant. A typical conflict situation is shown in the following tableau.

(160) **Constraint Conflict and Ranking Argument**

Candidates from /input_i/	C_1	C_2
☞ ω		*
z	* !	

This constitutes a *potential* empirical argument that C_1 dominates C_2. Are we then licensed to conclude that the domination relation $C_1 \gg C_2$ must be honored by the grammar under investigation? Could it be that another constraint in the grammar – call it D – is actually responsible for the victory of ω over z, mooting the clash of C_1 and C_2?

Indeed it could, but any such spoiler constraint must meet tight conditions. First of all, ω and z cannot tie on D; for if they do, D plays no role in deciding between them. Second, D cannot favor z over ω: no such constraint, disfavoring ω, can be responsible for its triumph over a competitor.

This leaves only the situation where D favors ω over z, exactly as C_1 does. Such constraints have the power to decide the competition in favor of ω. These are the ones to watch out for. If there are none, or if they have already been shown to be lower-ranked than C_2 by other considerations, then the ranking argument in (160) goes through and establishes a necessary condition on the grammar.[61]

To put it another way: a successful direct ranking argument shows that C_1 is the *rejector* of the candidate z in its contest against ω, i.e. that C_1 is the very constraint that puts an end to z's candidacy. The only type of constraint whose presence in the grammar would undermine the argument is another potential rejector of z *vis-à-vis* ω. (Should such a potential rejector exist, and should we have no reason to believe that it must be ranked below C_2, we can only conclude that C_1 *or* D is ranked above C_2.)

As a second point of useful ranking logic, we review the discussion of Pāṇini's Theorem on Constraint Ranking from §5.3. Intuitively, this theorem says that if a more general and a more specific constraint disagree, then they can only both be active in winnowing the candidate set of an input if the specific constraint dominates the general one. The first relevant case of this theorem in Lardil involves the more general constraint PARSE and the more specific constraint FREE-V which disagrees with the more general one on its more specialized domain, V-final stems.

Let us review the relevant definitions from chapter 5.

---

[61] This argument can be re-phrased in terms of the Cancellation/Domination Lemma below: ch. 8, (192), p. 153, and (238), p. 174. The Cancellation/Domination Lemma holds that each mark incurred by the overall winner ω must be canceled or dominated by the marks of any competitor. Let us suppose, without loss of generality, that we are looking at fully canceled tableaux, in which all common marks have been eliminated. The form ω has a mark $*C_2$; the claim of the comparison in tableau (160) is that C_1 crucially supplies the dominating mark for z. Of course, there might be another constraint around, D, which actually supplies the dominating mark. To fill this role, D would have to give a mark to z and no mark to ω, just like C_1.

(161)   Dfn. **Pāṇinian Constraint Relation**
Let $\mathbb{S}$ and $\mathbb{G}$ be two constraints. $\mathbb{S}$ *stands to* $\mathbb{G}$ *as special to general in a Pāṇinian relation* if, for any input i to which $\mathbb{S}$ applies non-vacuously, any parse of i which satisfies $\mathbb{S}$ fails $\mathbb{G}$.

A constraint applies *non-vacuously* to an input i if some of the parses of i violate the constraint while others satisfy it.

For example, the constraint FREE-V stands to PARSE as special to general in a Pāṇinian relation. Given any input to which FREE-V applies non-vacuously – an input with a stem-final vowel V – any parse of it which satisfies FREE-V by leaving V unparsed must for that very reason violate PARSE.

The other concept we need is:

(162)   Dfn. **Active**
Let $\mathbb{C}$ be a constraint in a constraint hierarchy $\mathbb{CH}$ and let i be an input. $\mathbb{C}$ is *active on* i *in* $\mathbb{CH}$ if $\mathbb{C}$ eliminates from consideration some candidate parses of i.

That is, among those candidate parses of i which survive the constraints which dominate $\mathbb{C}$ in the hierarchy $\mathbb{CH}$, some violate $\mathbb{C}$ and others satisfy it, so $\mathbb{C}$ eliminates those parses which violate it. (Recall that in harmonic ordering, if all the candidates left for consideration by $\mathbb{C}$ violate $\mathbb{C}$, then $\mathbb{C}$ does not eliminate any of these parses.)

Now the theorem asserts:

(163)   **Pāṇini's Theorem on Constraint Ranking** (PTC)
Let $\mathbb{S}$ and $\mathbb{G}$ stand as specific to general in a Pāṇinian constraint relation. Suppose these constraints are part of a constraint hierarchy $\mathbb{CH}$, and that $\mathbb{G}$ is active in $\mathbb{CH}$ on some input i. Then if $\mathbb{G} \gg \mathbb{S}$, $\mathbb{S}$ is not active on i.

Thus if both the general and specific constraints are active on a common input, the specific must dominate the general. We will see shortly how PTC can be used to help deduce the domination hierarchy of Lardil. For other examples of PTC and related patterns of argument, see Kirchner 1992bc and McCarthy & Prince 1993a.

PTC has obvious affinities with the Elsewhere Condition of Anderson 1969 and Kiparsky 1973c, which has played an important role in enriching and deepening the theory of Lexical Phonology. There is an important difference: PTC is merely a point of logic, but the Elsewhere Condition is thought of as a principle specific to UG, responsible for empirical results which could very well be otherwise. In Kiparsky 1973c, for example, the Elsewhere Condition is written to govern the relationship between rules whose structural changes are *the same* as well as incompatible (broadly, 'conflicting'). This enables him to claim that it is the Elsewhere Condition, rather than the interpretation of parentheses, that is responsible for disjunctive ordering in stress rules. Suppose a grammar has the two (adjacent) rules 'stress the penult' and 'stress the final syllable'. Since every word has a final syllable, but not every word a penult, it follows from the Elsewhere Condition that in longer words *only* the penult stress rule applies. It is logically possible that both rules would apply, stressing the last two syllables in longer words. Current prosodic theory yields a better understanding of the phenomenon. In reality, the two stress rules are incompatible: conflicting, not identical in structural change. If main-stress is at issue, then the relevant constraints entail that there can be only one such in a word. (Each rule then says "*the* main-stress is here.") The ranking decides which position is favored; and either is possible. If mere stress vs. unstress is at issue, then Foot Binarity decides the matter (not to mention anti-clash constraints).

Along the same lines, the Elsewhere Condition is sometimes said to entail that a given morphological category should have only one marking; double marking of e.g. plural by two different affixes, one specialized, the other of more general applicability, is then held to be an 'exception' to the Elsewhere Condition (Stump 1989). Here again, it should be clear that what's really at issue is a substantive matter: how morphological categories are expressed. A morphosyntactic feature [+PL] typically has one morpheme devoted to it in a string (Pinker 1984, Marcus et al. 1992); thus, different plural morphemes are *incompatible*. This allows for a special-case/general-case system, in which the logic of PTC determines the ranking that yields the observed facts. What double marking challenges is the assumption of incompatibility, without which the PTC is irrelevant. We conclude that the standard Elsewhere Condition folds together a point of logic (PTC) with additional claims about what linguistic phenomena are incompatible. With the incompatibility claims properly factored out into substantive constraints of various types, what's left is PTC; that is to say, nothing.

7.2.2   Ranking the Constraints

Let us now turn to the business at hand. We repeat the constraint list for convenience of reference.

(164)   **Constraints to be Ranked**
   a.   Basic Syllable Structure
         Ons, –Cod, Fill^{Ons}, Fill^{Nuc}, Parse, *Complex
   b.   Segmental Association
         CodaCond
   c.   Foot Structure
         FtBin
   d.   Morphology–Phonology Interface Constraints
         Lx≈Pr, Align, Free-V

Five of the constraints are never violated in Lardil, and are therefore not crucially dominated. In any given grammar, which imposes a total order on the constraint set, all but one of the five will be formally dominated; but permuting the ranking relations among the members of this set will have no effect on the outcome.

(165)   **Constraints Not Crucially Dominated**
ONS, CODACOND,*COMPLEX, LX≈PR, FTBIN

It remains to be determined how each of these top-rankable constraints is *enforced* via domination of a relevant faithfulness constraint. We will find direct evidence in the cases of ONS, LX≈PR, FTBIN. Note that the constraint *COMPLEX, which bans tautosyllabic sequences, is undominated in Lardil just as it is in the Basic Syllable Structure Theory of chapter 6 (123), p. 109.

Lardil is a member of the family $\Sigma^{CV(C)}_{del}$ of CV(C) languages (§6.1), with mandatory onset enforced by omitting stranded V's, as in VV, from syllable structure. From the discussion in chapter 6, we know how to define this family:

(166)   **Mandatory Onset Enforced by Failure to Parse**
ONS, FILL^{Ons} ≫ PARSE

Input sequences CVV are resolved as .CV.⟨V⟩, incurring a *PARSE violation, as seen in the postvocalic disappearance of -*i* in -*in* 'nonfuture accusative'. The alternatives which posit an Onsetless syllable .V., or an empty Onset position as in .□V., are declared less harmonic by this ranking. (Since we are not treating the resolution of VV in any depth here, we abstract away from the issue of deciding which V of VV is to remain unparsed, and we will therefore not offer a constraint discriminating C⟨V⟩V from CV⟨V⟩.)

(167)   **Coda Allowed**
FILL^{Nuc}, PARSE ≫ −COD

Syllables can have codas. Input CVCCV, for example, is syllabified faithfully (CODACOND willing), rather than submitted to aggressive over- or underparsing that would support the preconsonantal C with an empty nucleus (*FILL^{Nuc}) or eject it altogether from syllable structure (*PARSE).

Let us consider now the position of the pair LX≈PR and FTBIN, which jointly entail the minimality limitation on words. These two are clearly undominated, because never violated. In addition, they must be specifically ranked above certain other constraints. Operationally speaking, the minimal word size condition must *trigger* epenthesis and *block* deletion. In Optimality-theoretic terms, a constraint that is said to trigger or to block is simply dominant; there are no distinguished triggering and blocking relations. Consequently LX≈PR and FTBIN must be dominant over the FILL constraints, which militate against empty structure (*triggering* its appearance), and over the FREE-V constraint, which favors nonparsing of word-final V (*blocking* the nonparse).

To see the details, let's first examine the augmentation of subminimal stems. The constraints LX≈PR and FTBIN are enforced by positing empty syllabic nodes, sometimes unfilled Onset as well as unfilled Nucleus. It follows that:

(168)   **LX≈PR, FTBIN Enforced via Empty Structure**
LX≈PR, FTBIN ≫ FILL^{Nuc}, FILL^{Ons}

Parses such as *.maɽ.□□́.* are therefore optimal, despite violation of both Fɪʟʟ^Ons and Fɪʟʟ^Nuc. In any candidate without the additional syllable, fatal violation of the higher-ranked constraints Lx≈Pʀ or FᴛBɪɴ must occur. The tableau below shows only the Lx≈Pʀ violation, caused by failure to foot the input. Assigning the input a monomoraic foot would make it possible to satisfy Lx≈Pʀ, but at the unacceptable cost of violating FᴛBɪɴ.

/maɽ/	Lx≈Pʀ	Fɪʟʟ^Nuc	Fɪʟʟ^Ons
☞ [(꜀ .maɽ.□□́.)]_PrWd		*	*
.maɽ.	*!		

Notice that we are justified in ignoring the other constraints here. *Both* candidates fail –Cᴏᴅ; both satisfy Aʟɪɢɴ; so neither constraint can decide between them.

In forms that are precisely minimal, stem-final vowels are parsed in violation of Fʀᴇᴇ-V, because of the domination of Lx≈Pʀ and FᴛBɪɴ.

(169) **Lx≈Pʀ, FᴛBɪɴ Force Parsing of Stem-Final Vowels**
   Lx≈Pʀ, FᴛBɪɴ ≫ Fʀᴇᴇ-V

In vowel-final bimoraic stems CVCV, Fʀᴇᴇ-V conflicts with Lx≈Pʀ and FᴛBɪɴ. Parsing the final vowel violates Fʀᴇᴇ-V. Leaving it out produces a monosyllabic monomoraic output, violating either Lx≈Pʀ or FᴛBɪɴ. The conflict goes to Lx≈Pʀ and FᴛBɪɴ, of course. The following tableau shows the Lx≈Pʀ situation, considering candidates in which no monomoraic feet are assigned:

(170) **Failure of Truncation in Minimal Words**

/wiṭe/	Lx≈Pʀ	Fʀᴇᴇ-V
☞ [(.wi.ṭe.)]_PrWd		*
.wiṭ.⟨e⟩	*!	

This comparison validly establishes the relation between Lx≈Pʀ and Fʀᴇᴇ-V even though several other constraints beside Lx≈Pʀ favor the optimal candidate over its cited competitor: namely, Pᴀʀsᴇ, Aʟɪɢɴ, and –Cᴏᴅ. We will see momentarily that both Pᴀʀsᴇ and Aʟɪɢɴ must be ranked below Fʀᴇᴇ-V. And –Cᴏᴅ must in turn be ranked below Pᴀʀsᴇ because codas are allowed, as already remarked in (167). This leaves only Lx≈Pʀ to out-rank Fʀᴇᴇ-V and decide (170) in favor of the correct form.

The constraint Fʀᴇᴇ-V interacts with Pᴀʀsᴇ in the simple way covered by Pāṇini's Theorem. As mentioned in §7.2.1, Fʀᴇᴇ-V stands to Pᴀʀsᴇ as specific to general in a Pāṇinian relation: on those inputs where Fʀᴇᴇ-V applies non-vacuously, V-final stems, satisfying Fʀᴇᴇ-V entails violating Pᴀʀsᴇ.

Similarly, FREE-V stands to ALIGN as specific to general in the Pāṇinian relation: in V-final stems, satisfying FREE-V entails that the right MWord boundary (after V) is not a syllable boundary. Now let G_1 denote whichever of the general constraints PARSE and ALIGN is higher-ranked in Lardil, and G_2 the other. Consider the possibility that the special constraint S = FREE-V is dominated by G_1. Then G_1 must be active on supraminimal V-final stems, eliminating parses like .CV.CV.CVT.⟨V⟩, where T symbolizes a legal coda as in *yi.li.yil.⟨i⟩*, which violate no other constraints except G_2, which is lower-ranked than G_1. So by PTC, since the general constraint G_1 is active on V-final stems, the special constraint S = FREE-V cannot be active on these inputs: in other words, it may as well not be in the grammar, since it cannot do the work we require of it. Thus this possibility is ruled out: S must dominate G_1. Since by definition G_1 is the more dominant of PARSE and ALIGN, it follows that FREE-V must dominate *both* PARSE and ALIGN:

(171) **Pāṇini's Theorem (with respect to Final Vowel Parsing)**, Case 1
FREE-V ≫ PARSE

(172) **Pāṇini's Theorem (with respect to Final Vowel Parsing)**, Case 2
FREE-V ≫ ALIGN

Those who are skeptical of the power of pure reason may wish to examine the following tableau to see the Pāṇinian conclusion affirmed.

(173) **Pāṇini Vindicatus**

/yiliyili/	FREE-V	ALIGN	PARSE
☞ .yi.li.yil.⟨i⟩		*	*
.yi.li.yi.li.	* !		

A less obvious interaction between FREE-V and FILL^{Nuc} is implicated here as well. It is actually possible to omit the final vowel in /wiṭe/ from syllable structure while keeping the overall output bisyllabic: implant an empty final nucleus to replace, as it were, the unparsed vowel. The end-of-the-word structure would look like this:

(174) **Simultaneous Under- and Overparsing** /wiṭe/ → *wiṭa

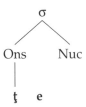

This analysis can be transcribed as *.wi.ʈ□́.⟨e⟩* if we keep in mind that no linear order holds between □́ = Nuc and the segment ⟨e⟩, as is apparent in the fuller diagram (174). The simultaneous truncation/augmentation analysis is plausible because both structures occur independently with other stems; why should they not be superimposed? That this devious analysis is not correct implies that the violation of FILL^{Nuc} by *.wi.ʈ□́.⟨e⟩* is worse than the violation of FREE-V incurred by *.wi.ʈe*. We must have FILL^{Nuc} dominating FREE-V, with results as shown in the following tableau:

(175) **No Truncation and Augmentation of the Same Stem**

/wiʈe/	FILL^{Nuc}	FREE-V
☞ .wi.ʈe.		*
.wi.ʈ□́.⟨e⟩	* !	

The required ranking is recorded here:

(176) **Unparsed Stem-Final Vowels not Replaced with Empty Nuc**
FILL^{Nuc} ≫ FREE-V

This ranking asserts that FREE-V will be sacrificed to avoid epenthesis.[62]

[62] A more interesting line of attack on this problem is potentially available within the present theory. Suppose that the constraint responsible for the truncation pattern is not, like FREE-V, in the mold of Bottom-Up Constructionism (of which extrametricality is a necessary adjunct), but pertains instead to the syllable structure, and, top-down, bans open syllables from final position. Such a constraint is recognizable as a specialization of the NONFINALITY family of §4.3. Instead of demanding that the head of a PrWd or the head of a Foot not stand in final position, this constraint demands that the head of a *syllable* not be final. Call this constraint NONFINSYLHD. Forms like *.ŋa.lu.⟨k⟩* and *.muŋ.ku.mu.⟨ŋku⟩* satisfy the constraint because no syllable head is truly final, the head of the *last* syllable being separated from the word-edge by unparsed segmental material. Crucially, augmentation also violates NONFINSYLHD. Thus both *.wi.ʈe.* and *.wi.ʈ□́.⟨e⟩* violate NONFINSYLHD equally. The analysis *.wi.ʈ□́.⟨e⟩*, which both truncates and augments, has additional marks *ALIGN, *PARSE, and *FILL^{Nuc}, which will sink it no matter where those constraints are ranked. It now follows that simple augmentation cannot coexist with truncation, without having to specify a ranking between FILL^{Nuc} and the constraint that drives truncation – an attractive result. This analysis successfully embodies the idea that augmentation does not go with truncation for the simple reason that augmentation merely recreates the structure that truncation serves to eliminate. Furthermore it releases FILL^{Nuc} from having to dominate ALIGN, so that it can join FILL^{Ons} in a contiguous package of Faithfulness constraints, perhaps simplifying the overall structure of the analysis.

    The problem with the proposal is that NONFINSYLHD faces yet another method of circumvention: *closing* the final syllable with an empty Coda. The aimed-for optimum *.wi.ʈe.* now faces other competitors: *.wi.ʈe□.* and *.wi.ʈ□́□.⟨e⟩*. (Notice that the coda-epenthesized form does not satisfy FREE-V and so is not a serious competitor in the analysis proposed in the text.) Depending on details of formulation, one or both of these candidates are likely to satisfy NONFINSYLHD, which *.wi.ʈe.* fails. (A similar issue arises with respect to whole-syllable augmentation: *.maɻ.□□́□.*

ALIGN is involved in one last ranking. This constraint forces certain forms to be augmented by an entire empty syllable, rather than by a partly empty one. An extra empty node is needed to complete the empty syllable; FILL violation is driven beyond its absolute minimum. The crucial examples are cases like *.maɾ.□□.* where the stem-final consonant ɾ is a possible coda. Compared to the alternative *.ma.ɾ□́.*, the optimal parse has an additional mark *FILL^{Ons}. In order that the FILL^{Ons} defect be rendered harmless, we must have dominant ALIGN.

(177) **Augment with Complete Syllable**
       ALIGN ≫ FILL^{Ons}

The following tableau lays it out:

(178) **ALIGN Compels Extra Structure**

/maɾ/	ALIGN	FILL^{Ons}
☞ .maɾ.□□́.		*
.ma.ɾ□́.	* !	

We have now determined a set of domination relations between pairs or triples of constraints by considering candidate comparisons where they conflict. These constraint dominations are *necessary* in order that the overall constraint ranking be consistent with the Lardil facts. If any one of these dominations failed to hold, then the conflicts we have examined would be resolved differently, and an actual Lardil parse would be less harmonic than at least one competitor, and it could not appear in the output of the grammar.

At this point in the analysis we must combine these necessary domination relations to determine whether they are consistent with some single constraint domination hierarchy. Then we must check that such a hierarchy is logically *sufficient* to explain the Lardil facts. This final step is required because in establishing each two- or three-way domination relation, we have only examined one input and one competitor to the actual Lardil parse. It remains to demonstrate, for the entire spectrum of inputs, that the Lardil parse is more harmonic than all competing parses, when all constraints are taken into consideration simultaneously.

---

now begins to look better than *.maɾ.□□́.*) Since NonFinSylHd must dominate ALIGN to allow e.g. *muŋ.ku.mu.⟨ŋku⟩* – ALIGN favors the parsing of stem-final material – the coda-epenthesized forms cannot be allowed to triumph through victory on NonFinSylHd.

The issue appears to demand a principled resolution, since syllable amplification is not a well-known response to constraints of the NonFinality family. Pending such resolution, we put the matter aside, noting the promise of the approach, both conceptually (it brings truncation into the purview of NonFinality) and analytically (it affects the structure of Lardil grammar in ways that may count as simplification).

The constraint domination relations we must now unify into a hierarchy are those in (165–169, 171–172, 176–177). The unification is performed incrementally in the following table, working down the hierarchy, starting with the superordinate constraints.

(179)   **Lardil Constraint Hierarchy Derived**

Constraint	Ranking justification		Remarks
*Complex, CodaCond, Ons, FtBin, Lx≈Pr ≫	None crucially dominated	(165)	All are unviolated; all force violations
Fill^{Nuc} ≫	Lx≈Pr ≫ Fill^{Nuc}	(168)	Empty Nuc to meet word minimality
Free-V ≫	Fill^{Nuc} ≫ Free-V	(176)	Truncation & augmentation don't mix
Align ≫	Free-V ≫ Align	(172)	Final V *is* free
Fill^{Ons} ≫	Align ≫ Fill^{Ons}	(177)	Whole empty σ possible to get Align
Parse ≫	Fill^{Ons} ≫ Parse	(166)	Avoid hiatus by nonparsing of V
–Cod	Parse ≫ –Cod	(167)	Admit codas

Note that this overall ranking is consistent with the following five domination relations, which were established above in (166–171) as necessary, but which are not among the six used to deduce the hierarchy in (179):

Ons ≫	Parse	(166)	Avoid hiatus by nonparsing of V
Fill^{Nuc} ≫	–Cod	(167)	Don't make potential codas into onsets
Lx≈Pr ≫	Fill^{Ons}	(168)	Can use whole empty σ to get minimal word
Lx≈Pr ≫	Free-V	(169)	Don't truncate minimals
Free-V ≫	Parse	(171)	Final V *is* free

Of the undominated constraints, we have provided specific evidence for the ranking of FtBin and Lx≈Pr above Fill^{Nuc} (168), and for the ranking of Ons above Parse (166). *Complex and CodaCond could in principle be enforced by breach of Fill^{Nuc} (with epenthesis to resolve the problematic consonant cluster) or of Parse (with deletion of one of the cluster members). Because Fill^{Nuc} ≫ Parse is required, it follows that Parse violation will be the least serious infraction in any choice where both are at play. Therefore, *Complex and CodaCond must crucially dominate only Parse. We will not emphasize this refinement, however, and we will persist in representing all undominated constraints as grouped together at the top.

7.3   Verification of Forms

In §7.2, working from pairwise candidate competitions over which constraints were in conflict, we examined interactions which each involved only those constraints relevant to the competition at hand. A set of relative domination relations among locally conflicting constraints was thereby determined. We then unified these relations into an entire constraint hierarchy (179). If any hierarchy of the constraints in (164) can account for the Lardil facts, it must include the ranking relations required in *this* one. We arrived at this conclusion by showing, in a variety of cases, that a desired optimum was better than *one* of its competitors. To show that the desired optimum is in fact optimal, and uniquely so, we must establish that it is better than *all* of its competitors. More importantly, we must determine whether this hierarchy correctly generates the complete set of alternation patterns under scrutiny: the 'language' conceived in its generality, not just the pieces of data that happen to have come our way. To this end, we will traverse the systematic classification of (159), and check that the actual Lardil parse is optimal in each case, as determined by the constraint hierarchy (179).

Global verification is not a new kind of burden imposed on grammarians by the present approach. Generative theories of phonology with rule-ordering, assignment of rules and constraints to various levels, specification of triggering and blocking relations, repair strategies, persistent rules, and so on, all give rise to complex systems that are often argued for on the basis of small-scale interactions. These grammars too can be left unverified overall only at the analyst's peril. In Optimality Theory, as in all interactionist theories, it is important to verify the analysis because interactions often arise which are not obvious to local inspection – indeed, this must be so, because getting interesting consequences from simple assumptions is the very rationale for interactionism.

In the verification arguments presented here, we will employ a useful methodology for testing the predictions of Optimality-theoretic grammars. To verify that a domination hierarchy yields the correct output, it is necessary to show that all competing analyses of the input are less harmonic than the correct analysis. This requires a clear grasp of Gen, and control of a method for establishing optimality. The method we will use is this:

(180)   **The Method of Mark Eliminability**
    To show that a particular analysis is optimal, consider each of its marks m, and show that any way of changing the analysis to eliminate m results in at least one worse mark.[63]

We proceed systematically through the summary of patterns provided in (159), starting with the C-final stems.

---

[63] The logic behind this method is given by the Cancellation/Domination Lemma, stated in (192) and (238) of ch. 8, pp. 153 and 174, and proved in §A.1 of the Appendix.

7.3.1 Consonant-Final Stems

Stems ≥ μμ. Stem-final consonants, in stems ≥ μμ, non-subminimals, are parsed if they satisfy the Coda Condition, unparsed otherwise. Examples (159a–b) are treated in the following tableau:

(181) **Consonant-Final Stems ≥ μμ**

	*COMPLEX, FTBIN, CODACOND, ONS, LX≈PR	FILL^Nuc	FREE-V	ALIGN	FILL^Ons	PARSE	−COD
A. i. ☞ .ken.ta.pal.							**
ii. .ke.n◻.ta.pa.⟨l⟩		*!		*		*	
B. i. ☞ .wa.ŋal.⟨k⟩				*		*	*
ii. .wa.ŋalk.	*! [*COMPLEX] *! [CODACOND]						*
iii. .wa.ŋal.k◻.		*!		*			*
C. i. ☞ .ŋa.lu.⟨k⟩				*		*	
ii. .ŋa.luk.	*! [CODACOND]						*

When the stem-final consonant satisfies CODACOND, as in /kentapal/, it appears as a coda in the optimal parse (181 A.i). Optimality is readily established. The only marks against (181 A.i) are the two *–CODs, incurred from parsing *n, l* as codas. Any more harmonic parse would have to eliminate one or both of these marks:

- To do so by failing to parse either segment violates the higher-ranked PARSE constraint.
- To parse either *l* or *n* as an onset would require positing an empty nucleus node after it, violating higher-ranked FILL^Nuc.

A competitor combining these attempts is shown in (181 A.ii), along with the marks which show it to be less harmonic than the correct output.

This provides a concrete example of the general analysis in chapter 6 showing that codas are possible when −COD ranks lower than both PARSE and FILL^Nuc. The basic syllable theory analysis applies without modification, because the only constraints coming into play are those of the basic theory, plus ALIGN, which provides a further incentive to parse a stem-final consonant as a Coda.

Henceforth, we will not comment on the violation marks *–COD that may be incurred in parses claimed to be optimal, since, as we have just seen, any attempt to avoid such marks always leads to more serious violations. Since −COD violations do not play a decisive role in the competitions of interest, we will omit −COD from all further tableaux.

A further constraint comes into play when the final consonant is not a pure coronal, for in that case parsing it as a coda violates CODACOND. We see that in the optimal parse of /waŋalk/ (181 B.i), the final *k* is *not* parsed, thereby violating both PARSE and ALIGN. This analysis is nonetheless optimal:

- The only way to avoid both these marks is to parse the final *k* as a coda (181 B.ii), violating the highest-ranked *COMPLEX and CODACOND.
- Trying to rescue the *k* by putting it in the onset of a final syllable with an empty nucleus (181 B.iii) still incurs the mark *ALIGN, and trades *PARSE for the worse mark *FILL^{Nuc}.

The same argument applies in the case of /ŋaluk/ (181 C.i–ii). The difference is only that the penultimate segment is a vowel rather than a possible coda consonant, so the optimal form doesn't violate –COD and the competitor doesn't violate *COMPLEX. This doesn't affect the conclusion, since any attempt to parse the *k* still violates CODACOND (when parsed as a coda) or FILL^{Nuc} (when parsed as an onset), both worse than *PARSE and *ALIGN.

Stems < μμ. With subminimal stems the constraints LX≈PR and FTBIN come into play, as shown below in the tableau (182), which displays examples from (159 c–e). Satisfying these constraints requires positing a second syllable with at least one empty position (namely, Nuc).

(182) **Subminimal Consonant-Final Stems**

		*COMPLEX, CODACOND, ONS, FTBIN, LX≈PR	FILL^{Nuc}	FREE-V	ALIGN	FILL^{Ons}	PARSE
A. i. ☞	.maṛ.□◌́.		*			*	
ii.	.maṛ.	* ! [LX≈PR]					
iii.	.ma.ṛ◌́.		*		* !		
B. i. ☞	.ṛel.k◌́.		*		*		
ii.	.ṛel.⟨k⟩	* ! [LX≈PR]			*		*
C. i. ☞	.ya.k◌́.		*		*		
ii.	.yak.□◌́.	* ! [CODACOND]	*			*	
D. i. ☞	.kaŋ.□◌́.		*			*	
ii.	.ka.ŋ◌́.		*		* !		

In the first example, /maṛ/, the optimal parse (182 A.i) violates FILL^{Nuc}, FILL^{Ons}, and –COD [omitted]:

- Any attempt to avoid the worst mark, *FILL^{Nuc}, will have to give up on the possibility of a second syllable, as in the faithful parse (182 A.ii). This fatally violates Lx≈PR or FTBIN, since the monosyllabic parse does not admit binary feet. To avoid violating Lx≈PR or FTBIN, it is necessary to posit an empty Nuc node; we need only consider such parses, then, when seeking optimal parses.[64] All such parses incur the mark *FILL^{Nuc}, so we can therefore ignore this mark in subsequent comparisons. (Note that the null parse, in which no segment is parsed, violates Lx≈PR and cannot therefore be optimal.)
- The remaining two marks of the parse (182 A.i), *FILL^{Ons} and *–COD, can both be avoided by parsing the stem-final consonant ɾ not as a Coda but rather as an Onset (182 A.iii). Parsing ɾ as an Onset violates ALIGN, fatal because the mark *ALIGN outranks the marks *FILL^{Ons} and *–COD that would thereby be avoided. It follows that form (182 A.i) is optimal.[65]

The situation changes, though, when the stem-final consonant (or cluster) is not a legal coda. Now the final consonant is optimally parsed as an onset. With /ɾelk/ (182 B) and /yak/ (182 C), parsing the final *k* as an onset violates ALIGN, but there is no alternative that is more harmonic. This mark *ALIGN could only be avoided by analyzing final *k* as a Coda, which would violate the superordinate constraint CODACOND (and in (182 B) also *COMPLEX) – yielding a less harmonic parse.

It is instructive to compare the fate of the final *k* in /ɾelk/ (182 B) to that in /waɳalk/ (181 B). In the longer word, the final *k* is not parsed (incurring *PARSE), whereas in the subminimal case, the *k* is parsed as an Onset (incurring *FILL^{Nuc}).

When Lx≈PR and FTBIN are not involved, as with /waɳalk/, the fact that FILL^{Nuc} dominates PARSE entails that nonparsing of *k* is optimal, since *PARSE is the lower-ranked mark. Syllabic well-formedness is achieved through omission of

---

[64] Lardil does not employ vowel lengthening to parse subminimal stems as bimoraic feet. For discussion of the constraints relevant to this limitation, see Black 1991, Piggott 1992, Itô & Mester 1992. As argued in McCarthy & Prince 1993a for the parallel case of Axininca Campa, vowel lengthening is already ruled out for stems CV, because of ALIGN; the pattern .CV.□Ó. preserves MWord/syllable alignment while .CV□. destroys it. For Lardil, this is 50% welcome: we have ɾu.WA. but .tʸaA, of which the latter remains inexplicable on the present account (unless it is underlyingly /tʸ/).

More generally, Lardil does not use any kind of internal epenthesis to satisfy minimality requirements. Thus, from /maɾ/ we could expect either .ma□ɾ. with a long vowel, or bisyllabic .ma.□Óɾ. or .mÓ.□aɾ., both of which are properly aligned. Although the .ma□ɾ. type is cross-linguistically attested (see McCarthy & Prince 1986, Lombardi & McCarthy 1991) and therefore suitable for being controlled by a rankable constraint, internal syllabic augmentation appears to be unknown and therefore requires a deeper and more stable explanation.

[65] Recall that .maɾ.□Ó. is distinguished from .□Ó.maɾ. on the grounds of proper alignment, as discussed in §7.1, p. 127. By ALIGN in the text we mean ALIGN-R, pertaining to final edges. It is Lx≈PR, construed in the Chen–Selkirk manner as requiring initial-edge alignment, that rules out prothesis.

refractory segmental material, rather than through supplying empty structure to support it. But when undominated Lx≈PR and FTBIN become relevant, as with /ṛelk/, they mask the fact that FILL^Nuc dominates PARSE, and the result reverses. In the competing analyses of /ṛelk/ in (182 B), it is no longer relevant that PARSE is dominated by FILL^Nuc, since the low-ranked PARSE violation now comes along with a superordinate failure on Lx≈PR or FTBIN, the minimality enforcers.

The final case of /kaŋ/ (182 D) works just like the first case (182 A) of /maṛ/, given proper formulation of CODACOND, a matter discussed in fn. 60, p. 126.

7.3.2 Vowel-Final Stems

Stems > μμ.   The most aggressive truncations in Lardil are observed with supraminimal vowel-final stems. The final vowel is unparsed, as are all the preceding consonants which cannot be parsed as codas without violating CODACOND. The examples from (159 f–g) illustrating one, two, and three final unparsed segments are treated in the tableau (183).

(183)   **Supraminimal Vowel-Final Stems**

		*COMPLEX, CODACOND, ONS, FTBIN, Lx≈PR	FILL^Nuc	**FREE-V**	ALIGN	FILL^Ons	PARSE
A. i. ☞	.yi.li.yil.⟨i⟩				*		*
ii.	.yi.li.yi.li.			*!			
B. i. ☞	.yu.kař.⟨pa⟩				*		**
ii.	.yu.kařp.⟨a⟩	*! [*COMPLEX] *! [CODACOND]			*		*
iii.	.ya.kař.p□.⟨a⟩		*!		*		*
C. i. ☞	.ŋa.wu.ŋa.⟨wu⟩				*		**
ii.	ŋa.wu.⟨ŋawu⟩				*		***!*
D. i. ☞	.muŋ.ku.mu.⟨ŋku⟩	*! [CODACOND]			*		***
ii.	.muŋ.ku.muŋ.⟨ku⟩				*		**

Most striking here is the way that the domination hierarchy permits such flagrant violations of PARSE as those observed in *.muŋ.ku.mu.⟨ŋku⟩*, while controlling these violations so that in each case only the correct number of segments are left unsyllabified.

PARSE is ranked low enough in the hierarchy so as to be out-ranked by several constraints which conflict with it: relevantly, CODACOND, FILL^Nuc, and FREE-V.

With these three in dominant position, it is optimal to leave segments out of syllable structure (*PARSE) if

- for vowels, parsing them violates FREE-V;
- for consonants, assigning them to coda position violates CODACOND or assigning onset status violates FILL^{Nuc}.

On the other hand, while ranked low, PARSE is nonetheless operative in Lardil grammar (as in every grammar). Any failure to parse which is not required to meet a higher-ranked constraint renders the overall parse less harmonic, due to the avoidable marks *PARSE thereby incurred.

To see how these constraint interactions play out in the actual cases, consider first /yiliyili/ (183 A). The optimal parse incurs the marks *ALIGN, *PARSE, and *–COD (the last being unmentioned in the tableau):

- To avoid the two highest marks, *ALIGN and *PARSE, the final segment would have to be parsed. But this would violate FREE-V, a higher-ranked constraint (183 A.ii).
- As mentioned above in the discussion of (181 A), the lowest mark, *–COD, cannot be avoided without incurring higher marks, because the constraints FILL^{Nuc}, PARSE, and –COD are ranked in a pattern characteristic of coda-permitting languages (167), p. 133. Thus (183 A.i) is optimal.

The relative overall Harmonies of .yi.li.yil.⟨i⟩ (183 A.i) and .yi.li.yi.li. (183 A.ii) pointedly illustrate the *strictness* of strict domination. Fully parsed .yi.li.yi.li. is less harmonic than truncated .yi.li.yil.⟨i⟩ even though it violates only one constraint, while the truncated form violates three of the four lower-ranked constraints (including –COD). Indeed, a form like .yi.li.yi.li. would seem on first glance to be a perfect parse, consisting as it does entirely of optimal CV syllables, and constituting a perfectly faithful parse in which underlying segments are in one-to-one correspondence with syllable positions. Such is the strength of FREE-V in Lardil, and of the strictness of strict domination, that the sole mark *FREE-V renders the form less harmonic than the optimal output, which violates fully three of the four constraints ranked lower than FREE-V.

The fate of the stem /yukaṛpa/ (183 B) is almost identical to that of /yiliyili/ (183 A), the only difference being that in the optimal parse, the penultimate consonant (*p*) remains unsyllabified:

- Any attempt to avoid *ALIGN and *PARSE by syllabifying the final vowel violates higher-ranked FREE-V, just as with /yiliyili/.
- Attempts to save the penultimate consonant, and thereby remove the second *PARSE mark, must also decrease Harmony. Parsing *p* with *ṛ* in a single coda (183 B.ii) violates the superordinate constraints *COMPLEX and CODACOND. Parsing it as an onset (183 B.iii) requires a following empty Nuc node, thus incurring a mark *FILL^{Nuc} which is worse than the mark *PARSE thereby avoided.

The stem /ŋawuŋawu/ (183 C) is identical in all relevant respects to /yukařpa/ (183 B) except that the antepenultimate segment is a vowel; in the optimal output, the last parsed segment is a vowel. The proof of optimality is virtually the same as that just given.

The resulting phonetic form [ŋawuŋa] is vowel-final; derivational accounts with a final-vowel-deletion rule (as in previous interpretations of the phenomenon) must ensure that this rule cannot reapply to further delete the now-final *a* and, presumably, with it the preceding illicit coda consonant *ŋ*. This would result in the form [ŋawu], which is subject to further truncation, blocked then by a minimal word constraint. In (183 C.ii) we show the competing output [ŋawu], phonologically, .ŋa.wu.⟨ŋawu⟩, to allay any fears that such iterated truncation, with more than one vowel unparsed, can arise to plague the present account. Because the second *a* is not a *word-final* vowel, it plays no role in assessing violations of FREE-V. Parsing it (183 C.i) is quite irrelevant to the constraint FREE-V. Consequently, the additional mark *PARSE that results from leaving it unparsed (183 C.ii) is entirely unjustifiable, as it avoids no other marks. The additional PARSE violation is fatal to the overtruncated [ŋawu].

The conclusion still holds if the preceding consonant were not *ŋ* but, say, *n*, which could safely be parsed as a coda, thereby eliminating the fourth *PARSE mark from (183 C.ii). The fourth mark is superfluous; the third *PARSE incurred by not parsing *a*, a single step beyond necessity, is sufficient to decide the competition.

The final example .muŋ.ku.mu.⟨ŋku⟩ (183 D) works just like the others. It is of some interest that the antepenultimate segment *ŋ* is unparsed even though it is followed by *k*. In a derivational account, the sequence of rules which accounts for this is: delete final vowel *u*, delete illegal coda consonant *k*, delete illegal coda consonant *ŋ*. These steps are serially ordered, since prior to deleting *u*, the *k* is parsable as an onset; and prior to deleting *k*, the *ŋ* is parsable as a coda. In the present account, there is no derivational sequence and no deletion. The entire final parse is evaluated once and for all; everything follows from the primary syllabification of the input string. In the optimal analysis, *u* is not syllabified; neither is *k*; nor *ŋ*. Parsing any or all of these segments introduces violations of the constraints on syllabification and on the morphology/prosody relation, violations more serious than the three *PARSE marks incurred by not syllabifying the segments in question. The one case not seen before is the alternative of parsing only *ŋ*, shown in (183 D.ii). The undominated constraint CODACOND is violated because the coda *ŋ* is linked to no following onset. There is an appropriate underlying *segment*, of course: *k*; but in the total parse under evaluation, there is no following *onset*.

Stems = μμ.   Unlike longer stems just reviewed, those vowel-final stems which are exactly minimal must have their final vowel parsed. The example (159 h) is shown in the following tableau:

(184)   **Minimal Vowel-Final Stems**

	*COMPLEX, CODACOND, FTBIN, ONS, Lx≈PR	FILL^Nuc	FREE-V	ALIGN	FILL^Ons	PARSE
i. ☞ .wi.ţe.			*			
ii. .wiţ.⟨e⟩	* ! [Lx≈PR]			*		*
iii. .wiţ.□□́.⟨e⟩		* !		*	*	*
iv. .wi.ţ□́.⟨e⟩		* !		*		*

In minimal stems, FREE-V conflicts with Lx≈PR and FTBIN. The optimal parse violates FREE-V, because failing to parse the final vowel leads to violation of Lx≈PR or FTBIN (184 ii), unless empty nodes are also posited. Such empty nodes are optimal in subminimal consonant-final stems (182), and we must consider them here. In (184 iii), ţ is parsed as a Coda and followed by an empty Onset and Nucleus; in (184 iv), ţ is parsed as an Onset and followed by an empty Nucleus. In both cases, the high-ranking mark *FILL^Nuc, absent in the optimal parse, proves fatal.

7.4   Discussion

Several features of the analysis deserve specific comment.

Grammar building.   The typical result in Part I involves the ranking of only a few constraints. The Lardil analysis shows that the formal principles laid out in Part I apply smoothly and without enrichment to an intricate grammatical system. Other work in the theory offers similar demonstrations; we refer the interested reader to the works cited at the end of chapter 1.

Pitfalls of pre-theoretic intuitions of Harmony.   Lardil *Final Vowel Deletion* is taken by Goldsmith (1991) to be a plainly 'anti-harmonic rule' – one whose application *reduces* the Harmony of the representation. This construal motivates his proposal that linguistic derivations involve a set of non- or even anti-harmonic rule applications between levels, in addition to serial harmonic rule applications within levels.

   Harmonic rule application is characterized as follows: ". . . phonological rules apply . . . just in case their output is better than their input with respect to some criteria specified by a phonotactic (of the relevant level)" (Goldsmith 1991: 252). He then observes that "word-final vowels are perfectly satisfactory" in Lardil. Since there is no *phonotactic* involved – no descriptively true generalization about surface word structure – he is led to conclude that harmonic considerations are irrelevant. The claim is, of course, untenable: the truncation pattern respects minimality limitations that are the direct consequence of prosodic well-formedness constraints (Wilkinson 1986, 1988).

Although we have full sympathy with the general programmatic notion that harmonic considerations are central to the assignment of linguistic form, we suggest that the problem with the Goldsmith proposal for Lardil lies in its reliance on pre-theoretic notions of Harmony, which are simply too ill-defined to provide much of a guide to real-world complexities. Although it seems reasonable that rules ought to apply when their output is better "with respect to some criteria specified by a phonotactic," in realistic situations the output is just as likely to be *worse* by some criteria specified by other phonotactics, and this worseness can very well be crucial. And, if we are right about the universality and generality of constraints, the motivating factors are unlikely to be limited to anything as parochial as a phonotactic presumably is.

Goldsmith states, plausibly, that "the bulk of phonological rules apply in order to arrive at representations that *maximally satisfy constraints* (or, equivalently, schemata) that involve structuring phonological information [emphasis supplied]." But without a well-defined notion of what it is to *maximally satisfy* a set of potentially conflicting constraints, there is in general no way to ascertain whether a given process is harmonic or the direct opposite; intuition, even steeped in scholarship, offers no sure guide.

In the account developed here, the Harmony of the Lardil analysis is defined in such a way that supraminimal words with final unparsed vowels are *more* harmonic than those with final parsed vowels. In the appropriate theoretical framework, then, we can formally acknowledge a constraint, FREE-V, which asserts that, all other things being equal, leaving word-final vowels unparsed is optimal. This constraint not only fits into the overall constraint hierarchy of Lardil, along with other pre-theoretically more intuitive constraints; it is recognizable (indeed, as is already observed in Wilkinson 1986) as a slightly peculiar member of a universal family of 'extrametricality' constraints, which deal with the nonfinality of prominence. Understood in this way, its interaction with minimality considerations – patently harmonic in character – is entirely expected.

Relevance of the Basic Syllable Structure Theory.   The Basic Syllable Structure Theory assumes a certain level of idealization in order to explicate fundamental universal aspects of syllable structure theory. Nonetheless, it forms without modification a crucial sub-structure within the Lardil analysis, indicating that further progress in developing and applying the syllable theory can proceed by addition to the basic module rather than by catastrophic renovation of its premises.

Relation between universal and language-particular phonology.   The Basic Syllable Structure constraints and the additional constraints brought forth in the Lardil analysis are either strictly universal or mildly parametrized versions of recognizably universal constraints. The general approach to typological analysis exemplified by the Basic Syllable Structure Theory, like the substantive content of its constraints, is carried over intact into the more richly detailed context of

Lardil. As promised in our characterization of the theory, Universal Grammar provides a set of constraints (some parametrized) and the primary mechanism of cross-linguistic variation is the different dominance rankings which are chosen by individual languages.

Generalization patterns. All decisions required to determine the correct analysis of a given stem are handled by the single notion of constraint domination. This includes interactions that would be described in other accounts as involving *constraints* and *rules*, ontologically quite different and with problematic interaction. A complete explication is given for how a constraint can appear to trigger or block the application of a rule. Such effects are handled by the same mechanism that handles basic syllabification and all other components of structural analysis: maximizing Harmony, as defined through a constraint hierarchy.

Strictness of strict domination. In several examples the correct analysis violates many constraints, and its optimality rests crucially on the fact that competitors with a cleaner record overall happen to violate some single dominant constraint. Recall the discussion of /yiliyili/ in §7.3.2: a strong contender violating just one constraint is bested by an optimal parse violating three of the four less dominant constraints. This effect highlights the content of the central evaluative hypothesis of Optimality Theory, and sets the theory apart from others in which richer notions of 'weighting' and 'trade-off' are entertained.

Parallelism and representation. The theory operates by evaluating a total candidate parse, which contains the underlying form, over the entire constraint hierarchy. This non-sequential approach offers at least two advantages in the Lardil analysis. First, since the underlying form is present in the structure being evaluated, the status of a vowel as word- or stem-final does not change; thus the constraint FREE-V can unproblematically refer to word-final vowels. This constraint is then *not* violated by the plethora of Lardil forms containing phonetically final vowels that are not phonologically final, analyses where the last parsed segment is a vowel which is followed by unparsed segments. This eliminates the issue that arises in serial theories of whether a rule of *Final Vowel Deletion* can reapply during the derivation (see the discussion of /ŋawuŋawu/ in §7.3.2).

The second advantage involves the parallel assessment of constraints on a total analysis. Consider the stem /kaŋ/, which is analyzed as .kaŋ.□□́., phonetic [kaŋka] (182 D.i). As observed in Kirchner 1992a, serialist theories have difficulty explaining how ŋ surfaces as a coda.

Suppose there are rules *Syllabification* and *Augmentation* that must apply in sequential steps. Syllabification must have a chance to apply before Augmentation in order to establish the needed distinction between /maṛ/ → [.maṛ.ṭa.] (182 A.i), in which the stem forms a syllable, and /yak/→ [.ya.ka.] (182 C.i), in which the stem-final consonant is attached to the next syllable over. Augmentation inserts an onset only when the stem-final consonant is *already* parsed as a coda.

Now consider /kaŋ/. When Syllabification applies, the ŋ is no more syllabifiable as a coda than the *k* of /yak/ – ŋ can only be a coda when linked to a following onset. The situation is obviously not improved by trying to allow Augmentation to precede Syllabification, with the aim of making it possible for ŋ to be syllabified as a coda, for then it would be unclear why stem-final consonants should ever be parsed as anything but onsets. In short, Syllabification and Augmentation are mutually interdependent: each 'triggers' the other. Augmentation triggers the syllabification of a coda, which itself triggers the insertion of an onset (which itself triggers coda-syllabification, which itself . . .). This kind of ordering pathology is an artifact of the derivational treatment, which resembles but exceeds in severity the problems discussed above for Bottom-Up Constructionism in prosodic theory. Interestingly, it is not resolvable by allowing Syllabification to apply *freely* in a serial derivation, an approach which Itô 1986 successfully uses to solve other similar problems. We conclude that the coincidence of stem and syllable edges cannot be successfully derived from serial (including cyclic) application of syllabification rules.

When all of the relevant constraints are assessed in parallel, as in Optimality Theory, an entire completed parse is subject to evaluation. At the point where the status of ŋ as a licit coda is judged, each candidate analysis has already committed once and for all to the presence or absence of a following onset node. The necessity of this kind of information flow is a key prediction of the present theory, and a number of further cases of crucial parallelism are discussed in McCarthy & Prince 1993a. The crux of the matter is that the grammar must determine which *total* analysis is well-formed – a task impeded by the use of serial algorithms to build structure step-by-step.

Chapter 8

Universal Syllable Theory: Ordinal Construction of C/V and Onset/Coda Licensing Asymmetry

Syllabification must reconcile two conflicting sources of constraint: from the bottom up, each segment's inherent featural suitability for syllable peak or margin; and from top down, the requirements that syllables have certain structures and not others. The core conflict can be addressed in its most naked form through the idealization provided by CV theory. Input C's need to be parsed as margins; input V's need to be parsed as peaks. Syllables need to be structured as Onset–Peak–Coda; ideally, with an onset present and a coda absent. In the Basic Theory, only one input segment is allowed per syllable position. Problematic inputs like /CCVV/ are ones which bring the bottom-up and top-down pressures into conflict. These conflicts are resolved differently in different languages, the possible resolutions forming the typology explored in chapter 6.

The CV theory gives some articulation to the top-down pressures: syllable shapes deviate from the Onset–Peak ideal in the face of bottom-up pressure to parse the input. By contrast, the bottom-up is construed relatively rigidly: C and V either go into their determined positions, or they remain unparsed. In real syllabification, of course, a richer set of possibilities exists. A segment ideally parsed as a peak may actually be parsed as a margin, or vice versa, in response to top-down constraints on syllable shape. One of the most striking examples of the role of optimality principles in syllabification, Tashlhiyt Berber (chapter 2), exploits this possibility with maximal thoroughness. Berber syllabification on the one hand and CV syllabification on the other constitute extremes in the flexibility with which input segments may be parsed into different syllable positions in response to top-down pressure. In between the extremes lies the majority of languages, in which some segments can appear only as margins (like C in the CV theory), other segments only as peaks (like V), and the remaining segments, while ideally parsed into just one of the structural positions, can under sufficient top-down pressure be parsed into others.

In this section we will seek to unify the treatments of the two extremes of syllabification, Berber and the CV theory. Like the CV theory, the theory developed here will deal with an abstract inventory of input segments, but instead of just two abstract segments, each committed to a structural position, the inventory will consist of abstract elements distinguished solely by the property of *sonority*, taken to define a strict order on the set of elements. For mnemonic value we denote these elements $a, i, \ldots, d, t$; but it should be remembered that all dimensions other than sonority are idealized away. In the CV theory, the universally superordinate constraints *M/V and *P/C prohibit parsing V as a margin or C as a peak. In the more realistic theory we now turn to, the corresponding constraints are not universally superordinate: the constraints against parsing any segment α as a margin (*M/α) or as a peak (*P/α) may vary cross-linguistically in their rankings. What Universal Grammar requires is only that more sonorous segments make more harmonic peaks and less harmonic margins.

From these simple assumptions there will emerge a universal typology of inventories of possible onsets, peaks, and codas. The inventories will turn out to be describable in terms of derived parameters π_{Ons}, π_{Nuc}, and π_{Cod}, each with values ranging over the sonority order. The margin inventories are the sets of segments *less* sonorous than the corresponding parameter values π_{Ons} or π_{Cod}, and the peak inventory is the set of segments *more* sonorous than the value of π_{Nuc}. Languages in which $\pi_{Ons} > \pi_{Nuc}$ are therefore languages with ambidextrous segments, which can be parsed as either onset or nucleus. The following diagram pictures the situation; the double line marks the zone of overlap.

(185)   **Languages with Ambidextrous Segments**

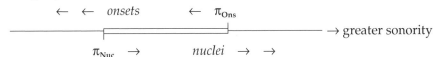

The theory entails a universal licensing asymmetry between onsets and codas: codas can contain only a subset, possibly strict, of the segments appearing in onsets. This fundamental licensing asymmetry will be shown to follow from the asymmetry between Onset and Coda in the Basic Syllable Structure Constraints. From the fact that onsets should be present and codas absent, it will follow in the theory that Coda is a weaker licenser.[66] To our knowledge, no other approach has been able to connect the structural propensities of syllables with the licensing properties of syllabic positions, much less to derive one from the other. This is surely a significant result, one that indicates that the theory is on the right track in a fundamental way. The exact nature of the obtained licensing asymmetry has some empirical imperfections which can be traced to the oversimplified analysis of codas in the internal structure of the syllable, and we suggest possible refinements.

The present section constitutes a larger-scale exploration of our general line of attack on the problem of universal typology. Universal Grammar provides a fixed set of constraints, which individual languages rank differently in domination hierarchies; UG also provides certain universal conditions on these hierarchies,

[66] The demonstration will require some work, however; perhaps this is not surprising, given the simplicity of the assumptions.

which all languages must respect. The results obtained here involve a further development of the basic idea: *parametrization by ranking*. The parameters π_{Ons}, π_{Nuc}, and π_{Cod} are epiphenomenal, in that they do not appear at all in Universal Grammar, or indeed, in particular grammars: they are not, for example, mentioned in any constraint. These parameters are not explicitly set by individual languages. Rather, individual languages simply rank the universal constraints, and it is a *consequence* of this ranking that the (derived, descriptive) parameters have the values they do in that language. The procedures for reading off these parameter values from a language's constraint domination hierarchy are not, in fact, entirely obvious.

The analysis developed here introduces or elaborates several general concepts of the theory:

(186)   **Push/Pull Parsing**
        The parsing problem is analyzed in terms of the direct conflict between two sets of constraints:

   a.   *ASSOCIATE* constraints
        PARSE, FILL, ONS, and the like, which penalize parses in which input segments or structural nodes *lack* structural associations to a parent or child;
   b.   *DON'T-ASSOCIATE* constraints
        *M/V, *P/C, and −COD and their like, which penalize parses which *contain* structural associations of various kinds.

(187)   **Universal Constraint Sub-Hierarchies**
        The DON'T-ASSOCIATE constraints *M/V, *P/C, superordinate in the CV theory, are replaced by an articulated set of anti-association constraints *M/a, *M/i, . . . , *M/d, *M/t; *P/a, *P/i, . . . , *P/d, *P/t which penalize associations between Margin or Peak nodes on the one hand and particular input segments on the other. Universal Grammar requires that the domination hierarchy of each language rank these constraints *M/α, *P/α relative to one another in conformity with the following universal domination conditions:
        $$*M/a \gg *M/i \gg \cdots \gg *M/d \gg *M/t \qquad \text{(Margin Hierarchy)}$$
        $$*P/t \gg *P/d \gg \cdots \gg *P/i \gg *P/a \qquad \text{(Peak Hierarchy)}$$
        The Margin Hierarchy states that it's less harmonic to parse *a* as a margin than to parse *i* as a margin, less harmonic to parse *i* as a margin than *r*, and so on down the sonority ordering. The Peak Hierarchy states that it's less harmonic to parse *t* as a peak than *d*, and so on up the sonority order.

(188)   **Associational Harmony**
        The universal Margin and Peak Hierarchies ensure the following universal ordering of the Harmony of possible associations:
        $$M/t > M/d > \cdots > M/i > M/a$$
        $$P/a > P/i > \cdots > P/d > P/t$$

These represent the basic assumption that the less sonorous an element is, the more harmonic it is as a margin; the more sonorous, the more harmonic it is as a peak.

(189)   **Prominence Alignment**
These universal rankings of constraints (187) and ordering of associational Harmonies (188) exemplify a general operation, Prominence Alignment, in which scales of prominence along two phonological dimensions are harmonically aligned. In this case, the first scale concerns prominence of structural positions within the syllable:

Peak > Margin

while the second concerns inherent prominence of the segments as registered by sonority:

$a > i > \cdots > d > t$

(190)   **Encapsulation**
It is possible to greatly reduce the number of constraints in the theory by encapsulating sets of associational constraints *M/α, *P/α into defined constraints which explicitly refer to *ranges* of sonority. This corresponds to using a coarse-grained sonority scale, obtained by collapsing distinctions. This must be done on a language-specific basis, however, in a way sensitive to the language's total constraint hierarchy: which sets of associational constraints can be successfully encapsulated into composite constraints depends on how the language inserts other constraints such as PARSE, FILL, ONS, and so on, into the Margin and Peak Hierarchies, and how these two Hierarchies are interdigitated in the language. Encapsulation opens the way to developing a substantive theory of the sonority classes operative in syllable structure phenomena.

Along with these conceptual developments, this section introduces a collection of useful techniques for reasoning about constraint domination hierarchies in complex arenas such as that defined by the segmental syllable theory. A few of these techniques are:

(191)   **Harmonic Bounding for Inventory Analysis**
In order to show that a particular kind of structure φ is not part of a universal or language-particular inventory, we consider any possible parse containing φ and show constructively that there is some competing parse (of the same input) which is more harmonic; thus no structure containing φ can ever be optimal, as it is always bounded above by at least one more-harmonic competitor. (This form of argument is used to establish the distribution of epenthesis sites in §6.2.3.)

(192)   **Cancellation/Domination Lemma**
In order to show that one parse A is more harmonic than a competitor B which does not incur an identical set of marks, it suffices to show that

every mark incurred by A is either (i) cancelled by an identical mark incurred by B, or (ii) dominated by a higher-ranking mark incurred by B. That is, for every constraint violated by the more harmonic form A, the losing competitor B either (i) matches the violation exactly, or (ii) violates a constraint ranked higher.

(193)   **The Method of Universal Constraint Tableaux**
A generalization of the method of language-specific constraint tableaux is developed; it yields a systematic means for using the Cancellation/Domination Lemma to determine which parse is optimal, not in a specific language with a given constraint hierarchy, but in a typological class of languages whose hierarchies meet certain domination conditions but are otherwise unspecified.

Exposition proceeds as follows. In §8.1 we define the Basic Segmental Syllable Theory; using our analyses of Berber and the Basic CV Syllable Structure Theory as starting points, we develop most of the basic notions mentioned above, including Associational Harmony and Prominence Alignment.

The Basic Segmental Syllable Theory defined in §8.1 is then subjected to extended analysis in §8.2. The formal techniques mentioned above are introduced and applied, leading ultimately to a set of necessary and sufficient constraint domination conditions involving $*M/\alpha$ (or $*P/\alpha$) which govern whether the segment α is a possible onset (or nucleus). Some nontrivial analysis is required, because we are answering the following nontrivial question: considering all possible orderings of (a fair number of) constraints, and considering all possible input strings, when is parsing some segment α as an onset more harmonic than all possible alternative parses? It is possible to skim the detailed analysis; this should suffice for reading the rest of chapter 8, which is considerably less technical.

The necessary and sufficient conditions derived in §8.2 are then cashed in (§8.3) for a universal typology of inventories of onset and nucleus segments. We consider codas, and derive and discuss the onset/coda licensing asymmetry result. We also derive the procedures for extracting a language's parameters π_{Ons}, π_{Nuc}, and π_{Cod} from its constraint hierarchy.

In §8.4 we develop and briefly discuss the Encapsulated Segmental Syllable Theory.

Given that this section contains a considerable amount of analysis, it is worth taking a moment at the outset to see a bit more clearly why extended analysis is necessary to establish the results we will obtain. The most complex result is the onset/coda licensing asymmetry, which can be stated as follows:

(194)   Cross-linguistically, the inventory of possible codas is a subset of the inventory of possible onsets, but not vice versa.

To see just what we'll need to show in order to establish this result, we will give a step-by-step reduction of (194) to the elements in terms of which it must actually be demonstrated:

(194) a. For all languages admitted by Universal Grammar, the inventory of possible codas is a subset of the inventory of possible onsets, but not vice versa.

b. For all constraint hierarchies CH formed by ranking the universal syllable structure constraints as allowed by Universal Grammar, the inventory of possible codas is a subset of the inventory of possible onsets, but not vice versa.

c. For all rankings CH of the universal syllable structure constraints allowed by Universal Grammar, and
    for all segments λ,
        if λ is a possible coda in the language given by CH
        then λ is a possible onset in CH,
but not vice versa.

d. For all rankings CH of the universal syllable structure constraints allowed by Universal Grammar, and
    for all segments λ,
        if there is an input string I_λ
            containing λ
            for which the optimal parse (with respect to CH) is one in which λ is associated to Cod,
        then there is an input string I_λ'
            containing λ
            for which the optimal parse (with respect to CH) is one in which λ is associated to Ons;
but not vice versa.

e. **For all** rankings CH of the universal syllable structure constraints allowed by Universal Grammar, and
    for all segments λ,
        if there exists an input string I_λ
            containing λ
            for which **there is** a parse $B_{Cod/\lambda}$ in which λ is associated to Cod
            such that
                if C is any other candidate parse of I_λ,
                then $B_{Cod/\lambda}$ is more harmonic than C with respect to the ranking CH ($B_{Cod/\lambda} >_{CH}$ C),
        then there exists an input string I_λ'
            containing λ
            for which **there is** a parse $B_{Ons/\lambda}'$ in which λ is associated to Ons
            such that
                if C' is any other candidate parse of I_λ'
                then $B_{Ons/\lambda}'$ is more harmonic than C' with respect to the ranking CH ($B_{Ons/\lambda}' >_{CH}$ C');
but **not** vice versa.

In the final formulation, as in all the others, the phrase 'but not vice versa' means that if 'Cod' and 'Ons' are interchanged in the proposition which precedes, then the resulting proposition is false. The logical quantifiers and connectives in this assertion have been set in boldface in order to indicate the logical structure of the proposition without resorting to predicate calculus. The innermost embedded propositions ($B_{Cod/\lambda} >_{CH} C$, and likewise for the primed parses) are themselves somewhat complex propositions, defined in §5.1, which involve comparisons of the hosts of marks incurred by parses of entire strings.

The strategy pursued in this chapter is to approach the complexity inherent in such a result incrementally, demonstrating the onset/coda licensing asymmetry after accumulating a series of increasingly complex results on segmental inventories. We begin with the most fundamental notion, Associational Harmony.

8.1   Associational Harmony

To move from the Basic CV Syllable Structure Theory to the Basic Segmental Syllable Structure Theory, we need to move from CV strings to segmental string inputs. All we will need to do, in fact, is to replace the CV association constraints *M/V (121) and *P/C (122), p. 109, with constraints that are sensitive to the relative Harmonies of pairings between, on the one hand, different segments λ, and, on the other, structural nodes of type M (margin: Ons and Cod) or P (peak: Nuc). Thus we will need to replace *M/V and *P/C by constraints such as *M/λ and *P/λ which refer to particular segments λ. From these, we will reconstruct categories of segments which behave to first approximation as C and V do in the CV theory.

We have already seen in Berber the need to make the Harmony of P/λ associations sensitive to the sonority of λ; more sonorous segments make more harmonic syllable peaks. This was embodied in the constraint Hnuc; it was the central element in our Berber analysis and we claimed it to be an element of universal syllable structure theory. Now is the time to spell out this aspect of harmonic syllable structure theory; considerable elaboration of the ideas is necessary, and we can motivate the necessary development by returning to Berber to inspect a minor detail the consequences of which for the general theory turn out to be substantial.

8.1.1   Deconstructing Hnuc: Berber, Take 1

In our earlier analysis of Berber, we assumed that over- and underparsing (a.k.a. epenthesis and deletion) are forbidden, that syllable positions are non-complex, and that onsets (except phrase-initially) are required. Together, these had the consequence that in certain cases even highly sonorous segments such as *i* and *u* will be parsed as onsets (and realized as *y* and *w*, respectively). It turns out, however, that the most sonorous segment, *a*, can *never* be parsed as a margin; it is the only segment in Berber that fails to be parsable both as an onset and as a nucleus. Since Berber morphology can in fact generate an input containing /aa/, one of our simplifying assumptions must give way; in fact, in this one situation, Berber tolerates overparsing, generating an empty onset, so that /aa/ → .á.□á (phonetically *aya*; Guerssel 1986).

We can apply the Basic Syllable Structure Theory results of chapter 6 to incorporate this fact about /a/ into our Berber analysis as follows. The syllable structure is $\Sigma^{CV(C)}_{ep}$, so according to the Onset Theorem (136), since onsets are required, enforced via overparsing, we must have

(195) **Berber Onsets**
{ONS, PARSE} $\gg$ FILL^{Ons}

By the Coda Theorem (138), since codas are not prohibited, we must also have

(196) {FILL^{Nuc}, PARSE} $\gg$ −COD.

The superordinate constraint *M/V (121) is replaced by

(197) ***M/*a*: *a* must not be parsed as a margin.

The segment *a* is the one segment (like V in CV theory) that is so unacceptable as a margin that it is more Harmonic to posit an empty onset and thereby violate FILL^{Ons}; thus we must have:

(198) **Berber Epenthesis**
*M/*a* $\gg$ FILL^{Ons} $\gg$ HNUC

That FILL^{Ons} must dominate HNUC follows from the fact that, aside from *M/*a*, no other constraint can force epenthesis; in particular, HNUC cannot; otherwise, an onset would be epenthesized before every underlying segment, allowing it to be parsed as a nucleus and thereby increasing nuclear Harmony.

Now corresponding to *P/C (122) in the CV theory, in our Berber analysis we have HNUC. Whereas *P/C says that C must not be parsed as a peak, HNUC gives an articulated scale for the Harmony of associations P/λ, governed by the sonority of λ. For now, then, we will replace *P/C by HNUC. As we have seen earlier, the onset requirement in Berber takes precedence over the forming of more Harmonic nuclei, but nuclear Harmony dominates avoidance of codas, so

(199) **Berber Onset/Nucleus/Coda Interaction**
ONS $\gg$ HNUC $\gg$ −COD

We can now assemble these relative domination conditions into a constraint hierarchy for Berber:

(200) **Berber Hierarchy**
{ONS, PARSE, FILL^{Nuc}, *M/*a*} $\gg$ FILL^{Ons} $\gg$ HNUC $\gg$ −COD

Thus we see in the following tableau, for example, how /aa/ does indeed trigger epenthesis, whereas /ia/ or /ai/ or /tk/ does not (as usual, we are assuming that ONs in Berber treats the beginning of a phrase as an acceptable onset). Here, as elsewhere in this chapter, we analyze hypothetical inputs which contain only the material necessary to establish the analytical point at hand, factoring out irrelevant complexities and distractions.

(201) **Berber Exceptional Epenthesis**

	ONS	PARSE	FILL^{Nuc}	*M/a	FILL^{Ons}	HNUC	−COD
/aa/ →							
☞ .á.□á.					*	á á	
.aá.				* !		á	
.á⟨a⟩.		* !				á	
.á.á.	* !					á á	
/ia/ →							
☞ .iá.						á	
.í.□á.					* !	á í	
.ía.				* !		í	*
/ai/ →							
☞ .ái.						á	*
.á.□í.					* !	á í	
.aí.				* !		í	
/tk/ →							
☞ .tḱ.						ḱ	
.t□k.			* !				*

While this solution is adequate descriptively, it is somewhat unsatisfactory explanatorily. For the constraint *M/a we have introduced expresses the markedness of a as a Margin; and of course the strong affinity of a, the most sonorous segment, for the Peak position is already expressed in HNUC. It seems no coincidence that it is a that has surfaced in a high-ranking constraint disfavoring Margin position, yet there is nothing in our theory so far that would have prevented, say, *M/r from having suddenly appeared in place of *M/a. It is almost as if HNUC were a *complex* of constraints governing the affinity of segments with varying sonority to the Peak and Margin positions – and while most of them are contiguous in the hierarchy, occupying the position we have marked Hnuc, the strongest of them, pertaining to *a*, has detached itself from the rest and drifted above certain other constraints: crucially, Fill^{Ons}.

Now while the behavior of *a* is in a sense atypical within Berber – it is the only segment that cannot be parsed into both Peaks and Margins, and this fact only reveals itself in the event that an input contains /aa/ – such behavior is of course the *norm* in more familiar languages; the class of segments that can fill both Peak and Margin positions commonly consists of at most a few segments, whereas in Berber it consumes all the segments except *a*. So the need for high-ranking constraints such as *M/*a* in Berber will extend in most languages to the majority of segments; these constraints are primarily responsible for distinguishing consonants from vowels, as we shall now see, and they do a lot of work in typical languages. They function in the segmental theory as did *M/V (121) and *P/C (122) in the CV theory.

So the program now is to 'explode' Hnuc into many segment-specific constraints like *M/*a*, so that those that need to may rise high in the domination hierarchy and prevent pure vowels from being parsed into Margins and pure consonants into Peaks. (In the sense intended here, Berber has one pure vowel, *a*, and no pure consonants.)

8.1.2   Restricting to Binary Marks

As a glance at the preceding tableau immediately reveals, Hnuc stands out from the other constraints in its non-binarity; whereas the other constraints invoke a simple '*' when violated, Hnuc is a graded constraint favoring more sonorous peaks. The explosion of Hnuc now required, which liberates the like of *M/*a*, begins in fact as a recasting of the single, multi-valued Hnuc constraint into a set of binary-valued constraints. Recall that

(202)   **Hnuc**
          $á > í > \cdots > \hat{t}$ [generally, $\hat{\lambda} > \hat{\tau}$ if $|\lambda| > |\tau|$]

At this point it is convenient to re-write this as follows:

(203)   **Peak Harmony**
          $P/a > P/i > \cdots > P/t$

Now we can achieve this *Harmony scale* via an exactly corresponding *binary constraint hierarchy* of the form:

(204)   **Peak Hierarchy**
          $*P/t \gg \cdots \gg *P/i \gg *P/a$

formed from the constraints:

(205) ***P/λ**
   λ must not be parsed as a syllable Peak (i.e., associated to Nuc).

The tableau makes this equivalence clear:

(206) **Hɴᴜᴄ Reduced to Binary Constraints**

	*P/t	...	*P/i	*P/a
P/a = á				*
P/i = í			*	
⋮		...		
P/t = t́	*			

If we take any two segments λ and τ with |λ| > |τ|, and compare their Harmonies using this constraint hierarchy, we see that λ̂ > t̂.

In anticipation of later analysis we point out that the Peak Hierarchy is not completely equivalent to Hɴᴜᴄ. As far as the harmonic ordering of individual peaks is concerned, the two are indeed equivalent, but when entire parses containing multiple peaks are compared, a difference emerges. On whole parses, Hɴᴜᴄ compares the multiple nuclei from most harmonic to least harmonic (as discussed in §5.2.1.2). The Peak Hierarchy, however, evaluates all violations in a parse of *P/t first, and so on down the Peak Hierarchy; and the violations of *P/t are incurred by the *least* harmonic nuclei. Thus the Peak Hierarchy evaluates whole parses by comparing the multiple nuclei from least to most harmonic. We will return to this issue in a later discussion of Berber in §8.3.3. In the meantime, we turn our attention to the consequences of the Peak Hierarchy for syllabification universally.

Paralleling this hierarchy of Peak association constraints, there is another hierarchy for Margins, with opposite polarity:

(207) **Margin Hierarchy**
   *M/a ≫ *M/i ≫ ⋯ ≫ *M/t

The constraints here are in direct correspondence to the Peak counterparts (205):

(208) ***M/λ**
   λ must not be parsed as a syllable Margin (i.e., associated to Ons or Cod).

The most dominant constraint, as promised in the earlier discussion of Berber, is *M/a. This Margin Hierarchy generates the following Harmony scale:

(209) **Margin Harmony**
$$M/t > \cdots > M/i > M/a$$

The single non-binary constraint HNUC and the Peak Hierarchy (204) of binary constraints each generate the same Harmony scale (203) for Nuc/segment associations (202). The power of the Peak Hierarchy is greater, however, since it will function as does HNUC to correctly rank all the peaks *regardless of whether all the constraints *P/λ are contiguous in the hierarchy*. That is, other constraints may be interspersed within the sequence prescribed by the Peak Hierarchy (204), and similarly for the Margin Hierarchy (207). This allows Berber, for example, to rank *M/a high in the hierarchy (200, 201) – crucially, higher than F_{ILL}^{Ons} – and all the other Margin constraints $*M/i \gg \cdots \gg *M/t$ lower than F_{ILL}^{Ons} in the hierarchy. This will (eventually) lead to another, more explanatory, analysis of Berber which is equivalent to the analysis in (200) and (201); cf. §8.3.3. More importantly, the separated association constraints of the Peak and Margin Hierarchies will enable us to handle the typological variation among languages in the degree of flexibility with which they permit segments to move between Margin and Peak positions.

The Peak and Margin Hierarchies exemplify a general treatment of the problem of producing Harmony scales in the association of two dimensions of structure D_1 and D_2, one of them binary, by 'aligning' two pre-defined (non-Harmony) scales on D_1 and D_2. Here, D_1 is the binary structural dimension Peak/Margin, with the prominence scale:

(210) **Syllable Position Prominence**
$$P > M$$

and D_2 is the segment inventory with the prominence scale given by sonority:

(211) **Segmental Sonority Prominence**
$$a > i > \cdots > t$$

(Recall that '*i*' denotes a sonority level, not a full bundle of distinctive features.) The process of *alignment* of these two prominence scales, (210) and (211), is an operation which by definition generates two Harmony scales on the associations between the two dimensions: precisely the two scales (203) and (209).

(212) **Alignment**
Suppose given a binary dimension D_1 with a scale $X > Y$ on its elements {X, Y}, and another dimension D_2 with a scale $a > b > \cdots > z$ on its elements. The *harmonic alignment* of D_1 and D_2 is the pair of Harmony scales:
H_X: $X/a > X/b > \cdots > X/z$
H_Y: $Y/z > \cdots > Y/b > Y/a$
The *constraint alignment* is the pair of constraint hierarchies:
C_X: $*X/z \gg \cdots \gg *X/b \gg *X/a$
C_Y: $*Y/a \gg *Y/b \gg \cdots \gg *Y/z$

C_X and C_Y are to be understood as sub-hierarchies of a language's total constraint hierarchy; e.g., C_X asserts that scattered within the constraint hierarchy of a language are the constraints *X/z, ⋯ , *X/b, *X/a, and that they fall in that order (from most to least dominant), with other constraints possibly falling above, below, and among these constraints.

The idea of harmonic alignment is easily described in cases like the present one where the two scales are prominence scales along two dimensions (syllable structure and sonority): the more prominent position X prefers the more prominent elements (ideally, a); the less prominent position Y prefers the less prominent elements (ideally, z). Constraint alignment says that associating less prominent elements (like z) to the more prominent position X produces the most dominant marks; similarly for associating more prominent elements (like a) to the less prominent position Y.

As illustrated above (206), constraint alignment entails harmonic alignment; conversely, the constraints *X/α and *Y/α must be ordered according to constraint alignment if they are to be consistent with harmonic alignment. Thus there are two essentially equivalent ways to enter the alignment of two dimensions into Universal Grammar. The first is to assert that the constraint hierarchies C_X, C_Y of constraint alignment are universal, that they must be incorporated into the particular constraint hierarchy of any language. The second is to assert that the Harmony scales H_X, H_Y of harmonic alignment and the constraints *X/α, *Y/α are universal; particular languages must order these constraints in a way consistent with H_X, H_Y. It then follows as a consequence that individual languages' constraint hierarchies will always contain the sub-hierarchies C_X, C_Y, i.e. satisfy constraint alignment.

We assume the following principle of Universal Grammar:

(213)   **Universal Syllable Position/Segmental Sonority Prominence Alignment**
The syllable position (210) and segmental sonority (211) prominence scales are universally aligned: the harmonic alignments are the Peak (203) and Margin (209) Harmony scales; the constraint alignments are the Peak (204) and Margin (207) Constraint Hierarchies.

Note that while (213) fixes universally the relative Harmonies $P/\lambda > P/\tau$ and $M/\tau > M/\lambda$ (when $|\lambda| > |\tau|$), *it leaves the relative Harmonies of P/λ and M/λ open for cross-linguistic variation.* In sum, the segment λ is always a better peak than the segment τ, and always a worse margin, but individual languages will freely decide whether having λ as a peak is better or worse than having λ as a margin.

We now explore the possibilities that arise when a given language fixes the relative rankings of the Peak, Margin, and Basic Syllable Structure Constraints. That is, we develop the following theory:

(214)   **Basic Segmental Syllable Theory**
- The constraints governing syllable structure are the Peak and Margin association constraints (205, 208), and the syllable structure constraints ONS, −COD, PARSE, and FILL (114–117) and NUC and *COMPLEX (119–120).

- The constraints NUC (119) and *COMPLEX (120) are universally undominated, while the remaining, lower-ranking constraints can be ranked in any domination hierarchy, limited only by universal Syllable Position/ Segmental Sonority Prominence Alignment (213).

In other words, we study the factorial typology induced by these constraints. Our focus will be on the distribution of various segments across syllable positions. For now we take as given the segment inventory of a language; in §9.1.2 we will show how the theory can address typological variation in the inventories themselves.

In the Basic CV Syllable Structure Theory, the inputs to be parsed were taken to be all possible CV strings {C,V}$^+$. Likewise, in the Basic Segmental Syllable Theory, we abstract away from omissions in the lexicon, and consider the set of inputs to be parsed in a language to be the set of all possible strings of our idealized segments $a, i, \ldots, d, t$. We postpone until chapter 9 our discussion of the issue of structure in the lexicon.

In this chapter we show how the theory can elucidate the consequences for Universal Grammar of alignments such as that of sonority and syllable position prominence; while focusing on the role of sonority in syllable-internal segment distribution, we are of course not blind to the role of other dimensions and constraints. It is for future research to determine the extent to which the methods developed here, or their extensions, can also shed new light on the role of factors other than sonority.

We shall see that from the ranking of constraints in a given language, a series of parameter values can be computed, each of which sets a sonority value that delimits a distributional class of segments. All segments more sonorous than a parameter we call π_{Nuc} are possible nuclei; all those less sonorous than another parameter π_{Ons} are possible onsets. If there are any segments in common, these are ambidextrous: they are both possible nuclei and onsets (185). The possible codas are those segments less sonorous than a parameter π_{Cod}, which may have a lower, but not a higher, sonority value than π_{Ons}; the set of possible codas in some languages may be a smaller set than the set of possible onsets, but never the reverse.

In addition to establishing particular results such as these, the theoretical development to follow in this chapter has two other goals. First, the methods that will be developed are quite general and can be applied to a variety of other problems. Secondly, the discussion will show how the theory enables a surprisingly rich set of conclusions to be formally extracted from a starting point as simple as the Basic Segmental Syllable Theory (214), which involves only simple universal constraints, simple universal operations such as Alignment, and simple means of generating cross-linguistic variation such as the Factorial Typology.

We will ultimately be concerned to derive the previously mentioned licensing asymmetry between onsets and codas. Until we take up this asymmetry, however, we will ignore codas and focus on the distribution of segments within onsets and nuclei.

8.2   Reconstructing the C and V Classes: Emergent Parameter Setting via Constraint Ranking

In this section we introduce most of the formal techniques summarized at the beginning of the chapter, and apply them to the problem of determining the conditions on constraint hierarchies under which segments may be optimally parsed into onset and nucleus positions. These conditions are assembled in (239) at the beginning of §8.3, in which section they form the basis of our typology of inventories of onsets and nuclei. On a first reading, it may be desirable to skim up to §8.3, as the formal and logical development of §8.2 is rather involved.

8.2.1   Harmonic Completeness of Possible Onsets and Peaks

We begin by observing a direct consequence of the universal Margin and Peak Hierarchies for the role of sonority in the distribution of segments within syllables. The universal Margin Hierarchy says that less sonorous segments make more harmonic onsets; *Harmonic Completeness* implies that if some segment is a possible onset, then so are all less sonorous segments.

(215)   **Harmonic Completeness: Possible Onsets and Nuclei**
If $|\lambda| > |\tau|$ and λ is a possible onset, then so is τ. If $|\alpha| > |\lambda|$ and λ is a possible nucleus, then so is α.

The validity of (215) follows from a basic lemma concerning the Harmonic Ordering of Forms (HoF):

(216)   **Cancellation Lemma**
Suppose two structures S_1 and S_2 both incur the same mark *m. Then to determine whether $S_1 > S_2$, we can omit *m from the list of marks of both S_1 and S_2 ('cancel the common mark') and compare S_1 and S_2 solely on the basis of the remaining marks. Applied iteratively, this means we can cancel *all* common marks and assess S_1 and S_2 by comparing only their unshared marks.

This lemma is proved below in the Appendix, part of some formal analysis of HOF which we have postponed. That (215) follows from (216) requires a slightly involved argument; a first approximation to the argument runs as follows. By assumption, λ is a possible onset, so there must be some input I containing λ which is assigned an analysis S in which λ is parsed as an onset, i.e., S contains the association Ons/λ (which incurs the mark *M/λ). Replacing this occurrence of λ by τ in I and S produces a new input I' and a new structure S'; we claim that S' is the structure assigned to I', and that therefore τ too is a possible onset.

I: ---λ---	S: ---Ons/λ---
I': ---τ---	S': ---Ons/τ---

The central point is that the marks earned by S′ are the same as those earned by S, except that a mark *M/λ has been replaced by *M/τ; by the Cancellation Lemma, in comparing S and S′ we can cancel all their common marks and determine which is more harmonic solely on the basis of their unshared marks, *M/λ for S and *M/τ for S′. Since |λ| > |τ|, by (207) *M/λ ≫ *M/τ so we conclude that S′ > S. Since S is the output assigned by the grammar to I, it is optimal, that is, more harmonic than all its competitors. Since S′ > S, it is tempting to conclude that S′ is therefore also optimal, giving the desired conclusion that S′ is the output assigned to I′, and that therefore τ is a possible onset. Unfortunately, the fact that S is more harmonic than all its competitors does *not* entail that S′ is more harmonic than all *its* competitors: the competitors to S′ as analyses of I′ *also have λ replaced by τ*, and so they too, like S′, can be more harmonic than their λ-counterparts. Here, then, is the actual proof:

Proof of (215)
Let I,S and I′,S′ be as above. Now consider a competitor C′ as an output for I′; we must show that S′ > C′. Let C be the corresponding competitor to S (with λ in place of τ).

I: ---λ---	S: ---M/λ---	C: ---⟨λ⟩--- or ---P/λ--- or ---M/λ---
I′: ---τ---	S′: ---M/τ---	C′: ---⟨τ⟩--- or ---P/τ--- or ---M/τ---

As pointed out above, we know that S′ > S and that S > C. We would be done if C ≥ C′, but this need not be case; it depends on the analysis in C (C′) of λ (τ):

Case 1: λ is unparsed in C, i.e. ⟨λ⟩ in C, and therefore ⟨τ⟩ in C′. In this case, the same mark, *Parse, is earned by both λ and τ so C and C′ incur exactly the same marks: C ≈ C′. Thus S′ > S > C ≈ C′ and we are done.

Case 2: λ is parsed as a peak P/λ in C, and therefore τ is parsed as P/τ in C′. Now the difference in marks incurred by C and C′ is that C incurs *P/λ while C′ incurs *P/τ. By the Peak Hierarchy (204), *P/τ ≫ *P/λ, so C > C′ and again we are done: S′ > S > C > C′.

Case 3: λ is parsed as a margin M/λ in C, so τ is parsed as M/τ in C′. Now, since *M/λ ≫ *M/τ, we have C′ > C, and we are *not* done. Since *M/λ is incurred in *both* S and C, however, it cannot be responsible for the fact that S > C. That is, in comparing the marks incurred by S and by C to determine which is more harmonic, the mark *M/λ cancels out of the comparison; the fact that S > C must therefore follow from the remaining marks. But these are exactly the same as the marks that remain in the comparison of S′ to C′, since *M/λ has been replaced by *M/τ in both S′ and C′, and it cancels in this comparison as well. So just as the marks remaining after cancellation of *M/λ determine that S > C, so these same marks entail after cancellation of *M/τ that S′ > C′.

An immediate typological consequence of Harmonic Completeness (215) is:

(217)   **Possible Onset and Nuclei Parameters**
The cross-linguistic variation in the sets of possible onsets and nuclei are governed by two parameters, π_{Ons} and π_{Nuc}, which are sonority cut points in the Margin and Peak Hierarchies. The possible onsets are those segments with sonority less than or equal to π_{Ons}:
  $\text{PossOns} = \{\tau : |\tau| \leq \pi_{Ons}\};$
The possible peaks are those segments with sonority greater than or equal to π_{Nuc}:
  $\text{PossPeak} = \{\alpha : |\alpha| \geq \pi_{Nuc}\}$

Exactly characterizing what determines these cut points π_{Ons} and π_{Nuc} is a main goal of the following analysis: these are not primitive parameters directly set in the grammar of a particular language; rather their values are derived consequences of the language's ranking of the universal constraints. (The results are (247) and (248) of §8.3.)

To facilitate the discussion, it will be convenient to adopt the following:

(218)   **Definition of t and a**
In a given language, let t denote a segment of minimal sonority and a a segment of maximal sonority.

It is clear from (217) that if a language has any possible onsets, then t is one; if any possible peaks, then a. The reason for the qualification is that the theory as developed so far does not rule out a language in which all onsets or all nuclei are epenthesized. We assume henceforth that in every language, such a possible onset t and possible nucleus a exist.

8.2.2   Peak- and Margin-Affinity

In the present theory, the most obvious question concerning the relation between individual segments and syllable positions is: for a given segment λ, is the association to Peak, P/λ, or to Margin, M/λ, more harmonic? This question dichotomizes the segment inventory in a particular language:

(219)   **Syllable Position Affinity**
If in a given language $P/\lambda > M/\lambda$, or equivalently $*M/\lambda \gg *P/\lambda$, then λ is a *peak-preferring* segment; otherwise λ is *margin-preferring*.

The universal Peak and Margin Hierarchies have a sharp consequence for affinity:

(220)   **The Affinity Cut Theorem**
Suppose $|\lambda| > |\tau|$. Then if τ is peak-preferring, so is λ. If λ is margin-preferring, so is τ. Thus there is a cut in the sonority scale, above which all

segments are peak-preferring and below, margin-preferring. The only parameter of cross-linguistic affinity variation is the sonority level π_{Aff} of this cut point.

To see this, select for concreteness $\lambda = a$ and $\tau = i$. Suppose that in a given language i is peak-preferring. Then the following ranking of constraints must hold in the language:

(221) $*\text{M}/a \gg *\text{M}/i \gg *\text{P}/i \gg *\text{P}/a$

The first and last rankings are parts of the universal Margin and Peak Hierarchies, (207) and (204) respectively; the middle ranking $*\text{M}/i \gg *\text{P}/i$ simply asserts our hypothesis that i is peak-preferring. Reading off the left and right ends of (221), we see that $*\text{M}/a \gg *\text{P}/a$, i.e., that a too is peak-preferring. The situation can be illustrated as follows, the unshaded portions corresponding directly to (221):

(222) **Interleaving of Margin and Peak Hierarchies**, given $*\text{M}/i \gg *\text{P}/i$

Universal Peak Hierarchy (204)	$*\text{P}/t \gg$	$\cdots \gg$	$*\text{P}/l \gg$	$*\textbf{P}/\textbf{i} \gg$	$*\text{P}/a$
Language-particular				$\gg$	
Universal Margin Hierarchy (207)		$*\text{M}/a \gg$	$*\textbf{M}/\textbf{i} \gg$	$*\text{M}/l \gg$	$\cdots \gg$	$*\text{M}/t$

This diagram represents the large number of hierarchies gotten by unifying the Margin and Peak Hierarchies into a single hierarchy, in such a way that $*\text{M}/i \gg *\text{P}/i$. The diagram shows immediately that the same relation, $*\text{M}/a \gg *\text{P}/a$ follows, and in general, that $*\text{M}/\iota \gg *\text{P}/\iota$ for one segment ι will entail the same domination relation for any more sonorous segment α: if ι is peak-preferring, so must be α. This means that if ι denotes the least sonorous peak-preferring segment, the least sonorous segment obeying the property $*\text{M}/\iota \gg *\text{P}/\iota$ displayed by $\iota = i$ in (222), then all segments more sonorous than ι are peak-preferring also, and all less sonorous segments are margin-preferring (else there would be a segment less sonorous than ι which is peak-preferring, contrary to the definition of ι). Thus the 'cut point' π_{Aff} of the Affinity Cut Theorem (220) lies between the sonority level of ι and the next sonority level lower: more sonorous segments (starting with ι) are peak-preferring, less sonorous segments are margin-preferring:

(223) **Affinity Parameter**
π_{Aff} is located as follows between two adjacent sonority levels, that of the most sonorous margin-preferring segment and that of the least sonorous peak-preferring segment:
$$\max_\lambda\{|\lambda| : *\text{P}/\lambda \gg *\text{M}/\lambda\} < \pi_{\text{Aff}} < \min_\iota\{|\iota| : *\text{M}/\iota \gg *\text{P}/\iota\} \,.$$

As with the sonority values for the parameters π_{Ons} and π_{Nuc} introduced above, the sonority value π_{Aff} is not a primitive parameter set directly by a grammar, but rather a value determined by the language's ranking of universal constraints, as illustrated in (222).

8.2.3   Interactions with PARSE

In and of itself, the affinity of a segment does not determine its distribution. In general, there will be conflicts between respecting the segment's affinity and other constraints. The easiest such interaction to analyze involves PARSE.

Suppose *M/α is ranked above PARSE. Then parsing α as a Margin is so low in Harmony as to be even less harmonic than phonetically deleting the entire input string containing α – that is, assigning no structure to it at all (i.e., the Null Parse of §4.3.1). For while assigning no structure incurs many *PARSE marks (one for each segment in the input string), the one mark *M/α that is sure to be incurred in any analysis in which α is parsed as an M is less harmonic than any number of *PARSEs, by the hypothesis that *M/α strictly dominates PARSE. This observation illustrates a useful general technique of analysis:

(224)   **Harmonic Bounding**
In order to show that a particular structure φ does not appear in the outputs of a grammar, it suffices to show that any candidate structure A containing φ is less harmonic than *one* competing candidate B (of the same input). (B provides a *harmonic (upper) bound* for A).

Note that the competing candidate B need not be the *most* harmonic one, it need only be *more* harmonic than A, i.e. B > A. In the case at hand, to show the impossibility of the association $\varphi = M/\alpha$, we have identified a structure B, the Null Parse, which harmonically bounds any structure containing φ. For the vast majority of inputs, the Null Parse B will not be the *optimal* analysis; but it nonetheless suffices as a harmonic upper bound. (The optimal analysis of an input containing α may, for example, involve failing to parse only α; or it may involve parsing α as a peak.)

Thus a major dichotomy in the segments is induced by the location of PARSE within the Margin Hierarchy of constraints:

(225)   **Untenable Associations**
A segment α is defined to be an *untenable margin* iff *M/α ≫ PARSE, i.e., if α is more harmonic deleted $\langle \alpha \rangle$ than parsed as a margin M/α. τ is an *untenable peak* iff *P/τ ≫ PARSE. If λ is both an untenable peak and an untenable margin, then λ is an *untenable surface segment*. If α is an untenable margin then it is not a possible margin; likewise for peaks.

Note that this result gives us a bit of information about the values of the parameters π_{Ons} and π_{Nuc}. The highest π_{Ons} can possibly be is the highest sonority level $|\tau|$ at which PARSE dominates *M/τ; for higher sonority levels $|\alpha| > |\tau|$, *M/α dominates PARSE and thus α is an untenable margin hence not a possible onset. This situation is illustrated in (226) with $\tau = i$ (compare (222)):

(226)   **Untenable Margins**
$$*M/a \gg \textsc{Parse} \gg \quad *M/i \gg *M/l \gg \cdots \gg *M/t$$

----

a: untenable margin $\Big|$ $\qquad \Big| \rightarrow \rightarrow \rightarrow \rightarrow \pi_{\text{Ons}} (?) \rightarrow \rightarrow \rightarrow \rightarrow$

The maximum sonority of possible onsets, π_{Ons}, cannot be higher than the sonority level $|i|$, because a is an untenable margin ($*M/a \gg \textsc{Parse}$). A corresponding illustration for possible peaks (again, compare (222)) is:

(227)   **Untenable Peaks**
$$*P/t \gg \quad \cdots \quad *P/n \gg \textsc{Parse} \gg \quad *P/l \gg *P/i \gg *P/a$$

----

t–n: untenable peaks $\Big|$ $\qquad \Big| \rightarrow \rightarrow \rightarrow \pi_{\text{Nuc}} (?) \rightarrow \rightarrow \rightarrow$

While we have shown that $*M/\alpha \gg \textsc{Parse}$ entails the impossibility of α associating to M in an output, we have yet to examine the converse, whether $\textsc{Parse} \gg *M/\tau$ entails that M/τ can sometimes appear in an output. It will turn out that the answer is affirmative if τ is margin-preferring; if τ is peak-preferring, then whether it may associate to M turns out to depend on the ranking of other syllable structure constraints such as $\textsc{Ons}$ and $\textsc{Fill}^{\text{Ons}}$.

Thus, while it has been easy to find a *necessary* condition for τ to be a possible margin (viz., $\textsc{Parse} \gg *M/\tau$), finding *sufficient* conditions will be much harder. To find a necessary condition for M/τ to surface in a well-formed structure, it sufficed to find *one* competitor (total phonetic deletion) that must be surpassed. To find a *sufficient* condition requires showing that for *all* universally possible orderings of constraints, there is *some* input in which an analysis containing M/τ is more harmonic than *all* its competing analyses. Establishing such a conclusion is rather involved, and we find it prudent to proceed via a series of incrementally developed results, worthwhile in themselves. The result will be necessary and sufficient conditions for a segment to be a possible onset or nucleus; from these conditions will follow a typology of segmental inventories, with respect to syllable structure distribution, and a universal asymmetry in the licensing of segments in codas and onsets.

8.2.4   Restricting Deletion and Epenthesis

In order to limit the set of candidate analyses we will need to consider, we pause here to establish results restricting the environments where under- and overparsing (a.k.a. deletion and epenthesis) is possible. The underparsing result concerns the special case of optimal syllables:

(228)   **No Deletion of Tenable Segments in Optimal Syllables**
Suppose τ is a tenable margin and α a tenable peak. Then the structure assigned to /$\tau\alpha$/ can involve no underparsing.

For the obvious analysis .$\tau\acute{\alpha}$., while not necessarily optimal, is more harmonic than any analysis involving $\langle\tau\rangle$ or $\langle\alpha\rangle$. Since it represents the universally optimal syllable structure (128), .τά. incurs only the marks {*M/τ, *P/α}, with no marks for syllable structure constraint violations. On the other hand, any structure containing either ⟨τ⟩ or ⟨α⟩ will incur at least one mark *PARSE. Now to assume that τ and α are a tenable margin and peak, respectively, is precisely to assume that PARSE ≫ *M/τ and PARSE ≫ *P/α (225); thus any alternative containing them which fails to parse either τ or α is less harmonic than .τά. (In other words, .τά. harmonically bounds (224) the set of all candidates containing either ⟨τ⟩ or ⟨α⟩.)

The second result is just the Epenthesis Sites theorem (145) of the CV theory (§6.2.3): it holds in the segmental theory we are now developing as well, in which the families of constraints *M/λ and *P/λ have replaced *M/V (121) and *P/C (122) of the CV theory. The demonstration of (145) proceeded via a series of four propositions. Re-examination of these shows that in Propositions 1 and 2, all the Harmony comparisons involved only *unfilled* syllable positions, and no segments, so no constraints involving segments were relevant to the comparisons; thus exactly the same arguments go through in the present theory. Proposition 3 showed that epenthesis into the environment .(□)□̂C. is impossible because of the more harmonic alternative .C□̂. Here, the segment C (now call it λ) is parsed as a coda in the first analysis and as an onset in the second; but since both involve the same constraint *M/λ of the current theory, this common mark cancels, and the original conclusion still stands. (This would not be the case if we were to distinguish two families of constraints, *Ons/λ and *Cod/λ, but the theory we are now developing lumps these into *M/λ.) Finally, the new result of Proposition 4 was the impossibility of .C□̂.□V., because it is less harmonic than .CV.; again, since .τ□̂.□ά. and .τά. both incur the association marks {*M/τ, *P/α}, these cancel, and the argument from the CV theory goes through as before. Thus all the Propositions 1–4 still hold in the present segmental theory, therefore so does the FILL Violation Theorem (possible epenthesis sites), a direct consequence of these four propositions.

8.2.5   Further Necessary Conditions on Possible Onsets and Nuclei

We now proceed to find necessary and sufficient conditions for segments to be possible onsets and nuclei. One set of necessary conditions was given in the earlier analysis of untenable associations (225); in this section we derive the following further necessary conditions:

(229)   **Possible Onset Condition**
   If τ is a possible onset in a language, then:
   [1]   *P/τ or ONS ≫ *M/τ
   and
   [2]   *P/τ or *M/□ ≫ *M/τ

(230)   **Possible Peak Condition**
   If α is a possible peak in a language, then:
   [3]   *M/α or *P/□ ≫ *P/α

Here we have adopted the notations $*M/\square \equiv \text{FILL}^{\text{Ons}}$ and $*P/\square \equiv \text{FILL}^{\text{Nuc}}$ in order to explicitly represent the conceptual parallelism between the two FILL constraints and the families of $*M/\lambda$ and $*P/\lambda$ constraints. And of course $*P/\tau$ or ONS $\gg *M/\tau$ means $*P/\tau \gg *M/\tau$ or ONS $\gg *M/\tau$.

The virtual isomorphism between the Possible Onset and Possible Peak Conditions is more evident in the following pair of alternative, logically equivalent, formulations:

(231)   **Possible Onset Condition, Alternate Version**
Condition '[1] AND [2]' of (229) is equivalent to the condition:
either
    [i] τ is margin-preferring $(*P/\tau \gg *M/\tau)$,
or
    [ii] $\{\text{ONS}, *M/\square\} \gg *M/\tau \gg *P/\tau$.
If τ is a possible onset, then exactly one of [i] or [ii] must hold.

(232)   **Possible Peak Condition, Alternate Version**
Condition [3] of (230) can be re-written:
either
    [iii] α is peak-preferring $(*M/\alpha \gg *P/\alpha)$,
or
    [iv] $*P/\square \gg *P/\alpha \gg *M/\alpha$.
If α is a possible peak, then exactly one of [iii] or [iv] must hold.

The nucleus condition arises from the onset condition by exchanging P and M, and ONS and NUC. However, NUC is universally superordinate, whereas the domination position of ONS may vary; so while ONS must be explicitly mentioned in [ii], NUC need not be mentioned in the corresponding condition [iv].

The results expressed in conditions (231) and (232), and their justifications, can be rendered informally as follows. We start with (232), which is slightly simpler.

In order for α to be a possible nucleus, either [iii] it must be less harmonic to parse α as a margin than as a peak (because α is peak-preferring), or, if α prefers to be a margin [iv], then an unfilled Nuc node that could be created by disassociating α from Nuc and parsing it instead as a margin must generate a mark $*\text{FILL}^{\text{Nuc}}$ which is worse than the mark $*P/\alpha$ incurred by parsing α into its dispreferred peak position.

The situation in (231) is similar. In order for τ to be a possible onset, either [i] it must be less harmonic to parse τ as a peak than as an onset (because τ is margin-preferring), or, if τ prefers to be a peak [ii], then the marks incurred in either removing the Ons node so vacated $(*\text{ONS})$, or in leaving it in place but unfilled $(*\text{FILL}^{\text{Ons}})$, must dominate τ's inherent preference.

We now make these informal explanations precise. The technique we use runs as follows. Suppose we are given a language in which α can be parsed as a peak. Then there must be some input I containing α whose optimal parse O contains Nuc/α. This means that for any competing parse C of I in which α is not parsed as a nucleus, we must have O > C. By choosing C so that it forms a kind of minimal pair with O, we can show that O > C can only hold if the constraint hierarchy in the language meets some domination condition, viz., [3] of (230).

So suppose that α is a possible peak, i.e., that there is some input containing α whose analysis O contains Nuc/α. To generate the competitor C, we simply take O and reassociate α to Ons:

(233) **Marks for Nuc/α and a Competitor with Ons/α**

    O: ---$\acute{\alpha}$---   *P/α

    C: ---$\Box$.$\alpha\acute{\Box}$---   *P/$\Box$, *M/α, *P/$\Box$

The mark *P/α incurred by O is exchanged in C for {*P/$\Box$, *M/α, *P/$\Box$}; all the other marks incurred by O (not involving α) are shared by C and thus cancel (216). Thus in order that O > C, it must be that at least one of the marks *P/$\Box$ or *M/α dominates *P/α; this establishes [3] (230).

Now consider onsets. Suppose that τ is a possible onset, i.e., that there is some input I containing τ whose optimal parse O contains Ons/τ. We compare O to two competing parses of I, C_1 and C_2, in which τ associates to Nuc (i.e., $\acute{\tau}$):

(234) **Marks for Ons/τ and Competitors with Nuc/τ**

    O: ---.$\tau\acute{\alpha}$---   *M/τ

    C_1: ---.$\Box\acute{\tau}$.$\Box\acute{\alpha}$---   *M/$\Box$, *P/τ, *M/$\Box$

    C_2: ---.$\acute{\tau}$.$\acute{\alpha}$---   *ONS, *P/τ, *ONS

Since τ is an onset in O, it must be followed by a Nuc position; in (234) this has been notated $\acute{\alpha}$, with the understanding that α may either be an underlying segment associated to Nuc, or $\Box$, in the case the Nuc following τ is unfilled.

The marks incurred by O and its competitors are indicated in (234). O incurs *M/τ; this is traded for *P/τ in C_1 and C_2, along with a pair of *M/$\Box$ marks in C_1 and a pair of *ONS marks in C_2; all other marks incurred by O (not involving τ; including those incurred by α) are shared by both C_1 and C_2 and thus cancel. In order that O > C_1, either *P/τ or *M/$\Box$ must dominate *M/τ. In order that O > C_2, either *P/τ or *ONS must dominate *M/τ. If O is to be the optimal structure, *both* these conditions must hold. Thus we get (229).

In assuming that the languages under study possess a possible onset t and a possible nucleus a, we are thus implicitly assuming that (229) holds with $\tau = t$ and that (230) holds with $\alpha = a$.

8.2.6 Sufficient Conditions on Possible Onsets and Nuclei

Now we move on to the main task, to show that the preceding necessary conditions (225, 229, 230) are indeed *sufficient* for segments to be possible onsets and nuclei:

(235) **Possible Peak Sufficient Condition**
    If α is a tenable peak and satisfies [3], then α is a possible peak.

(236) **Possible Onset Sufficient Condition**
   If τ is a tenable margin and satisfies both [1] and [2], then τ is a possible onset.

Our strategy will be to show that segments τ meeting the necessary conditions for possible onsets do indeed surface as onsets in /τa/, and that segments α meeting the necessary conditions for possible nuclei surface as such in /tα/.

   We start with peaks, and consider /tα/; we want to show that no matter how a language ranks its constraints, consistent with the strictures of Universal Grammar, the analysis .tά. is optimal. The competitors we must consider have been limited by (228), which rules out all deletions for this input (t by assumption is a possible hence tenable onset); and the possible Epenthesis Sites have been limited by (145). The table (237) below – a *universal tableau* – shows all the remaining competitors and the constraints they violate. *The ordering of columns does not represent strict domination ranking* since we are reasoning about universal and not language-particular constraint interactions, and there is no particular ranking of the constraints that we can assume; this means that drawing the relevant conclusions from this universal tableau will require somewhat more involved analysis than is needed in a language-particular tableau in which the columns are ordered by the domination hierarchy in that language. As we examine the universal tableau, we will see that some of the relative positions of the columns have been designed to reflect the domination relations which must hold as a consequence of the hypotheses we have made concerning t and α.

(237) **Universal Tableau for /tα/**

/tα/→	ONS	*P/t	*M/□	*P/□	*M/α	*M/t	*P/α	-COD
a. ☞ .tά.						*	*	
b. .tα.	*	*PH			*MH	MH	PH	*
c. .t□α.				*3	*3	[*]	3	*
d. .t́.ά.	**1	*1				1	[*]	
e. .t́.□ά.	*1	*1	*			1	[*]	
f. .t́.αĺ.	*1	*1		*3	*3	1	3	
g. .□t́.ά.	*	*2	*2			2	[*]	
h. .□t́.□ά.		*2	**2			2	[*]	
i. .□t́.αĺ.		*2	*2	*3	*3	2	3	
j. .t□.ά.	*			*		[*]	[*]	
k. .t□.□ά.			*	*		[*]	[*]	
l. .t□.αĺ.				**3	**3	[*]	3	

In constructing this large universal tableau, we have exhaustively listed altern-atives, rather than following our customary practice with language-particular tableaux of omitting many of the least harmonic candidates. This for the simple reason that here it is not at all clear which *are* the least harmonic candidates, since we are not reasoning about a specific language-particular hierarchy.

So our first task is to verify that the candidates [a–l] are indeed the only ones we need consider. Since legal epenthesis sites (145) all involve either a filled onset or a filled nucleus, with only two underlying segments in /tɑ/, analyses with more than two syllables must involve illegal epenthesis. Given that deletion is impossible for this input (228), the only possible monosyllabic parses are those shown in rows [a–c]. Given the constrained epenthesis sites, disyllabic parses are limited to those in which the first syllable contains *t* and the second contains α. There are three possible monosyllables containing *t*, given the impossibility of epenthesis into coda position: .ŧ́., .□ŧ́., and .tŧ̂. These three possibilities are repres-ented in candidates [d–f], [g–i], and [j–l], respectively. There are also the corres-ponding three possible monosyllables containing α, and the nine bisyllabic parses [d–l] comprise all combinations – the Cartesian product – of the three *t* parses with the three α parses: [d–l] = {.ŧ́., .□ŧ́., .tŧ̂.} × {.ɑ́., .□ɑ́., .αɑ̂.}. (Actually, one of these bisyllabic candidates [k] involves two adjacent epentheses, already ruled out as legal epenthesis sites (145); we have included [k] in order to exhibit the Cartesian product structure of the bisyllabic candidate set.)

One of these candidates has already been implicitly compared to .tɑ́. in the process of deriving the Possible Peak Condition [3] which, by hypothesis, holds of α. The condition [3] was derived as necessary to ensure that a parse ---ɑ́--- is more Harmonic than the alternative ---□.αɑ̂--- (233). A special case of this com-parison is that of [a] to [l]. Thus [3] by construction entails (as we shortly verify) that [a] > [l].

Similarly, since *t* is assumed to be a possible onset, it must meet the conditions [1] and [2] necessary of all possible onsets. So the Harmony comparisons used to derive [1] and [2] have also implicitly been assumed to favor parsing *t* as an onset. Those comparisons were of ---.t--- to ---.□ŧ́.□--- and to ---.ŧ́.---. Thus since *t* satisfies [1] and [2], it will follow that [a] is more harmonic than [h] and [d].

Unfortunately this still leaves eight competitors left to check, and we must resort to examination of the table of marks. It will only be necessary to discuss a few of the cases. The procedure illustrates a general technique, the *Method of Universal Tableaux*, which is useful in other applications. This method relies on the following lemma concerning HOF, derived below in the Appendix:

(238)   **Cancellation/Domination Lemma**
   Suppose two parses B and C do not incur identical sets of marks. Then B > C iff every mark incurred by B which is not cancelled by a mark of C is dominated by an uncancelled mark of C.

For the case at hand, this idea should be intuitively clear. We want to show that B = [a] is more harmonic than each of the competitors C in the set [b–l]. [a] incurs two marks, *M/*t* and *P/*α. If a competitor C's marks include neither of [a]'s, then in order to show that [a] is more harmonic than C, we must show that each of [a]'s marks is dominated by one of C's marks: this is both necessary and sufficient for showing that among the marks of [a] and C, the worst mark is incurred by C, and that therefore [a] is more harmonic. If one of [a]'s marks is shared by C, we can exploit the Cancellation Lemma and cancel this shared mark from both [a] and C, and then show that the remaining mark of [a] is dominated by a remaining mark of C. If both of [a]'s marks are shared by C, then both cancel, and if C has any other marks at all, it is less harmonic than [a].

In other words, what we need to show is that for any competitor C, the mark *M/t of [a] is either *cancelled* by the same mark in C or *dominated* by other uncancelled marks of C; and similarly for [a]'s second mark *P/α. Pursuant to this strategy, the Universal Tableau (237) is annotated according to the method for handling each of [a]'s two marks. In the *M/t column for a given competitor C is an annotation indicating whether this mark of [a] is cancelled or dominated by a mark of C. We will have demonstrated that [a] is optimal if we can place an appropriate annotation in both the *M/t and *P/α columns of every competitor.

The annotation scheme is as follows. If [a]'s mark *M/t is *cancelled*, then it must be shared by C, so a * must occur in the *M/t column of C; we enclose this in brackets [*] to indicate that this mark cancels its counterpart in [a]. If the mark *M/t of [a] is *dominated* by a mark of C, then the *M/t column of C is annotated with the label of a previously established constraint domination condition which demonstrates this domination; in this case, the particular mark(s) of C which dominate *M/t are annotated with the same label. The labels are: 'MH', Margin Hierarchy (207); 'PH', Peak Hierarchy (204), and '1', '2', '3' for conditions [1], [2], and [3] of (229) and (230). MH and PH hold universally; by hypothesis, [1] and [2] hold of $\tau = t$ and [3] holds of α.

So consider the first competitor, [b]. The table indicates that *M/t is dominated by *M/α in virtue of the Margin Hierarchy; this is the case assuming that $|\alpha| > |t|$, which will hold in general since t is of minimal sonority. (That is, t makes a more harmonic onset than α.) The only exception will be if α also is of minimal sonority (e.g., if $\alpha = t$), in which case the two marks *M/t and *M/α are of equal domination rank and therefore cancel. The table also indicates that *P/α is dominated by *P/t in virtue of the Peak Hierarchy; the same sonority argument applies. (That is, α makes a more harmonic peak than t.) Thus the marks of [a] are dominated by those of [b], unless α happens to be of minimum sonority, in which case both of [a]'s marks are cancelled, which still leaves [b] with the two uncancelled marks *ONS and *–COD. (That is, even if α is of the same minimal sonority as t, the syllable structure of [a] is more harmonic than that of [b].) So for any α, [a] > [b].

In the second competitor, [c], t is parsed as an onset, as in [a], so [a]'s first mark *M/t is cancelled by [c]. [a]'s second mark *P/α is not cancelled, since α is not parsed as a peak in [c]; however, condition [3] of (230) ensures that *P/α is dominated either by *M/α or by *P/$\square$, and these two marks are both incurred by [c]. Therefore the assumption that the constraint hierarchy of the language satisfies [3] for segment α ensures that [a] > [c]. The situation is annotated in row [c] of the universal tableau by putting '3' under *P/α and next to the two marks *P/$\square$ and *M/α of [c] which together ensure by [3] that *P/α is dominated.

We can now revisit the issue of the ordering of the columns in the universal tableau. Consider the annotations in row [b]. The Peak Hierarchy ensures that *P/t dominates *P/α, which is suggested by placing the column *P/t to the left of the column *P/α. (Unless $|\alpha| = |t|$, in which case these columns are really the same.) Similarly for the Margin Hierarchy and the columns for *M/α and *M/t. Note, however, that there is no reason at all to assume that *P/t dominates *M/α; the relative ordering of this pair of columns is not significant. Now consider the annotations in row [c]. Condition [3] says that *either* *P/$\Box$ *or* *M/α dominates *P/α, so that if the columns were ordered for a given language to reflect constraint domination, *at least one* of the columns for the constraints *P/$\Box$ or *M/α would be left of the column for *P/α; but universally we have no right to assume that *both* are. Thus the placement in the universal tableau of both *P/$\Box$ and *M/α left of *P/α must be given this appropriate disjunctive interpretation. And of course, there is no universal significance at all to the relative ordering of the columns *P/$\Box$ and *M/α with respect to each other nor to all the other columns left of *M/t. In effect, the annotations indicate that *M/t and *P/α are dominated in every language by certain of the columns to their left, but beyond that, the order of columns cannot be given a more definite universal interpretation. It is really the constraint domination conditions indicated by the annotations rather than the ordering of the columns in the universal tableau which is critical to assessing the relative harmonies of [a] and its competitors.

We return to the tableau now to consider the remaining, bisyllabic, competitors. Consider [d] = .$\acute{t}.\acute{\alpha}$., for example. Since both [d] and [a] parse α as a peak, their common marks *P/α cancel. The other mark of [a], *M/t, is, according to [1], dominated either by ONS or by *P/t; since both marks *ONS and *P/t are incurred by [d], [1] guarantees that *M/t is dominated. Thus we have annotated the *M/t column of [d] with '1', and used '1' to annotate the relevant pair of [d]'s dominating marks, *ONS and *P/t. We have ordered ONS and *P/t left of *M/t as a mnemonic for [1], which says that one – but not necessarily both – of these constraints must dominate *M/t. Note that the second *ONS is not appealed to in this argument; in general, a second mark in any column of the table is not required to demonstrate the greater Harmony of [a]. Neither is any mark *–COD (which appears at the far right since no domination condition ranks it higher than *M/t or *P/α).

By tracing the role of [1] in showing that [a] > [d], we have verified a claim made a few paragraphs earlier, that the argument we originally used to derive [1] entails [a] > [d] as a special case. The reasoning just followed, however, extends also to cases [e] and [f], for which the earlier argument does not directly apply. As with [d], in [e] the mark *P/α is cancelled and the mark *M/t dominated by virtue of [1]; in [f], *M/t is also dominated via [1], but now *P/α no longer cancels. Instead, it too is dominated, in virtue of [3], which says that *P/α is dominated by either *P/$\Box$ or *M/α.

The Cartesian product structure of the bisyllabic competitor set [d–l], namely

$$\{.\acute{t}., .\Box\acute{t}., .t\hat{\Box}.\} \times \{.\acute{\alpha}., .\Box\acute{\alpha}., .\alpha\hat{\Box}.\}$$

is directly manifest in the *M/t and *P/α columns for these candidates. The mark *M/t incurred by t in [a] is dominated via [1] for .$\acute{t}$., and via [2] for .$\Box\acute{t}$.; it is cancelled for .$t\Box$., which like [a] parses t as a margin. [a]'s other mark *P/α incurred by α is cancelled for both .$\acute{\alpha}$. and .$\Box\acute{\alpha}$., both of which parse α as a peak; *P/α is dominated by [3] in .$\alpha\Box$. These dominations via the conditions [1], [2], and [3] are hardly surprising; as already discussed, these three conditions were derived precisely to ensure just these dominations. What the table and all the arguments behind it show, however, is a conclusion that is new and nonobvious: that these domination conditions – together with the universal Margin and Peak Hierarchies, and the assumption that t and α are respectively a tenable margin and peak, therefore not deletable in /$t\alpha$/ (228) – are also *sufficient* to prove that α is a possible peak. We have thus proved (235).

The proof of (236) proceeds analogously. To show that in a language in which τ satisfies the domination conditions [1] and [2], τ can appear as an onset, we apply the same technique to prove that .$\tau\acute{a}$. is the optimal analysis of the input /τa/. In fact, the same argument goes through exactly as before, with τ replacing t and a replacing α. This is because the properties [1] and [2] which we now hypothesize to hold of τ were in the proof of (236) required to hold of t, which is by assumption a possible onset; similarly, the possible peak a must satisfy the same property [3] that was hypothesized to hold of α in the proof of (235).

8.3   The Typology of Onset, Nucleus, and Coda Inventories

In this section we first derive from the results of §8.2 a typology of onset and peak inventories (§8.3.1), showing explicitly how to extract from the constraint domination hierarchy of a language the values in that language for the parameters π_{Ons} and π_{Nuc} which determine these inventories. We then obtain the corresponding results for codas, and derive an onset/coda licensing asymmetry (§8.3.2). We close the section by returning to Berber to exemplify the results for an actual language (§8.3.3).

8.3.1   The Typology of Onset and Nucleus Inventories

Putting together the results (225, 229–232, 235–236) of the preceding sections, we have the following:

(239)   **Typology of Possible Onsets and Peaks**
   For τ to be a possible onset, it is necessary and sufficient that
   either
      [i] {PARSE, *P/τ} ≫ *M/τ (τ a *willing onset*)
   or
      [ii] {PARSE, ONS, *M/$\Box$} ≫ *M/τ ≫ *P/τ (τ a *coercible onset*).

For α to be a possible peak, it is necessary and sufficient that
either

[iii]   {Parse, *M/α} $\gg$ *P/α (α a *willing peak*)

or

[iv]   {Parse, *P/$\square$} $\gg$ *P/α $\gg$ *M/α (α a *coercible peak*).

The onset conditions [i, ii] are the same as those in (231), except that Parse has been included explicitly to capture the requirement that τ be a tenable margin (225). Similarly for [iii, iv] and (232).

In (239) we have distinguished the possible onsets satisfying each of the mutually exclusive conditions [i] and [ii], calling the former *willing* and the latter *coercible*; willing onsets are margin-preferring tenable margins, while coercible onsets are peak-preferring tenable margins which can be coerced to override their affinity by higher-ranking syllable-structure constraints, Ons and *M/$\square$ = Fill^{Ons}. And analogously for peaks.

We can draw many conclusions from (239). The first concerns affinity (219):

(240)   **Affinity and Possibility**

Suppose λ is a tenable surface segment. Then if λ is margin-preferring, it is a possible onset; if peak-preferring, a possible peak.

This conclusion follows immediately from (239): if λ is margin-preferring, then by definition M/λ > P/λ, i.e., *P/λ $\gg$ *M/λ; if λ is a tenable surface segment, then Parse must dominate either *P/λ or *M/λ, i.e., Parse must dominate the lowest constraint, *M/λ. This establishes [i], so λ is a possible (indeed a willing) onset. And correspondingly if λ is peak-preferring.

Using (239) the segmental inventory in a given language can now be divided into a number of overlapping classes. These are illustrated in the following table, for the case of a language with ambidextrous segments. The horizontal axis is the sonority scale, increasing to the right.

(241)   **Segmental Classes (with Ambidextrous Segments)**

		Increasing Sonority $\rightarrow$		
t	π_{Nuc}	π_{Aff}	π_{Ons}	*a*
$\leftarrow$	willing onsets	$\rightarrow\leftarrow$	willing peaks	$\rightarrow$
	$\leftarrow$ coercible peaks $\rightarrow\leftarrow$ coercible onsets $\rightarrow$			
$\leftarrow$		possible onsets	$\rightarrow$	
	$\leftarrow$	possible peaks		$\rightarrow$
$\leftarrow$ pure onsets $\rightarrow\leftarrow$	ambidextrous segments		$\rightarrow\leftarrow$ pure peaks	$\rightarrow$

This analysis of the segment classes is a direct logical consequence of (239). The reasoning depends on the following results:

(242)   **Segment Classes**
  (a)   A coercible onset is a willing peak; a coercible peak is a willing onset.
  (b)   The set of *ambidextrous segments*, those which are both possible onsets and possible peaks, is the set of coercible segments. Each ambidextrous segment λ satisfies
  $\qquad$ PARSE $\gg$ {*M/λ, *P/λ}.
  (c)   The set of *impossible surface segments*, those which are neither possible onsets nor possible peaks, is the set of untenable surface segments (225), i.e., those λ for which
  $\qquad$ {*M/λ, *P/λ} $\gg$ PARSE.
  (d)   The set of possible onsets, $\{\lambda : |\lambda| \leq \pi_{\mathrm{Ons}}\}$, is the union of the sets of willing and coercible onsets.
  (e)   The set of possible peaks, $\{\lambda : |\lambda| \geq \pi_{\mathrm{Nuc}}\}$, is the union of the sets of willing and coercible peaks.
  (f)   The set of *pure onsets*, those segments which are possible onsets but not possible peaks, is the set of willing onsets minus the set of coercible peaks.
  (g)   The set of *pure peaks*, those segments which are possible peaks but not possible onsets, is the set of willing peaks minus the set of coercible onsets.

These observations are all immediate consequences of (239) and (217).

For example, (242a) follows from (239) since a coercible onset is a segment λ which satisfies [ii] with $\tau = \lambda$, which includes the requirement that

$$\text{PARSE} \gg {}^*\mathrm{M}/\lambda \gg {}^*\mathrm{P}/\lambda;$$

then necessarily [iii] holds with $\alpha = \lambda$, so λ is also a willing peak. The second part of (242a) follows by exactly analogous reasoning.

Then the first part of (242b) follows immediately, since (242a) entails that all coercible segments are ambidextrous (and no segment can be ambidextrous unless it is coercible). The second part of (242b) follows since, from [ii] and [iv] we see that, among other things, a coercible segment λ must satisfy

$$\text{PARSE} \gg \{{}^*\mathrm{M}/\lambda, {}^*\mathrm{P}/\lambda\}.$$

The argument for (242c) is slightly more involved. Suppose λ is an impossible surface segment. Like any segment, λ is either peak-preferring or margin-preferring. Suppose the former:

($\aleph$) ${}^*\mathrm{M}/\lambda \gg {}^*\mathrm{P}/\lambda$.

Then if we had

$$\text{PARSE} \gg {}^*\mathrm{P}/\lambda,$$

λ would be a willing peak; so, since λ is an impossible surface segment, we must have instead

$$*P/\lambda \gg \text{PARSE}.$$

Thus, given ($\aleph$), we must have

$$\{*M/\lambda, *P/\lambda\} \gg \text{PARSE},$$

the desired conclusion. If instead λ is margin-preferring, the same conclusion follows by exchanging M and P in the argument.

The remaining points (242d–g) are obvious, given (242a), and serve only to introduce terminology and reintroduce the parameters π_{Ons} and π_{Nuc} from (217).

The diagram (241) above illustrates a language possessing ambidextrous segments but no impossible surface segments. It turns out that:

(243)   No language can have both ambidextrous and impossible surface segments.

To show this, we derive a contradiction from supposing that a single language has an impossible surface segment λ and an ambidextrous segment α. From (242b), α must satisfy

$$\text{PARSE} \gg \{*M/\alpha, *P/\alpha\}.$$

From (242c), λ must satisfy the opposite domination,

$$\{*M/\lambda, *P/\lambda\} \gg \text{PARSE}.$$

Combining these, we get:

$$\{*M/\lambda, *P/\lambda\} \gg \text{PARSE} \gg \{*M/\alpha, *P/\alpha\}$$

But this contradicts the Peak and Margin Hierarchies (204, 207). For by the Margin Hierarchy,

$$*M/\lambda \gg *M/\alpha \text{ entails } |\lambda| > |\alpha|$$

while by the Peak Hierarchy,

$$*P/\lambda \gg *P/\alpha \text{ entails } |\lambda| < |\alpha|.$$

Statement (243) asserts that languages divide into those with ambidextrous segments, those with impossible surface segments, and those with neither. The diagram corresponding to (241) for a language with impossible surface segments is simpler:

(244)   **Segmental Classes (with Impossible Surface Segments)**

Increasing Sonority →				
t	π_{Ons}	π_{Aff}	π_{Nuc}	a
← willing onsets →			← willing peaks →	
← possible onsets →			← possible peaks →	
← pure onsets →	← impossible surface segments →		← pure peaks →	

In the context of the current Basic Segmental Theory, it is unclear what role could be played in such a language by the impossible surface segments. There seems to be no way to distinguish the case in which such a segment is present in a morpheme – and necessarily left unparsed regardless of what other segments the morpheme may combine with in an input – and the case in which such a segment is simply not present underlyingly, and indeed not part of the segmental inventory of the language. Thus it would appear that there is no need to postulate underlying segments at sonority levels which correspond to impossible surface segments (and indeed the acquisition theory introduced in §9.3 will entail that learners would not posit underlying forms containing such segments). *Henceforth, we will restrict attention to languages without such impossible surface segments.* In theories richer than the Basic Segmental Theory (214), impossible surface segments could of course function in a language: there would need to be additional constraints which are sensitive to such segments even though they are not parsed into syllable structure and not phonetically realized.[67]

Our assumption that the languages under study are all without impossible surface segments has the following consequence:

(א)   PARSE ≫ *M/τ when τ is margin-preferring.

For if not,

(ב)   *M/τ ≫ PARSE

and since τ is margin-preferring,

*P/τ ≫ *M/τ,

---

[67] Such a situation was, in a sense, illustrated in our analysis of Lardil (ch. 7), where the FREE-V constraint asserted that word-final vowels must not be parsed; parsed vowels which are surface-final but followed by unparsed underlying segments do **not** violate this constraint. Thus /wuŋkunuŋ/ ['queen-fish', §7.1 (150a)] surfaces as [wuŋkunu] parsed as .wuŋ.ku.nu⟨ŋ⟩.; the final underlying segment ŋ functions in the language via FREE-V to allow the parsing of the last *u*. The unparsed segment is of course, however, not an impossible type of surface segment; even that particular token of ŋ in fact surfaces in other inflections of the same stem.

and hence

$$\{{}^{*}P/\tau, {}^{*}M/\tau\} \gg \textsc{Parse}.$$

Then τ is an untenable surface segment and by (242c), τ is an impossible surface segment. This contradicts our assumption on the language so (ב) must be incorrect and (א) correct. By exchanging margin and peak, the same argument shows that

(ל) $\textsc{Parse} \gg {}^{*}P/\alpha$ if α is peak-preferring.

Now (א) entails that [i] of (239) holds, so a margin-preferring segment τ is a possible onset. Similarly, (ל) implies [iii] of (239), so a peak-preferring segment α is a possible peak. Thus:

(245)   In a language without impossible surface segments, all margin-preferring segments are possible (hence willing) onsets, and all peak-preferring segments are possible (hence willing) peaks.

This situation is illustrated in (241): recall that the margin-preferring segments are those left of (less sonorous than) π_{Aff}, and the peak-preferring segments are those right of (more sonorous than) π_{Aff}, as seen in (220) and (223).

Using (239) we can now derive explicit expressions for the parameters π_{Ons} and π_{Nuc} which govern the segment classes of (241) and (242). First, define:

(246)   **Critical Constraints**
   $C_{\text{Ons}} \equiv \min\{\textsc{Parse}, \textsc{Ons}, {}^{*}M/\square\}$; $C_{\text{Nuc}} \equiv \min\{\textsc{Parse}, {}^{*}P/\square\}$

That is, in a particular language, C_{Ons} names the least dominant of the three constraints $\textsc{Parse}$, $\textsc{Ons}$, and ${}^{*}M/\square = \textsc{Fill}^{\text{Ons}}$. This is the constraint which, according to (239 [ii]), determines which peak-preferring segments λ are coercible onsets: they are the ones for which $C_{\text{Ons}} \gg {}^{*}M/\lambda$. π_{Ons} is by definition (217) the highest sonority level at which this condition holds. Thus we have:

(247)   **Onset Inventory Parameter Value**
   $\pi_{\text{Ons}} = \max_{\lambda}\{|\lambda| : C_{\text{Ons}} \gg {}^{*}M/\lambda\}$

That is, the value of the parameter π_{Ons} in a given language is the sonority value of the most sonorous segment λ for which ${}^{*}M/\lambda$ is dominated by C_{Ons}. For segments α more sonorous than this, parsing the segment as an onset incurs a worse mark (${}^{*}M/\alpha$) than the mark (${}^{*}\textsc{Parse}$, or ${}^{*}\textsc{Ons}$, or ${}^{*}M/\square$) which would be incurred by some alternative in which α is not parsed as an onset (as the analysis of §8.2 has shown).

By exactly analogous reasoning,

(248)   **Nucleus Inventory Parameter Value**
   $\pi_{\text{Nuc}} = \min_{\lambda}\{|\lambda| : C_{\text{Nuc}} \gg {}^{*}P/\lambda\}$

That is, π_{Nuc} is the sonority value of the least sonorous segment λ for which $*P/\lambda$ is dominated by C_{Nuc}.

We can illustrate how the ordering of constraints in a particular hypothetical language sets these parameters by showing how to go from (222) to (241) via (223), (247), and (248). (In §8.3.3 we consider an actual language, Berber.)

(249)   **Deriving Segmental Class Parameters π_{Nuc} and π_{Ons}:** An Example

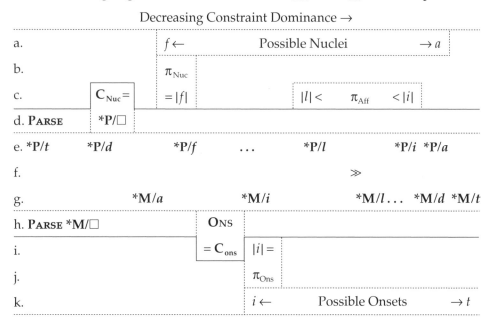

Decreasing Constraint Dominance →

a. $f \leftarrow$ Possible Nuclei $\rightarrow a$

b. π_{Nuc}

c. $C_{\mathrm{Nuc}}=$ $=|f|$ $|l| <$ π_{Aff} $< |i|$

d. **PARSE** $*P/\square$

e. $*P/t$ $*P/d$ $*P/f$ . . . $*P/l$ $*P/i$ $*P/a$

f. $\gg$

g. $*M/a$ $*M/i$ $*M/l$ . . . $*M/d$ $*M/t$

h. **PARSE** $*M/\square$ **ONS**

i. $= C_{\mathrm{ons}}$ $|i| =$

j. π_{Ons}

k. $i \leftarrow$ Possible Onsets $\rightarrow t$

In (249), constraints are indicated in boldface in rows c–i, between the solid lines. They are arranged, as usual, with the most dominant constraints to the left. (Note that, unlike (241), the horizontal axis shows constraint domination and not sonority.) This is an example of a particular language, so the constraints form a strict domination hierarchy. For clarity, we have vertically separated the constraints into the rows c–i, but they are nonetheless strictly ranked left-to-right. Rows e–g are a copy of (222); we have suppressed the explicit domination symbols '$\gg$' except in row f, which shows the cross-over point in the domination hierarchy (as in diagram (222)). To the left of this point are the constraints $*P/\tau$ which dominate their counterparts $*M/\tau$; these are the margin-preferring segments. In the example illustrated here, this cross-over point occurs between the sonority levels $|l|$ of the most sonorous margin-preferring segments, and $|i|$ of the least sonorous peak-preferring segments. As indicated in line c, this cross-over point on the sonority scale is the affinity parameter π_{Aff} (223).

To determine the sonority values of the other two parameters π_{Nuc} (248) and π_{Ons} (247), we need first to identify the critical constraints C_{Nuc} and C_{Ons} (246). The constraints relevant to identifying C_{Nuc} are shown on line d; the least dominant one in this example is $*P/\square$, which has therefore been identified in line c as C_{Nuc}. According to (248), the value of π_{Nuc} is the lowest sonority value $|\lambda|$ of those segments λ for which $C_{Nuc} \gg$ *P$/\lambda$; this value is $|f|$ here, so lines b–c indicate that in this language $\pi_{Nuc} = |f|$. That is, all segments at least as sonorous as f are possible nuclei (217); this is noted in line a.

Analogously, the constraints relevant to determining C_{Ons} are shown in line h (one of them, Parse, was also shown in line d). The lowest ranking is $C_{Ons} = $ Ons, as noted in line i. Then (247) tells us that the value of π_{Ons} is the sonority value $|\lambda|$ of the most sonorous segment λ for which $C_{Ons} \gg$ *M$/\lambda$; in this example, this value is $|i|$, as noted in lines i–j. That is, as noted in line k, all segments at most as sonorous as i are possible onsets (217).

Note that for reading off the possible nuclei, we consult the constraints *P$/\lambda$, which are arrayed in order of *increasing* sonority (line e), following the Peak Hierarchy (204), while for identifying the possible onsets, we examine the constraints *M$/\lambda$, arrayed with *decreasing* sonority (line g), as demanded by the Margin Hierarchy (207). Hence the opposite segment ordering indicated in lines a and k.

In this example, the ambidextrous segments are those λ with sonority values at least $|f|$ and at most $|i|$; these are segments for which *P$/\lambda$ finds itself to the right of C_{Nuc} *and* *M$/\lambda$ falls to the right of C_{Ons}. The set of ambidextrous segments is not directly evident in the diagram (249), but rather inferred as the intersection of the nucleus inventory displayed in line a and the onset inventory identified in line k.

8.3.2   Onset/Coda Licensing Asymmetries

In this section, we derive necessary and sufficient conditions for a segment to be a possible coda. The analysis takes the form of a high-speed recapitulation of the methods applied earlier to onsets and nuclei. Once the conditions for possible codas are in hand, we can extract the typological consequences, including a licensing asymmetry.

In order for a language to permit any codas at all, we must have

(250)   **Codas Allowed**
   {Parse, *P$/\square$} $\gg$ −Cod

as in the Coda Theorem (138), p. 114, of CV Theory. We will re-derive this condition for the present Segmental Theory in the course of establishing the following result:

(251)   **Necessary Condition for Possible Codas**
   If τ is a possible coda, then it must meet conditions [i] or [ii] for possible onsets (239). *In addition*, **either**
      [v]   {Ons, *M$/\square$} $\gg$ −Cod
   or
      [vi]   *P$/\tau \gg$ −Cod
   must hold as well.

To see this, consider any input containing τ the optimal parse of which is a structure O in which τ is parsed as a coda. Such a structure can be represented ---$\acute{\alpha}\tau$.--- since a coda is necessarily preceded by a nucleus. (Any unparsed segments that may intervene between α and τ can be ignored.) This structure O must be more harmonic than all its competitors, including the four shown below:

(252) **Marks for Cod/τ and Competitors**

O:	---$\acute{\alpha}\tau$.---	*–Cod, *M/τ
C_1:	---$\acute{\alpha}\langle\tau\rangle$.---	*Parse
C_2:	---$\acute{\alpha}.\tau\hat{\square}$.---	*M/τ, *P/$\square$
C_3:	---$\acute{\alpha}.\hat{\tau}$.---	*Ons, *P/τ
C_4:	---$\acute{\alpha}.\square\hat{\tau}$.---	*M/$\square$, *P/τ

Each competitor C_i is identical to the parse O except in how τ is parsed. As in the corresponding analyses for nuclei (233) and onsets (234), we have ignored in (252) all the marks incurred by O and C_1–C_4 except those directly incurred by τ, since these other marks all cancel in comparing O to each competitor (216).

According to the Cancellation/Domination Lemma, (192) and (238), if O is to be optimal, each of O's two marks *–Cod and *M/τ must be cancelled or dominated by the marks incurred by each of these competitors. Thus, considering C_1, since *M/τ is not cancelled, it must be dominated:

(א) Parse $\gg$ *M/τ

i.e., τ must be a tenable margin. Also *–Cod must be dominated, so we must have

(ב) Parse $\gg$ –Cod,

as claimed above in (250). Considering next C_2, since the marks *M/τ cancel, we deduce that O's mark *–Cod must be dominated by C_2's remaining mark:

(ג) *P/$\square$ $\gg$ –Cod.

(ב) and (ג) re-derive (250).

Next we consider the competitors C_3 and C_4, which cancel neither of O's marks. In order for O's mark *M/τ to be cancelled in these two cases, we must have, for C_3:

(ד) *P/τ $\gg$ *M/τ **or**   Ons $\gg$ *M/τ

and, for C_4:

(ה) *P/τ $\gg$ *M/τ **or**   *M/$\square$ $\gg$ *M/τ

In other words, (including PARSE from (ℵ)) **either**:

[i]   {PARSE, *P/τ} ≫ *M/τ

(in which case the common left half of (ר) and (ה) holds), **or**

[ii]   {PARSE, ONS, *M/□} ≫ *M/τ

(in which case the right halves of (ר) and (ה) hold). These necessary conditions [i, ii] for a possible coda are identical to the conditions for a possible onset (239). So we have established the first part of the Necessary Condition for Possible Codas (251).

But O incurs another mark, *–COD, which also must be dominated in C_3 and C_4. The conditions are the same as for *M/τ, which is now simply replaced by *–COD: 'either [i] or [ii]' becomes (omitting PARSE now, since it is already covered by (250))

either
    [vi]   *P/τ ≫ –COD
or
    [v]   {ONS, *M/□} ≫ –COD.

Condition [v] does not refer to the segment τ; it is a condition on the ranking of the Basic Syllable Structure Constraints in the domination hierarchy of a language which may or may not be satisfied. It is completely independent of the condition (250) which admits codas into the language. It says that the language's aversion to codas (–COD) is less strong than its aversion to onsetless syllables (ONS) and unfilled margins (*M/□):

(253)   A language satisfying (251 [v]):
            {ONS, *M/□} ≫ –COD
        is said to be **weakly coda averse.**

In languages which are *not* weakly coda averse, the segment-specific condition [vi] must hold of τ for it to be a possible coda. In weakly coda averse languages, on the other hand, the Necessary Condition for Possible Codas (251) reduces to just the condition for possible onsets.

This establishes (251). The idea at the core of this argument is very simple: associating a segment τ to a Cod node incurs the same mark *M/τ as associating it to an Ons node, and *in addition* the mark *–COD. The asymmetry in the Basic Syllable Structure Constraints between the Ons (114) and Cod (115) nodes entails that the Cod association is inherently more marked than the Ons association. Therefore additional domination conditions must be met for the association Cod/τ to be optimal, above and beyond those conditions necessary for Ons/τ to be optimal. These additional conditions can, as we will soon see, exclude certain possible onsets from the coda inventory, in languages where the mark *–CoD is sufficiently dominant, i.e., in languages which are not weakly coda averse.

An immediate corollary of (251) is:

(254) **Possible Coda ⇒ Possible Onset**
      If τ is a possible coda, then it is a possible onset.

Next we show:

(255) **Sufficient Conditions for Possible Codas**
      The conditions of (251) are sufficient for τ to be a possible coda (in a language permitting codas).

To see this, consider the input /taτ/; we show that the conditions of (251) entail that the optimal analysis is .táτ., in which τ is parsed as a coda. This conclusion follows from the following lemma:

(256) **Lemma**
      The initial substring /ta/ of /ta---/ is parsed as .tá⋯.

      Proof
      .tá. is an optimal syllable (128) which violates no Basic Syllable Structure Constraints; its only marks are the associational ones *M/t and *P/a. The presence of the following '---' in the input does not afford opportunities to eliminate any syllable structure constraint violations in .tá., since there aren't any; alternative parses can only introduce new such violations, while possibly trading the marks *M/t and *P/a for alternative associational marks (if t and a are reassigned to different syllable positions). But we already know that all of these alternatives generate marks which dominate those of .tá., for this was established by the argument based on the universal tableau (237). This investigation of /tα/ showed that, assuming t to be a possible onset and α to be a possible nucleus, the marks incurred by .t$\acute{\alpha}$. are dominated by those incurred by all its competitors. Thus if we reiterated all those competitors, with $\alpha = a$, combining them in all possible ways with the possible analyses of '---', to form the universal tableau for /ta---/, we would simply end up showing that the marks incurred by t and a in any structure of the form .tá⋯. are dominated by the marks they incur in any of the competing analyses that parse the initial substring /ta/ differently.

From this lemma we see that the only competitors to the analyis O = .táτ. that we need consider are those of the form .tá⋯, with '⋯' denoting all possible parses of τ. But this is exactly the set of competitors considered in (252), where the pre-τ segment denoted '---$\acute{\alpha}$' in (252) is taken to be '.tá' and the post-τ segment denoted '---' in (252) is taken to be empty. The necessary conditions of (251) were just those needed to ensure that O was indeed more harmonic than its four competitors in (252). Thus these necessary conditions are also sufficient.

The Necessary (251) and Sufficient (255) Conditions for Possible Codas entail:

(257)   **Possible Coda Parameter**
  The possible codas are those segments with sonority value less than or equal to a cut-off parameter π_{Cod}:
  $$\text{PossCod} = \{\tau : |\tau| \leq \pi_{\text{Cod}}\}.$$
  In a weakly coda averse language, the value of π_{Cod} is given by:
  $$\pi_{\text{Cod}} = \pi_{\text{Ons}};$$
  otherwise,
  $$\pi_{\text{Cod}} = \min\{\pi_{\text{Ons}}, \max_\lambda\{|\lambda| : {}^*\text{P}/\lambda \gg -\text{Cod}\}\}.$$

For (251) says that if [v] holds, then the conditions on a possible coda are exactly the same as on a possible onset, so PossCod = PossOns, and the parameters characterizing the two segmental classes have the same value. So assume the language is not weakly coda averse, i.e., that [v] does not hold. Then a possible coda τ must be a possible onset, but in addition, [vi] must hold:

[vi] ${}^*\text{P}/\tau \gg -\text{Cod}.$

Note that if this condition [vi] is satisfied for any segment τ, it is also satisfied by any less sonorous segment λ, for the Peak Hierarchy (204) ensures that

$${}^*\text{P}/\lambda \gg {}^*\text{P}/\tau \gg -\text{Cod}.$$

Thus in order for τ to be a possible coda, its sonority value $|\tau|$ must be less than or equal to that of the most sonorous segment λ for which

$${}^*\text{P}/\lambda \gg -\text{Cod},$$

as well as being less than the maximum sonority value π_{Ons} of possible onsets. This is just what the last line of (257) says.
  Now (257) establishes:

(258)   **Onset/Coda Licensing Asymmetry**
  There are languages in which some possible onsets are not possible codas, but no languages in which some possible codas are not possible onsets.

The second half of this asymmetry was already established in (254). The first half follows from (257), which asserts that the most sonorous possible onsets λ will not be possible codas in any language which is not weakly coda averse and in which

$$-\text{Cod} \gg {}^*\text{P}/\lambda.$$

Since there are no universal principles violated in such languages, they are indeed possible according to the Basic Segmental Syllable Theory (214). Tableau (259) illustrates a language in which *d* but not *i* is a possible coda, while both are possible onsets.

(259) **Example Tableau for a Language in which Codas License Fewer Segments than Onsets**

	PARSE	*M/□	*P/d	*P/□	–COD	ONS	*M/i	*P/i	*M/d
/tad/ →									
☞ .tád.					*				*
.tá.d□́.				* !					*
.tá.d́.			* !			*			
.tá.□d́.		* !		*					
.tá.⟨d⟩	* !								
/tai/ →									
.tái.					* !		*		
.tá.i□́.				* !			*		
☞ .tá.í.						*		*	
.tá.□í.		* !						*	
.tá.⟨i⟩	* !								
/ia/ →									
☞ .iá.							*		
.í.á.						* ! *	*		
.□í.□á.		* ! *					*		
.⟨i⟩á.	* !					*			

In this tableau, we have omitted the marks incurred by *t* and *a*. By (256), for the two inputs of the form /taλ/, we need only consider candidate parses beginning .tá···., and in all these candidates the marks for *tá* cancel. For /ia/, it follows that the optimal parse is .iá. by the proof (at the very end of §8.2.6: p. 177) of (236), in which /τa/ was shown to be parsed as .ƭá. whenever τ satisfies the Possible Onset Conditions; these are satisfied for τ = *i* because (231 [ii]) holds by inspection of (259):

{ONS, *M/□} ≫ *M/*i* ≫ *P/*i*

is satisfied for $\tau = i$. In (259) we show some competitors simply for illustration. Since all these competitors also parse a as a peak, we can omit the cancelling marks *M/a.

This tableau (259) illustrates that d is a possible coda (/tad/ → .tád.), and while i is a possible onset (in /ia/ → .iá.), it is not a possible coda (/tai/ → .tá.í.).

This same example of a language in which codas license fewer segments than onsets is analyzed more completely in the following diagram (260), which shows the crucial ranking dependencies. Here the example illustrated in (249) has been extended to show the possible codas, delimited by π_{Cod}. The possible nuclei shown in (249) have been omitted here, but the possible onsets have been retained for comparison with the possible codas.

(260) **Deriving the Possible Coda Parameter π_{Cod}: An Example**

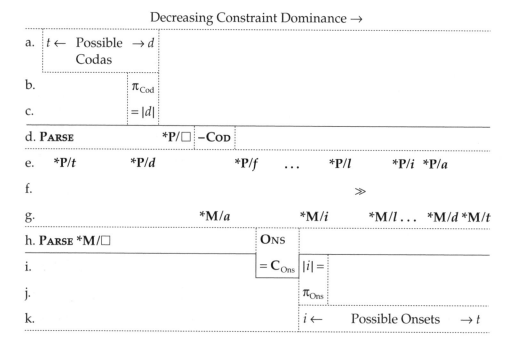

Lines e–k of (260) are identical to lines e–k of (249). In line d, we have shown that –Cod is lower-ranked than Parse and *P/□, as required by (250) in order than any codas be possible. The ranking of –Cod relative to the associational constraints *P/□ and *M/□ now determines π_{Cod} (257). We must first find the most sonorous segment λ for which *P/λ ≫ –Cod; this is d. We must then set π_{Cod} equal to the lower of the sonority values $|d|$ and $\pi_{Ons} = |i|$; so $\pi_{Cod} = |d|$, as noted in lines b–c. This means that all segments at most as sonorous as $|d|$ are possible codas (257), as noted in line a. Here we see an example where codas are more restricted than onsets, comparing lines a and k. As in (249), however, the figure is potentially a bit confusing because the direction of the sonority scales in lines a and k is reversed. This arises for the same reason here as it did in (249); like nuclei, the possible codas are determined (in part) by the locations of the constraints *P/λ, while the possible onsets are determined only by the locations of the constraints *M/λ. The figure does not explicitly show that a possible coda is necessarily a possible onset.

In this example, the segments with sonority levels higher than $\pi_{Cod} = |d|$ but not higher than $\pi_{Ons} = |i|$ are possible onsets but not possible codas. These same segments are also possible nuclei (249). Indeed this is always the case:

(261) **PossOns – PossCod ⊂ PossNuc**
In a language with some possible codas, if λ is a possible onset but not a possible coda, then λ must also be a possible nucleus.

Proof
The language must not be weakly coda averse, for if it were, all possible onsets would be possible codas (257), and no such λ would exist. Given that the language is not weakly coda averse, and that λ is a possible onset, λ must fail to be a possible coda in virtue of failing to satisfy condition (251 [vi]); i.e., we must have:
   –Cod ≫ *P/λ.
Since codas are possible in the language, by (250) we must in addition have
   {Parse, *P/□} ≫ –Cod ≫ *P/λ.
This implies that λ satisfies the Possible Peak Condition (230 [3]):
   *P/□ or *M/λ ≫ *P/λ
and that λ is a tenable peak (225):
   Parse ≫ *P/λ;
these two properties mean that λ satisfies the Possible Peak Sufficient Condition (235).

There are two aspects of our onset/coda licensing asymmetry which must be distinguished. On the one hand, from the fact that –Cod asserts that Cod is a marked structural position, we derive the fact that universally, inventories of codas are more restricted than those of onsets. The structural markedness of Cod entails that it is a weak licenser.

On the other hand, there is the particular nature of the relative restrictiveness of codas *vis-à-vis* sonority: that of the onset inventory the portion admitted into the coda inventory are the *least* sonorous segments. This is empirically unsatisfactory in that the most harmonic codas are generally regarded to be those which are *most* sonorous (Prince 1983, Zec 1988, 1994, Clements 1990). This inadequacy can be traced to the fact that we have treated codas and onsets identically as 'margins', in contrast with peaks. This is a reasonable first step beyond the CV theory, of course, since codas and margins are both 'C' positions in contrast to the 'V' position of peaks. On the other hand, refinements of this first step are clearly desirable. We have captured the commonality of coda and onset, but have ignored the fact that compared to the onset, the coda position is more structurally close to the peak: perhaps in the sense that both comprise the rime, or in that both are moraic.

So a refinement of the account presented above which immediately suggests itself is the following. If a segment λ is parsed in onset position, it incurs the associational mark *M/λ; if in peak position, *P/λ; if in coda position, *both* *M/λ and *P/λ: the former because the coda is a margin position, the second because it is moraic (or in the rime). This refinement captures the relationship of coda to both onset and to nucleus.

The way these relationships are captured, however, makes the coda position symmetrically related to both onset and nucleus, going too far in the direction of respecting the coda/nucleus relationship. For if the kind of analysis we have presented in this section is repeated with this new approach, the conclusion turns out to be that a possible coda must be an ambidextrous segment. This result is not surprising given that the marks a segment incurs when parsed as a coda include as a proper subset the marks it would incur as either an onset or a nucleus. And this result succeeds in shifting the coda inventory from the least to the most sonorous portion of the onset inventory – but overenthusiastically, including only those onsets which are so sonorous as to be themselves possible nuclei.

And assigning two marks {*M/λ, *P/λ} to Cod/λ while only one mark to either Ons/λ and Nuc/λ makes the coda position inherently more marked than the other positions, above and beyond the structural mark *–Cod which is the sole source of the greater markedness of Cod in the approach developed above. There are several related alternatives which assign two marks to *all* syllable positions, the simplest of which assigns {*M/λ, *P/λ} to Cod/λ, {*P/λ, *P/λ} to Nuc/λ, and {*M/λ, *M/λ} to Ons/λ. A somewhat more complex approach introduces a separate Rime Hierarchy of constraints *R/λ which is aligned with sonority like the Peak Hierarchy (more sonorous segments making more harmonic rimes); in such an account, Cod/λ incurs {*M/λ, *R/λ}; Nuc/λ incurs {*P/λ, *R/λ}, and Ons/λ {*M/λ, *M/λ}. This last approach breaks the symmetry of the relations between Cod and Nuc on the one hand and Cod and Ons on the other, a symmetry afflicting the previous alternatives. And this has the consequence that possible codas are necessarily possible onsets but not necessarily possible nuclei.

The merits of these more complex approaches relative to each other and to the simplest account developed in this section are largely yet to be explored. One conclusion, however, should be clear. The basic result at the core of the onset/coda licensing asymmetry which comes out of Optimality Theory is that the structural markedness of Cod entails that it is a weak licenser. The particular *nature* of the restrictions applying to codas, however, depends on details of the treatment of codas which are yet to be seriously explored; in this section, we have examined only the very simplest of possibilities.

8.3.3 An Example: Berber, Take 2

We now illustrate the Basic Segmental Theory (214) by applying our results to the analysis of Berber. We repeat for convenience our previously determined constraint hierarchy (200):

(262) **Berber Hierarchy**
{Ons, Parse, *P/□, *M/a} ≫ *M/□ ≫ Hnuc ≫ –Cod

First, from (262) we see that Berber is weakly coda averse (253):

{Ons, *M/□} ≫ –Cod.

Thus the possible codas are the same as the possible onsets; we can refer to them simply as the possible margins. The hypothetical example illustrated in (249) can be modified to accommodate the domination hierarchy (200) of Berber. We also modify it to reflect the fact that in Berber, all segments are possible peaks and all segments except a are possible margins:

(263) **Determining Parameters for Berber**
Decreasing Constraint Dominance →

a.	$t \leftarrow$	Possible Nuclei	$\rightarrow a$
b.	π_{Nuc}		
c. $\mathbf{C_{Nuc}}$ =	= |t|		
d. {**Parse, *P/□**}			
e.	*P/t	⋯	*P/a
f.		??	
g.	*M/a	*M/i ⋯	*M/t
h. {**Parse, Ons**}	*M/□		
i.	= $\mathbf{C_{Ons}}$	|i| =	
j.	π_{Ons}		
k.	$i \leftarrow$	Possible Margins	$\rightarrow t$

The relative ranking of the associational constraints {*P/t, ⋯, *P/a} and {*M/i, ⋯, *M/t} need to be determined by considering the Dell–Elmedlaoui algorithm, which resolves in a certain way the inherent conflict between trying to maximize nuclear vs. marginal Harmony, or, to minimize nuclear vs. marginal markedness. Consider the following hypothetical inputs:

(264) **Berber Peak and Margin Hierarchies**

	*M/f	*M/d	*M/t	*P/t	*P/d	*P/f
/tkt/ →						
☞ .t̑.kt̑.			[*]	{*} *		
.tkt̑.			[*] * !	{*}		
/fdt/ →						
☞ .f̑.dt̑.		*		*		*
.fdt̑.	* !		*		*	

The Dell–Elmedlaoui algorithm gives .f̑.kt̑. as the correct parse of /tkt/. It is instructive to compare this correct parse to the competitor .tkt̑., shown in the tableau (264). This tableau shows the relevant portions of the Peak (204) and Margin (207) Hierarchies; at this point we do not know how these rank relative to one another. Comparing these two alternative parses, we have cancelled a matching pair of *M/t marks, enclosed in square brackets, and a pair of *P/t marks enclosed in curly brackets. The two remaining marks are *P/t for the correct parse and *M/t for the incorrect parse (remembering that since |k| = |t|, k is treated like t by the constraints of both hierarchies). That is, since all sonority values are equal, the correct parse has one more peak (incurring *P/t) and the incorrect parse one more margin (earning *M/t). In order that the correct parse (the one with more peaks) be the more harmonic, we must have *M/t ≫ *P/t. Since *M/t is the bottom of the Margin Hierarchy and *P/t the top of the Peak Hierarchy, this entails that the entire Margin Hierarchy must be ranked higher than the entire Peak Hierarchy.

The second example illustrated in (264) is perhaps clearer. The least harmonic peak in the correct parse of /fdt/, t̑, is less harmonic than the least harmonic peak in the incorrect parse, d̑. Thus if the Peak Hierarchy were dominant, the incorrect parse would be chosen, in order to avoid the least harmonic peak. The correct result does, however, arise by placing the Margin Hierarchy above the Peak Hierarchy: for the least harmonic margin in the incorrect parse, f, is less harmonic than the least harmonic margin in the correct parse, d.

As pointed out in fn. 10 of chapter 2, p. 20, and briefly mentioned in §8.1.2, there are two equivalent harmonic ways of viewing the Dell–Elmedlaoui algorithm. The simplest is as a procedure which scans unsyllabified material in a string for the most harmonic nucleus, and makes it the nucleus of a new syllable. The other is as a procedure which scans for the least harmonic potential margin, and it makes the nucleus of a new syllable.

The operations performed under either description are identical. While the first formulation has the virtue of simplicity, it has a decided disadvantage as far as the current enterprise is concerned: it evaluates (nuclei) from most to least harmonic. As long as this is confined within a single constraint HNUC, this falls within the purview of Optimality Theory (as formally explained in §5.2.1.2).

But in chapter 8 the work done within the single constraint Hnuc is now distributed over multiple constraints in the Peak and Margin Hierarchies. The marks assessed by these constraints are scattered across the columns of constraint tableaux, and these marks operate in harmonic evaluation from worst to best, i.e., from those incurred by the least harmonic structures first. The 'worst first' aspect of harmonic evaluation concords with the second formulation of the Dell–Elmedlaoui algorithm, which scans for the least harmonic potential margin and parses it as a nucleus. This is a consequence of the fact derived through (264), that the Margin Hierarchy dominates the Peak Hierarchy in Berber. In the example of /fdt/ (264), the most sonorous segment f controls the parsing by means of the highest-ranked (relevant) margin constraint *M/f, which must be satisfied if at all possible, and not by the lowest-ranked (relevant) peak constraint *P/f.

Another way of seeing why the Dell–Elmedlaoui algorithm in effect places the Margin Hierarchy higher than the Peak Hierarchy can be understood through the notion of affinity introduced earlier. Since the entire Margin Hierarchy outranks the entire Peak Hierarchy, we have for *every* segment λ that:

$$*M/\lambda \gg *P/\lambda,$$

i.e., that

$$P/\lambda > M/\lambda.$$

That is, *every segment is peak-preferring*: most harmonic when parsed as a nucleus. For the Dell–Elmedlaoui algorithm descends the *entire* sonority hierarchy, preferring to construct (the most harmonic possible) peaks, being undeterred even by voiceless stops. As long as this does not prevent (via other constraints such as Ons) a more sonorous segment from being parsed as a nucleus, even ts will be parsed as peaks rather than margins.[68]

So what aspects of the Dell–Elmedlaoui algorithm are explained by the Optimality-theoretic treatment of Berber? We have seen how the algorithm is a result of the operation of the Peak and Margin Hierarchies, when the Margin Hierarchy is dominant. Our analysis would also permit a language (Berber') in which the Peak Hierarchy dominated the Margin Hierarchy. In Berber', the winners and losers in (264) are exchanged: the parsing is driven to avoid the least harmonic peaks, thereby getting the most harmonic margins, rather than the other way around, as in Berber. The variant of the Dell–Elmedlaoui algorithm which implements syllabification in Berber' scans the sonority hierarchy from least to most sonorous, at each stage constructing a new syllable in which the least-sonorous possible segment is parsed as a margin.

---

[68] In fact, as pointed out in §2.1, we are abstracting away from certain complications which are not handled by the Dell–Elmedlaoui algorithm, including effects which Dell and Elmedlaoui treat with subsequent desyllabification rules operating at word boundaries. It may well be possible to incorporate such additional complexities into the present account via constraints which are sensitive to boundaries, and perhaps by reconsidering whether the Margin Hierarchy *completely* dominates the Peak Hierarchy (that is, whether even the obstruents are all peak-preferring).

At the level of individual syllables Berber and Berber' involve the same notion of syllabic well-formedness: minimum-sonority margins, maximum-sonority peaks. They differ only in multisyllabic comparisons, minimal cases of which are illustrated in (264). In multisyllabic parses, conflicts can arise between optimizing the nuclear Harmony of one syllable and optimizing the marginal Harmony of an adjacent syllable; Berber and Berber' differ in whether the former or the latter has priority. And since harmonic ordering works by filtering out constraint violators starting with the worst, the Berber priority on optimizing nuclear Harmony is achieved by filtering out first those parses in which the most harmonic potential nuclei have been parsed as margins, that is, those with the least harmonic margins. In Berber, the Margin Hierarchy dominates, giving rise to multisyllabic parses in which optimizing nuclear Harmony has higher priority than optimizing marginal Harmony. The reverse is true in Berber'. But both Berber and Berber' share the universal Harmony scales determining what constitutes a more harmonic nucleus or a more harmonic margin.

What is important to note is that our theory completely rules out syllabification systems which construct syllables with minimum-sonority nuclei or maximum-sonority margins. Such systems would arise from a variant of the Dell–Elmedlaoui algorithm in which the sonority scale was descended from top to bottom, and at each stage the most sonorous available segment was parsed as a margin. Or a variant in which the sonority scale was mounted from bottom to top, the least sonorous available segment being parsed as a nucleus. Such syllabification systems ruled out by our theory correspond to harmonic syllable systems in which the Peak Hierarchy is inverted (*P/a ≫ ⋯ ≫ *P/t) and likewise for the Margin Hierarchy. In other words, our theory universally restricts the ranking of constraints within the Peak sub-Hierarchy which determine the relative Harmony of different nuclei, and similarly for margins. What it leaves open for cross-linguistic variation is the way the Peak and Margin Hierarchies rank relative to each other. If the entire Margin Hierarchy dominates the entire Peak Hierarchy, all segments are peak-preferring and we get Berber; the other way around, and we get Berber'. As the analysis in this chapter has shown, if the two hierarchies intersect, we get more typical syllabic systems in which some number of the more sonorous segments can be peaks, and some number of the less sonorous can be margins.

We can now return to the overall analysis of Berber which helped motivate the Segmental Theory in the first place. The Berber constraint hierarchy (262) can now be given as:

(265)   **Berber**
{ONS, PARSE, *P/□, *M/a} ≫ *M/□ ≫ [*M/i ≫ ⋯ ≫ *M/t]
≫ {−COD, [*P/t ≫ ⋯ ≫ *P/a]}

The constraint 'HNUC' of (200) has been replaced by the lower portion of the Margin Hierarchy [*M/i ≫ ⋯ ≫ *M/t], and the Peak Hierarchy [*P/t ≫ ⋯ ≫ *P/a] has been ranked beneath the Margin Hierarchy. The relative ranking of −COD and the Peak Hierarchy appears to have no empirical consequences, so we leave this ranking unspecified.

As a simple illustration of (265), the following tableau shows one hypothetical example:

(266) **Berber**

/iun/ →	Ons, Parse, *P/□	*M/a	*M/□	*M/i	*M/n	*M/t	–Cod	*P/t	*P/n	*P/i	*P/a
☞ .í.uń.				*					*	*	
.iún.				*	*!		*			*	
.í.□ún.		*!			*		*			**	
.iú.n□.	*!			*	*					*	

In this tableau, we have abbreviated the sonority hierarchy to $a > \{i, u\} > n > t$ and considered a hypothetical input which involves only these segments. (Recall that *M/i refers to high vowels, encompassing both i and u.) We have arbitrarily positioned –Cod left of the Peak Hierarchy, suggesting this arbitrariness by using a dotted line to separate them. The dashed lines are only used to help bind together the adjacent portions of the Margin and Peak Hierarchies, in anticipation of the next development.

8.4 Simplifying the Theory by Encapsulating Constraint Packages

8.4.1 Encapsulating the Association Hierarchies

The typology of segment classes we have developed, illustrated in the diagrams (249) and (260), suggests that we may reduce the number of constraints, and enhance the interpretability of the analysis, by encapsulating portions of the Peak and Margin Hierarchies into the following derived (parametrized) constraints:

(267) **Poss-Nuc(π_{Nuc})**
    Interpretation: Segments with sonority less than π_{Nuc} may not be parsed as peaks.
    Abbreviates: [*P/t ≫ ⋯ ≫ *P/τ], where τ is the most sonorous segment with $|\tau| < \pi_{Nuc}$.
    Ranking: Above C_{Nuc}. Hence, unviolated.

(268) **Poss-Mar(π_{Ons})**
    Interpretation: Segments with sonority greater than π_{Ons} may not be parsed as margins.
    Abbreviates: [*M/a ≫ ⋯ ≫ *M/α] where α is the least sonorous segment with $|\alpha| > \pi_{Ons}$.
    Ranking: Above C_{Ons}. Hence, unviolated.

(269)   **Poss-Cod(π_{Cod})**

 Interpretation: Segments with sonority greater than π_{Cod} may not be parsed
  as codas.[69]

 Ranking: Sufficiently high to be unviolated.

(270)   ***P**

 Interpretation: The lower $|\lambda|$, the more marked the association P/λ.

 Abbreviates: [*P/$\zeta \gg \cdots \gg$ *P/a], where $|\zeta| = \pi_{Nuc}$.

 Ranking: Below C_{Nuc}.

(271)   ***M**

 Interpretation: The higher $|\lambda|$, the more marked the association M/λ.

 Abbreviates: [*M/$\rho \gg \cdots \gg$ *M/t], where $|\rho| = \pi_{Ons}$.

 Ranking: Below C_{Ons}.

Together with the Basic Syllable Structure Constraints (114–120), these constraints
define the **Encapsulated Segmental Syllable Theory.** We discuss them in turn.

  The constraints Poss-Nuc and Poss-Mar are unviolated by construction. Poss-
Nuc and Poss-Mar each encapsulates by definition exactly those associational
constraints *P/λ or *M/λ which we have through rather extensive analysis shown
to be unviolated in all outputs. They also both encapsulate just those associational
constraints which dominate what we have shown to be a critical constraint (246):
either C_{Ons} (the lowest-ranked of Parse, Ons, and *M/$\square$) or C_{Nuc} (the lowest-
ranked of Parse and *P/$\square$). Thus the positions of Poss-Nuc and Poss-Mar in
the constraint hierarchy must reflect this, and the restrictions on the allowed
rankings of these constraints are noted in (267) and (268). That the derived constraint Poss-X (X = Nuc or Mar) dominates the corresponding Basic Syllable
Structure Constraint C_X is sufficient (as our analysis has shown) to ensure that it
is unviolated, and so it does not matter *where* each is ranked above C_X.

  It is clear that Poss-Nuc and Poss-Mar constitute a reconstruction within the
Basic Segmental Syllable Theory (214) of the analogs of the two universally high-
ranked constraints of the Basic CV Syllable Theory (123):

*P/C: C may not be parsed as a peak (122), and

*M/V: V may not be parsed as a margin (121).

  The constraint Poss-Cod is less directly constructed. In languages without
onset/coda licensing asymmetries, where $\pi_{Cod} = \pi_{Ons}$, such a constraint is not
needed; Poss-Mar suffices to block illegal associations to both Ons and Cod. So
consider a language in which there is a segment λ which is a possible onset but
not a possible coda ($\pi_{Cod} < \pi_{Ons}$). Associations Cod/λ must be blocked, but not by
blocking M/λ, since Ons/λ is legal. The arrangement of Basic Segmental Syllable

---

[69] The discussion at the end of §8.3.2 introduces several possible refinements of the account of
codas developed here. All these refinements have as a consequence that the coda inventory is
governed by *two* parameters ranging over the sonority scale: a lower limit as well as an upper
limit.

Theory constraints that conspires to block Cod/λ is more spread out than that which blocks Ons/α for an illegal onset α (simply, *M/$\lambda \gg$ C$_{\text{Ons}}$). Included is the requirement (257) that $-$Cod $\gg$ *P/λ, but neither $-$Cod nor *P/λ can be absorbed into a derived constraint Poss-Cod. We therefore simply define Poss-Cod by its interpretation in (269), without reducing its definition to an abbreviation of associational constraints. We also simply assert that it must be sufficiently highly ranked to be unviolated, without stating precisely what constitutes a high enough ranking to ensure this.

The constraints *P and *M encapsulate the lower portions of the Peak and Margin Hierarchies, respectively: the portions remaining after the highest parts have been incorporated into the Poss-Nuc and Poss-Mar constraints. As discussed in §8.3.3 in the context of Berber, the constraint *P constitutes a reconstruction of Hnuc, but with a subtle change: *P evaluates marks from worst to best, whereas Hnuc evaluates marks from best to worst. (This difference among constraints was discussed formally at the end of §5.2.1.2 in terms of the order in which constraints list the marks incurred by entire parses.) Like Hnuc, the constraints *P and *M are non-binary, and their use in ranking competing structures is a bit more complex than with the binary constraints they encapsulate. Remembering that they are mere abbreviations for portions of the Peak and Margin Hierarchies, respectively, it is clear that to use them in a constraint tableau, under *P one lists all the marks *P/λ incurred by a candidate, starting from the worst. Then to compare two candidates' violations of *P, we tick off their respective marks *P/λ starting from the worst. When the two candidates share a particular mark *P/λ, that mark cancels. As soon as one candidate reaches a mark that is not cancelled by the other, the candidate with the worst mark loses. We illustrate with our canonical example.

8.4.2   An Example: Berber, Take 3

Using the encapsulated constraints, we can re-write the Berber constraint domination hierarchy (265) as follows:

(272)   **Berber**
      {Ons, Parse, *P/$\square$, Poss-Mar} $\gg$ *M/$\square \gg$ *M $\gg$ {$-$Cod, *P}

Poss-Cod is unnecessary, merely repeating Poss-Mar, since there is no onset/ coda licensing asymmetry. Poss-Mar is simply *M/a, since in Berber only a is not a possible margin. Note that Poss-Mar is indeed ranked higher than C$_{\text{Ons}} \equiv$ min{Parse, Ons, *M/$\square$} = *M/$\square$ in Berber, as required by (268). *M encapsulates all the Margin Hierarchy except *M/a = Poss-Mar, and, as required by (271), *M ranks lower than C$_{\text{Ons}}$. Since all segments are possible nuclei in Berber, Poss-Nuc vanishes, and *P is the entire Peak Hierarchy. As required by (270), *P ranks lower than C$_{\text{Nuc}} \equiv$ min{Parse, *P/$\square$} in Berber.

We illustrate this encapsulated account of the Berber analysis (272) by showing the resulting tableau which encapsulates (266):

(273) **Berber**

/iun/ →	ONS, PARSE, *P/□	POSS-MAR *M/a	*M/□	*M/i	*M/n	*M/t	−COD	*P/t	*P/n	*P/i	*P/a
☞ .í.uń.			*i						*n	*i	
.iún.				*i	*n !		*			*i	
.í.□ún.		* !			*n		*			*i *i	
.iú.n□.	* !			*i	*n					*i	

8.4.3 Sufficiency and Richness of the Encapsulated Theory

In the preceding analysis of Berber, the Encapsulated Segmental Syllable Theory was sufficient to re-express the earlier Basic Segmental Syllable Theory analysis. This is because it was not necessary to insert additional constraints into the midst of the portions of the Peak and Margin Hierarchies that are encapsulated by *P and *M. How generally this will turn out to be the case is an open question. There seems to be no obvious principle that would prevent such intrusions of additional constraints.

It is also somewhat unclear whether the Encapsulated Theory has sufficient expressive power to cover all analyses possible within the Basic Segmental Syllable Theory. For example, if *P and *M are ranked as wholes one above the other, as required by the Encapsulated Theory, this does not permit expression of the general patterns of interdigitating the Peak and Margin Hierarchies which are possible with the Basic Theory. We are no longer free, for example, to independently manipulate the parameter π_{Aff} which determines the sonority value separating peak- from margin-preferring segments.

It is, however, not clear whether this limitation reduces the languages which can be analyzed. We do know that some languages analyzable within the Basic Theory require −COD to be inserted within the constraints encapsulated by *P. Consider a language which allows:

$\{t, \cdots, i\}$ as onsets,
only $\{t, d\}$ as codas, and
$\{d, \cdots, a\}$ as peaks.

This possibility would be illustrated by (249) and (260), if in (249) *P/d were down-ranked slightly, below C_{Nuc} = *P/□. Encapsulating this analysis,

Poss-Nuc ≡ *P/t,

since t is the only impossible nucleus. Thus

$$^*P \equiv [^*P/d \gg {}^*P/f \gg \cdots \gg {}^*P/a].$$

But in order that d but not f be a possible coda, while both are possible onsets, we must have, by the Possible Coda Parameter expression (257):

$$^*P/d \gg -\text{Cod} \gg {}^*P/f.$$

So $-\text{Cod}$ must insert itself into the constraints encapsulated by $^*P$ in order to separate the legal from illegal codas.

However, this language *does* seem to be analyzable in the Encapsulated Theory, even though $-\text{Cod}$ cannot be inserted into $^*P$ now treated as a single constraint. This is achieved simply by setting $\pi_{\text{Cod}} = |d|$ in Poss-Cod.

Yet even if the Encapsulated Theory does turn out to offer less generality of analysis than the Basic Theory with its full hierarchies of associational constraints, it appears to be worthwhile determining whether analysis within the Encapsulated Theory is possible before resorting to the more complex Basic Theory. The general conception of constraint encapsulation can be applied in other ways than in (267)–(271), and other modes of encapsulation may be appropriate under certain ranking conditions.

Were it not for the influence of our primary example, Berber, where Hnuc has been the driving force for our analysis, one might have been tempted to try a more Boolean encapsulation strategy. The segmental inventory having been divided into the classes (242), we might try to simply define constraints that rule out all impossible associations, and leave it at that. Aside from the role of sonority in separating the classes of possible nuclei, possible onsets, and possible codas from one another, sonority would then play no role *within* the classes themselves. This would amount to adopting the parametrized high-ranking (unviolated) constraints Poss-Nuc, Poss-Mar, and Poss-Cod, but omitting the constraints $^*P$ and $^*M$ which serve to distinguish the relative Harmonies of possible associations. In such a theory, all the segments within a given class would be distributionally equivalent.

It is worth emphasizing that this alternative Boolean encapsulation would fail rather seriously to do justice to the Basic Segmental Syllable Theory. We have of course seen many examples of the role of sonority in governing syllabification within the large class of ambidextrous segments in Berber. Indeed, the following example shows that, at least in languages that permit codas, Berber-like syllabification is universal within the class of ambidextrous segments:

(274) **Sonority is Operative within the Class of Ambidextrous Segments**
   $/\text{tat}\lambda_1\lambda_2/ \rightarrow$

.tá.t $\hat{\lambda}_1\lambda_2$.	$^*P/\lambda_1$, $^*M/\lambda_2$
.tát.$\lambda_1\hat{\lambda}_2$.	$^*M/\lambda_1$, $^*P/\lambda_2$

Here λ_1 and λ_2 are two ambidextrous segments: possible nuclei, margins, and codas. By (256) we know that the initial /ta/ is parsed .tá. The question is whether the segments $\lambda_1\lambda_2$ will be parsed as the rime of a closed syllable starting with t, or as an open syllable, leaving the second t to close the first syllable. The marks incurred by λ_1 and λ_2 are shown in (274). Clearly, if $|\lambda_1| > |\lambda_2|$, then both the marks $*P/\lambda_1$ and $*M/\lambda_2$ of the first parse are dominated by the marks of the second, thanks to the Peak (204) and Margin (207) Hierarchies. For in this case λ_1 is a more harmonic peak *and* λ_2 is a more harmonic margin. If, on the other hand, $|\lambda_1| < |\lambda_2|$, then the reverse holds and the second parse is the optimal one. Thus within the ambidextrous segments, sonority operates within syllabification to find the optimal nuclei, as in Berber.

To see how sonority differences affect syllabification even within the classes of pure onsets and pure peaks, consider a deletion language, one where {Ons, $*M/\square = \text{Fill}^{\text{Ons}}$, $*P/\square = \text{Fill}^{\text{Nuc}}$} $\gg$ Parse. First suppose τ_1 and τ_2 are pure onsets: they are possible onsets but not possible peaks. Consider the following example:

(275)   **Sonority is Operative within the Class of Pure Onsets**

$$/\tau_1\tau_2 a/ \rightarrow$$

$$.\langle\tau_1\rangle\tau_2\acute{a}. \quad *M/\tau_2$$

$$.\tau_1\langle\tau_2\rangle\acute{a}. \quad *M/\tau_1$$

Since we are in a deletion language, the preferred outcome here involves deletion. The question is, which consonant will be deleted? If τ_1 is deleted, the onset incurs the mark $*M/\tau_2$; and likewise with 1 and 2 interchanged. The least marked onset will contain the least sonorous segment, so the more sonorous segment is the one to delete. Thus sonority differences within the class of pure consonants are operative in syllabification.

The parallel example for pure peaks α_1 and α_2 is:

(276)   **Sonority is Operative within the Class of Pure Peaks**

$$/t\alpha_1\alpha_2/ \rightarrow$$

$$.t\langle\alpha_1\rangle\acute{\alpha}_2. \quad *P/\alpha_2$$

$$.t\acute{\alpha}_1\langle\alpha_2\rangle. \quad *P/\alpha_1$$

Here, it is the *least* sonorous segment that deletes, to create the most harmonic nucleus.

Part III

Issues and Answers in Optimality Theory

Overview of Part III

Here we examine basic properties of Optimality Theory and its relation to other grammatical architectures.

We begin by showing, in chapter 9, how language-particular inventories are obtained in a theory where constraints and possible inputs are both entirely universal. Structures which never appear in optimal outputs are absolutely un-grammatical: inventories are therefore defined by the *outputs* of grammars. Cross-linguistic variation in inventories arises from differences in constraint ranking, which induce variation in patterns of optimal outputs, even given the same set of inputs.

- In this situation, standard considerations of theory construction dictate that the set of grammatical inputs be assumed universal, avoiding the need for further machinery to limit inputs. This is the principle of *Richness of the Base*.
- Without phoneme lists, underlying feature-combination filters, or morpheme structure constraints, the raw material that goes into the grammar (the set of possible inputs) is the same in all languages, and any apparent lexical regu-larities (among the set of actual lexical forms) are emergent con-sequences of the grammar. *Lexicon Optimization* entails that the limitations imposed by a grammar on its outputs casts a shadow back onto the lexicon.
- A central desirable result in inventory structure is *Harmonic Completeness*: if a structure is admitted by a grammar, then so are all other structures that are more harmonic – less marked – along a certain dimension. This property, when present, yields the implicational-universal characterization of markedness: if a language admits a more marked element, it will also admit a less marked element.
- Applying these ideas, chapter 9 derives a portion of the consonantal inven-tory of Yidin^y. A theory of coronal unmarkedness instantiates the general notion of a universal markedness constraint hierarchy. Formal tools for analyzing language-particular and universal inventories are brought into

play, including the method of *harmonic bounding* introduced in §6.2.3: a structure can be proved ungrammatical by showing that any output that contains it is less harmonic than some identifiable competing output, not itself necessarily optimal.

Chapter 10 situates Optimality Theory within the larger linguistic and computational landscape. Qualms about optimization are dismissed, as is the naive equation of grammar with computation. We identify some fundamental affinities and divergences between Optimality Theory and Connectionist (or 'neural network') architectures for optimization, which also embody systems of violable constraints. By comparative analysis of particular phonological examples, hierarchies of violable constraints are contrasted with various proposals for imposing (inviolable) constraints on re-write rule systems: Harmonic Phonology, Persistent Rule theory, and the Theory of Constraints and Repair Strategies. A general pattern is identified by which these 'Phonotactics + Repair' theories relate to Optimality Theory.

The distinctive conception of constraint conflict in Optimality Theory, inherently tied to violability of constraints, is contrasted with notions of conflict arising within systems of rules plus constraints. Given constraint violability, a theory with a single, uniform mechanism – ranking – avoids the unresolved conceptual and formal difficulties arising when inviolable constraints are grafted onto rule systems; at the same time, it becomes possible to include markedness centrally within the universal principles from which all grammars are directly constructed.

Chapter 9

Inventory Theory and
the Lexicon

All grammatical constraints are violable, in principle. A constraint such as Ons, 'syllables have onsets', in and of itself and prior to its interaction with other constraints, does not assert that syllables lacking onsets are impossible, but rather that they are simply less harmonic than competitors possessing onsets. Its function is to sort a candidate set by measuring adherence to (equivalently: divergence from) a formal criterion. Constraints therefore define relative rather than absolute conditions of ill-formedness, and it may not be immediately obvious how the theory can account for the absolute impossibility of certain structures, either within a given language or universally. Yet in the course of the preceding analyses we have seen many examples of how Optimality Theory explains language-particular and universal limits to the possible. In this section, we identify the general explanatory strategy that these examples instantiate, and briefly illustrate how this strategy can be applied to explaining segmental inventories. We then consider implications for the lexicon, proposing a general induction principle which entails that the structure of the constraints in a language's grammar is strongly reflected in the content of its lexicon. This principle, Lexicon Optimization, asserts that when a learner must choose among candidate underlying forms which are equivalent in that they all produce the same phonetic output and in that they all subserve the morphophonemic relations of the language equally well, the underlying form chosen is the one whose output parse is most harmonic.

9.1 Language-Particular Inventories

We begin by examining a simple argument which illustrates the central challenge of accounting for absolute ill-formedness in a theory of relative well-formedness:

For Optimality Theory, syllables without onsets are not absolutely ill-formed, but only relatively. The syllable .VC. (for example) is *more* ill-formed than the syllable

.CV., but .VC. is not *absolutely* ill-formed. How can Optimality Theory bar .VC. from any language's syllable inventory?

What Optimality Theory would need in order to outlaw such syllables is some additional mechanism, like a *threshold* on ill-formedness, so that when the graded ill-formedness of syllables passes this threshold, the degree of ill-formedness becomes absolutely unacceptable.

The fallacy buried in this argument has two facets: a failure to distinguish the inputs from the outputs of the grammar, coupled with an inappropriate model of grammar in which the ill-formed are those *inputs* which are rejected by the grammar. In Optimality Theory, the job of the grammar is not to accept or reject *inputs*, but rather to assign the best possible structure to every input. The place to look for a definition of ill-formedness is in the set of *outputs* of the grammar. These outputs are, by definition, well-formed; so what is ill-formed – absolutely ill-formed – is any structure which is never found among the outputs of the grammar. To say that .VC. syllables are not part of the inventory of a given language is not to say that the grammar rejects /VC/ and the like as input, but rather that no *output* of the grammar ever contains .VC. syllables.

We record this observation in the following remark:

(277)   **Absolute Ill-Formedness**

A structure φ is (absolutely) ill-formed with respect to a given grammar iff there is no input which when given to the grammar leads to an output that contains φ.

Note further that in a demonstration that .VC. syllables are ill-formed according to a given grammar, the input /VC/ has no *a priori* distinguished status. We need to consider every possible input in order to see whether its output parse contains a syllable .VC. Of course, /VC/ is a promising place to start the search for an input which would lead to such a parse, but, before concluding that .VC. syllables are barred by the grammar, we must consider all other inputs as well. Perhaps the optimal parse of /C/ will turn out to be .□C., providing the elusive .VC. syllable. It may well be possible to show that if *any* input leads to .VC. syllables, then /VC/ will – but in the end such an argument needs to be made.

If indeed .VC. syllables are ill-formed according to a given grammar, then the input /VC/ must receive a parse other than the perfectly faithful one: .VC. At least one of the Faithfulness constraints PARSE and FILL must be violated in the optimal parse. We can therefore generally distinguish two paths that the grammar can follow in order to parse such problematic inputs: violation of PARSE, or violation of FILL. The former we have called 'underparsing' the input, and in some other accounts would correspond to a 'deletion repair strategy'; the latter, overparsing, corresponds to an 'epenthesis repair strategy'. (In §10.3 we explicitly compare Optimality Theory to some repair theories.) These two means by which a grammar may deal with problematic inputs were explicitly explored in the Basic CV Syllable Structure Theory of chapter 6. There we found that .VC. syllables were barred by either

1 requiring onsets: ranking either Parse or Fill^{Ons} lower than Ons; or

2 forbidding codas: ranking either Parse or Fill^{Nuc} lower than −Cod.

One particularly aggressive instantiation of the underparsing strategy occurs when the optimal structure assigned by a grammar to an input is the *null* structure: no structure at all. This input is then grammatically completely unrealizable, as discussed in §4.3.1. There is some subtlety to be reckoned with here, which turns on what kinds of structure are asserted to be absent in the null output. In one sense, the *null* means 'lacking in realized phonological content', with maximal violation of Parse, a possibility that can hardly be avoided in the candidate set if underparsing is admitted at all. In another sense, the null form will fail to provide the morphological structure required for syntactic and semantic interpretation, violating M-Parse. To achieve full explicitness, the second move requires further development of the morphological apparatus; the first requires analogous care in formulating the phonetic interpretation function, which will be undefined in the face of completely unparsed phonological material. In this discussion, we will gloss over such matters, focusing on the broader architectural issues.

It would be a conceptual misstep to characterize null parsing as *rejection of the input* and to appeal to such rejection as the basis of a theory of absolute ill-formedness. For example, it would be wrong to assert that a given grammar prohibits .VC. syllables because the input /VC/ is assigned the null structure; this is a good hint that the grammar may bar .VC. syllables, but what needs to be demonstrated is that *no* input leads to such syllables. In addition, a grammar which assigns some non-null structure to /VC/, for example .□V.⟨C⟩, might nonetheless prohibit .VC. syllables.

Subject to these caveats, it is clear that assigning null structure to an input is one means a grammar may use to prevent certain structures from appearing in the output. The Null Parse is a possible candidate which must always be considered and which may well be optimal for certain particularly problematic inputs. We have already seen two types of examples where null structures can be optimal. The first example emerged in the analysis of the Latin minimal word phenomenon in §4.3.1, where, given a certain interpretation of the data, under the pressure of FtBin and Lx≈Pr, the optimal parse of the monomoraic input is null (but see Mester 1992, as 1994: 20–3). The second was in the CV Syllable Structure Theory of chapter 6, where it was shown that the structure assigned to /V/ is null in any language requiring onsets and enforcing Ons by underparsing: that is, where Parse is the least significant violation, with {Ons, Fill^{Ons}} ≫ Parse; as in ex. (134), p. 113.

9.1.1 Harmonic Bounding and Nucleus, Syllable, and Word Inventories

Absolute ill-formedness, explicated in (277), is an emergent property of the interactions in a grammar. Showing that a structure φ is ill-formed in a given language requires examination of the system. One useful strategy of proof is to proceed as follows. First we let A denote an arbitrary candidate parse which contains the (undesirable) structure φ. Then we show how to modify *any such analysis* A to produce a particular (better) competing candidate parse B of the same input, where B does not contain φ and where B is provably more harmonic than A. This is sufficient to establish that no structure containing φ can ever be optimal. The structure φ can never occur in any output of the grammar, and is thus absolutely ill-formed. We have called this method of proof 'Harmonic Bounding' – it establishes that every parse containing the structure φ is bettered by, bounded above by, one that lacks φ.

The strategy of Harmonic Bounding was implicitly involved, for example, in the analysis of the minimal word phenomenon (§4.3.1). In this case, the impossible structure is φ = [μ]$_{PrWd}$. We examined the most important type of input, a monomoraic one like /re/, and showed that the analysis containing φ, A = [[ré]$_F$]$_{PrWd}$, is less harmonic than a competitor B = ⟨re⟩, the Null Parse, which lacks φ. The method of constructing B from A is simply to replace structure with no structure.

To complete the demonstration that the Latin constraint hierarchy allows no monomoraic words in the output, we must consider every input that could give rise to a monomoraic word. We need to examine inputs with less than one mora, showing that they do not get overparsed as a single empty mora: [[□̂$_μ$]$_F$]$_{PrWd}$. We also must consider inputs of *more than one* mora, showing that these do not get underparsed, with only one mora being parsed into the PrWd: [[μ]$_F$]$_{PrWd}$⟨μ···⟩. Both of these are also harmonically bounded by the Null Parse of the relevant inputs. On top of whatever violation marks are earned by complete structuring of monomoraic input – marks that are already sufficient to establish the superiority of the Null Parse – these moraic over- and underparses incur *FILL and *PARSE marks as well, and it is even clearer that a monomoraic parse cannot be optimal.

Similarly, in the analysis of Lardil in chapter 7, we provided the core of the explanation for why no words in its inventory can be monomoraic. The result is the same as in Latin, but enforcement of Lx≈Pr and FtBin for monomoraic inputs is now by *over*parsing rather than by *under*parsing, due to differences in the constraint ranking. The structure we wish to exclude is again φ = [μ]$_{PrWd}$, and, as in Latin, we examined monomoraic inputs such as /maɻ/ (182), p. 141, to see if their parses contained φ. In each case, the optimal parse is a bisyllabic competitor B with an unfilled second mora. We also examined vowel-final *bimoraic* inputs (184), p. 146, because, for longer inputs, a final vowel is optimally *un*parsed, a pattern which would lead to monomoraicity if universally applied. However, both moras in bimoraic inputs must be parsed, so again we fail to produce a monomoraic output. Inputs with three or more moras leave a final vowel unparsed, but parse all the others (183), p. 143. Thus, there are no inputs, long or short, which produce monomoraic outputs.

It is worth emphasizing that, even though the lack of monomoraic words in the Latin and Lardil inventories is a result of the high ranking of Lx≈Pr and FtBin in the domination hierarchy, it would be distinctly incorrect to summarize the Optimality Theory explanation as follows: "Lx≈Pr and FtBin are superordinate therefore unviolated, so any monomoraic input is thereby rendered absolutely ill-formed." An accurate summary is: "Lx≈Pr and FtBin dominate a

FAITHFULNESS constraint (PARSE in Latin; FILL in Lardil), so for *any input at all* – including segmentally monomoraic strings as a special case – monomoraic parses are always less harmonic than available alternative analyses (Null Parse for Latin, bisyllable for Lardil); therefore outputs are never monomoraic."

Successful use of the Harmonic Bounding argument does not require having the optimal candidate in hand; to establish *φ in the absolute sense, it is sufficient to show that there is always a B-without-φ that is better than any A-with-φ. Whether any such B is optimal is another question entirely. This can be seen clearly in the kind of argument pursued repeatedly above in the development of the Basic Segmental Syllable Theory in chapter 8. For example, as part of the process of deriving the typology of segmental inventories licensed by various syllable positions, we showed that the inventory of possible nuclei could not include a segment α in any language in which $*P/\alpha \gg \{\text{FILL}^{\text{Nuc}}, *M/\alpha\}$).[70] These are languages in which it is

1   more important to keep α out of the Nucleus (P = 'peak') than to fill the Nucleus, and
2   more important to keep α out of the Nucleus than to keep it out of the syllable margins.

The φ we want to see eliminated is the substructure Nuc/α, in which the segment α is dominated by the node Nucleus. Let A denote an arbitrary parse containing Nuc/α = $\acute{\alpha}$, so that a segment α appearing in the input string is parsed as a nucleus: A = ~$\acute{\alpha}$~. The bounding competitor B is identical to A except that the structure in question, Nuc/α, has been replaced by the string in which α is an onset sandwiched between two empty nuclei: B = ~□.α□~. In terms of the slash-for-domination notation, the crucial replacement pattern relating A to B can be shown as

A = . . . Nuc/α . . .   B = . . . Nuc/□. Ons/α Nuc/□. . . . .

We have then the following argument:

(278)   **Harmonic Bounding Argument** showing α is an impossible nucleus
    a.   Assumed constraint ranking
        $*P/\alpha \gg \{\text{FILL}^{\text{Nuc}}, *M/\alpha\}$

    b.   Structures
        i.   φ = $\acute{\alpha}$ (segment α *qua* nucleus)
        ii. A = ~ $\acute{\alpha}$ ~   (any parse taking α to be a nucleus)
        iii. B = ~ □.α□ ~ (analysis A modified in a specific way to make α nonnuclear)

    c.   Argument: show that B bests A.

---

[70] Here, $*M/\alpha$ and $*P/\alpha$ are the constraints against parsing α as a Margin (Onset, Coda) and as a Peak (Nucleus), respectively; this is the contrapositive of the Possible Peak Condition (230).

It should be clear that B is always more harmonic than A in the given languages. The mark *P/α incurred by nucleizing α in A is worse than both the marks *M/α (for marginalizing α) and *F$_{\text{ILL}}$^{Nuc} (for positing empty nuclei) that are incurred by B. Hence, in such a grammar the optimal parse can never include $\varphi = \text{Nuc}/\alpha$, no matter what the input. The conclusion is that α is not in the inventory of possible nuclei for these languages. However, we cannot conclude that every occurrence of α is in onset position, as in the bounding analysis B, or indeed, without further argument, that *any* occurrence of α is in onset position. There may be other analyses that are even more harmonic than B in specific cases; but we are assured that α will never be a nucleus in any of these. (In fact, under certain rankings consistent with (278a) α will be banned from the surface altogether, barred from the onset as well as the nucleus, as an 'untenable association', (225), p. 168.)

The Harmonic Bounding strategy is explicitly carried out for syllable inventories in the CV theory in the Appendix, and is implicitly involved in a number of other results derived above. Samek-Lodovici (1992a) makes independent use of the same method of proof (taking B to be a kind of Null Parse) to establish the validity of his Optimality-theoretic analysis of morphological gemination processes.

9.1.2   Segmental Inventories

Having illustrated the way prosodic inventories are delimited, from the structural level of the syllable position (e.g. Nuc) up through the syllable itself to the word, we can readily show how the technique extends downward to the level of the segment. Now we take as inputs not strings of already formed segments, but rather strings of feature sets. These must be optimally parsed into segments by the grammar, just as (and at the same time as) these segments must be parsed into higher levels of phonological structure. The segmental inventory of a language is the set of segments found among the optimal *output parses* for all possible inputs.

We now illustrate this idea by analyzing one particular facet of the segmental inventory of Yidin^{y} (Kirchner 1992b). Our scope will be limited: the interested reader should examine the more comprehensive analysis of the Yidin^{y} inventory developed in Kirchner's work, which adopts the general Optimality Theory approach to inventories, but pursues different analytic strategies from the ones explored here.

The consonant inventory of Yidin^{y} looks like this:

Labial	Coronal	Retroflex coronal	Palatalized coronal	Velar
b	d		d^{y}	g
m	n		n^{y}	ŋ
	l			
	r	ɽ		

Here [r] is a "trilled apical rhotic" and [ɹ] an "apical postalveolar (retroflex) rhotic continuant," according to Dixon (1977: 32).

Complex articulations are found only at coronal place of articulation; this is the generalization we wish to derive. The complexities include palatalization in [dʸ, nʸ] and the retroflexion in [ɹ]. (A similar but more articulated system is found in Lardil; see (148), §7.1, p. 121.) We propose to analyze the normal and palatalized coronals as follows, along lines developed in Clements 1976, 1991 and Hume 1992. On this view, the PLACE node in segment-internal structure may dominate a C-Place node, which holds the primary place of articulation for a consonant; or a V-Place node, which holds the place of articulation for a vowel; or both, in which case the V-Place node expresses the secondary place of articulation of the consonant.

(279)   **Representation of Coronals**

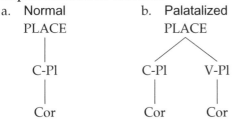

    a.   Normal   b.   Palatalized

In line with the findings of Gnanadesikan 1992 and Goodman 1993, we hold that retroflexion is dorsalization rather than coronalization (as it is in Kirchner 1992b). Among the complex segments, to focus the discussion, we will deal only with the palatalized ('coronalized') coronals (279b). As a compact representation of these structures, we will use bracketing to denote the structure of the Place node, according to the following scheme:

(280)   **Bracketing Notation for Place Geometry**
    a.   [α]   'feature α occupies C-Place, there is no V-Place' node
    b.   [α β]   'feature α occupies C-Place and feature β occupies V-Place'

With this notation, structure (279a) is denoted by [Cor] and structure (279b) by [Cor Cor].

In this representational system, the palatalized coronals are literally *complex*, with two places of articulation, while the other, unmarked, coronals are literally simple. The generalization is now clear: of all the possible structurally complex places, only one is admitted into the Yidinʸ lexicon: the one in which the primary and secondary places are both Cor – generally held to be the unmarked place of articulation (Avery & Rice 1989, and see especially the papers in Paradis & Prunet 1991, reviewed in McCarthy & Taub 1992).

Informally speaking, two generalizations are involved:

(281)   **Coronal Unmarkedness (Observation)**
    "Don't have a place of articulation other than Coronal."

(282)   **Noncomplexity (Observation)**
"Don't have structurally complex places of articulation."

Our goal is to analyze the interaction between coronal unmarkedness and complexity markedness. This is of particular interest because it exemplifies a common pattern of interaction: each constraint is individually violated, but no form is admitted which violates both of them at once. There are consonants with single Labial or Velar specifications, violating coronal unmarkedness, and there are consonants with two place specifications, violating noncomplexity. But no consonant with any noncoronal place feature has a complex specification. We dub this generalization pattern *banning the worst of the worst*.

The worst-of-the-worst interaction is absent in the Basic CV Syllable Structure Theory. The two dimensions of well-formedness there – Onset well-formedness (more harmonic when present) and Coda well-formedness (more harmonic when absent) – operate independently. Requiring Onset, prohibiting Coda will generate the entire Jakobson Typology; languages which ban only the worst-of-the-worst do not appear. Such a language would allow onsets to be absent, and codas to be present, but not in the same syllable; its inventory would include CV, V, CVC, but exclude VC. This inventory is not possible according to the Basic CV Syllable Structure Theory, and we know of no reason to believe that this is anything but a desirable result.

The techniques already developed enable a direct account of the interaction between coronality and structural complexity. We assume that the input to the grammar is a string of root nodes each with a set of (unassociated) features. The output is an optimal parse in which these features are associated to root nodes (with the root nodes associated to syllable-position nodes, and so on up the prosodic hierarchy). To minimize distractions, let's assume a universally superordinate constraint requiring root nodes to have a child PL (Place) node. (This parallels the assumption made in chapter 6 that the syllable node always has a child Nuc, due to universal superordinance (123) of the relevant constraint Nuc (119), p. 108.) For the present analysis of consonant inventories, we similarly assume a universally superordinate constraint, or restriction on Gen, to the effect that in consonants the presence of V-Place entails the presence of C-Place. (This head/dependent type of relationship is conveniently encoded in the bracketing notation of (280), because the configuration [α is always interpreted as *α is C-Pl*.)

Our focus will be on which of the place features in an input feature set gets associated to the PL node. As always, unparsed input material is phonetically unrealized; underparsing is therefore a principal means of barring certain feature combinations from the inventory. If certain infelicitous combinations of features should appear in an input feature set, the grammar may simply leave some of them unparsed; the feature combinations which surface phonetically define a segmental inventory from which certain ill-formed feature combinations have been absolutely banned.

In Yidin^y, the feature set {Cor, Cor} gets completely parsed. Both Cor features are associated to the PL node in the optimal parse, and the segment surfaces as

d^y or n^y, depending on which other features are in the set. On the other hand, the set {Lab, Lab} does *not* get completely parsed: the inventory does not include complex labials. In contrast, the unit set {Lab} does get completely parsed; the language has simple labials.

To minimize notation we will deal only with Cor and Lab; any other noncoronal place features receive the same analysis for present purposes as Lab.

Coronal unmarkedness can be formally stated as the following universal Harmony scale:

(283)   **Coronal Unmarkedness: Harmony Scale**
        PL/Cor > PL/Lab

The notation 'PL/Cor' refers to a structural configuration in which PL dominates Cor, understood to be through some intermediate node – either C-Pl or V-Pl. The simplest theory, which we develop here, treats the two intermediate nodes alike for purposes of Harmony evaluation.

Following the same analytic strategy as for Universal Syllable Position/ Segmental Sonority Prominence Alignment (213), chapter 8, p. 162, we convert this Harmony scale to a domination ranking of constraints on associations:

(284)   **Coronal Unmarkedness: Domination Hierarchy**
        *PL/Lab ≫ *PL/Cor

Following the general 'Push/Pull' approach to grammatical parsing summarized in §8.1 (186), the idea here is that all associations are banned, some more than others. The constraint hierarchy (284) literally says that it is a more serious violation to parse labial than to parse coronal. Coronal unmarkedness in general means that to specify PL as coronal is the least offensive violation. The constraint *PL/ Lab is violated whenever Lab is associated to a PL node; this constraint universally dominates the corresponding constraint *PL/Cor because Lab is a less well-formed place than Cor. In addition to these two associational constraints we have the usual Faithfulness constraints PARSE and FILL. They are parametrized by the structural elements they pertain to; in the present context, they take the form:

(285)   **PARSE**[Feat]
        An input feature must be parsed into a root node.

(286)   **FILL**[PL]
        A PL node must not be empty (unassociated to any features).

Just as with the Segmental Syllable Theory, we have a set of deeply conflicting universal constraints: association constraints (*PL/Lab, *PL/Cor), which favor no associations, and Faithfulness constraints which favor associations (PARSE[Feat] from the bottom up, FILL[PL] from the top down). This conflict is resolved differently in different languages by virtue of different domination hierarchies. The four constraints can be ranked in 4! = 24 ways overall; Universal Grammar, in the guise of Coronal Unmarkedness (283), rules out the half of these in which *PL/Lab is ranked below *PL/Cor, leaving 12 possible orderings, of which 8 are distinct. These induce a typology of segment inventories which includes, as we will shortly see, the Yidin^y case.

In languages with a wider variety of complex segments than Yidin^y, we need to distinguish an input which will be parsed as [Cor Vel] – a velarized coronal like [t^y] – from an input which will be parsed as [Vel Cor] – a palatalized velar like [k^y]. (Both these segments occur, for example, in Irish and Russian.) For this purpose we assume that the feature set in the first input is {Cor, Vel'} and in the second, {Cor', Vel}; the notation f' means that the feature f is designated in the feature set as secondary, one which is most harmonically parsed in the secondary place position. That is, we have the constraint:

(287) *[f'
       f' is not parsed as the primary place of articulation (not associated to C-Pl).

Since f and f' designate the same place of articulation, parsing either of them incurs the same mark *PL/f; there are no separate marks *PL/f' because *PL/f refers only to the place of articulation f.

Now we are ready to analyze the interaction between coronal unmarkedness and complexity in Yidin^y. The analysis is laid out for inspection in table (288).

The size of the table gives a misleading impression of intricacy. The idea behind this analysis is quite simple. Association must be forced, since the anti-association constraints *PL/α militate against it. The location of PARSE amid the anti-association constraints marks a kind of cut-off point: those *PL/α below PARSE are overruled and association of their α is compelled; those above PARSE, by contrast, are under no bottom-up pressure to associate. Only the top-down pressure of FILL will compel association – but since violations must be minimal, only minimal association can be forced. Glancing across the top of the tableau, one can see that all Cor's will be forced into association by PARSE, but Lab-association, driven only by FILL, will be minimal.

Here we give the details of the argument just outlined. Since *PL/Lab ≫ PARSE^{Feat}, it is more harmonic to leave Lab features unparsed (incurring *PARSE^{Feat}) than to associate them to PL (incurring *PL/Lab). Thus, *ceteris paribus*, Lab features remain unparsed.

The only reason that Lab nodes are ever parsed at all is to satisfy FILL^{PL}, which dominates *PL/Lab. FILL is exactly the *ceteris* that is not *paribus*. If the only features available in the set are Lab features, then failing to parse all of them would leave PL unfilled, earning a worse mark *FILL^{PL} than is incurred by parsing one of the Lab nodes.

On the other hand, only *one* Lab feature need be parsed to satisfy FILL^{PL}. When two are available, as in (f–h), parsing both would only increase the degree of violation of *PL/Lab. Since violations are minimal, the least concession necessary

(288) **Segmental Inventory**

Input POA's	Candidates	FILL^PL	*PL/Lab	*Parse^Feat	*PL/Cor	*[f'
Coronalized coronal	a. ☞ [Cor Cor']				* *	
	b. [Cor' Cor]				* *	* !
{PL, Cor, Cor'}	c. [Cor] ⟨Cor'⟩			* !	*	
	d. [Cor'] ⟨Cor⟩			* !	*	*
t^y ↣ t^y	e. [ ] ⟨Cor, Cor'⟩	* !		* *		
Labialized labial {PL, Lab, Lab'}	f. [Lab Lab']		* *!			
	g. ☞ [Lab] ⟨Lab'⟩		*		*	
p^w ↣ p	h. [ ] ⟨Lab, Lab'⟩	* !			* *	
Coronalized labial	i. [Lab Cor']		* !		*	
	j. [Lab] ⟨Cor'⟩		* !	*		
{PL, Lab, Cor'}	k. ☞ [Cor'] ⟨Lab⟩			*	*	*
p^y ↣ t	l. [ ] ⟨Lab, Cor'⟩	* !		* *		
Labialized coronal	m. [Cor Lab']		* !		*	
	n. ☞ [Cor] ⟨Lab'⟩			*	*	
{PL, Cor, Lab'}	o. [Lab'] ⟨Cor⟩		* !	*		*
t^w ↣ t	p. [ ] ⟨Cor, Lab'⟩	* !		* *		
Simple coronal {PL, Cor}	q. ☞ [Cor]				*	
t ↣ t	r. [ ] ⟨Cor⟩	* !		*		
Simple labial {PL, Lab}	s. ☞ [Lab]		*			
p ↣ p	t. [ ] ⟨Lab⟩	* !		*		

is made to FILL^PL. If two Labs are available in the set, one of them satisfies its intrinsic tendency to remain unparsed, while the other sacrifices this for the higher goal of ensuring that PL is not completely empty.

The situation is reversed for Cor, however; it is more harmonic to parse these features than to leave them unparsed, because Parse^Feat ≫ *PL/Cor.

As we see from the tableau, the Yidin^y inventory includes simple labials, as in rows (g,s), simple coronals, as in rows (k,n,q), and complex coronals as in row (a), but no other complex Places.[71] The grammar foils the attempt to create a complex labial from the input {PL, Lab, Lab'} in rows (f–h) by underparsing this set: a simple labial is output, as in (g), with one of the Lab features unparsed. The input {PL, Lab, Cor'} in rows (i–l) also fails to generate a complex segment, because the grammar parses only the Cor feature, outputting a simple coronal, row (k). The same output results from the input {PL, Cor, Lab'} of rows (m–p). This then is an instance of what we called 'Stampean Occultation' in §4.3.1; potential complex places involving Lab cannot surface, because the grammar always interprets them as something else, behind which they are effectively hidden. In the simplest case, the learner would never bother to posit them (see §9.3 for discussion).

9.2   Universal Inventories

In addition to language-particular inventories, any theory must make possible an account of universal inventories. We have already seen a number of examples of universal inventory construction, and the preceding analysis of segmental inventories provides yet another, which we will now explore. The general issue of universal inventories has two aspects which we will exemplify; the following statements are intended to fix the terms of the discourse.

(289) **Absolute Universal Inventory Characterizations**
  a. **Absence.** A structure φ is absent from the universal inventory if, for every possible grammar and every possible input, the optimal output parse of that input for that grammar lacks φ.
  b. **Presence.** A structure φ is universally present in language inventories if, for any possible grammar, there is some input whose optimal parse in that grammar contains φ.

(290) **Relative Universal Inventory Characterizations**
  An *implicational universal* of the form 'ψ in an inventory implies φ in the inventory' holds if, for every possible grammar in which there is some input whose optimal parse includes ψ, there is an input whose optimal parse in that same grammar includes φ.

The phrase 'possible grammar' refers to the well-formedness constraints provided by Universal Grammar, interacting via a particular domination hierarchy consistent with the domination conditions imposed by Universal Grammar.

---

[71] In the tableau, a label like 'Labialized Labial' for the input {PL, Lab, Lab'} is keyed to what *would result* from a faithful parse. The actual grammar underparses this input, and the output is a simple labial. Such labels are intended to aid the reader in identifying the input collocation and do not describe the output.

9.2.1   Segmental Inventories

The segmental inventory of Yidin^{y}, barring only the worst-of-the-worst (complex, with at least one noncoronal Place), is but one of the inventories in the universal typology generated by the 12 possible domination hierarchies which can be constructed from the four constraints *PL/Cor, *PL/Lab, F$_{ILL}$^{PL}, P$_{ARSE}$^{Feat}, consistent with the universal domination condition (284) that yields Coronal Unmarkedness. This typology includes, for example, inventories which exclude all segments with complex places, and inventories which exclude all labials. The basic sense of the typology emerges from a couple of fundamental results, demonstrated below; these results correspond directly to the informal observations of Noncomplexity (282) and Coronal Unmarkedness (281), taken as implicational universals:

(291)   **Complex ⇒ Simple**   [π ψ'] ⇒ [π], [ψ]
If the segment inventory of a language includes a complex segment with primary place π and secondary place ψ, it has a simple segment with place π and a simple segment with place ψ.

(292)   **Lab ⇒ Cor**   [···Lab···] ⇒ [···Cor···]
If the segment inventory of a language admits labials, it admits coronals.

   a.   **Harmonic Completeness with respect to Simple Segments:**
   [Lab] ⇒ [Cor]
   If a language has simple labials, then it has simple coronals.

   b.   **Harmonic Completeness with respect to Primary Place:**
   [Lab ψ'] ⇒ [Cor ψ']
   If a language has a complex segment with primary place Lab and secondary place ψ, then it has a complex segment with primary place Cor and secondary place ψ.

   c.   **Harmonic Completeness with respect to Secondary Place:**
   [π Lab'] ⇒ [π Cor']
   If a language has a complex segment with secondary place Lab and primary place π, then it has a complex segment with secondary place Cor and primary place π.

   Recall that we are using *Lab* to denote any noncoronal place of articulation. All noncoronals satisfy these implicational universals, because like Lab they all satisfy the Coronal Unmarkedness constraint domination condition (284). Both *Lab* and *Cor* should be taken here as no more than concrete place-holders for 'more marked entity' and 'less marked entity'.
   Harmonic completeness means that when a language admits forms that are marked along some dimension, it will also admit all the forms that are less marked along that dimension. More specifically, if some structure is admitted

into a language's inventory, and if a subpart of that structure is swapped for something more harmonic, then the result is also admitted into that language's inventory. Like the syllable structure results – for example, (215) of §8.2.1, p. 164 – the implications **Complex** ⇒ **Simple** and **Lab** ⇒ **Cor** ensure harmonic completeness in exactly this sense.

These results entail that *only* harmonically complete languages are admitted by the constraint system, no matter what rankings are imposed. In other words, harmonic completeness in POA is a necessary condition for the admissibility of a language under the constraint system at hand. This result is not as strong as we would like: it leaves open the possibility that there are nevertheless some harmonically complete languages that the system does not admit. For example, if the factorial typology turned out to generate only those languages where the distinctions among the coronals were *exactly the same* as those among the labials, the theorems **Complex** ⇒ **Simple** and **Lab** ⇒ **Cor** would still hold true, for such languages are harmonically complete. (In fact, we know by construction that this is not the case: the Yidin^y hierarchy allows secondary articulations among the coronals but nowhere else.) What we want, then, is that harmonic completeness be also a sufficient condition for admissibility, so that *all* harmonically complete languages are admitted. Let us single out and name this important property:

(293)   **Strong Harmonic Completeness (SHARC) Property**
        If a typology admits *all and only* the harmonically complete languages, then we say that it has Strong Harmonic Completeness (SHARC).

If a typology has the SHARC, then it manifests what has been referred to in the literature as 'licensing asymmetry'. For place of articulation, in the circumscribed realm we have been examining, this comes out as follows:

(294)   **POA Licensing Asymmetry**
        In any language, if the primary place Lab licenses a given secondary place, then so does Cor; but there are languages in which the secondary places licensed by Cor are a strict superset of those licensed by Lab.

In the common metaphor, Cor is a 'stronger' licenser of secondary places than Lab. With the SHARC, there is the broader guarantee that every asymmetric system is possible. We know that the system of constraints examined here has the POA licensing asymmetry property, because harmonic completeness is a necessary property of admitted languages, and because we have produced at least one (Yidin^y) where the secondary articulations among the coronals are a strict superset of those permitted with labials. The factorial typology of the constraint system presented here does not in fact have the SHARC, as the reader may determine, but is a step in that direction.

It is worth noting that the SHARC is undoubtedly not true of POA systems in languages, and therefore not true of the entire UG set of constraints pertaining to POA. Indeed, it is unlikely that harmonic completeness is even a necessary condition on POA systems, as John McCarthy has reminded us. With respect to labialization, for instance, many systems have k^w or g^w with no sign of t^w or d^w. With respect to **Simple ⇒ Complex**, one recalls that Irish has velarized labials and palatalized labials, but no plain labials. McCarthy points to the parallel case of Abaza, which has pharyngealized voiceless uvulars but not plain ones. We do not see this as cause for dismay, however. Virtually any theory which aims to derive implicational universals must include subcomponents which, in isolation, predict the necessity of harmonic completeness and even its sufficiency as well. The constraints discussed here are a very proper subset of those relevant to POA. In particular, the key domination hierarchy is concerned only with context-free comparison of single features, and contains no information about effects of combination (labial + velar, round + back, ATR + high, etc.), which greatly alter the ultimate predictions of the system (Chomsky & Halle 1968: ch. 9, Cairns 1969, Kean 1974, Stevens & Keyser 1989, Archangeli & Pulleyblank 1992). Optimality Theory, by its very nature, does not demand that individual constraints or constraint groups must be *true* in any simple a-systematic sense. What this means is that an established subsystem or module can be enriched by the introduction of new constraints, without necessarily revising the original impoverished module at all. (We have already seen this in the transition from the Basic Syllable Structure Theory to the analysis of Lardil.) This fact should increase one's Galilean confidence that finding a subtheory with the right properties is a significant advance.

The POA subtheory examined here derives the relative diversity of coronals in inventory from the single fact of their unmarkedness. These two characteristics are so commonly cited together that it can easily be forgotten that underspecification theory cannot relate them. This important point comes from McCarthy & Taub 1992:

> Equally important as evidence for the unmarked nature of coronals is the fact that they are extremely common in phonemic inventories, where they occur with great richness of contrast . . . [The] phonetic diversity of coronals is represented phonologically by setting up a variety of distinctive features that are dependent on the feature coronal. . . .
>
> As explanations for different aspects of coronal unmarkedness, underspecification and dependent features are distinct or even mutually incompatible. By the logic of dependency, a segment that is specified for a dependent feature . . . must also be specified for the corresponding head feature . . . For example, even if the English plain alveolars *t, d, l, r* and *n* are underspecified for [coronal] the dentals θ/ð and palato-alveolars č/ǰ/š/ž must be fully specified to support the dependent features [distributed] and [anterior]. As a consequence, the dentals and palato-alveolars should not participate in the syndrome of properties attributed to coronal underspecification, and conversely, the plain alveolars should not function as a natural class with the other coronals until application of the [coronal] default rule.

It seems clear that the only way out is to abandon underspecification in favor of markedness theory (cf. Mohanan 1991). This is an ill-advised maneuver if it means embracing nothing more substantial than an elusive hope. The present theory shows that solid formal sense can be made of the notion of markedness, and, more significantly, that results about subtleties of inventory structure – permitted featural combinations – can be deduced from hypotheses about the relative markedness of individual atomic features. The coronal diversity result parallels the result in §8.3.2 that onsets are stronger licensers of segments than codas. In the syllable structure case, it is the structural markedness of the Cod node relative to the Ons node which impairs its ability to license segments. Here, licensing is diminished by the markedness of Lab as a place relative to Cor. Formally, the relationship of licenser to licensed is quite different in the two cases, but in both cases the markedness of the licenser governs its ability to license. We have, then, a very general mode of subtheory construction within Optimality Theory which allows us to argue from the markedness of atomic components to limitations on the structure of systems.

We now turn to the demonstrations of (291) and (292), with the goal of identifying a general technique for establishing such implicational universals.[72]

---

[72] Another related technique, used in ch. 8 and to an extended degree in Legendre, Raymond, & Smolensky 1993, can be effectively used here as well; the results are more general but the technique is a bit more abstract. This other technique, which might be called the Technique of Necessary and Sufficient Conditions, goes as follows. Step 1: Determine necessary and sufficient conditions on the ranking of constraints in a hierarchy in order that each of the relevant structures be admitted into the inventory by that constraint ranking. Step 2: Examine the logical entailments that hold among these conditions: arguments of the form: in order to admit structure ϕ it is necessary that the constraints be ranked in such-and-such a way, and this entails that the constraint ranking meets the sufficient conditions to admit structure ψ. To carry out Step 1, to determine the necessary and sufficient conditions for a structure ϕ to be admitted, one takes a general parse containing ϕ and compares it to all alternative parses of the same input, and asks, how do the constraints have to be ranked to ensure that ϕ is more harmonic than all the competitors? And this in turn is done by applying the Cancellation/Domination Lemma, (192), p. 153, and (238), p. 174: for each mark *m incurred by ϕ, and for each competitor C, if *m is not cancelled by an identical mark incurred by C then it must be dominated by at least one mark of C.

In the present context, this technique gives the following results (Step 1):

(i)   In order that [χ] be admitted into an inventory it is necessary and sufficient that:
      either Parse^{Feat} or Fill^{PL} ≫ *PL/χ
(ii) In order that [π ψ] be admitted into an inventory it is necessary and sufficient that:
      a.   Parse^{Feat} ≫ *PL/ψ, and
      b.   either Parse^{Feat} or *[f' ≫ *PL/π, and
      c.   either Parse^{Feat} or Fill^{PL} ≫ *PL/π

From here, Step 2 is fairly straightforward. The result Complex ⇒ Simple (291) for the secondary place ψ follows immediately, since (ii a) ⇒ (i) for χ = ψ. The result Complex ⇒ Simple for the primary place π follows similarly since (ii c) ⇒ (i) for χ = π.

For the Harmonic Completeness results (292), we use the Coronal Unmarkedness domination condition (284):

*PL/Lab ≫ *PL/Cor

This means that whenever any of the domination conditions in (i) or (ii) hold of the feature Lab, it must also hold of the feature Cor; for in that case, each asserts that some constraint must dominate *PL/Lab, which means the same constraint must also dominate *PL/Cor since *PL/Lab ≫ *PL/Cor. Spelling this observation out in all the cases a–c of (292) proves the result Lab ⇒ Cor.

The argument establishing (291) runs as follows:

(295) **Proof of Complex $\Rightarrow$ Simple**
For the case of the secondary place, i.e., proof that if a language has [π ψ′] it has [ψ]:

    a. By definition of admission into the inventory, the output [π ψ′] must appear in an optimal parse of some input; the only possible such input is {PL,π,ψ′}.

    b. This means that [π ψ′] (incurring two marks *PL/π, *PL/ψ) must be more harmonic than all competing parses of the input {PL,π,ψ′}, including [π]⟨ψ′⟩ (incurring the marks *PL/π, *Parse^{Feat}).

    c. This entails that Parse^{Feat} must dominate *PL/ψ.

    d. This in turn implies that with the input {PL,ψ}, the parse [ψ] (incurring *PL/ψ) is more harmonic than its only competitor, [ ]⟨ψ⟩ (incurring *Parse^{Feat} [as well as *Fill^{PL}]), hence [ψ] is the optimal parse.

    e. Which means that the simple segment [ψ] is admitted into the segmental inventory.

Broadly put, the argument runs like this. Association must be compelled, over the resistance of the anti-association constraints. Either Parse or Fill can be responsible. The existence of [π ψ′] in an optimal output guarantees that association of ψ is in fact compelled by the grammar and indeed compelled by Parse, since Fill would be satisfied by merely parsing π. Therefore, the association [ψ] must also occur, driven by Parse. A similar but slightly more complex argument also establishes that [π] must be admitted.

The parallel argument establishing (292) is just a little more complicated:

(296) **Proof of Lab $\Rightarrow$ Cor**
For the case of simple segments, (292a):

    a. If a grammar admits simple labials, then the feature Lab in some input feature set must get associated to PL: [Lab] must appear in the optimal parse of this input.

    b. In order for this to happen, the association [Lab, incurring *PL/Lab, must be more harmonic than leaving Lab unparsed (incurring *Parse^{Feat}, and also possibly *Fill^{PL} if there are no other features in the set to fill PL).

    c. This means the language's domination hierarchy must meet certain conditions: either

        [i] Parse^{Feat} $\gg$ *PL/Lab

      or

        [ii] Fill^{PL} $\gg$ *PL/Lab.

    d. These conditions [i–ii] on the ranking of *PL/Lab entail that the same conditions must hold when *PL/Lab is replaced by the universally lower-ranked constraint *PL/Cor: since *PL/Lab $\gg$ *PL/Cor, by Coronal Unmarkedness (283), if [i], then:

       [i'] $\text{Parse}^{\text{Feat}} \gg \text{*PL/Lab} \gg \text{*PL/Cor}$;
   if [ii], then:
       [ii'] $\text{Fill}^{\text{PL}} \gg \text{*PL/Lab} \gg \text{*PL/Cor}$.

  e. This in turn entails that parsing Cor must be better than leaving it unparsed: the input {PL,Cor} must be parsed as [Cor] (incurring *PL/Cor), since the alternative [ ]⟨Cor⟩ would incur both *Fill^{PL} and *Parse^{Feat}, at least one of which must be a worse mark than *PL/Cor by (d).

  f. This means that coronals are admitted into the inventory.

Again, the argument can be put in rough-and-ready form. Association must be compelled, either bottom-up (by Parse) or top-down (by Fill). The appearance of [Lab – primary labial place – in an optimal output of the grammar guarantees that labial association has in fact been compelled one way or the other. Either a dominant Parse or a dominant Fill forces violation of *PL/Lab 'don't have a labial place'. The universal condition that labial association is worse than coronal association immediately entails that the less drastic, lower-ranked offense of coronal association is also compelled, by transitivity of domination.

    The two proofs, (295) and (296), illustrate a general strategy:

(297) **General Strategy for Establishing Implicational Universals ψ ⇒ φ**

  a. If a configuration ψ is in the inventory of a grammar G, then there must be some input I_ψ such that ψ appears in the corresponding output, which, being the optimal parse, must be more harmonic than all competitors.

  b. Consideration of some competitors shows that this can only happen if the constraint hierarchy defining the grammar G meets certain domination conditions.

  c. These conditions entail – typically by dint of universal domination conditions – that an output parse containing φ (for some input I_φ) is also optimal.

9.2.2 Syllabic Inventories

The general strategy (297) was deployed in chapter 8 for deriving a number of implicational universals as part of developing the Basic Segmental Syllable Theory. One example is the Harmonic Completeness of the inventories of Possible Onsets and Nuclei (215), which states that if τ is in the onset inventory, then so is any segment less sonorous than τ, and if α is in the nucleus inventory, then so is any segment more sonorous than α. A second example is (254), which asserts that if τ is in the inventory of possible codas, then τ is also in the inventory of possible onsets. That the converse is *not* an implicational universal is the content of Onset/Coda Licensing Asymmetry (258).

    So far, our illustrations of universal inventory characterizations have been of the implicational or relative type (290). Examples of the absolute type (289) may be found in the Basic CV Syllable Structure Theory of chapter 6. A positive example is the result (128), p. 111, that every syllable inventory contains CV, the universally optimal syllable. A negative example is the result (144), p. 117, which states that, in syllabic theory (which does not include constraints like Lx≈Pʀ), two adjacent empty syllable positions (phonetically realized as two adjacent epenthetic segments) are universally impossible: the universal word inventory, under the Basic Theory, includes no words with two adjacent epenthetic segments.

9.3   Optimality in the Lexicon

The preceding discussions have been independent of the issue of what inputs are made available for parsing in the actual lexicon of a language. Under the thesis that might be dubbed *Richness of the Base*, which holds that *all* inputs are possible in all languages, distributional and inventory regularities follow from the way the universal input set is mapped onto an output set by the grammar, a language-particular ranking of the constraints. This stance makes maximal use of theoretical resources already required, avoiding the loss of generalization entailed by adding further language-particular apparatus devoted to input selection. (In this we pursue ideas implicit in Stampe 1969, 1973/79, and deal with Kisseberth's grammar/lexicon 'duplication problem' by having no duplication.) We now venture beyond the Richness of the Base to take up, briefly, the issue of the lexicon, showing how the specific principles of Optimality Theory naturally project the structure of a language's grammar into its lexicon.

Consider first the task of the abstract learner of grammars. Under exposure to phonetically interpreted grammatical outputs, the underlying inputs must be inferred. Among the difficulties is one of particular interest to us: the many-to-one nature of the grammatical input-to-output mapping, arising from the violability of Faithfulness. To take the example of the Yidin^y segmental inventory illustrated above in the tableau (288), two different inputs surface as a simple labial: the input {PL, Lab} which earns the faithful parse [Lab], and the input {PL, Lab, Lab'} which is parsed [Lab]⟨Lab'⟩. These outputs are phonetically identical: which underlying form is the learner to infer is part of the underlying segmental inventory? Assuming that there is no morphophonemic evidence bearing on the choice, the obvious answer – posit the first of these, the faithfully parsable contender – is a consequence of the obvious principle:

(298)   **Lexicon Optimization**[73]
        Suppose that several different inputs $I_1, I_2, \ldots, I_n$ when parsed by a grammar G lead to corresponding outputs $O_1, O_2, \ldots, O_n$, all of which are

---

[73] The term 'lexicon' here is really overly restrictive, since this is actually a principle for inducing underlying forms in general, not just those of lexical entries. For example, it can apply in syntax as well. The rules of the syntactic base might well generate structures such as [[[[[he]_{DP}]_{DP}]_{DP}]_{DP}]_{DP} as well as simple [he]_{DP}. But, as we shall see, the principle (298) will imply that the simpler alternative will be selected as the underlying form.

realized as the same phonetic form Φ – these inputs are all *phonetically equivalent* with respect to G. Now one of these outputs must be the most harmonic, by virtue of incurring the least significant violation marks: suppose this optimal one is labelled O_k. Then the learner should choose, as the underlying form for Φ, the input I_k.

This is the first time that parses of *different inputs* have been compared as to their relative Harmony. In all previous discussions, we have been concerned with determining the output that a given input gives rise to; to this task, only the relative Harmony of competing parses of the same input is relevant. Now it is crucial that the theory is equally capable of determining which of a set of parses is most harmonic, even when the inputs parsed are all different.

Morphophonemic relations can support the positing of input–output disparities, overriding the Lexicon Optimization principle and thereby introducing further complexities into lexical analysis. But for now let us bring out some of its attractive consequences. First, it clearly works as desired for the Yidin[y] consonant inventory. Lexicon Optimization entails that the analysis of the Yidin[y] constraint hierarchy (288) simultaneously accomplishes two goals: it produces the right *outputs* to provide the Yidin[y] inventory, and it leads the learner to choose (what we hypothesize to be) the right *inputs* for the underlying forms. The items in the Yidin[y] lexicon will not be filled with detritus like feature sets {PL, Cor, Lab'} or {PL, Lab, Lab'}. Since the former surfaces just like {PL, Cor} and the latter just like {PL, Lab}, and since the parses associated with these simpler inputs avoid the marks *PARSE[Feat] incurred by their more complex counterparts, the needlessly complex inputs will never be chosen for underlying forms by the Yidin[y] learner.[74]

Lexicon Optimization also has the same kind of result – presumed correct under usual views of lexical contents – for many of the other examples we have discussed. In the Basic CV Syllable Structure Theory, for example, Lexicon Optimization entails that the constraints on surface syllable structure will be echoed in the lexicon as well. In the typological language family $\Sigma^{CV}_{del,del}$, for example, the syllable inventory consists solely of CV. For any input string of Cs and Vs, the output will consist entirely of CV syllables; mandatory onsets and forbidden codas are enforced by underparsing (phonetic nonrealization). Some inputs that surface as [CV] are given here:

(299)   **Sources of CV in $\Sigma^{CV}_{del,del}$**
  a.   /CVV/   → .CV.⟨V⟩
  b.   /CCVV/   → ⟨C⟩.CV.⟨V⟩
  c.   /CCCVVV/ → ⟨C⟩⟨C⟩.CV.⟨V⟩⟨V⟩

The list can be extended indefinitely. Clearly, of this infinite set of phonetically equivalent inputs, /CV/ is the one whose parse is most harmonic (having no marks at all); so *ceteris paribus* the $\Sigma^{CV}_{del,del}$ learner will not fill the lexicon with

---

[74] The Yidin[y] system follows the pattern called 'Stampean Occultation' in §4.3.1 above. The principle of Lexicon Optimization thus makes explicit the content of the occultation idea.

supererogatory garbage like /CCCVVV/ but will rather choose /CV/. Ignoring morphological combination (which functions forcefully as *ceteris imparibus*) for the moment, we see that CV-language learners will never insert into the lexicon any underlying forms that violate the (surface) syllable structure constraints of their language; that is, they will always choose lexical forms that can receive faithful parses given their language's syllable inventory.

Morphological analysis obviously enlivens what would otherwise be a most boringly optimal language, with no deep/surface disparities at all. So let's add to our CV language some stem + affix morphology. Away from the stem/affix boundary, the lack of deep/surface disparities will clearly remain, but at this boundary we can see a bit of interesting behavior beginning. As an example, we consider the CV idealization (with slight simplification) of the justly celebrated case of deep/surface disparity in Maori passives discussed in Hale 1973. The language is in the typological class we've called $\Sigma^{(C)V}$: onsets optional, codas forbidden; the paradigm of interest is illustrated in (300):

(300)   **CV Inflectional Paradigm** (phonetic surface forms cited)

	uninflected	inflected
a.	CVCV	CVCV*V*
b.	CVCV	CVCV*CV*

The inflected form is composed exactly of the uninflected form followed by additional material, which in case (300a) consists only of V, and in case (300b) consists of CV. At issue is how to analyze the suffix. One analysis is shown in (301):

(301)   **Phonological Analysis**

	stem	+affix	uninflected	inflected
a.	CVCV	+*V*	.CV.CV.	.CV.CV.*V*.
b.	CVCVC	+*V*	.CV.CV.⟨C⟩	.CV.CV.*CV*.

This analysis runs as follows: the inflection is a suffix +V; there are two classes of stems: V-final (a), and C-final (b); the means used to enforce the prohibition on codas is underparsing, so that in the uninflected form, the final C is not parsed. (In terms of the CV Syllable Structure Theory of chapter 6, the language is $\Sigma^{(C)V}_{del}$.)

In his discussion of Maori, Hale calls this analysis the *phonological* analysis; in derivational terms, it calls on a phonological rule of final C deletion. This is to be contrasted with what Hale calls the *conjugation* analysis, shown in (302):

(302)   **Conjugation Analysis**

	stem	+affix	uninflected	inflected
I.	CVCV	+**V**	.CV.CV.	.CV.CV.**V**.
II.	CVCV	+**CV**	.CV.CV.	.CV.CV.**CV**.

Here class-I and class-II stems are distinguished in the lexicon with a diacritic whose force is to select different forms for the inflectional affix: +V in the first case and +CV in the second.

The question now is this: how do these two analyses fare with respect to the Lexicon Optimization principle (298)? In the conjugation analysis, the parses are completely faithful, incurring no marks at all. By contrast, the phonological analysis requires underparsing for uninflected C-final (class-II) stems: this incurs a *PARSE mark. Thus, as stated in (298), the Lexicon Optimization principle would appear to favor the conjugation analysis. Indeed, in general it favors analyses that minimize deep/surface disparities, and that maximize faithful parsing, thereby avoiding *PARSE and *FILL marks. Yet it is clear that in many circumstances, phonological analyses like (301) are to be preferred to conjugational analyses like (302). The deficiency in the formulation (298) of Lexicon Optimization is that it attempts a form-by-form optimization, without taking into consideration, for example, the optimization (minimization) of the number of allomorphs associated with an affix.

In general, morphological analysis entails that morphemes will appear in multiple combinations with other morphemes; the underlying form for a morpheme which is optimal (in the sense of Lexicon Optimization) when it appears in some combinations will not be optimal when it appears with others. The conjugational analysis avoids this by limiting the possible combinations (the class-I form of the affix, +V, can only co-occur with class-I stems), at the obvious cost of not minimizing the number of allomorphs for the affix. It seems clear that Lexicon Optimization must be reformulated so that, instead of form-by-form optimization, a more global optimization of the lexicon is achieved, in which more deep/surface disparities are accepted in order to minimize the constraints on allowed morphological combination which are part and parcel of conjugational analyses.

One simple way of formulating such a global lexicon optimization would be in terms of minimizing the totality of underlying material contained in the lexicon. Applied to the problem of deciding between the phonological and conjugational analyses illustrated by our CV example, such a Minimal Lexical Information approach would go something like this. The conjugation and phonological analyses share a common core consisting of a set of uninflected stems and the affix +V. In addition to this core, the conjugational analysis requires an additional allomorph for the affix, +CV, and a diacritic for each stem indicating which allomorph it takes. (In an actual language, an additional allomorph instantiating +CV would be needed for each possible consonant that can instantiate C.) The phonological analysis requires, in addition to the shared core, additional final Cs on the class-II stems. (In an SPE-style segmental derivational theory, the phonological analysis also requires an extra final C deletion rule, but in any modern syllabic theory this comes for free, courtesy of the same grammatical structure – for us, constraint hierarchy – that determines the syllable inventory in the first place.) Specification of all the stem-final Cs in the phonological analysis, and specification of all the diacritics distinguishing the conjugational classes in the conjugational analysis, require basically the same amount of lexical information – depending on details of accounting and of distribution of possible final Cs which we set aside here. What is left to differentiate the quantity of lexical information required by the two analyses is simply the additional allomorphic material +CV in the conjugational analysis. Thus, if the omitted details are properly handled, the principle of Minimal Lexical Information would appear to favor the phonological analysis – if only by the barest of margins.

It is quite possible that this accounting grossly underassesses the costs of multiple allomorphs. The true cost of unnecessary allomorphs may not be that of *having* them – as assessed by the additional underlying material they contain – but rather in the increased difficulty of *learning* them; more precisely, of learning to identify a morpheme which has multiple exponents, each with its own idiosyncratic limitation on the other allomorphs or stems with which it can combine. The problem of detecting the combinatorial structure underlying stem + affix may well be *much* easier when the affix has a unique exponent, even when compared to the case of just two allomorphs. Evidence bearing indirectly on this claim comes from a series of learning experiments carried out by Brousse & Smolensky (1989) and Brousse (1991) using connectionist ('neural') network learning techniques. Networks were trained to identify inputs which possessed the structure *stem + affix*, where *stem* was any member of a set S and *affix* any member of another set A; the network had to learn the classes S and A as well as the means of morphologically decomposing the inputs into *stem + affix*. This task was very robustly learnable; from a tiny proportion of exclusively positive examples, the networks acquired a competence (under a somewhat subtle definition) extending far beyond the training examples. Next, limitations on legal combination were imposed: networks had to learn to identify inputs with either of the legal forms $stem_I + affix_I$ or $stem_{II} + affix_{II}$, distinguishing them from other inputs, such as those with the illegal forms $stem_I + affix_{II}$ or $stem_{II} + affix_I$. (Here $stem_I$ is any member of a set S_I of 'class-I stems', $stem_{II}$ any member of a set S_{II} of 'class-II stems', $affix_I$ any member of a set A_I of 'class-I affixes', and $affix_{II}$ any member of a set A_{II} of 'class-II affixes'.) This task was completely unlearnable by the same networks that had no trouble at all in learning the first task, in which stem/affix combination is not constrained in the way it must be in conjugational analyses. Thus there may be very strong learnability pressure to minimize combinatorial constraints, i.e., to minimize conjugational classes and the number of exponents of each morpheme.

While properly reformulating Lexicon Optimization from a form-by-form optimization to a global lexicon optimization is a difficult problem, one that has remained open throughout the history of generative phonology, a significant step towards bringing the Minimal Lexical Information principle under the scope of Lexicon Optimization as formulated in (298) is suggested by a slight reformulation, the Minimal Lexical Redundancy principle: to the maximal extent possible, information should be excluded from the lexicon which is predictable from grammatical constraints. Such considerations figure prominently, e.g., in discussions of underspecification. An example of the consequences of this principle, if taken to the limit, is this: in a language in which *t* is the epenthetic consonant, a *t* interior to a stem which happens to fall in an environment where it would be inserted by epenthesis if absent in underlying form should for this very reason *be* absent in the underlying form of that stem. A rather striking example of this can be provided by the CV Theory. Consider a $\Sigma^{(C)V}_{ep}$ language (onsets not required; codas forbidden, enforced by overparsing – 'epenthesis'). The Minimal Lexical Redundancy principle would entail that a stem that surfaces as .CV.CV.CV. must be represented underlyingly as /CCC/, since this is overparsed as .Cʊ́.Cʊ́.Cʊ́., which is phonetically identical to .CV.CV.CV.: it is redundant to put the V's in the lexicon of such a language. Given the constraints considered thus far, Lexicon Optimization as stated in (298) selects /CVCVCV/ and not /CCC/ in this case; again, avoiding deep/surface disparities whenever possible. But this is at odds with the principle that the lexicon should not contain information which can be predicted from the grammar.

The approach to parsing we have developed suggests an interesting direction for pursuing this issue. As stated in (186), the Push/Pull Parsing approach views parsing as a struggle between constraints which *prohibit* structure and constraints which *require* structure. As noted in §3.1, the most general form of the structure-prohibiting constraint is *Struc which penalizes any and all structure. There is a specialization of it which would be invisible during parsing but which can play an important role in learning:

(303)   ***Spec**
Underlying material must be absent.

Each underlying feature in an input constitutes a violation of this constraint.[75] But these violations cannot influence parsing since the underlying form is fixed by the input, and no choice of alternative output parses can affect these violations of *Spec. But Lexicon Optimization is an inverse of parsing: it involves a fixed phonetic *output*, and varying underlying *inputs*; thus, among phonetically equivalent inputs, *Spec favors those with fewest featural and segmental specifications.

Now an interesting change occurs if *Spec outranks Faithfulness: Lexicon Optimization (298) selects /CCC/ over /CVCVCV/ in the CV theory example – since minimizing Faithfulness violations (and thereby deep/surface disparities) is now less important than minimizing underlying material. If, on the other hand, Faithfulness dominates *Spec, we are back to /CVCVCV/ as the optimal underlying form.

Clearly a great deal of work needs to be done in seriously pursuing this idea. Still, it is remarkable how the addition of *Spec to the constraint hierarchy can allow Lexicon Optimization – in its original straightforward formulation (298) – to capture an important aspect of the Minimal Lexical Information and Minimal Lexical Redundancy principles. It remains to be seen whether a constraint like

---

[75] Compare the informal featural measure of lexical complexity suggested in passing in Chomsky & Halle 1968: ch. 8, p. 381, which however does not deal with the lexicon as a whole but rather with redundancy rules describing it.

*SPEC can supplant other possible constraints aimed specifically at limiting allomorphy, demanding (for example) a 1:1 relation between a grammatical category and its morphemic exponent. It is important to note that the addition of *SPEC makes no change whatever to any of the analyses we have considered previously. This raises the intriguing question of whether there are other constraints which are invisible to parsing – the operation of the grammar – but which play indispensable roles in grammar acquisition.

Chapter 10

Foundational Issues and Theory-Comparisons

> If this is the best of all possible worlds, what are the others like?
> – Candide ou l'Optimisme, ch. VI

10.1 Thinking about Optimality

10.1.1 Fear of Optimization

We distinguish three species of qualm that have dissuaded people from thinking about optimality-based theories of linguistic form.

Q1. *Computation*. "Optimization is computationally intractable. Even simple optimization problems typically turn out to be inordinately expensive in terms of computational time and space. Many problems based on satisfaction of well-formedness conditions (much less *relative* well-formedness conditions) are even undecidable."

Q2. *Loss of Restrictiveness*. "In order to handle optimality, you must use numbers and use counting. The numerical functions required belong to a vast class which cannot be constrained in a reasonable way. Arbitrary quantization will be required, both in the weighting of degrees of concordance with (and violation of) individual constraints and in the weighting of the importance of disparate constraints with respect to each other. The result will be a system of complicated trade-offs (e.g. '*one* serious violation of A can be overcome when *three* moderate agreements with B co-occur with *two* excellent instances of C'), giving tremendous descriptive flexibility and no hope of principled explanation. Therefore, the main goal of generative grammatical investigation is irredeemably undermined."

Q3. *Loss of Content*. "Appeal to scalar constraints – degrees of well-formedness – leads inevitably to a functionalizing narrative mush of the 'better for this/better for that' sort. By means of such push-pull, any imaginable state-of-affairs can be comfortably (if hazily) placed in a best of all possible worlds. Vagueness of formulation is reinstated as the favored mode of discourse, and Pullum's worst fears are realized."

10.1.2   The Reassurance

Q1. *Computation*. This qualm arises from a misapprehension about the kind of thing that grammars are. It is not incumbent upon a grammar to compute, as Chomsky has emphasized repeatedly over the years. A grammar is a function that assigns structural descriptions to sentences; what matters formally is that the function is well-defined. The requirements of explanatory adequacy (on theories of grammar) and descriptive adequacy (on grammars) constrain and evaluate the space of hypotheses. Grammatical theorists are free to contemplate any kind of formal device in pursuit of these goals; indeed, they *must* allow themselves to range freely if there is to be any hope of discovering decent theories. Concomitantly, one is not free to impose arbitrary additional meta-constraints (e.g. 'computational plausibility') which could conflict with the well-defined basic goals of the enterprise.

In practice, computationalists have always proved resourceful. All available complexity results for known theories are stunningly distant from human processing capacities (which appear to be easily linear or sublinear), yet all manner of grammatical theories have nonetheless been successfully implemented in parsers, to some degree or another, with comparable efficiency (see e.g. Barton, Berwick, & Ristad 1987; Berwick, Abney, & Tenny 1991.) Furthermore, it is pointless to speak of relative degrees of failure: as a failed image of psychology, it hardly matters whether a device takes twice as long to parse five words as it takes to parse four words, or a thousand times as long. Finally, real-world efficiency is strongly tied to architecture and to specific algorithms, so that estimates of what can be efficiently handled have changed radically as new discoveries have been made, and will continue to do so. Consequently, there are neither grounds of principle nor grounds of practicality for assuming that computational complexity considerations, applied directly to grammatical formalisms, will be informative.

Q2. *Loss of Restrictiveness through Arithmetic*. Concern is well-founded here. As we have shown, however, recourse to the full-blown power of numerical optimization is not required. *Order*, not *quantity* (or *counting*), is the key in Harmony-based theories. In Optimality Theory, constraints are ranked, not weighted; harmonic evaluation involves the abstract algebra of order relations rather than numerical adjudication between quantities.

Q3. *Loss of Content through Recourse to the Scalar and Gradient*. Here again there is a real issue. Recourse to functional explanations, couched in gradient terms, is often accompanied by severe loss of precision, so that one cannot tell how the purported explanation is supposed to play out over specific cases. A kind of informal terminological distinction is sometimes observed in the literature: a 'law' is some sort of functional principle, hard to evaluate specifically, which grammars should generally accord with, in some way or other, to some degree or other; a 'rule' is a precise formulation whose extension we understand completely. Thus, a 'law' might hold that 'syllables *should* have onsets', where a 'rule' would be: 'adjoin C to V'. 'Laws' typically distinguish better from worse, marked from unmarked; while 'rules' construct or deform.

Linguistic theory cannot be built on 'laws' of this sort, because they are too slippery, because they contend obscurely with partly contradictory counter-'laws', because the consequences of violating them cannot be assessed with any degree of precision. With this in mind, one might feel compelled to view a grammar as a more-or-less arbitrary assortment of formal rules, where the principles that the rules subserve (the 'laws') are placed entirely outside grammar, beyond the purview of formal or theoretical analysis, inert but admired. It is not unheard of to conduct phonology in this fashion.

We urge a re-assessment of this essentially formalist position. If phonology is separated from the principles of well-formedness (the 'laws') that drive it, the resulting loss of constraint and theoretical depth will mark a major defeat for the enterprise. The danger, therefore, lies in the other direction: clinging to a conception of Universal Grammar as little more than a loose organizing framework for grammars. A much stronger stance, in close accord with the thrust of recent work, is available. When the scalar and the gradient are recognized and brought within the purview of theory, Universal Grammar can supply the very substance from which grammars are built: a set of highly general constraints which, through ranking, interact to produce the elaborate particularity of individual languages.

10.2   The Connectionism Connection, and Other Computation-Based Comparisons

10.2.1   Why Optimality Theory Has Nothing To Do with Connectionism

The term 'Harmony' in Optimality Theory derives from the concept of the same name proposed in 'Harmony Theory', part of the theory of connectionist (or abstract neural) networks (Smolensky 1983, 1984, 1986; Smolensky & Riley 1984). It is sometimes therefore supposed that Optimality Theory should be classified with the other connectionist approaches to language found in the literature (McClelland & Kawamoto 1986; Rumelhart & McClelland 1986; Lakoff 1988, 1989; McMillan & Smolensky 1988; Stolcke 1989; Touretzky 1989, 1991; Elman 1990, 1991, 1992; Goldsmith & Larson 1990; Larson 1990, 1992; Legendre, Miyata, & Smolensky 1990abc, 1991ab; Hare 1990; Rager & Berg 1990; St. John & McClelland 1990; Berg 1991; Jain 1991; Miikkulainen & Dyer 1991; Touretzky & Wheeler 1991; Goldsmith 1992; Wheeler & Touretzky 1993 is a small sample of this now vast literature; critiques include Lachter & Bever 1988, Pinker & Prince 1988). Despite their great variety, almost all of these connectionist approaches to language fall fairly near one or the other of two poles, which can be characterized as follows:

(304)   **Eliminativist Connectionist Models**
        Representing the mainstream connectionist approach to language, the primary goals of these models are to show:

(a) that basic analytic concepts of generative theory 'can be eliminated' in some sense;

(b) that numerical computation can eliminate computing with symbolically structured representations;

(c) that knowledge of language can be empirically acquired through statistical induction from training data.

(305) **Implementationalist Connectionist Models**
At the other pole, these models aim to contribute to the theory of language by studying whether (and how) more-or-less standard versions of concepts from generative grammar or symbolic natural language processing can be computationally implemented with connectionist networks. As with symbolic computational approaches, the claim is that limitations on what can be (efficiently) computed bear importantly on issues of language theory.

The conspicuous absence of connectionist models in this work shows how far Optimality Theory is from either of these poles; both eliminativist and implementationalist connectionism depend crucially on the study of specific connectionist networks. All three of the prototypical objectives in eliminativist research (304a–c) are completely antithetical to Optimality Theory. And as for the implementationalist approach, rather than arguing for the contribution of Optimality Theory based on issues of connectionist implementation, we have not even entertained the question.[76]

10.2.2 Why Optimality Theory Is Deeply Connected to Connectionism

That Optimality Theory has nothing to do with eliminativist or implementationalist connectionism is related to the fact that, fundamentally, Harmony Theory itself has little to do with eliminativist or implementationalist connectionism. Harmony Theory develops mathematical techniques for the theory of connectionist computation which make it possible to *abstract away* from the details of connectionist networks. These techniques show how a class of connectionist networks can be analyzed as algorithms for maximizing Harmony, and, having done so, how Harmony maximization itself, rather than the low-level network algorithms used to implement it, can be isolated as one of the central characteristics of connectionist computation. Optimality Theory constitutes a test of the hypothesis that *this* characterization of connectionist computation is one which can enrich – rather than eliminate or implement – generative grammar: by bringing into the spotlight optimization as a grammatical mechanism.

[76] It is clear that Optimality Theory can be readily implemented using non-connectionist computation, and study of implementational issues in both connectionist and non-connectionist systems is a large open area for research.

Optimality Theory has abstract conceptual affinities with Harmonic Grammar (Legendre, Miyata, & Smolensky 1990c), a grammar formalism which is mathematically derivable from Harmony Theory and general principles concerning the realization of symbolic structure within distributed connectionist networks (Dolan 1989, Dolan & Dyer 1987, Legendre, Miyata, & Smolensky 1991ab, Smolensky 1987, 1990; relatedly, Pollack 1988, 1990). Harmonic Grammar is more intimately connected than Optimality Theory to a connectionist substrate: the relative strengths of constraints are encoded numerically, rather than through non-numerical domination hierarchies. Harmonic Grammar has been applied to the formulation of a detailed account of the complex interaction of syntactic and semantic constraints in unaccusativity phenomena in French (Legendre, Miyata, & Smolensky 1990ab, 1991a; Smolensky, Legendre, & Miyata, 1992).

It is instructive to ask what happens to Optimality Theory analyses when they are recast numerically in the manner of Harmonic Grammar. Suppose we assess numerical penalties for violating constraints; the optimal form is the one with the smallest total penalty, summing over the whole constraint set. A relation of the form $C_1 \gg C_2$ means considerably more than that the penalty for violating C_1 is greater than that for violating C_2. The force of strict domination is that *no* number of C_2 violations is worth a single C_1 violation; that is, you can't compensate for violating C_1 by pointing to success on C_2, no matter how many C_2 violations are thereby avoided. In many real-world situations, there will be a limit to the number of times C_2 can be violated by any given input; say, 10. Then if p_k is the penalty for violating C_k, it must be that p_1 is greater than $10 \times p_2$.

The same reasoning applies on down the constraint hierarchy $C_1 \gg C_2 \gg \cdots \gg C_n \gg \cdots$. If C_3 admits a maximum of 10 violations, then $p_2 > 10 \times p_3$, and $p_1 > 10 \times 10 \times p_3$. For p_n, we'll have $p_1 > 10^{n-1} \times p_n$, if we cling artificially to 10 as the standard number of possible violations per constraint. The result is that, in order to represent the domination relation, the penalties must grow exponentially. Optimality Theory, on this practical construal, represents a very specialized kind of Harmonic Grammar, with exponential weighting of the constraints.

When we remove the artifice of limiting the number of violations per constraint, it becomes clear that the real essence of the domination idea is that the penalty for violating C_1 is *infinitely* greater than the penalty for violating C_2. The notion of Harmony in Optimality Theory, then, cannot be faithfully mapped into any system using standard arithmetic. Nevertheless, Optimality Theory is recognizable as a regimentation and pushing to extremes of the basic notion of Harmonic Grammar. The interested reader is referred to Smolensky, Legendre, & Miyata 1992, in which the relations between Harmonic Grammar, Optimality Theory, and principles of connectionist computation are subjected to detailed scrutiny.

10.2.3   Harmony Maximization and Symbolic Cognition

The relation of Optimality Theory to connectionism can be elaborated as follows (for extended discussion, see Smolensky 1988, 1995). In seeking an alternative to eliminativist and implementationalist connectionism, a natural first question to ask is whether, and how, connectionist principles might be capable of informing generative grammar. Suppose connectionism is viewed as a computational hypothesis concerning the structure of cognition at a level lower than that assumed in standard symbolic cognitive theory – a level closer to, but not as low as, the neural level. The question then becomes, how can connectionist computational principles governing this lower level of description constructively interact with principles operating at the higher level of description where grammar has traditionally been carried out? As a first step toward a reconciliation of the kinds of processes and representations assumed by connectionism to operate at the lower level with those assumed to operate in grammar, it seems necessary to find ways of introducing symbolic principles into connectionist theory and means of importing connectionist principles into symbolic theory. The former can take the form of new principles of structuring connectionist networks so that their representational states can be formally characterized at a higher level of analysis as symbolically structured representations.

In the reverse direction, principles of connectionist computation need to be introduced into symbolic grammatical theory. What principles might these be? Perhaps the most obvious are the principles of mutual numerical activation and inhibition which operate between connectionist units (or 'abstract neurons'). Work along these lines includes Goldsmith and Larson's *Dynamic Linear Model* (DLM), in which the levels of activity of mutually exciting and inhibiting units are taken to represent, typically, levels of prominence of adjacent phonological elements, e.g., derived sonority, stress (Goldsmith 1992, Goldsmith & Larson 1990, Larson 1990, 1992). As Goldsmith and Larson have shown, linguistically interesting behaviors are observed in these models; a variety of results to this effect have been proven in Prince 1993, which provides detailed formal analysis of the models, including explicit mathematical expressions characterizing their behavior. (It must also be noted that this analysis reveals a number of nonlinguistic behaviors as well.)

Principles of mutual activation and inhibition are the lowest-level principles operating in connectionist networks. Rather than attempting to import such low-level principles to as high-level a theoretical enterprise as the theory of grammar, an alternative strategy is to identify the highest-level principles to emerge from connectionist theory, and attempt to import these instead. Such high-level principles are presently in very short supply. One of the few available is Harmony maximization.

Stripping away the mathematical technicalities, the principle of Harmony maximization can be couched in the following quite general terms:[77]

---

[77] This principle, and an appreciation of its generality and importance, is the result of the work of a number of people, including Hopfield 1982, 1984; Cohen & Grossberg 1983; Hinton & Sejnowski 1983, 1986; Smolensky 1983, 1986; Golden 1986, 1988; and Rumelhart, Smolensky, McClelland, & Hinton 1986. There are almost as many names for the Harmony function as investigators: it (or its negative) also goes by the names Lyapunov-, energy-, potential-, or goodness-function.

(306) **Connectionist Harmony Maximization**
In a certain class of connectionist network, the network's knowledge consists in a set of conflicting, violable constraints which operate in parallel to define the numerical Harmonies of alternative representations. When the network receives an input, it constructs an output which includes the input representation, the one which best simultaneously satisfies the constraint set – i.e., which has maximal Harmony.

That Harmony maximization could be imported into phonological theory as a leading idea was suggested by Goldsmith (1990), working within the context of concerns about the role of well-formedness constraints in influencing derivations; it plays a central role in the model called Harmonic Phonology (Goldsmith 1990, 1991, 1993; Bosch 1991; Wiltshire 1992). (Immediately below, we examine some features of the class of models to which this belongs.) In line with our assessment of fundamentally different modes of interaction between connectionist and symbolic theories, it is important to recognize that the Dynamic Linear Model is conceptually and technically quite distinct from the family of linguistic models employing notions of Harmony, and in understanding its special character it is necessary to be aware of the differences. The DLM is a discrete approximation to a forced, heavily-to-critically damped harmonic oscillator. The networks of the DLM do not conform in general to the formal conditions on activation spread which guarantee Harmony maximization (either equally weighted connections going in both directions between all units, or no feedback – see Prince & Smolensky 1991b for discussion). To the best of our knowledge, no Harmony function exists for these networks. Further, while Harmonic Phonology is based on symbol structures, the representations in the DLM are crucially numerical and non-structural. Thus, even if a Harmony function existed for the networks, it is unlikely that the activation passing in them can be construed as Harmonic Rule Application.

Optimality Theory, by contrast, seeks to strengthen the higher-level theory of grammatical form. It can be viewed as abstracting the core idea of the principle of Harmony maximization and making it work formally and empirically in a purely symbolic theory of grammar. We see this as opening the way to a deeper understanding of the relation between the cognitive realm of symbol systems and the subcognitive realm of activation and inhibition modelled in connectionist networks. The property of strict domination is a new element, one quite unexpected and currently unexplainable from the connectionist perspective,[78] and one which is crucial to the success of the enterprise.

10.3 Analysis of 'Phonotactics + Repair' Theories

As discussed in chapter 1, Optimality Theory is part of a line of research in generative syntax and phonology developing the explanatory power of output

---

[78] For a possible line of explanation, see Smolensky, Legendre, & Miyata 1992 (§3.3).

constraints. Most other research in this line has been derivational and in phonology has tended to use constraints only for surface- (or level-)[79] unviolated conditions: *phonotactics*. The fact that these phonotactics are surface-true arises in these derivational theories from a variety of factors, including the blocking of phonological processes which would lead to violation of a phonotactic, and the triggering of repair rules which take representations violating a phonotactic and modify them in one way or another so that the phonotactic holds of the result.

In these *Phonotactics + Repair* theories, interactions between phonotactics and repair rules can be handled in a variety of ways, across and within particular theories. An individual repair may be associated with individual phonotactics or not; they may be ordered with respect to other phonological rules or not; a phonotactic may block a rule or not. As we have observed throughout this work, all these patterns of interaction between phonotactics and repair rules have effects which are obtained in Optimality Theory from the single device of constraint domination. Domination yields not only the effects of phonotactic/repair interactions, but also accomplishes all the other work of the grammar, including the prosodic parse and the effects of what in derivational theories are general phonological processes. This constitutes a pervasive unification of what is expressed in other theories through a fragmented diversity of incommensurable mechanisms.

In this section we explicitly compare Optimality Theory to two representatives of the family of Phonotactics + Repair theories: the persistent rule theory (Myers 1991), and the Theory of Constraints and Repair Strategies (Paradis 1988ab). We will focus on one issue of central importance: comparing the notions of conflict which operate in Optimality Theory on the one hand and in Phonotactics + Repair theories on the other. We will see how a special case of Optimality-theoretic resolution of constraint conflict by ranking directly yields results which Phonotactics + Repair theories achieve by regulating phonotactic/rule interaction. The configuration at issue is one in which certain phonological rules are *not blocked* by a phonotactic, leading to intermediate derivational states in which the phonotactic is violated, at which point one of a set of possible repair rules is selected to restore compliance with the phonotactic. The cases we examine are treated within Optimality Theory via a straightforward interaction pattern which is quite familiar from descriptive work in the theory. While we will not consider Harmonic Phonology explicitly here, the general comparative analysis we will provide is relevant to it as well, as a member of the Phonotactics + Repair (henceforth, 'P+R') family of theories.

The interaction of phonotactics, repair rules, and the general rules implementing phonological processes is structured in Harmonic Phonology in the following way (Goldsmith 1990, 1991, 1993, Bosch 1991, Wiltshire 1992). The overall derivation involves several levels of representation. At each level certain specified phonotactics apply. At each level there is a set of rules, essentially repair rules, which apply freely within that level, governed by the principle of Harmonic Rule Application: "phonological rules apply . . . just in case their output is better than

---

[79] Throughout this section, properties predicated of the 'surface' will refer to properties which hold either level-finally or derivation-finally.

their input with respect to some criteria specified by a phonotactic (of the relevant level)" (Goldsmith 1991: 252). Rules apply one at a time within a level, but the derivational step to another level involves a parallel application of a specified set of rules which are not subject to Harmonic Rule Application. As with the P+R theories we treat specifically below, rules are used to achieve results which in Optimality Theory arise through the interaction of violable constraints. Optimality Theory differs crucially in explicitly assessing Harmony using constraints many of which are surface- (or level-) violated. A specific comparison on this point was provided in the Lardil analysis, §7.4; all effects in the Optimality-theoretic account are the result of harmonic evaluation, while the Harmonic Phonology perspective requires that crucial parts of the analysis be attributed to cross-level rules to which harmonic principles do not apply. The main reason for this difference is that crucial well-formedness conditions in the Optimality-theoretic analysis are *not* surface-unviolated phonotactics. The constraints, unlike phonotactics, come from Universal Grammar – they cannot be gleaned from inspection of surface forms. Indeed, there is no hope of constructing UG in this way if its constraints must be inviolable, and conversely, no hope of constructing individual grammars from inviolable constraints if they must be universal. In this situation, we argue, it is necessary to go for a strong UG rather than cling to the notion that constraints are *a priori* inviolable.

The central idea, then, which distinguishes Optimality Theory from other related proposals in the generative literature, notably Phonotactics + Repair theories, is this: constraints which are violated on the surface do crucial work in the grammar.[80] In alternative approaches, the work done in Optimality Theory by surface-violable constraints is generally performed by derivational rules. The issue of *conflict* is central here, since in Optimality Theory, surface violations of constraints arise only when they are forced by conflicts with more dominant constraints. Such conflicts between constraints in Optimality Theory are related in nonobvious ways to conflicts which arise in other theories between surface-unviolated constraints and derivational rules. Clarifying the relation between constraint/constraint conflict in Optimality Theory and rule/phonotactic conflict in P+R theories is a main goal of this section.

Examining the relation between these two kinds of conflict will allow us to compare Optimality Theory to a few specific P+R proposals in the literature. Our goal is to explicitly relate an important class of accounts based on a combination of surface-true constraints and derivational rules to Optimality-theoretic accounts based exclusively on constraints, both surface-true and surface-violated, and in the process to relate rule/phonotactic conflict in other theories to constraint/constraint conflict in Optimality Theory. For this purpose we will sketch particular Optimality-theoretic accounts of phonological interactions which are kept as close as possible to selected P+R accounts; and we will flesh out these Optimality-theoretic accounts just sufficiently to allow us to concretely illustrate the following general observations, for an interesting class of cases:

---

[80] We are grateful to Robert Kirchner and John McCarthy for clarificatory discussion. See Kirchner 1992bc.

(307) **The Rule/Constraint Divide**

 (a)   The work done in P+R theories by specific repair rules is included under Optimality Theory in the consequences of general, violable constraints which function generally within the grammar to ensure correct parsing. In many cases, they are kinds of Faithfulness constraints, versions of PARSE and FILL.

 (b)   P+R theories distinguish sharply between phonotactics and repair rules, which must be treated entirely differently. Optimality Theory makes no such distinction, exploiting the single theoretical construct of the violable constraint: higher-ranked constraints end up surface-unviolated; lower-ranked ones, surface-violated. Avoiding the ontological phonotactic/repair-rule distinction considerably strengthens Universal Grammar, because the same constraint which is surface-violated in one language (correlating with a repair rule) is surface-unviolated in another (corresponding to a phonotactic). Universal Grammar provides violable constraints which individual grammars rank; whether a constraint appears as surface-violated ('repair-like') or surface-unviolated ('phonotactic-like') in a given language is a consequence of the constraint's ranking in the grammar.

 (c)   Under Optimality Theory, the universally fixed function Gen supplies all structures; there are no special structure-building or structure-mutating processes that recapitulate the capacities of Gen in special circumstances. Because of Gen, the correct form is somewhere out there in the universe of candidate analyses; the constraint hierarchy exists to identify it. In a nut-shell: all constraint theories, in syntax as well as phonology, seek to eliminate the *Structural Description* term of rules; Optimality Theory also eliminates the *Structural Change*.

(308) **Conflict and Violation**

 (a)   Conflict between a phonotactic $\mathbb{C}$ and a phonological rule R does *not* correspond in Optimality Theory to conflict between $\mathbb{C}$ and the constraint $\mathbb{C}_R$ which does the main work of the rule R; both $\mathbb{C}_R$ and $\mathbb{C}$ are surface-unviolated, hence the two constraints cannot be in conflict.

 (b)   Instead, the conflict in Optimality Theory is between the pair $\{\mathbb{C}, \mathbb{C}_R\}$ on the one hand, and a third constraint $\mathbb{C}_{\text{rstr}}$ on the other: this third constraint is one which is violated by the repair rule which is used in the P+R theory to enforce the phonotactic $\mathbb{C}$.

 (c)   One consequence of the P+R approach is the conclusion that constraints which are unviolated on the surface must nonetheless be violated at intermediate stages of derivations. In Optimality Theory, surface-violable constraints which do some of the work of repair rules eliminate the need for temporary violation of surface-unviolated constraints.

It is clear that the very idea of *repair strategies* demands that surface-inviolable constraints be violated in the course of derivations: a repair strategy is a derivational process which takes a representation in which a constraint is violated and mutates it into a representation in which the constraint is satisfied. Such a process cannot take place unless representations violating the constraint are present in the derivation.

A derivational process is by definition a sequential procedure for converting an input into an output; a sharp ontological distinction between input and output is not possible since there is a host of intermediate representations bridging them. Constraints need to be evaluated over all such representations, and part of the reason theoretical complexities arise is that constraints which are unviolated on the surface may be violated in underlying forms (especially after morphological combination) and then at least for some time during the derivation; or constraints may be initially vacuously satisfied because they refer to structure that is not yet constructed, but as soon as the relevant structure is built, violation occurs. In the non-serial version of Optimality Theory, however, there is a sharp ontological difference between inputs and outputs: Markedness constraints are evaluated only with respect to the output; and Faithfulness constraints, which value realization of the input, must also look to the output to make their assessments. Any surface-unviolated constraint is therefore literally entirely unviolated in the language, as it would be a basic category error to say that the constraint is violated by underlying forms.

While it is obvious that a repair strategy approach requires that surface-unviolated constraints be violated at least temporarily during derivations, it is much less obvious, of course, that the work of repair strategies can in fact be done by violable constraints, the violations of which are governed by domination hierarchies. Evidence for this conclusion is implicit in most of the preceding sections, since many of the Optimality-theoretic analyses we have presented use the freedom of Gen and constraint violation to do work which is performed in other accounts by repair rules. In this section, we focus on explicit comparison between Optimality-theoretic and a few P+R accounts from the literature. It turns out that several of these comparisons have a structure which is already implicit in one of our basic analyses, the CV syllable structure typology of chapter 6. So before turning to our comparisons, we set up their general structure by examining this simplest case.

10.3.1   CV Syllable Structure and Repair

Consider syllabification in the typological class $\Sigma^{CV(C)}_{ep}$: onsets are mandatory, enforced by overparsing. In §6.2.2.1 we examined the input /V/, and saw that it was parsed as .□V., surfacing as a CV syllable with an epenthetic onset (133). A simple analysis of this situation using a surface-unviolated phonotactic and a repair rule runs as follows. The language has a syllable structure constraint SYLLSTRUC given by the template CV(C). (In the terminology of chapter 6, SYLLSTRUC encapsulates the constraint package {ONS, NUC, *COMPLEX}.) A syllabification rule R_{syll} erects a σ node and associates V to it (via a Nuc or μ node). This onsetless σ violates SYLLSTRUC and this violation triggers a repair rule R_{ep}: a C-epenthesis rule.

Even in this utterly simple situation, the most basic of the problematic issues which loom large in richer contexts are already present. Why doesn't the constraint SYLLSTRUC *block* the syllabification rule in the first place? (Indeed, this is just what might be assumed in a comparable analysis of the *under*parsing case, $\Sigma^{CV(C)}_{del}$.) What general principle licenses temporary violation of SYLLSTRUC?

These questions disappear when derivational rules are replaced by Optimality Theory's violable constraints. The work of the syllabification rule R_{syll} is done by the constraint PARSE, which happens to be surface-unviolated in this language. The work of the repair rule R_{ep} is performed by the constraint FILL (more precisely, FILL^{Ons}) which happens to be surface-violated in this language.

For theory comparison, the cross-theoretic relation between the derivational rule R_{syll} and the Optimality Theory constraint PARSE is an important one, for which it is convenient to have a name; we will say that PARSE is a *postcondition* of R_{syll}: the constraint PARSE gives a condition ('underlying material must be parsed into syllable structure') which is satisfied *after* the operation of the rule R_{syll}, which parses underlying material into syllable structure. There is not a unique postcondition associated with a rule; and not just any one will result in an Optimality-theoretic account that works. The theory comparison enterprise on which we now embark is certainly not a mechanical one. The postcondition relation is a strictly *cross*-theoretic notion; since it is not a notion internal to Optimality Theory, the fact that it is not uniquely defined in no way undermines the well-definition of Optimality Theory.

The relation between the repair rule R_{ep} and the constraint FILL is also cross-theoretically important, and different from that relating R_{syll} and PARSE. The repair rule R_{ep} does *not* apply *unless* it is necessary to save the SYLLSTRUC constraint; it is precisely the avoidance of FILL violations which prevents overparsing (epenthesis), except when necessary to meet SYLLSTRUC. A postcondition of the rule R_{ep} is thus SYLLSTRUC. FILL, on the other hand, is a *restraint* on the repair rule: it is *violated* when the rule fires. (Like postcondition, restraint is a cross-theoretic relation which is not uniquely defined.)

The Optimality Theory treatment employs the basic domination relation:

(309)   SYLLSTRUC $\gg$ FILL

This is central to achieving the same result as that obtained in the P+R account by stating that the repair rule applies *when necessary* to meet SYLLSTRUC (but otherwise not, 'in order to avoid violating FILL'). The domination (309) illustrates the general case: when a repair rule R_{rep} has as postcondition a (surface-unviolated) constraint (corresponding to a phonotactic) $\mathbb{C}_{tac}$, and when this rule is restrained by a (surface-violated) constraint $\mathbb{C}_{rstr}$, we must have:

(310) $\mathbb{C}_{tac} \gg \mathbb{C}_{rstr}$

The restraining constraint must be subordinate to the constraint corresponding to the phonotactic.

This situation is summarized in the following table:

(311) $\Sigma^{CV(C)}_{ep}$:

	Rule	Constraint
Repair/Phonotactic	R_{rep} = C-Epenthesis	C_{tac} = SYLLSTRUC
Process/Postcondition	R_{proc} = Syllabification	C_{proc} = PARSE
Restraining Constraint	*violated by R_{rep}*:	C_{rstr} = FILL

Ranking: $\{C_{tac}, C_{proc}\}$ $\gg C_{rstr}$
    i.e. {SYLLSTRUC, PARSE} $\gg$ FILL

This table, it turns out, captures the general structure of several more complex theory comparisons which will be spelled out in analogous tables below (314, 316, 318). It is important to note, however, that the labelled columns do not partition the theories, and a point-for-point occamite match-up is not on offer here. Along with the cited rules, the P+R theory includes an exact image of the Markedness constraint(s) SYLLSTRUC; and in addition includes a condition (functioning like PARSE) that causes the Syllabification rule to fire in the presence of unsyllabified material, and another condition, analogous to Faithfulness in general and here functioning like FILL, which restrains C-epenthesis, restricting repair to minimal modification. On the Optimality Theory side, there is Gen, which supplies candidates corresponding to those produced by C-Epenthesis and Syllabification (as well as many more).

In the P+R account, the parsing of /V/ involves a conflict between the constraint SYLLSTRUC and the rule R_{syll}: this is a case of rule/phonotactic conflict. The locus of conflict in the Optimality-theoretic account is elsewhere, however. The clearest Optimality-theoretic counterpart of the rule R_{syll} is its postcondition PARSE, and there is no conflict between SYLLSTRUC and PARSE; the conflict is between the pair of constraints {SYLLSTRUC, PARSE} on the one hand and FILL on the other: and it is FILL which gets violated. The rule/phonotactic conflict between SYLLSTRUC and R_{syll} arises in the P+R account from the fact that R_{syll} chooses to procedurally implement PARSE with a construction that implicitly also tries to implement FILL: for R_{syll} constructs a syllable with no unfilled nodes. To see the consequences of this, let's trace the status of the three constraints SYLLSTRUC, PARSE, and FILL during the simple derivation of /V/ $\rightarrow$.□V.

(312) **Constraint Violation History of a Simple Derivation**

Step	Form	Rule	SYLLSTRUC	PARSE	FILL
0	/V/			*	
1	.V.	R_{syll}	*		
2	.□V.	R_{ep}			*

The rule R_{syll} eliminates the PARSE violation by parsing V into a new σ, but chooses to construct this σ in such a way as to avoid violations of FILL; that is, it constructs a σ with no onset. The problem is that this then creates a violation of SYLLSTRUC which next needs repair. The P+R analysis requires a stage of derivation, step 1 (shaded), in which a phonological rule has been allowed to produce a violation of a surface-unviolated rule. And, of course, such a violation is necessary to trigger R_{ep}. The Optimality Theory account, however, involves no violation of the surface-unviolated constraint SYLLSTRUC: it involves a violation of the surface-violated constraint FILL.

10.3.2   General Structure of the Comparisons: Repair Analysis

The simple example of syllabification of /V/ in $\Sigma^{CV(C)}_{ep}$ illustrates a very general situation. In the P+R account, the story goes as follows. At one stage of a derivation, the conditions of a phonological process (e.g. Syllabification) are met; the process applies, creating a structure which violates a phonotactic; the conditions of a repair rule now being met, the repair applies; and then the phonotactic is satisfied.

The Optimality Theory view of this P+R account goes like this. The surface-unviolated phonotactic is a high-ranking constraint $\mathbb{C}_{tac}$. The phonological process achieves some postcondition, another constraint $\mathbb{C}_{proc}$. $\mathbb{C}_{proc}$ is not 'blocked' in any sense by $\mathbb{C}_{tac}$ because in fact the two *do not conflict*: there is a way of satisfying them both, at the expense of a third constraint $\mathbb{C}_{rstr}$ which is lower-ranked than both $\mathbb{C}_{tac}$ and $\mathbb{C}_{proc}$.

There is no constraint/constraint conflict between $\mathbb{C}_{proc}$ and $\mathbb{C}_{tac}$ even though there is rule/phonotactic conflict between R_{proc} and $\mathbb{C}_{tac}$. This is because the rule R_{proc} enforcing $\mathbb{C}_{proc}$ introduces a stage of derivation in which $\mathbb{C}_{tac}$ is violated in order to meet $\mathbb{C}_{proc}$. But the subsequent repair produces an ultimate structure which meets both $\mathbb{C}_{tac}$ and $\mathbb{C}_{proc}$, which is possible only because there is no constraint/constraint conflict between these two constraints. The constraint/constraint conflict is actually between the pair {$\mathbb{C}_{tac}$, $\mathbb{C}_{proc}$} on the one hand, and $\mathbb{C}_{rstr}$ on the other. In this conflict, $\mathbb{C}_{rstr}$ loses: it is the constraint violated by the repair rule.

The Optimality Theory account of the same situation is simply this (from (311)):

(313)   {$\mathbb{C}_{tac}$, $\mathbb{C}_{proc}$} ≫ $\mathbb{C}_{rstr}$

In an unproblematic input (e.g., /CV/ above), $\mathbb{C}_{tac}$, $\mathbb{C}_{proc}$, and $\mathbb{C}_{rstr}$ are all satisfied. In a problematic input (e.g. /V/ above), $\mathbb{C}_{tac}$ and $\mathbb{C}_{proc}$ together force the violation of $\mathbb{C}_{rstr}$.

This general comparative analysis can be applied to relate a variety of P+R accounts to Optimality Theory accounts of the same phenomena, as we now see. It is useful to have a name for this strategy: we call it *Repair Analysis*.

We reiterate the importance of distinguishing theory-comparative and Optimality Theory-internal notions in this discussion. Within Optimality Theory, all constraints have exactly the same status. The theory does not recognize, for example, a difference between 'violable' and 'inviolable' constraints. All constraints are *potentially* violable, and which ones happen to emerge as violated on the surface is a logical *consequence* of the domination hierarchy, the set of inputs, and the content of the constraints (which determines which of them conflict on the inputs). Similarly, although Repair Analysis distinguishes constraints as $\mathbb{C}_{tac}$, or $\mathbb{C}_{proc}$, or $\mathbb{C}_{rstr}$, this distinction is entirely theory-comparative: from the Optimality Theory-internal perspective, they are all simply violable constraints, interacting in the only way sanctioned by the theory: strict domination. The distinction between $\mathbb{C}_{tac}$, $\mathbb{C}_{proc}$, and $\mathbb{C}_{rstr}$ arises only in comparing an Optimality Theory account to a P+R account; they are constraints which relate to elements (e.g., phonotactics and repair rules) which have markedly different theoretical status in the P+R account – the constraints have identical theoretical status in Optimality Theory.

Two major features of subsequent Repair Analyses are also simply illustrated in the example of syllabification in $\Sigma^{CV(C)}_{ep}$. The first feature is generality: the constraints involved in the Optimality Theory account are extremely general ones, which function pervasively in the grammar to define well-formedness. The effects of a specific repair rule (epenthesis in a specific kind of environment) are derived consequences of the interaction of general well-formedness constraints.

The constraints in the Optimality Theory account are general in another sense, beyond their general applicability within the given language: the constraints in question are the same ones which operate in other languages exemplifying typologically different syllabification classes – this was exactly the point of the CV Syllable Structure Theory developed in chapter 6. Thus the second important feature illustrated in this example is universality. From the perspective of comparison to P+R theories, the point is this: a constraint $\mathbb{C}$ may happen to be surface-unviolated in language L_1 and formalized as a phonotactic in a P+R theory, and the same constraint may well be operative but surface-violated in another language L_2 – and therefore not treatable as a phonotactic. $\mathbb{C}$ may play the role $\mathbb{C}_{tac}$ in L_1, but may be demoted to the role of a subordinate constraint $\mathbb{C}_{rstr}$ in L_2. In the Optimality Theory treatment, $\mathbb{C}$ may have exactly the same form in both languages; but in P+R theory, this is completely impossible.

This situation has been exemplified in a number of cases discussed in previous sections, and is quite clear in the syllable structure example. In the language $L_1 = \Sigma^{CV(C)}_{ep}$ discussed in §10.3.1, the surface-unviolated constraint is $\mathbb{C}_{tac} = \text{SYLLSTRUC} = \{\text{NUC}, \text{*COMPLEX}, \text{ONS}\}$ while the surface-violated constraint is $\mathbb{C}_{rstr} = \text{FILL}$. However, for a language L_2 in the family $\Sigma^{(C)V(C)}$, for example, the roles of ONS and FILL are interchanged: now ONS is surface-violated while FILL is surface-unviolated. The constraint ONS is part of the phonotactic $\mathbb{C}_{tac}$ in L_1; and similarly –COD is also part of the corresponding phonotactic for a language L_1' in the family Σ^{CV}. Yet at least one of ONS and –COD must be active in $L_2 = \Sigma^{(C)V(C)}$, although both are surface-violated: even though .CVC. and .V. are individually legal syllables in L_2, ONS or –COD must ensure that, as in all languages, /CVCV/ is syllabified .CV.CV. rather than .CVC.V. (recall the discussion at the end of §6.1, p. 107). To see how ONS and –COD are demoted from the status of $\mathbb{C}_{tac}$ in L_1

and L_1' to the status of $\mathbb{C}_{rstr}$ in L_2, consider the following P+R account of L_2. A Core Syllabification Rule builds core syllables, and if any unsyllabified segments remain after core syllabification, these defects are repaired by rules of Coda Attachment (for free Cs) and Onsetless Open Syllable Construction (for free Vs). The first repair rule is restrained by the constraint −Cod and the second by Ons. So in a Repair Analysis of this P+R account of L_2, Ons and −Cod fill the role of $\mathbb{C}_{rstr}$.

The fact that Optimality Theory has no equivalent of the phonotactic/rule dichotomy, but rather a single category of potentially violable constraints, makes it possible for Universal Grammar to simply specify a set of general constraints: the distinction between surface-violated and surface-unviolated, then, is a derived language-particular consequence of constraint ranking. These universal constraints capture generalizations which, in P+R terms, link what appear as phonotactics and postconditions in some languages to what are effectively restraining constraints on repair rules in others.

10.3.3   Persistent Rule Theory

In the preceding discussion we have been contrasting Phonotactics + Repair approaches, which use constraints for surface-unviolated phonotactics only, and Optimality Theory, which uses constraints much more widely. One recent analysis of the role of constraints in generative phonology is Myers 1991, which argues that constraints must be used *less* widely: only for a *subset* of phonotactics. Phonotactics are argued to divide into two classes which need to be theoretically treated in two different ways: one, as constraints which block phonological rules, the other, via *persistent rules* which do not block other phonological rules (but may in some cases undo their effects). The conclusion that the second class of phonotactics should not be treated as constraints but rather as the result of derivational rules is one which we now attempt to reconcile with Optimality Theory, in which such rules are eschewed in favor of constraints (surface-violated as well as surface-unviolated).

The repair rules of persistent rule theory (henceforth *PRT*) are 'persistent' in the sense that they are not ordered with respect to other rules, but rather apply whenever their conditions are met. The persistence of these rules does not, however, bear on the applicability of Repair Analysis: what matters is only that these rules are repair rules.

The arguments for PRT consist centrally in showing that a subset of phonotactics do not block phonological rules; that these rules apply, generating intermediate representations which violate the phonotactic, representations which are then repaired by a persistent rule. We will consider two such cases, and apply Repair Analysis to show how the necessary interactions fall out of very simple constraint interactions within Optimality Theory. We reiterate that our objective here is not at all to give full alternative treatments of these phenomena, but rather to illustrate the application of Repair Analysis to some relevant examples from the literature.

10.3.3.1   English closed syllable shortening

A simple application of Repair Analysis is to the Myers 1987b analysis (his §2.4) of English vowel length alternations like *keep/kept, deep/depth, resume/resumption*. The PRT analysis assumes a phonotactic which bars CVVC syllables; we can take this to be a constraint $*\mu\mu\mu$ barring trimoraic syllables. In the P+R account, this phonotactic does not block the process of Syllabification of, e.g., the final two consonants in *kept*, although the result of such syllabification is an illicit CVVC syllable, which then triggers a repair rule of Closed σ Shortening. The resulting derivation involves first associating the underlying long vowel of the stem *keep* to two syllabified moras, then associating *p* to a mora in the same syllable, then delinking the second mora for the vowel.

An Optimality Theory account of these interactions gives a straightforward application of Repair Analysis. The following table shows the relevant rules and constraints, in exact correspondence with the table for CV syllabification (311):

(314)   **English Closed Syllable Shortening**

	Rule	Constraint
Repair/Phonotactic	R_{rep} = Closed σ Shortening	$\mathbb{C}_{tac}$ = $*\mu\mu\mu$
Process/Postcondition	R_{proc} = Syllabification	$\mathbb{C}_{proc}$ = $\text{PARSE}^{\text{Seg}}$
Restraining Constraint	*violated by* R_{rep}:	$\mathbb{C}_{rstr}$ = PARSE^{μ}

Ranking: $\{\mathbb{C}_{tac}, \mathbb{C}_{proc}\}$ $\gg \mathbb{C}_{rstr}$ (313)
i.e. $\{*\mu\mu\mu, \text{PARSE}^{\text{Seg}}\} \gg \text{PARSE}^{\mu}$

The phonotactic is $\mathbb{C}_{tac} = *\mu\mu\mu$. The phonological process not blocked by the phonotactic is R_{proc} = Syllabification; the postcondition associated with this process is $\text{PARSE}^{\text{Seg}}$. The repair rule is R_{rep} = Closed σ Shortening. This is restrained by the constraint $\mathbb{C}_{rstr} = \text{PARSE}^{\mu}$ which says that moras must be parsed (see §4.5): this is the constraint which must be violated in order to perform shortening. Here we assume the following analysis of *keep/kept*, designed to be minimally different from the PRT analysis:

(315)

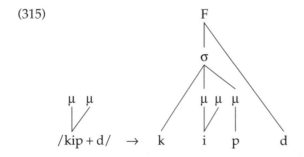

Like the PRT account, ours does not treat the segmental alternations i/ε, d/t. For comparative purposes, we retain Myers's assumption of a (superordinate) constraint entailing that the final consonant is extrasyllabic (at least at this level of representation); we assume that segments attached to prosodic structure at any hierarchical level (e.g., the foot F) are phonetically realized, and that the failure to parse the second μ of i means the vowel is phonetically realized as short. We use failure to parse the second μ of i into σ here, rather than the PRT delinking of i to the second μ, in conformity with the general Optimality-theoretic principle that a parse of an input must always include the entire input representation (here, including two μs and their associations to i). The constraint ranking in (314) ensures that the parse in (315), which incurs the mark *PARSE$^\mu$, is the optimal one.[81]

We observe that the Optimality-theoretic treatment involves no violation of *μμμ whatsoever: there is no need for an intermediate stage of derivation in which the long vowel is fully parsed into syllable structure in order to provide the conditions for a shortening rule; the second μ is simply never parsed. By using the (surface-violated, subordinate) constraint PARSE$^\mu$ instead of the derivational repair rule, the (surface-unviolated, superordinate) constraint *μμμ is spared even temporary violation.

In this case, the PRT account involves a conflict between the phonotactic *μμμ and the phonological process of Syllabification. But in the Optimality Theory account, without the Syllabification rule but with instead its postcondition PARSE^{Seg}, no conflict arises between this constraint and the constraint *μμμ; rather, the conflict is between the combination {*μμμ, PARSE^{Seg}} on the one hand, and the subordinate constraint PARSE$^\mu$ on the other. The Syllabification rule creates a conflict with *μμμ by doing syllabification in such a way as to satisfy PARSE$^\mu$ (in addition to PARSE^{Seg}): all μs are parsed into syllable structure, and this then needs to be undone by the repair rule.

In the Optimality Theory account, the correct interactions fall out directly from the simple constraint domination in (314), exactly the same domination pattern as in (311): the pattern characteristic of Repair Analysis. Furthermore, whereas repair rules (like Closed σ Shortening) are specialized rules which perform marked operations in order to overcome specific phonotactic violations created by phonological processes, the constraints which do the work in the Optimality Theory account are extremely general ones which are responsible for doing the central work in the grammar. Here, the repair rule of Closed σ Shortening performs the marked, anti-grammatical operation of Shortening or Delinking, in the very specifically circumscribed context of a Closed σ. By contrast, PARSE$^\mu$ and PARSE^{Seg} are extremely general constraints which do the main grammatical work of ensuring the underlying material gets parsed . . . except when doing so would violate more highly ranked constraints. The final 'except' clause is automatically furnished by the fundamental operation of the theory, and there is therefore no need to build the specific cases where this exception is realized into a specialized repair rule which undoes parsing exactly when it should never have occurred in the first place.

---

[81] An absolutely direct assault is available if we recognize the 'cancelled link' as a representational entity whose distribution is governed by a generalized version of PARSE.

10.3.3.2   *Shona tone spreading*

Our second example of an argument from Myers 1991 against formalizing phonotactics as constraints is more complex: Shona tone spreading. Here the phonotactic is a prohibition on contour tones. The phonological processes which are not blocked by this phonotactic are Association of Syllables to Tones, and Rightward Spread of High Tone. The repair rule is Simplification, which delinks the right tonal association of any syllable which has two tonal associations.

H tones are present in underlying forms, and L tones arise from a rule of Default. The basic spreading facts are that underlying H tones always dock and then spread right, unboundedly through a stem but only to the first σ after crossing a morphological boundary (which we'll denote '|'). The input /ku|mú| verengera/ – which has a single underlying H tone (denoted ´) on /mú/ – surfaces as *kumúvérengera*, with the underlying H tone spreading right one σ to yield *vé*, the remaining σs receiving default L tone.

The derivation of this output displays the now-familiar pattern in which the phonotactic is violated temporarily. On the first cycle, L tone is associated by default to the stem; next, with the innermost prefix /mú/ added, the underlying H tone spreads right to the first syllable of the stem, *ve*, which syllable is now doubly linked to both H and L, in violation of the phonotactic; this double-association then triggers Simplification, which delinks the right (L) association of this syllable, satisfying the phonotactic.

The situation is more complex, but, with appropriate flexing, Repair Analysis applies here as well. The table corresponding to tables (311) and (314) is:

(316)   **Shona Tone Spread**

		Rule	Constraint
Repair/Phonotactic	R_{rep} = Simplification (delink right T)		$\mathbb{C}_{tac}$ = *$\breve{σ}$
Process/Postcondition	$R_{proc}{}^{1}$ = Association		$\mathbb{C}_{proc}{}^{1}$ = Parse^{T}
	$R_{proc}{}^{2}$ = Spread H →		$\mathbb{C}_{proc}{}^{2}$ = *$\acute{σ}σ$
Subordinate Constraints	*potentially violated by $R_{proc}{}^{2}$:*		$\mathbb{C}_{rstr}{}^{1}$ = *T↑σ
	$R_{sub}{}^{2}$ = Spread H →		$\mathbb{C}_{proc}{}^{2'}$ = *$\acute{σ}σ$
	$R_{sub}{}^{3}$ = Default T is L		$\mathbb{C}_{rstr}{}^{2}$ = *$\acute{σ}$

$$\text{Ranking:} \quad \{\mathbb{C}_{tac}, \mathbb{C}_{proc}\} \qquad \gg \mathbb{C}_{rstr} \qquad (313)$$
$$\text{i.e.} \quad \{\mathbb{C}_{tac}, \mathbb{C}_{proc}{}^{1}, \mathbb{C}_{proc}{}^{2}\} \gg \mathbb{C}_{rstr}{}^{1} \gg \mathbb{C}_{proc}{}^{2'} \gg \mathbb{C}_{rstr}{}^{2}$$

The Optimality-theoretic constraint corresponding to the phonotactic is written *$\breve{σ}$, where $\breve{σ}$ denotes a doubly associated σ. The first phonological process not blocked by this phonotactic, Association, has a postcondition Parse^{T}. The second such process, Spread H→, requires a bit more discussion.

For present purposes, the following treatment of spreading will suffice. Under present assumptions, the phonological and morphological content of the input is assumed to be an identifiable part of every candidate output. In an output, let ó denote a syllable associated to H, and ő a syllable associated to a tautomorphemic H. Then we can capture Shona's rightward spreading as a pair of constraints, the first of which is *óσ: this is violated when an L-bearing σ follows an H-bearing σ. The second, higher-ranked constraint is *őσ, violated when an L-bearing σ follows a σ bearing a tautomorphemic H tone.[82]

We assume without further comment that a familiar set of constraints are imposed on the candidate sets generated by Gen: e.g., all σs must be associated to tones, association lines do not cross, the OCP.

The Default rule of L-association is motivated by a (lowest-ranked) constraint barring H-bearing syllables: *ó. The only remaining constraint is one which assesses a mark for each tonal association line which crosses a morphological boundary; we iconically name this constraint *T↑σ.

The Optimality Theory analysis follows the general form of the previous cases: compare the constraint ranking in (316) to those in (311) and (314). Now, however, the lower-ranking constraints corresponding to C_{rstr} are crucially ranked with respect to one another. Because *T↑σ is ranked lower than *őσ and higher than *óσ, it follows that H tones will spread rightward, exactly one syllable across a morphological boundary: the rightmost H-bearing σ is then ó rather than ő; so failing to continue to spread violates *óσ, but continuing to spread violates higher-ranked *T↑σ. Heteromorphemic H-tone association (violating *T↑σ) can only be forced by *őσ, which is satisfied by spreading a single syllable across the morpheme boundary. Because *ó is lowest-ranked, it will be violated in optimal forms in which H tones spread: but it ensures that any syllable not receiving H tone by spread from an underlying H tone will bear an L tone.

As in the preceding examples, in the Optimality Theory account, the constraint C_{tac} is not (even temporarily) violated. In /ku|mú|verengera/ → .ku|mú|vérengera., the syllable *ve* does not have the tonal association history ø → L → HL → H which it undergoes in the P+R account; it never receives L tone in the first place, and there is thus no need to revoke it. And like the previous example, the work of a specialized repair rule is done by extremely general constraints which are also responsible for doing the primary grammatical work of correctly assigning parses to inputs.

10.3.3.3 Summary

The analysis in this section is obviously preliminary, and the conclusion therefore a tentative one. According to Persistent Rule Theory, the role of constraints in grammar is restricted to that subset of surface-unviolated phonotactics

---

[82] A more complete analysis would attempt to capture the connection between *T↑σ, which penalizes heteromorphemic association, and the sub-hierarchy *őσ ≫ *óσ, which asserts that heteromorphemic associations are weaker licensers of 'spreading'.

which block phonological rules; other phonotactics arise as the consequence of persistent rules. We have seen that the failure of a phonotactic to block a phonological process is an inevitable outcome within a constraint-based theory in which there is no conflict between the constraint C_{tac} corresponding to the phonotactic and the constraint C_{proc} which is a postcondition of the phonological process; these two constraints can be simultaneously met, at the expense of a third subordinate constraint C_{rstr} which is surface-violated; this additional constraint is what is violated by the operation of the persistent repair rules in PRT. Optimality Theory handles such cases straightforwardly via the simple domination condition (313):

$$\{C_{tac}, C_{proc}\} \gg C_{rstr}$$

The constraints involved in the Optimality-theoretic account are highly general ones which do the primary work of the grammar: but because the complete set of constraints $C_{tac}, C_{proc}, C_{rstr}$ cannot all be simultaneously satisfied in certain special problematic cases, something has to give, and the domination hierarchy determines that it is C_{rstr}. The special situations in which this subordinate constraint is violated are a logical *consequence* of the account, rather than a stipulated environment hand-wired into a specialized repair rule. Recall that the labels on the constraints are intended merely as guides to cross-theory comparison. The root prediction is that all domination orders are possible, yielding a typology of different systems, in which of course, from the operationalist point of view, there would be different constraints and different repairs.

10.3.4 The Theory of Constraints and Repair Strategies

Whereas Myers 1991 argues for restricting the role of constraints in grammar, Paradis has forcefully argued the opposite position. Optimality Theory builds on her work and further promotes the role of constraints, adding a theory of constraint interaction in which lower-ranked constraints are violated in order to satisfy higher-ranked ones. In this section we explicitly consider key aspects of the relation between the approaches, concretely grounding the discussion in a specific illustrative analysis from Paradis 1988a (to which paper the page number citations in this section refer).

Like the theories considered previously, Paradis' Theory of Constraints and Repair Strategies (*TCRS*) is a derivational Phonotactics + Repair framework, in which all constraints explicitly treated as such are surface-unviolated phonotactics. Thus the constraints in TCRS cannot conflict in the sense of Optimality Theory. We need to properly understand, then, statements such as the following:

> All these facts lead me to conclude that phonological processes do not freely violate phonological constraints. Actually, violations occur when there is a *constraint conflict*, which must be solved in some way. I argue that this is accomplished by the PLH. (p. 90, emphasis added)

'PLH' refers to the "phonological level hierarchy . . . : metrical > syllabic > skeletal > segmental" (p. 89). An example of Paradis' sense of 'constraint conflict' is provided by her analysis of Fula, about which she says

> the constraint violation . . . follows from a *conflict of two constraints*: the obligatory Segmental Licensing Convention for skeletal slots . . . (no floating slot); and the constraint against continuant geminates . . . (p. 89, emphasis added)

The derivation she refers to has a now-familiar form (317).

(317)   **Fula Gemination**: An example derivation

Step	Form	Rule	*V:C:	*GemCont	Fill^X	Parse^X	Parse^{Feat}
0	XXXX XX l a w + i	Input			*	******	
1	σ σ XXXX XX l a w + i	Spreading, Nucleus Syllabification	*	*		***	
2	σ σ XXXX XX l a b + i	Feature Changing, Onset Syllabification				*	*
	blocked	Coda Syllabification					
3	σ σ XXXX XX l a b i	Segmental Delinking, Skeletal Deletion				*	*

Fula has a phonotactic barring geminate continuant consonants. This phonotactic is temporarily violated during the derivation (317), at step 1 (shaded).

The strategy of Repair Analysis applies to this analysis as well. The following table is the counterpart of (311), (314), and (316):

(318) **Fula Gemination**

	Rule	Constraint
Repair/Phonotactic	R_{rep}^{1} =Segmental Delinking and Skeletal Deletion	C_{tac}^{1} = *VːCː
	R_{rep}^{2} = [+cont] → [−cont]	C_{tac}^{2} = *GEMCONT
Process/Postcondition	R_{proc} = Spreading	C_{proc} = FILL^{X}
Restraining Constraint	*violated by* R_{rep}^{1}:	C_{rstr}^{1} = PARSE^{X}
	violated by R_{rep}^{2}:	C_{rstr}^{2} = PARSE^{Feat}

$$\text{Ranking:} \quad \{C_{tac}, C_{proc}\} \quad \gg C_{rstr} \quad (313)$$
$$\text{i.e.} \quad \{C_{tac}^{1}, C_{tac}^{2}, C_{proc}\} \gg \{C_{rstr}^{1}, C_{rstr}^{2}\}$$

There are two phonotactics involved; the first is the prohibition on geminate continuant consonants. In the Optimality-theoretic analysis, this is captured in a constraint *GEMCONT which is violated whenever a consonantal root node is associated to the feature [+cont] and to two skeletal positions (regardless of whether those skeletal positions are parsed into syllable structure). The other phonotactic (related to that of the English Closed σ Shortening example discussed in §10.3.3.1) is a prohibition on the sequence VːCː. In the Optimality-theoretic analysis this takes the form of a constraint *VːCː, which is violated if a V is associated to two Xs, a following C is associated to two Xs, and all four Xs are parsed into prosodic structure. (To focus on differences between the Optimality Theory and TCRS frameworks, rather than substantive phonological assumptions, we stick as close as possible to the substantive assumptions of Paradis 1988a.)

The phonological process which is not blocked by the phonotactics is Spreading; in step 1 of (317), this geminates a continuant consonant in violation of *GEMCONT. This violation is repaired by the rule [+cont] → [−cont] which changes w to b in step 2. A postcondition of the Spreading rule is that the Xs previously unassociated to underlying segments are now so associated: we dub this postcondition FILL^{X}.

At step 2 of the derivation (317) the first X associated to b is unparsed (its syllabification being blocked by *VːCː); this violates a 'no floating slot' constraint. The repair for this are rules of Segmental Delinking and Skeletal Deletion. In the TCRS treatment, the 'X' in step 3 has been deleted from the representation; in the Optimality-theoretic treatment, this skeletal position is part of the output (as it must be since it is part of the underlying form) but this 'X' is not parsed into prosodic structure and therefore the consonant b associated to it does not surface long. Thus in the Optimality-theoretic account, the constraint violated by the repair rule of Skeletal Deletion is PARSE^{X}.

The effects of the other repair rule, [+cont] → [−cont], arise naturally within an Optimality Theory account following the treatment of segment inventories in §9.1.2. We will assume that the underlying segment denoted w in the example (317) is actually a set of features which need to be parsed (associated to a root node) in order to surface. The feature [+cont] would normally be so parsed (to satisfy PARSE[feat]), except that in the particular problematic case of (317), parsing this feature would violate *GEMCONT, so underparsing is forced; we assume the segment is phonetically realized as [−cont] as a result of the failure to parse [+cont]. This failure to parse [+cont] constitutes a violation of PARSE[Feat], which is crucially lower-ranked than FILL[X] (318): this is why in the optimal analysis (the final representation in (317), with 'X' present but unparsed into syllable structure), the floating position 'X' of the suffix is filled (associated to 'b', with 'b' having an unparsed [+cont] feature) rather than unfilled (unassociated to a segmental root node).

In the TCRS derivation (317), the segment w/b is first associated (step 1) and later delinked (step 3) to a second X. From the perspective of the Optimality Theory account, there is another association/dissociation: the feature [+cont] of this same segment is first parsed into the root node (step 0) then unparsed (step 2). The intermediate stage (step 1) at which the phonotactic *GEMCONT is violated is necessary in the derivational account to trigger the repair rule [+cont] → [−cont] which applies only to geminate consonants. This derivation exhibits *opacity* in the sense of Kiparsky 1973b.

How does the Optimality Theory account explain the opaque outcome, where the consonant surfaces as b even though it does not surface long? That is, how does it explain the optimality of the final representation in (317)? As follows. High-ranked FILL[X] forces the floating 'X' to be filled, which is achieved by associating it to the root node of underlying w; *GEMCONT forces [+cont] not to be parsed into this root node, violating lower-ranked PARSE[Feat]; this explains why b surfaces. At the same time (and in fact, logically independently), *V:C: forces 'X' not to be parsed, violating lower-ranked PARSE[X]; this is why b surfaces short. Note that the exact formulation of the constraints *GEMCONT and *V:C: are crucial to this explanation. *GEMCONT, as formulated above, would be violated if [+cont] were parsed into the root node – even though one of the two skeletal positions to which this root node is associated, X, is not itself parsed into syllable structure. Furthermore, *V:C:, as formulated above, is not violated in the optimal parse precisely because X is unparsed.[83]

---

[83] The Fula analysis in Paradis 1988a has further complexities, and in (318) we have focused on the aspects most relevant to the issues under consideration in this section: a general Optimality-theoretic analysis of Phonotactics + Repair theories, with specific attention to what Paradis terms 'constraint conflict' in TCRS. Going beyond the elements displayed in (318), several additional factors involved in the Fula analysis are addressed in the text and footnotes of Paradis 1988a. Questions about the derivation (317) which must be addressed include these two:

(a)   Why is the free X in the suffix filled by spreading from the preceding consonant rather than from the following vowel?

(b)   Why does the long vowel in the stem not shorten in order to satisfy the *V:C: constraint?

We now return to the issue of constraint conflict within Paradis' account. As quoted earlier, she states that the constraint 'no floating slot' conflicts with the constraint *GᴇᴍCᴏɴᴛ; however, in the end, both constraints are satisfied, appropriate repairs having been made. The relevant sense of 'constraint conflict' here centers around the crucial step 1 of the derivation (317): gemination of underlying *w*, in conflict with *GᴇᴍCᴏɴᴛ, but necessary to trigger [+cont] → [–cont]. The question Paradis raises in her discussion is: why does gemination occur at step 1 rather than Skeletal Deletion (which, after all, does occur at step 3)? This is where the Phonological Level Hierarchy is invoked. Because skeletal > segmental in this hierarchy, Paradis observes that

> a slot, which has *priority* over a segment, cannot be deleted because of a segmental restriction (viz. a segmental feature). Therefore the spreading of the continuant consonant seems to be the last resort. It causes a minimal violation, that is a violation of a segmental type, which can be minimally repaired in changing the value of the feature. (p. 90, emphasis added)

Thus the issue comes down to a choice between two repairs: deleting a skeletal position or changing a feature. In the TCRS account, only one repair can apply

---

Like the core of the TCRS analysis displayed in (318), the core of the Optimality-theoretic analysis presented there must be supplemented in order to address these questions. Given that our objective here is not at all to provide a full treatment of Fula, we content ourselves with a few remarks about how the observations Paradis makes in answer to these questions straightforwardly suggest Optimality-theoretic constraints which satisfactorily complete the treatment of our example (317); properly testing these possible constraints across Fula goes beyond our goals here.

To question (a), Paradis offers two possible explanations: "[i] a nuclear segment does not spread to a non-nuclear position if a non-nuclear segment is available. Moreover, [ii] nouns cannot end with long vowels in Fula" (p. 90; numbers added). The second possible explanation [ii] refers to a surface-unviolated constraint which could obviously be added to the top of the constraint hierarchy in the Optimality-theoretic account. The first proposed explanation [i] is more interesting, and since it has the 'except when' structure, it is a natural product of an Optimality-theoretic treatment involving constraint conflict. One possible such analysis would involve a constraint against vowels associated to two skeletal positions (which may or may not be parsed into syllable structure): '*V:'. Obviously, this is surface-violated; violations are forced by a dominating constraint Fɪʟʟ^X. The constraint *V:, dominated by Fɪʟʟ^X, yields explanation [i] as a consequence: it entails that a free X will be associated to a vowel only if a consonant is not available. In (317), a consonant *is* available (even though it happens to be [+cont]).

Paradis does not explicitly address question (b) in the context of the derivation (317), but in a footnote discussing CV:C syllables generally, she observes that in a variety of environments, shortening does not occur to avoid such syllables (note 4). This discussion would suggest a surface-unviolated constraint with the effect that underlying long vowels surface long. One way to achieve this in the Optimality-theoretic analysis would be to assume, as we have done before, that underlying long vowels are distinguished by already being associated to two Xs or two μs in the input; and then to place superordinate in the Fula hierarchy a constraint which requires nuclear skeletal positions to be parsed. In this case, 'Pᴀʀsᴇ$^{X'}$' in (318) would be specialized to apply to C skeletal positions ('Pᴀʀsᴇ$^{C'}$') and another constraint Pᴀʀsᴇ^V for V positions would be inserted at the top of the hierarchy.

first, and the choice is crucial – even though, in the end, both repairs will be made. The repair lower in the phonological level hierarchy (feature change) is made first.

As in the previous applications of Repair Analysis, the Optimality-theoretic view of the conflicts inherent in this situation is rather different. In the TCRS account, the 'no floating slot' constraint is met in the surface representation because 'X' has been deleted. Thus in this account the constraint is surface-unviolated. In the Optimality-theoretic analysis, however, the constraint PARSE^X is in fact violated in the output; only when this constraint is treated as violable can it truly conflict with the other constraints, and be violated as a result. The other victim of conflict, from the perspective of the Optimality-theoretic account, is the constraint PARSE^{Feat}, which is therefore also surface-violated.

To summarize: from the TCRS perspective, it is the constraints 'no floating slot' and *GEMCONT which conflict, even though in the TCRS account both are surface-unviolated. In our view, such conflict arises only when the former constraint is treated as violable, PARSE^X, and is in fact violated in output forms. Furthermore, the mechanism which TCRS invokes in cases regarded as constraint conflict is a mechanism of choosing which repair rule to apply first; it is therefore formally very different from the Optimality-theoretic mechanism of constraint domination for resolving conflicts between constraints which cannot be simultaneously satisfied in a possible output. The Optimality-theoretic conflicts crucially involve other surface-violated constraints such as FILL^X and PARSE^{Feat} which are not part of the *constraint* component of TCRS, but rather correspond to *rules*, in much the same way as we have seen in the previous analyses of Phonotactics + Repair accounts.

The work of Paradis addresses a number of important and difficult issues which must be resolved in order to render well-defined those derivational theories in which various kinds of rules interact with constraints. We have argued that foregrounding constraints, their interactions, and their conflicts – giving due prominence to the crucial notion that linguistic constraints are violable – makes it possible to formulate phonological analyses which offer fresh substantive insights. The result is a strengthened theory of Universal Grammar, conceived as a set of violable constraints the interactions among which are determined on a language-particular basis. Among the principles of Universal Grammar are cognates of those formerly thought to be no more than loose typological and markedness generalizations. Formally sharpened, these principles now provide the very material from which grammars are built.

Appendix

A.1 The Cancellation and Cancellation/Domination Lemmas

For any harmonic ordering $>$, define $\geq$ in the obvious way: $A \geq B$ iff $A > B$ or $A \approx B$. Define $\leq$ analogously.

(216) **Cancellation Lemma.** Suppose two structures S_1 and S_2 both incur the same mark *m. Then to determine whether $S_1 > S_2$, we can omit *m from the list of marks of both S_1 and S_2 ('cancel the common mark') and compare S_1 and S_2 solely on the basis of the remaining marks. Applied iteratively, this means we can cancel *all* common marks and assess S_1 and S_2 by comparing only their unshared marks.

Proof. What the lemma claims more precisely is this. (105), p. 90, defines the relationship $A > B$ as a predicate over the marks incurred by A and B – the lists of lists of marks assigned to A and B by the constraint hierarchy $\mathcal{H}$: $\mathcal{H}(A)$, $\mathcal{H}(B)$. Let us call this predicate 'harmonic evaluation' $h_+(A, B)$: $A > B$ iff $h_+(A, B)$, by definition. Now suppose a constraint $\mathbb{C}$ assigns the same mark *m to both A and B – that is, $\mathbb{C}(A)$, the list of marks assigned by $\mathbb{C}$ to A, includes at least one token of the mark type *m, and so does $\mathbb{C}(B)$. Let $h_-(A, B)$ be the predicate $h_+(A, B)$ but with one token of *m removed from each of $\mathbb{C}(A)$ and $\mathbb{C}(B)$: this is the harmonic evaluation of A relative to B *after cancellation* of the pair of marks *m. Then the lemma asserts that $A > B$, i.e., $h_+(A, B)$ holds, iff $h_-(A, B)$ holds: harmonic evaluation after cancellation must give the same result as harmonic evaluation before cancellation.

   We will develop the proof in this direction: if $A > B$, then $h_-(A, B)$. This result leads quickly to its converse: if $h_-(A, B)$, then $A > B$, i.e., if harmonic evaluation favors A after mark cancellation, then truly $A > B$. This is because the predicate h defining harmonic evaluation is inherently anti-symmetric: it is impossible for it to declare both A > B and B > A. In other words, if $h\_(A, B)$ is true then $h\_(B, A)$ must be false. So suppose $h\_(A, B)$ holds. Then it cannot be that B > A, for then $h\_(B, A)$ would follow. So if $h\_(A, B)$ holds it must be that either A > B or A ≈ B. But the former must be true because, as we note shortly, if it were true that A ≈ B, then harmonic evaluation after cancellation could not favor A (or B): $h\_(A, B)$ could not be true.

We will spell out the proof that A > B entails $h\_(A, B)$ in full detail, to show how the formal apparatus of the definition (105) of harmonic ordering really works. This is a lengthy process, but the underlying ideas are very simple. The only complication that arises is that at any time, the process of harmonic evaluation compares one mark of A with one mark of B – but it need not be that the two marks *m being cancelled are directly compared with one another. (E.g., analogous to (103), in the Hnuc comparison of .txź.ńt. with .txź.nt́., the two mark-lists are Hnuc(.txź.ńt.) = (ń ź) and Hnuc(.txź.nt́.) = (ź t́). It is the ź marks that cancel, but harmonic evaluation compares the first marks ń vs. ź; after cancellation, harmonic evaluation compares ń vs. t́.)

To begin, let us assume that no constraint ℂ assesses two distinct marks $*m_1$ and $*m_2$ which are equally harmonic. For if this were the case, if ℂ evaluated $*m_2$ as equally harmonic to $*m_1$, we could just replace each token of $*m_2$ with a token of $*m_1$, and this would have no effect on harmonic ordering.

Next, note that we can assume that each cancelled mark *m is the first-listed token of its type. Since marks are listed in harmonic order, and marks of different types have different Harmony values, it follows that all marks of type *m must be contiguous in the list – it can't matter which *m token is omitted; for convenience, we can assume it's the first that is removed.

We need to show that the Harmony ordering of S_1 and S_2 is unaffected by removing a pair of identical marks *m, one from S_1, one from S_2. There are two possibilities: either S_1 and S_2 have the same Harmony, or one of them has greater Harmony. The first possibility is easily dispensed with.

Examination of the definition of harmonic ordering readily shows that the only way S_1 and S_2 can have the same Harmony is if they incur exactly the same marks on all constraints. (For suppose S_1 and S_2 were assessed different marks by some constraints; let the highest-ranked such constraint be ℂ. During harmonic evaluation, S_1 and S_2 would tie on the comparisons of all constraints higher than ℂ, but once evaluation passes to ℂ, a mark $*m_1$ assessed by ℂ to S_1 would be compared to a different mark $*m_2$ assessed by ℂ to S_2, and one of these different marks would necessarily be evaluated by ℂ to have higher Harmony.) So if the structures S_1 and S_2 are equally harmonic, they must incur identical marks on all constraints, and in that case, after omitting one *m from the ℂ-marks of each structure, they will still incur identical marks and therefore will still be rated equally harmonic.

So henceforth assume that one of the two structures has higher Harmony, and label that structure S_1. Thus S_1 is more harmonic than S_2, and what we need to show is that this remains true after cancelling a pair of ℂ-marks *m. Let the constraint hierarchy be $\mathcal{H}1 \equiv \mathbb{C}1 \gg \mathbb{C}2 \gg \cdots \gg \mathbb{C}n \gg \mathbb{C} \gg \mathbb{C}' \gg \cdots \gg \mathbb{C}''$. Now according to the definition of harmonic ordering (105), since $S_1 >_{\mathcal{H}1} S_2$, either (i$_1$) $S_1 >_{C1} S_2$, or

(ii$_1$) $S_1 \approx_{C1} S_2$ and $S_1 >_{[C2 \gg \cdots \gg C'']} S_2$

(The harmonic orders '>' here are more specifically $>^{parse}$, the ordering of whole parses for either a single constraint or for a constraint hierarchy, as indicated by the subscript.)

In the first case (i$_1$), cancelling $\mathbb{C}$-marks cannot make a difference since $>_{C1}$ does not involve the mark-lists generated by $\mathbb{C}$, only those generated by $\mathbb{C}1$; so we are done. Likewise, in the second case (ii$_1$), cancellation cannot change $S_1 \approx_{C1} S_2$, so it remains only to determine whether $S_1 >_{\mathcal{H}2} S_2$ remains true after cancellation. This returns the argument to the previous paragraph, except that now the hierarchy is reduced to $\mathcal{H}2 \equiv \mathbb{C}2 \gg \cdots \gg \mathbb{C}''$, the top constraint $\mathbb{C}1$ of $\mathcal{H}1$ having been removed.

Again there are two cases, (i$_2$) and (ii$_2$); these are just like (i$_1$) and (ii$_1$) above, but with $\mathbb{C}1$ replaced by $\mathbb{C}2$, etc. And again, if (i$_2$) holds, cancellation cannot matter, since only the marks assessed by $\mathbb{C}2$, and not those assessed by $\mathbb{C}$, are relevant; then we are done. If case (ii$_2$) holds, the question is now reduced to whether omitting the *ms can affect $S_1 >_{\mathcal{H}3} S_2$, with the new hierarchy $\mathcal{H}3$ resulting from removing the top-ranked $\mathbb{C}2$ from $\mathcal{H}2$.

Now if $S_1 \approx_{Ci} S_2$ for all the constraints dominating $\mathbb{C}$, $Ci = \mathbb{C}1, \mathbb{C}2, \ldots, \mathbb{C}n$, then finally we have $S_1 >_{[C \gg C' \gg \cdots \gg C'']} S_2$ and we must show that this relation still holds even after removing the *ms from the mark-lists assigned by $\mathbb{C}$ to S_1 and S_2, namely, $\mathbb{C}(S_1)$ and $\mathbb{C}(S_2)$.

Now since $S_1 >_{[C \gg C' \gg \cdots \gg C'']} S_2$, either

(i) $S_1 >_C S_2$, or

(ii) $S_1 \approx_C S_2$ and $S_1 >_{[C' \gg \cdots \gg C'']} S_2$

Case (ii) is simplest. If $S_1 \approx_C S_2$ then $\mathbb{C}$ must assess the same mark-set to both S_1 and S_2: $\mathbb{C}(S_1) = \mathbb{C}(S_2)$. (Otherwise, when recursively comparing first marks following (99), p. 86, at some point there would be a difference in the marks compared and $\mathbb{C}$ would declare one more harmonic.) But if $\mathbb{C}(S_1) = \mathbb{C}(S_2)$ then the sets $\mathbb{C}(S_1)$ and $\mathbb{C}(S_2)$ are still the same after the same mark *m has been removed from each set. So cancellation can't affect the $S_1 \approx_C S_2$ condition, and it can't affect the other condition either: $S_1 >_{[C' \gg \cdots \gg C'']} S_2$ does not involve the marks assessed by $\mathbb{C}$ at all.

For case (i), according to (99), $S_1 >_C S_2$ implies that either

(i$_0$) $FM(\mathbb{C}(S_1)) > FM(\mathbb{C}(S_2))$, or

(ii$_0$) $FM(\mathbb{C}(S_1)) \approx FM(\mathbb{C}(S_2))$ and $Rest(\mathbb{C}(S_1)) > Rest(\mathbb{C}(S_2))$

The harmonic order '>' here is more specifically $>_C^*$, the ordering of single $\mathbb{C}$-marks. Define *m$_i \equiv FM(\mathbb{C}(S_i))$ for $i = 1, 2$.

Start with case (i$_0$). Cancellation cannot affect whether $FM(\mathbb{C}(S_1)) > FM(\mathbb{C}(S_2))$ if *neither* of these first marks is *m; and the condition can't hold if *both* these first marks are *m (in that case we'd have (ii$_0$)). So we're done unless exactly one of the first marks is *m. Assume *m$_1$ = *m and *m$_2 \neq$ *m; we return to the opposite case in a moment. There are potentially two sub-cases to consider, depending on whether $\mathbb{C}$ lists its marks worst-first or best-first.

Suppose $\mathbb{C}$ lists its marks worst-first. Then $*m_2 < *m$, since $*m_2$ precedes $*m$ in the list. (To see why it's not possible that $*m_2 \approx *m$, recall that we are assuming that the omitted token $*m$ is the first-listed mark of its type; thus the only way the first-listed mark $*m_2$ can differ from $*m$ is if it is of a different type, in which case, it has different Harmony.) Thus in the first-mark comparison prior to $*m$-cancellation, when $*m_2$ is compared to $*m_1 = *m$, S_2 is declared less harmonic than S_1. After $*m$-cancellation, the first mark of S_2 is unchanged: it remains $*m_2 \neq *m$. But the new first mark of S_1 is the original second mark of S_1, $*m_1'$. Since this follows the omitted $*m$ in the original mark list, $*m \leq *m_1'$, and so the new first-mark comparison, $*m_2$ vs. $*m_1'$, yields $*m_2 < *m \leq *m_1'$, and, just as before cancellation, S_2 is judged less harmonic than S_1.

The previous paragraph actually shows that in the case $*m_1 = *m$ and $*m_2 \neq *m$ which we've been considering, it *must* be the case that $\mathbb{C}$ lists its marks worst-first, for otherwise we'd have $*m_2 > *m$ and the first-mark comparison $*m_2 > *m = *m_1$ would yield $S_2 > S_1$, contrary to fact.

Thus we see that the only remaining case is the reverse situation, where $*m_1 \neq *m$ and $*m_2 = *m$, in which case $\mathbb{C}$ must list its marks best-first, since $S_1 > S_2$. Then after cancellation the new first mark of S_2 is its original second mark $*m_2'$; the analogous argument to that of the previous paragraphs shows that the new first-mark comparison, $*m_1$ vs. $*m_2'$, becomes $*m_1 > *m = *m_2 \geq *m_2'$. Thus S_1 is still judged more harmonic than S_2 even after cancellation.

Now for case (ii$_0$), where the first marks are equally harmonic: $*m_1 \approx_C *m_2$, and $\text{Rest}(\mathbb{C}(S_1)) > \text{Rest}(\mathbb{C}(S_2))$. There are only two possibilities: either $*m_1 = *m_2 = *m$, and cancellation removes both $*m_1$ and $*m_2$, or $*m_1 = *m_2 \neq *m$, and mark cancellation removes neither. (Recall that the tokens of $*m$ omitted are the first-listed, so if $*m_1 \approx *m$ we must have $*m_2 = *m$; if $*m_1 \neq *m$, it follows that also $*m_2 \neq *m$.)

In the former case, omitting both $*m$s means both new first marks are the original second marks. The comparison of these is exactly what recursively initiates the definition of $\text{Rest}(\mathbb{C}(S_1)) > \text{Rest}(\mathbb{C}(S_2))$; this harmonic ordering, guaranteed by (ii$_0$), ensures that subsequent evaluation of the marks listed after the two cancelled $*m$s will yield the correct outcome $S_1 > S_2$.

In the latter case, $*m_1 = *m_2 \neq *m$, the to-be-omitted marks remain in the mark-lists evaluated by the condition $\text{Rest}(\mathbb{C}(S_1)) > \text{Rest}(\mathbb{C}(S_2))$. Evaluation of this condition after cancellation must yield the same result as evaluation, after cancellation, of the condition $S_1 >_C S_2$ with which we began. In $\text{Rest}(\mathbb{C}(S_1))$ and $\text{Rest}(\mathbb{C}(S_2))$, two identical marks $*m_1$ and $*m_2$ have been stripped off the fronts of the lists $\mathbb{C}(S_1)$ and $\mathbb{C}(S_2)$, respectively, leaving behind two shorter lists each containing a mark $*m$. Verifying that harmonic ordering is unchanged by omitting the $*m$ marks from those lists proceeds exactly as in the above argument. As first marks get stripped off, it must happen that at some point either one or both of the $*m$ marks appears as a first mark, yielding one of the cases already treated above.   □

(192, 238) **Cancellation/Domination Lemma**. Suppose two parses A and B do not incur identical sets of marks. Then A > B iff every mark incurred by A which is not cancelled by a mark of B is dominated by an uncancelled mark of B.

Proof. (Only if.) Suppose A > B. Then by the Cancellation Lemma, after cancelling all common marks, the remaining violations of A are more harmonic than those of B. Consider an uncancelled mark of A, $*m_i$, assessed by constraint $\mathbb{C}i$, where the hierarchy is $\mathbb{C}1 \gg \mathbb{C}2 \gg \cdots \gg \mathbb{C}i > \cdots \gg \mathbb{C}n$. Suppose, for contradiction, that among the uncancelled marks of B, there were no mark that dominates $*m_i$. Consider then the definition of harmonic ordering. First, violations of $\mathbb{C}1$ are evaluated. For B to be declared less harmonic than A at this stage of evaluation, it would have to incur a $\mathbb{C}1$ violation $*m_1$ more severe than any $\mathbb{C}1$ violation of A. In this case, $*m_1$ would dominate the $\mathbb{C}i$-mark $*m_i$, contrary to hypothesis. So B could not be declared less harmonic than A via $\mathbb{C}1$. Clearly the same argument holds for each $\mathbb{C}j$ with $j > i$. Now consider evaluation by $\mathbb{C}i$. For B to be declared less harmonic than A by $\mathbb{C}i$, B would have to incur a mark $*m_i'$ that dominates the mark $*m_i$ assessed to A by $\mathbb{C}i$. But again this is contrary to hypothesis. Thus the mark $*m_i$ incurred by A would have to dominate any $\mathbb{C}i$-mark $*m$ incurred by B (it could not be that $*m \approx *m_i$, for then these two marks would have cancelled). Thus $\mathbb{C}$ would declare A less harmonic than B, a contradiction. This establishes that if A > B, it must be that every uncancelled mark of A must be dominated by an uncancelled mark of B. In other words, every mark of A must be either cancelled by a mark of B, or dominated by one. (Note that each mark of A must be cancelled by a distinct mark of B, but after all cancellation, multiple marks of A can be dominated by a single mark of B.)

(If.) Suppose now that A and B do not incur identical sets of marks, and that every mark incurred by A which is not cancelled by a mark of B is dominated by one; we must show that then A > B. Now consider the evaluation of A with respect to the constraint hierarchy $\mathbb{C}1 \gg \mathbb{C}2 \gg \cdots \gg \mathbb{C}i \gg \cdots \gg \mathbb{C}n$. Consider evaluation by $\mathbb{C}1$. It cannot be that A incurs the highest uncancelled $\mathbb{C}1$-mark, for then there could be no dominating mark assessed to B, contrary to hypothesis. Either B incurs the highest-ranking uncancelled $\mathbb{C}1$ mark, in which case A > B and we are done, or there are no uncancelled $\mathbb{C}1$-marks, in which case harmonic evaluation passes to the next constraint, $\mathbb{C}2$. By exactly parallel reasoning, either B incurs the highest-ranking $\mathbb{C}2$-mark, hence A > B, or there are no uncancelled $\mathbb{C}2$-marks, in which case evaluation passes to $\mathbb{C}3$. It cannot be that there are no uncancelled $\mathbb{C}i$ marks for all $i = 1, 2, \ldots, n$, for in that case A and B would incur exactly identical sets of marks, contrary to hypothesis. It must be then that for some i in $1, 2, \ldots, n$, the highest-ranking $\mathbb{C}i$-mark is incurred by B; for the highest-ranked such $\mathbb{C}i$, the process of harmonic evaluation traced above terminates at $\mathbb{C}i$ with the conclusion that A > B.   □

A.2   CV Syllable Structure

(136)   **Onset Theorem** (Part). If Ons dominates either Parse or Fill^{Ons}, onsets are required in all syllables of optimal outputs.

Proof. In the Basic Syllable Structure Theory, an output consists of a sequence of syllables and unparsed elements $\langle C \rangle$ or $\langle V \rangle$. The syllable node expands to non-terminal sequences (Ons)^Nuc^(Cod) and the nonterminals may or may not dominate C or V. Ons and Cod may only dominate C; Nuc dominates only V.

Consider any output candidate A containing an onsetless syllable σ. Either σ = Nuc, or σ = Nuc Cod. Let us first dismiss those cases where one or both of Nuc and Cod are empty. Prop. 2, ch. 6, ex. (142), establishes that no entire syllable may be empty in an optimal parse. Prop. 3, ch. 6, ex. (143), establishes that no syllable may have Cod as its only filled position. Prop. 4, ch. 6, ex. (144), establishes that two adjacent empty positions never occur in an optimal parse. Taken together, these show that onsetless syllables may not contain empty positions in an optimal parse, regardless of the ranking of constraints.

The nodes Nuc and, if present, Cod in σ must therefore dominate terminal material. Nonterminals can contain at most one segment under the Basic Theory, so the syllable σ in A must take on one of two forms. If open, it takes the form σ = Nuc = .V. and if closed, it takes the form σ = Nuc Cod = .VZC., where Z is a string, possibly empty, of unparsed elements.

Write σ = .VX., where X = ZC or ∅. Then A = α.VX.β, where α and β are strings of syllables and unparsed elements. Now consider two alternative parses of the input underlying A: A′ ≡ α⟨VX⟩β, in which ⟨VX⟩ denotes a string of unparsed elements; and A″ ≡ α.□VX.β.

Since the constraints of the Basic Syllable Structure Theory do not refer to any cross-syllable relations and since they do not detect any relations between an unparsed element and anything outside it, the collection of marks incurred by A is exactly the union of the marks incurred by α, by .VX., and by β. Similarly, the collection of marks incurred by A′ = α⟨VX⟩β is exactly the union of the marks incurred by α, those incurred by ⟨VX⟩, and those incurred by β. And the collection of marks incurred by A″ is exactly the union of the marks incurred by α, by .□VX., and by β.

Thus when comparing A to A′, we can exploit the Cancellation Lemma: all marks incurred by α and by β cancel, reducing the Harmony comparison to the marks incurred by .VX. and by ⟨VX⟩. In addition, since X is shared, in case X = ZC, any marks incurred by Z, which occurs in the same (completely unparsed) form in both parses under discussion, will cancel. Thus, because it contains .VX., candidate A incurs the uncancelled mark (*Ons) if X = ∅ or the uncancelled marks (*Ons, *–Cod) if X = ZC. Candidate A′, by virtue of containing ⟨VX⟩, incurs uncancelled (*Parse) if X = ∅, or uncancelled (*Parse, *Parse) if X = ZC.

Similarly, the Harmony comparison of A with A″ reduces to the comparison of the uncancelled marks incurred by the individual syllables .VX. in A and .□VX. in A″. Since X is shared, and parsed the same way in both, any marks it incurs will cancel, and the uncancelled marks will be (*Ons) for A and (*Fill^{Ons}) for A″.

By the hypothesis of the theorem, Ons dominates either Parse or Fill^{Ons}. Thus in at least one of these comparisons, A's uncancelled mark, *Ons, will be higher than any uncancelled mark incurred by its competitor. Thus either A < A′ or A < A″. In either case, A cannot be optimal. Thus no candidate containing an onsetless syllable can possibly be optimal. Hence onsets are required in all syllables of optimal outputs.   □

Note that the method of proof here is Harmonic Bounding, discussed in §§8.2.3, 9.1.1: a structure (onsetless syllable) is shown to be suboptimal by identifying a more harmonic (but not necessarily optimal) candidate.

(138) **Coda Theorem** (Part). If $-$Cod dominates either Parse and Fill^{Nuc}, codas are forbidden in all syllables of optimal outputs.

Proof. The proof is directly analogous to that of (136). Any parse containing a closed syllable σ must have the form $A \equiv \alpha.XNC.\beta$, where $N = VZ$ or $\square Z$, and $X = CZ'$, or $\square$, or $\emptyset$, and Z and Z' are strings (perhaps empty) of unparsed elements. (If σ has no onset position, we take $X = \emptyset$; if σ has an onset, it is either empty, and $X = \square$, or it contains an input C, possibly separated from the syllable nucleus by unparsed segments Z', in which case $X = CZ'$. The possibility that a closed syllable in optimal parse might have an unfilled coda is eliminated by Prop. 1, ch. 6 (141). Hence the coda is C, perhaps separated from the nucleus by unparsed segments Z.) As competing parses we consider the results of unparsing the coda C, $A' \equiv \alpha.XN.\langle C \rangle \beta$, and of inserting an empty nucleus, $A'' \equiv \alpha.XN.C\square.\beta$. Suppose first that the nucleus is filled: $N = VZ$. Comparing A with A', all marks incurred by α and by β cancel, as do all marks generated by Z and Z', leaving as the remaining marks for A and A' (*–Cod) and (*Parse), respectively, if $X = CZ'$, or (*–Cod, *Fill^{Ons}) and (*Parse, *Fill^{Ons}) if $X = \square$, or (*–Cod, *Ons) and (*Parse, *Ons) if $X = \emptyset$. Thus regardless of the value of X, the A vs. A' comparison of uncancelled marks comes down to (*–Cod) vs. (*Parse). The same result obtains if the nucleus is empty, $N = \square Z$: each mark-list has an added *Fill^{Nuc}, but these all cancel. Similarly, A vs. A'' in all cases comes down to (*–Cod) vs. (*Fill^{Nuc}). Since by the hypothesis of the theorem, $-$Cod dominates either Parse or Fill^{Nuc}, it follows that either $A < A'$ or $A < A''$. Either way, A cannot be optimal, so any optimal output cannot contain a coda. $\square$

A.3 Pāṇini's Theorem on Constraint Ranking

As stated in the text, because of the complexity inherent in this issue, we treat only the case of constraints which are Boolean at the whole-parse level: constraints which assign a single mark to a candidate when they are violated, and no mark when they are satisfied.

Lemma. Suppose a form f is accepted by a constraint hierarchy $\mathbb{CH}$ which includes $\mathbb{C}$. Then either:

f satisfies $\mathbb{C}$, or $\mathbb{C}$ is not active on the input i.

Proof. Consider the filtering of the candidate set at $\mathbb{C}$; f must pass this filter since it passes all of $\mathbb{CH}$. Suppose f violates $\mathbb{C}$. Then f will be filtered out by $\mathbb{C}$ unless $\mathbb{C}$ is violated by all the candidates which pass the filtering in $\mathbb{CH}$ prior to $\mathbb{C}$, in which case $\mathbb{C}$ is not active on i. So if f violates $\mathbb{C}$ then $\mathbb{C}$ is not active on i. This is equivalent to the statement in the lemma. $\square$

(163)   **Pāṇini's Theorem on Constraint Ranking** (PTC). Let $\mathbb{S}$ and $\mathbb{G}$ stand as specific to general in a Pāṇinian constraint relation. Suppose these constraints are part of a constraint hierarchy $\mathbb{CH}$, and that $\mathbb{G}$ is active in $\mathbb{CH}$ on some input i. Then if $\mathbb{G} \gg \mathbb{S}$, $\mathbb{S}$ is not active on i.

Proof. Assume $\mathbb{S}$ so placed in the hierarchy; then any form which is subject to evaluation by $\mathbb{S}$ must have survived the filtering of the top portion of the hierarchy down to and including $\mathbb{G}$; call this subhierarchy T. Let i be an input for which $\mathbb{G}$ is active, which exists by hypothesis. Consider the candidate set Gen(i). By the lemma, any parse f in Gen(i) which survives T must satisfy $\mathbb{G}$. So every parse f which survives to be evaluated by $\mathbb{S}$ satisfies $\mathbb{G}$. But by the contrapositive of the Pāṇinian relationship, satisfying $\mathbb{G}$ entails failing $\mathbb{S}$. Since all the candidates which $\mathbb{S}$ gets to evaluate fail $\mathbb{S}$, $\mathbb{S}$ cannot filter any of them out, and $\mathbb{S}$ is therefore not active on the input i. $\square$

References

Square brackets enclose those items written or published after the original distribution of this work which contain or directly follow up material cited in the text, as well as those for which publication date differs significantly from date of circulation and use.

The Rutgers Optimality Archive (ROA) can be found at http://roa.rutgers.edu.

Allen, W. S. 1973. *Accent and rhythm*. Cambridge: Cambridge University Press.

Anderson, Stephen R. 1969. *West Scandinavian vowel systems and the ordering of phonological rules*. Doctoral dissertation, MIT, Cambridge, MA.

Anderson, Stephen R. 1972. On nasalization in Sundanese. *Linguistic Inquiry* 3, 253–68.

Anderson, Stephen R. 1982. The analysis of French schwa, or how to get something for nothing. *Language* 58, 534–73.

Aoun, Joseph. 1979. Is the syllable or supersyllable a constituent? In Kenneth J. Safir, ed., *MIT Working Papers in Linguistics 1: Papers on syllable structure, metrical structure, and Harmony processes*, pp. 140–8. Cambridge, MA: MIT Department of Linguistics.

Aoun, Joseph. 1986. *Generalized binding: the syntax and logical form of wh-interrogatives*. Studies in Generative Grammar 26. Dordrecht: Foris.

Archangeli, Diana. 1984. *Underspecification in Yawelmani phonology and morphology*. Doctoral dissertation, MIT, Cambridge, MA. [1988, New York: Garland Press.]

Archangeli, Diana and Douglas Pulleyblank. 1991. African tongue root harmony: optimal systems. Paper presented at NSF/LSA Conference on Phonological Feature Organization. University of California, Santa Cruz.

Archangeli, Diana and Douglas Pulleyblank. 1992. Grounded phonology. Ms. University of Arizona, Tucson and University of British Columbia, Vancouver. [1994, Cambridge, MA: MIT Press.]

Avery, Peter and Keren Rice. 1989. Segment structure and coronal underspecification. *Phonology* 6, 179–200.

Bach, Emmon. 1965. On some recurrent types of transformations. *Georgetown University Monograph Series on Languages and Linguistics* 18, 3–18.

Bach, Emmon and Deirdre Wheeler. 1981. Montague Phonology: a first approximation. In Wynn Chao and Deirdre Wheeler, eds., *University of Massachusetts Occasional Papers in Linguistics* 7, pp. 27–45. Amherst, MA: GLSA.

Barton, G. Edward, Robert C. Berwick, and Eric Sven Ristad. 1987. *Computational complexity and natural language*. Cambridge, MA: MIT Press.

Bell, Alan. 1971. Some patterns of occurrence and formation of syllable structures. In *Working Papers on Language Universals*, Number 6, pp. 23–137. Language Universals Project, Stanford University.

Bell, Alan and Joan Bybee Hooper. 1978. *Syllables and segments*. New York: Elsevier–North Holland.

Benton, Richard. 1971. *Pangasinán reference grammar*. Honolulu: University of Hawaii Press.

Berg, G. 1991. Learning recursive phrase structure: combining the strengths of PDP and X-Bar Syntax. Technical Report 91–5, Dept. of Computer Science, State University of New York, Albany.

Berwick, Robert, Steven Abney, and Carol Tenny, eds. 1991. *Principle-based parsing: computation and psycholinguistics*. Dordrecht: Kluwer.

Bird, Steven. 1990. *Constraint-based phonology*. Doctoral dissertation, University of Edinburgh.

Bittner, Maria. 1993. Cross-linguistic semantics. Ms. Rutgers University, New Brunswick. [1994, *Linguistics and Philosophy* 17, 57–108.]

Black, H. Andrew. 1991. The optimal iambic foot and reduplication in Axininca Campa. *Phonology at Santa Cruz* 2, 1–18. Santa Cruz: Dept. of Linguistics, University of California at Santa Cruz.

Black, H. Andrew. 1993. Constraint-ranked derivation: truncation and stem binarity in Southeastern Tepehuan. Ms. University of California, Santa Cruz.

[Black, H. Andrew. 1993. *Constraint-ranked derivation: a serial approach to optimization*. Doctoral dissertation, University of California, Santa Cruz.]

Borowsky, Toni. 1986a. *Topics in the lexical phonology of English*, Doctoral dissertation, University of Massachusetts, Amherst.

Borowsky, Toni. 1986b. Structure preservation and the syllable coda in English. *Natural Language and Linguistic Theory* 7, 145–66.

Bosch, Anna. 1991. *Phonotactics at the level of the phonological word*. Doctoral dissertation, University of Chicago.

Broselow, Ellen. 1982. On the interaction of stress and epenthesis. *Glossa* 16, 115–32.

Broselow, Ellen. 1992. Parametric variation in dialect phonology. In Ellen Broselow, Mushira Eid, and John J. McCarthy, eds., *Perspectives on Arabic linguistics IV*, pp. 7–47. Amsterdam: Benjamins.

Broselow, Ellen and John J. McCarthy. 1983. A theory of internal reduplication. *Linguistic Review* 3, 25–88.

Brousse, Olivier. 1991. *Generativity and systematicity in neural network combinatorial learning*. Doctoral dissertation. Dept. of Computer Science, University of Colorado, Boulder.

Brousse, Olivier and Smolensky, Paul. 1989. Virtual memories and massive generalization in connectionist combinatorial learning. In *Proceedings of the Eleventh Annual Conference of the Cognitive Science Society*, 380–7. Ann Arbor, MI: Erlbaum.

Browning, M. A. 1991. Bounding conditions on representation. *Linguistic Inquiry* 22, 541–62.

Burzio, Luigi. 1987. English stress. In Pier Marco Bertinetto and Michele Loporcaro, eds., *Certamen Phonologicum: Proceedings of the 1987 Cortona Phonology Meeting*. Turin: Rosenberg and Sellio.

Burzio, Luigi. 1992a. Metrical consistency. Abstract of paper presented at DIMACS Workshop, Princeton University.

Burzio, Luigi. 1992b. *Principles of English stress*. Ms. Johns Hopkins University. [1994, New York: Cambridge University Press.]

Bybee, Joan. 1985. *Morphology: a study of the relation between meaning and form*. Amsterdam: Benjamins.

Cairns, Charles. 1969. Markedness, neutralization and universal redundancy rules. *Language* 45, 863–85.

Cairns, Charles. 1988. Phonotactics, markedness, and lexical representation. *Phonology* 5, 209–36.

Cairns, Charles and Mark Feinstein. 1982. Markedness and the theory of syllable structure. *Linguistic Inquiry* 13, 193–226.

Calabrese, Andrea. 1988. *Towards a theory of phonological alphabets*. Doctoral dissertation, MIT, Cambridge, MA.

Carlson, Lauri. 1978. Word stress in Finnish. Ms. MIT, Cambridge, MA.

Chen, Matthew Y. 1987. The syntax of Xiamen tone sandhi. *Phonology Yearbook* 4, 109–50.

Chomsky, Noam. 1951. *Morphophonemics of Modern Hebrew*. Master's thesis, University of Pennsylvania, Philadelphia.

Chomsky, Noam. 1961. On the notion "rule of grammar". In *Proceedings of the Twelfth Symposium in Applied Mathematics*. [Reprinted 1964 in Jerry A. Fodor and Jerrold J. Katz, eds., *The structure of language: readings in the philosophy of language*, pp. 119–36. Englewood Cliffs: Prentice-Hall.]

Chomsky, Noam. 1965. *Aspects of the theory of syntax*. Cambridge, MA: MIT Press.

Chomsky, Noam. 1981. *Lectures on government and binding*. Dordrecht: Foris.

Chomsky, Noam. 1986. *Barriers*. Cambridge, MA: MIT Press.

Chomsky, Noam. 1989. Some notes on economy of derivation and representation. In Itziar Laka and Anoop Mahajan, eds., *MIT Working Papers in Linguistics* 10, pp. 43–7. Cambridge, MA: MIT, Dept. of Linguistics.

Chomsky, Noam. 1992. *A minimalist program for linguistic theory*. MIT Occasional Papers in Linguistics #1. Cambridge, MA: Dept. of Linguistics, MIT. [1993, in Ken Hale and S. J. Keyser, eds., *The view from building 20: essays in linguistics in honor of Sylvain Bromberger*, pp. 1–52. Cambridge, MA: MIT Press.]

Chomsky, Noam and Morris Halle. 1968. *The sound pattern of English*. New York: Harper and Row.

Churchward, Clerk Maxwell. 1953. *Tongan grammar*. London: Oxford University Press.

Churchyard, Henry. 1991. Biblical Hebrew prosodic structure as the result of preference-ranked constraints. Ms. University of Texas, Austin.

[Churchyard, Henry. 1999. *Topics in Tiberian Biblical Hebrew metrical phonology and prosodics*. Doctoral dissertation, University of Texas, Austin.]

Clements, G. N. 1976. Palatalization: linking or assimilation? In Salikoko S. Mufwene, Carol A. Walker, and Sanford B. Steever, eds., *Papers from the Twelfth Regional Meeting of the Chicago Linguistic Society*, pp. 96–109. Chicago: Chicago Linguistic Society.

Clements, G. N. 1990. The role of the sonority cycle in core syllabification. In John Kingston and Mary Beckman, eds., *Papers in Laboratory Phonology* I, pp. 283–333. New York: Cambridge University Press.

Clements, G. N. 1991. Place of articulation in vowels and consonants: a unified theory. [1993, as "Lieu d'articulation des consonnes et des voyelles: une théorie unifiée." In Bernard Laks and Annie Rialland, eds., collections "Sciences du Langage", *Architecture des représentations phonologiques*, pp. 101–45. Paris: Editions du CNRS.]

Clements, G. N. and S. J. Keyser. 1983. *CV phonology*. Cambridge, MA: MIT Press.

Cohen, Michael A. and Steven Grossberg. 1983. Absolute stability of global pattern formation and parallel memory storage by competitive neural networks. *IEEE Transactions on Systems, Man, and Cybernetics* 13, 815–25.

Cole, Jennifer S. 1992. Eliminating cyclicity as a source of complexity in phonology. UIUC-BI-CS Technical Report, Beckman Institute, University of Illinois. [1995, in Jennifer S. Cole, Jerry L. Morgan, and Georgia Green, eds., *Linguistics and Computation*, pp. 255–79. Stanford, CA: CSLI.]

Coleman, John. 1991. *Phonological representations – their names, forms, and powers*. Doctoral dissertation, University of York.

Davis, Stuart. 1988a. Syllable weight hierarchies and stress assignment. Ms. Indiana University, Bloomington.

Davis, Stuart. 1988b. Syllable onsets as a factor in stress rules. *Phonology* 5, 1–19.

Dell, François. 1973. *Les règles et les sons*. Paris: Hermann. [Tr. 1980 as *Generative Phonology* (= Part 1), and *Generative phonology and French phonology*, Catherine Cullen, trans. New York: Cambridge University Press.]

Dell, François and Mohamed Elmedlaoui. 1985. Syllabic consonants and syllabification in Imdlawn Tashlhiyt Berber. *Journal of African Languages and Linguistics* 7, 105–30.

Dell, François and Mohamed Elmedlaoui. 1988. Syllabic consonants in Berber: some new evidence. *Journal of African Languages and Linguistics* 10, 1–17.

Dell, François and Mohamed Elmedlaoui. 1989. Quantitative transfer in the nonconcatenative morphology of Imdlawn Tashlhiyt Berber. *Journal of Afroasiatic Languages* 3, 89–125.

[Dell, François and Mohamed Elmedlaoui. 2003. *Syllables in Tashlhiyt Berber and Moroccan Arabic*. Kluwer International Handbooks of Linguistics, vol. 2. Dordrecht: Kluwer.]

Devine, A. M. and Laurence Stephens. 1980. Latin prosody and meter: brevis brevians. *Classical Philology* 75, 142–57.

Dixon, R. M. W. 1977. *A grammar of Yidiny*. Cambridge: Cambridge University Press.

Dixon, R. M. W. 1988. *A grammar of Boumaa Fijian*. Chicago: University of Chicago Press.

Dolan, Charles P. 1989. *Tensor Manipulation Networks: connectionist and symbolic approaches to comprehension, learning, and planning*. Doctoral dissertation, Dept. of Computer Science, University of California, Los Angeles.

Dolan, Charles P. and Michael G. Dyer. 1987. Symbolic schemata, role binding, and the evolution of structure in connectionist memories. In *Proceedings of the IEEE First International Conference on Neural Networks*, vol. II, pp. 287–98. San Diego, CA: IEEE.

Dressler, Wolfgang. 1985. On the predictiveness of natural morphology. *Journal of Linguistics* 21, 321–37.

Elman, Jeffrey L. 1990. Finding structure in time. *Cognitive Science* 14, 179–211.

Elman, Jeffrey L. 1991. Distributed representations, simple recurrent networks, and grammatical structure. *Machine Learning* 7, 195–226.

Elman, Jeffrey L. 1992. Grammatical structure and distributed representations. In Steven Davis, ed., *Connectionism: theory and practice*, pp. 138–78. New York: Oxford University Press.

Emonds, Joseph. 1970. *Root and structure-preserving transformations*. Doctoral dissertation, MIT, Cambridge, MA.

Everett, Daniel. 1988. On metrical constituent structure in Pirahã. *Natural Language and Linguistic Theory* 6, 207–46.

French, Koleen Matsuda. 1988. *Insights into Tagalog reduplication. Infixation and stress from non-linear phonology*. MA thesis, University of Texas, Arlington. SIL and University of Texas, Arlington, Publications in Linguistics No. 84.

Furby, Christine. 1974. *Garawa phonology*. Pacific Linguistics Series A, No. 37. Canberra: Australian National University.

Giegerich, Heinz. 1985. *Metrical phonology and phonological structure*. Cambridge: Cambridge University Press.

Gnanadesikan, Amalia. 1992. The feature geometry of coronal subplaces. Ms. University of Massachusetts, Amherst. [1993, in Tim Sherer, ed., *University of Massachusetts Occasional Papers in Linguistics* 16, 27–68. Amherst: GLSA.]

Golden, Richard M. 1986. The "Brain-State-in-a-Box" neural model is a gradient descent algorithm. *Mathematical Psychology* 30/31, 73–80.

Golden, Richard M. 1988. A unified framework for connectionist systems. *Biological Cybernetics* 59, 109–20.

Goldsmith, John. 1976. *Autosegmental Phonology*. Doctoral dissertation, MIT, Cambridge, MA. [1979, New York: Garland Publishing.]

Goldsmith, John. 1990. *Autosegmental and metrical phonology*. Oxford: Basil Blackwell.

Goldsmith, John. 1991. Phonology as an intelligent system. In Donna Jo Napoli and Judy Kegl, eds., *Bridges between psychology and linguistics: a Swarthmore Festschrift for Lila Gleitman*, pp. 247–67. Hillsdale, NJ: Erlbaum.

Goldsmith, John. 1992. Local modeling in phonology. In Steven Davis, ed., *Connectionism: theory and practice*, pp. 229–46. New York: Oxford University Press.

Goldsmith, John. 1993. Harmonic Phonology. In John Goldsmith, ed., *The last phonological rule*, pp. 21–60. Chicago: University of Chicago Press.

Goldsmith, John and Gary Larson. 1990. Local modeling and syllabification. In Michael Ziolkowski, Manuela Noske, and Karen Deaton, eds., *Papers from the 26th Annual Regional Meeting of the Chicago Linguistic Society*, vol. 2: *Parasession on the syllable in phonetics and phonology*, pp. 129–42. Chicago: Chicago Linguistic Society.

Goodman, Beverley. 1993. *The integration of hierarchical features into a phonological system*. Doctoral dissertation, Cornell University, Ithaca.

Green, Tom. 1992. Core syllabification and the grid: explaining quantity sensitivity. In K. Broderick, ed., *Proceedings of NELS 22*, pp. 179–93. Amherst, MA: GLSA.

Grimshaw, Jane. 1993. Minimal projection, heads, and inversion. Ms. Rutgers University, New Brunswick. ROA-4. [Revised as "Projection, heads, and optimality," ROA-68; appeared 1997, as "Minimal projection, heads, and optimality," *Linguistic Inquiry* 28, 373–422.]

Guerssel, Mohammed. 1986. Glides in Berber and syllabicity. *Linguistic Inquiry* 17, 1–12.

Haiman, John. 1972. Phonological targets and unmarked structures. *Language* 48, 365–77.

Hale, Kenneth. 1973. Deep–surface canonical disparities in relation to analysis and change: an Australian example. *Current Trends in Linguistics* 11, 401–58.

Hale, Kenneth and A. Lacayo Blanco. 1988. *Vocabulario preliminar del ULWA (Sumu meridional)*. Centro de investigaciones y documentación de la Costa Atlantica, Karawala, Zelaya Sur, Nicaragua and Center of Cognitive Science, MIT, Cambridge, MA.

Halle, Morris. 1973. Stress rules in English, a new version. *Linguistic Inquiry* 4, 451–64.

Halle, Morris and Jean-Roger Vergnaud. 1987. *An essay on stress*. Cambridge, MA: MIT Press.

Hammond, Michael. 1984. *Constraining metrical theory: a modular theory of stress and destressing*. Doctoral dissertation, University of California, Los Angeles.

Hammond, Michael. 1992. Deriving ternarity. Ms. University of Arizona, Tucson. [1996, in Colleen M. Fitzgerald and Andrea Heiberg, eds., *Coyote Papers* 9, pp. 39–58. Tucson: Dept. of Linguistics, University of Arizona.]

Hare, Mary. 1990. The role of similarity in Hungarian vowel harmony: a connectionist account. *Connection Science* 2, 123–50.

Hayes, Bruce. 1980. *A metrical theory of stress rules*. Doctoral dissertation, MIT, Cambridge, MA.

Hayes, Bruce. 1982. Extrametricality and English stress. *Linguistic Inquiry* 13, 227–76.

Hayes, Bruce. 1984. The phonology of rhythm in English. *Linguistic Inquiry* 15, 33–74.

Hayes, Bruce. 1985. Iambic and trochaic rhythm in stress rules. In Mary Niepokuj, Mary VanClay, Vassiliki Nikiforidou, and Deborah Feder (with Claudia Brugman, Monica Macaulay, Natasha Beery, and Michele Emanatian), eds., *Proceedings of the Eleventh Annual Meeting of the Berkeley Linguistics Society: parasession on poetics, metrics, and prosody*, pp. 429–46. Berkeley: Berkeley Linguistics Society.

Hayes, Bruce. 1987. A revised parametric metrical theory. In Joyce McDonough and Bernadette Plunkett, eds., *Proceedings of the North East Linguistics Society* 17, pp. 274–89. Amherst: GLSA.

Hayes, Bruce. 1991/95. *Metrical stress theory: principles and case studies*. Ms. University of California, Los Angeles. [1995, Chicago: University of Chicago Press.]

Hewitt, Mark. 1992. *Vertical maximization and metrical theory*. Doctoral dissertation, Brandeis University, Waltham, MA.

Hewitt, Mark and Alan Prince. 1989. OCP, locality, and linking: the N. Karanga verb. In E. Jane Fee and Katherine Hunt, eds., *Proceedings of the Eighth West Coast Conference on Formal Linguistics*, pp. 176–91. Stanford: Stanford Linguistics Association.

Hinton, Geoffrey E. and Sejnowski, Terrence J. 1983. Optimal perceptual inference. In *Proceedings of the IEEE Computer Society Conference on Computer Vision and Pattern Recognition*, pp. 448–53. Silver Spring, MD: IEEE Computer Society Press.

Hinton, Geoffrey E. and Sejnowski, Terrence J. 1986. Learning and relearning in Boltzmann Machines. In David E. Rumelhart, James L. McClelland, and the PDP Research Group, eds., *Parallel Distributed Processing: explorations in the microstructure of cognition*, pp. 282–317. Cambridge, MA: MIT Press/Bradford Books.

Hooper, Joan Bybee. 1972. The syllable in linguistic theory. *Language* 48, 525–40.

Hopfield, John J. 1982. Neural networks and physical systems with emergent collective computational abilities. *Proceedings of the National Academy of Sciences, USA*, 79, 2554–8.

Hopfield, John J. 1984. Neurons with graded response have collective computational properties like those of two-state neurons. *Proceedings of the National Academy of Sciences, USA*, 81, 3088–92.

Howard, Irwin. 1973. *A directional theory of rule application*. Doctoral dissertation, MIT. Bloomington: Indiana University Linguistics Club.

Howard, Richard. 1990. The victor vanquished. *Antaeus* 64/65, 61–2. New York: Ecco Press.

Hudson, Grover. 1974. The role of SPC's in Natural Generative Phonology. In Anthony Bruck, Robert A. Fox, and Michael W. LaGaly, eds., *Papers from the parasession on Natural Phonology*, pp. 171–83. Chicago: Chicago Linguistic Society.

Hulst, Harry van der. 1984. *Syllable structure and stress in Dutch*. Dordrecht: Foris.

Hulst, Harry van der. 1992. The independence of stress and rhythm. Ms. Rijksuniversiteit te Leiden.

Hume, Elizabeth V. 1992. *Front vowels, coronal consonants, and their interaction in Nonlinear Phonology*. Doctoral dissertation, Cornell University, Ithaca.

Hung, Henrietta. 1992. Relativized suffixation in Choctaw: a constraint-based analysis of the verb grade system. Ms. Brandeis University, Waltham, MA.

Hung, Henrietta. 1994. *The rhythmic and prosodic organization of edge constituents*. Doctoral dissertation, Brandeis University, Waltham, MA. [1995, as *The rhythmic and prosodic organization of edge constituents: an Optimality-Theoretic account*. Bloomington: Indiana University Linguistics Club Publications.]

Hyman, Larry. 1985. *A theory of phonological weight*. Dordrecht: Foris.

Inkelas, Sharon. 1989. *Prosodic constituency in the lexicon*. Doctoral dissertation, Stanford University.

Itô, Junko. 1986. *Syllable theory in prosodic phonology*. Doctoral dissertation, University of Massachusetts, Amherst.

Itô, Junko. 1989. A prosodic theory of epenthesis. *Natural Language and Linguistic Theory* 7, 217–60.

Itô, Junko, Yoshihisa Kitagawa, and R. Armin Mester. 1992. Prosodic type preservation in Japanese: evidence from *zuuja-go*. SRC-92-05, Syntax Research Center, University of

California, Santa Cruz. [1996, Revised as "Prosodic faithfulness and correspondence: evidence from a Japanese argot," ROA-146.]

Itô, Junko and R. Armin Mester. 1992. Weak layering and word binarity. Report LRC-92-09, Linguistics Research Center, University of California, Santa Cruz.

Itô, Junko and R. Armin Mester. 1993. Licensed segments and safe paths. In Carole Paradis, Darlene LaCharité, and Emmanuel Nikiema, eds., *Constraint-based theories in multilinear phonology*, special issue of *Canadian Journal of Linguistics* 38, 197–213.

Jackendoff, Ray. 1983. *Semantics and cognition.* Cambridge, MA: MIT Press.

Jackendoff, Ray. 1987. *Consciousness and the computational mind.* Cambridge, MA: MIT Press.

Jackendoff, Ray. 1991. Musical parsing and musical affect. *Music Perception* 9, 199–230.

Jain, Ajay N. 1991. Parsing complex sentences with structured connectionist networks. *Neural Computation* 3, 110–20.

Jakobson, Roman. 1962. *Selected writings 1: phonological studies.* The Hague: Mouton.

Johnson, C. Douglas. 1972. *Formal aspects of phonological description.* The Hague: Mouton.

Kager, René. 1989. *A metrical theory of stress and destressing in English and Dutch = Een metrische theorie over klemtoon en klemtoonverlies in het Engels en het Nederlands.* Dordrecht: ICG.

Kager, René. 1992a. Are there any truly quantity-insensitive systems? In Laura A. Buszard-Welcher, Lionel Wee, and William F. Weigel, eds., *Proceedings of the Eighteenth Annual Meeting of the Berkeley Linguistics Society*, pp. 123–32. Berkeley: Berkeley Linguistics Society.

Kager, René. 1992b. Shapes of the generalized trochee. In J. Mead, ed., *Proceedings of the Eleventh West Coast Conference on Formal Linguistics* 11, 298–311. Stanford: CSLI.

Kager, René. 1993. Alternatives to the Iambic-Trochaic Law. *Natural Language and Linguistic Theory* 11, 381–432.

Kager, René and Ellis Visch. 1984a. *Een metrische analyse van ritmische klemtoonverschuiving.* MA thesis, Instituut de Vooys voor Nederlanse taal- en letterkunde, Rijksuniversiteit Utrecht.

Kager, René and Ellis Visch. 1984b. Syllable weight and Dutch word stress. In Hans Bennis and W. U. S. van Lessen Kloeke, eds., *Linguistics in the Netherlands 1984*, pp. 197–205. Dordrecht: Foris.

Kahn, Daniel. 1976. *Syllable-based generalizations in English phonology.* Doctoral dissertation, MIT, Cambridge, MA.

Kaye, Jonathan. 1990. 'Coda' licensing. *Phonology* 7, 301–30.

Kaye, Jonathan and Jean Lowenstamm. 1981. Syllable structure and markedness theory. In Adriana Belletti, Luciana Brandi, and Luigi Rizzi, eds., *The theory of markedness in generative grammar*, pp. 287–315. Pisa: Scuola Normale Superiore.

Kaye, Jonathan and Jean Lowenstamm. 1984. De la syllabicité. In François Dell, Daniel Hirst, and Jean-Roger Vergnaud, eds., *Forme sonore du langage*, pp. 123–59. Paris: Hermann.

Kaye, Jonathan, Jean Lowenstamm, and Jean-Roger Vergnaud. 1985. The internal structure of phonological elements: a theory of Charm and Government. *Phonology Yearbook* 2, 305–28.

Kean, Mary-Louise. 1974. *The theory of markedness in generative grammar.* Doctoral dissertation, MIT, Cambridge, MA.

Kelkar, Ashok R. 1968. *Studies in Hindi-Urdu I: introduction and word phonology.* Deccan College, Poona.

Kiparsky, Paul. 1973a. How abstract is phonology? In Osama Fujimura, ed., *Three dimensions of linguistic theory*, pp. 5–56. Tokyo: TEC.

Kiparsky, Paul. 1973b. Abstractness, opacity and global rules. In Osama Fujimura, ed., *Three dimensions of linguistic theory*, pp. 57–86. Tokyo: TEC.

Kiparsky, Paul. 1973c. "Elsewhere" in phonology. In Stephen Anderson and Paul Kiparsky, eds., *A Festschrift for Morris Halle*, pp. 93–106. New York: Holt, Rinehart, and Winston.

Kiparsky, Paul. 1981. Vowel harmony. Ms. MIT, Cambridge, MA.

Kiparsky, Paul. 1982. Lexical phonology and morphology. In I. S. Yang, ed., *Linguistics in the Morning Calm*, pp. 3–91. Seoul: Hanshin.

Kiparsky, Paul. 1991. Quantity sensitivity and the nature of templatic parsing. Undated handout. Berkeley Linguistics Society, Berkeley, CA.

Kiparsky, Paul. 1992. Catalexis. Ms. Stanford University, Stanford, CA.

Kirchner, Robert. 1992a. Lardil truncation and augmentation: a morphological account. Ms. University of Maryland, College Park.

Kirchner, Robert. 1992b. *Harmonic Phonology within one language: an analysis of Yidiny*. MA thesis, University of Maryland, College Park.

Kirchner, Robert. 1992c. Yidiny prosody in Harmony Theoretic Phonology. Ms. University of California, Los Angeles.

Kisseberth, Charles. 1970a. On the functional unity of phonological rules. *Linguistic Inquiry* 1, 291–306.

Kisseberth, Charles. 1970b. Vowel elision in Tonkawa and derivational constraints. In Jerrold M. Sadock and Anthony L. Vanek, eds., *Studies presented to Robert B. Lees by his students*, pp. 109–37. Edmonton: Linguistic Research Inc.

Kisseberth, Charles. 1972. On derivative properties of phonological rules. In Michael K. Brame, ed., *Contributions to generative phonology*, pp. 201–28. Austin: University of Texas Press.

Klokeid, Terry Jack. 1976. *Topics in Lardil grammar*. Doctoral dissertation, MIT, Cambridge, MA.

Kuryłowicz, Jerzy. 1968. *Indogermanische Grammatik. Band II: Akzent. Ablaut.* Heidelberg: Carl Winter.

Lachter, Joel and Bever, Thomas G. 1988. The relation between linguistic structure and associative theories of language learning – a constructive critique of some connectionist learning models. *Cognition* 28, 195–247.

Lakoff, George. 1965. *On the nature of syntactic irregularity*. Doctoral dissertation, Harvard University, Cambridge, MA. Harvard Computational Lab Report NSF-16.

Lakoff, George. 1988. A suggestion for a linguistics with connectionist foundations. In David Touretzky, Geoffrey Hinton, and Terrence Sejnowski, eds., *Proceedings of the 1988 Connectionist Models Summer School*. San Mateo, CA: Morgan Kaufmann.

Lakoff, George. 1989. Cognitive phonology. Paper presented at the UC-Berkeley Workshop on Rules and Constraints, May 1989.

Lakoff, George. 1993. Cognitive phonology. In John Goldsmith, ed., *The last phonological rule*, pp. 117–45. Chicago: University of Chicago Press.

Lapointe, Steven and Mark Feinstein. 1982. The role of vowel deletion and epenthesis in the assignment of syllable structure. In Harry van der Hulst and Norval Smith, eds., *The structure of phonological representations. Part II*, pp. 69–120. Dordrecht: Foris.

Larson, Gary. 1990. Local computational networks and the distribution of segments in the Spanish syllable. In Michael Ziolkowski, Manuela Noske, and Karen Deaton, eds., *Papers from the 26th Annual Regional Meeting of the Chicago Linguistic Society*, vol. 2: *Parasession on the syllable in phonetics and phonology*, pp. 257–72. Chicago: Chicago Linguistic Society.

Larson, Gary. 1992. *Dynamic computational networks and the representation of phonological information*. Doctoral dissertation, Dept. of Linguistics, University of Chicago.

Legendre, Géraldine, Yoshiro Miyata, and Paul Smolensky. 1990a. Can connectionism contribute to syntax? Harmonic Grammar, with an application. In Michael Ziolkowski,

Manuela Noske, and Karen Deaton, eds., *Papers from the 26th Annual Regional Meeting of the Chicago Linguistic Society*, pp. 237–52. Chicago: Chicago Linguistic Society.

Legendre, Géraldine, Yoshiro Miyata, and Paul Smolensky. 1990b. Harmonic Grammar – a formal multi-level connectionist theory of linguistic well-formedness: an application. In *Proceedings of the Twelfth Annual Conference of the Cognitive Science Society*, pp. 884–91. Cambridge, MA: Erlbaum.

Legendre, Géraldine, Yoshiro Miyata, and Paul Smolensky. 1990c. Harmonic Grammar – a formal multi-level connectionist theory of linguistic well-formedness: theoretical foundations. In *Proceedings of the Twelfth Annual Conference of the Cognitive Science Society*, pp. 388–95. Cambridge, MA: Erlbaum.

Legendre, Géraldine, Yoshiro Miyata, and Paul Smolensky. 1991a. Unifying syntactic and semantic approaches to unaccusativity: a connectionist approach. In Laurel A. Sutton and Christopher Johnson (with Ruth Shields), eds., *Proceedings of the Seventeenth Annual Meeting of the Berkeley Linguistics Society*, pp. 156–67. Berkeley: Berkeley Linguistics Society.

Legendre, Géraldine, Yoshiro Miyata, and Paul Smolensky. 1991b. Distributed recursive structure processing. In Richard P. Lippman, John E. Moody, and David S. Touretzky, eds., *Advances in Neural Information Processing Systems 3*, pp. 591–7. San Mateo, CA: Morgan Kaufmann.

Legendre, Géraldine, William Raymond, and Paul Smolensky. 1993. An Optimality-Theoretic typology of case marking and grammatical voice. In Joshua S. Guenter, Barbara A. Keyser, and Cheryl C. Zoll, eds., *Proceedings of the Nineteenth Annual Meeting of the Berkeley Linguistics Society*, pp. 464–78. Berkeley: Berkeley Linguistics Society. ROA-3.

Lerdahl, Fred and Ray Jackendoff. 1983. *A generative theory of tonal music*. Cambridge, MA: MIT Press.

Levelt, Clara. 1991. Samoan reduplication: how to behave as a plural and other good manners. In John van Lit, René Mulder, and Rint Sybesma, eds., *Proceedings of the Leiden Conference for Junior Linguists 2*. Leiden: University of Leiden.

Levin, Juliette [Blevins]. 1985. *A metrical theory of syllabicity*. Doctoral dissertation, MIT, Cambridge, MA.

Liberman, Mark. 1975. *The intonational system of English*. Doctoral dissertation, MIT, Cambridge, MA.

Liberman, Mark and Alan Prince. 1977. On stress and linguistic rhythm. *Linguistic Inquiry* 8, 249–336.

Lombardi, Linda and John J. McCarthy. 1991. Prosodic circumscription in Choctaw morphology. *Phonology* 8, 37–71.

Lowenstamm, Jean and Jonathan Kaye. 1986. Compensatory lengthening in Tiberian Hebrew. In Leo Wetzels and Engin Sezer, eds., *Studies in compensatory lengthening*, pp. 97–132. Dordrecht: Foris.

Marcus, Gary, Steven Pinker, Michael Ullman, Michelle Hollander, T. John Rosen, and Fei Xu. 1992. *Overregularization in language acquisition*. Monographs of the Society for Research in Child Development, 57 (4, Serial No. 228). Also MIT CCS Occasional Paper No. 41.

McCarthy, John J. 1979. *Formal problems in Semitic phonology and morphology*. Doctoral dissertation, MIT, Cambridge, MA.

McCarthy, John J. 1981. A prosodic theory of nonconcatenative morphology. *Linguistic Inquiry* 12, 373–418.

McCarthy, John J. 1986. OCP effects: gemination and antigemination. *Linguistic Inquiry* 17, 207–63.

McCarthy, John J. 1993. A case of surface constraint violation. In Carole Paradis, Darlene LaCharité, and Emmanuel Nikiema, eds., *Constraint-based theories in multilinear phonology*, special issue of *Canadian Journal of Linguistics* 38, 169–95.

McCarthy, John J. 1994. On coronal 'transparency'. Handout from TREND, Santa Cruz, CA.

McCarthy, John J. 2002. *A thematic guide to Optimality Theory*. Cambridge: Cambridge University Press.

McCarthy, John J. and Alan Prince. 1986. *Prosodic Morphology*. Ms. University of Massachusetts at Amherst and Brandeis University, Waltham, MA. [1996, as *Prosodic Morphology 1986*, RuCCS-TR-32, Technical Reports of the Rutgers Center for Cognitive Science. Piscataway: Rutgers University. http://ruccs.rutgers.edu/ruccs/publications.html.]

McCarthy, John J. and Alan Prince. 1988. Quantitative transfer in reduplicative and templatic morphology. In Linguistic Society of Korea, ed., *Linguistics in the Morning Calm* 2, pp. 3–35. Seoul: Hanshin.

McCarthy, John J. and Alan Prince. 1990a. Foot and word in Prosodic Morphology: the Arabic broken plurals. *Natural Language and Linguistic Theory* 8, 209–82.

McCarthy, John J. and Alan Prince. 1990b. Prosodic Morphology and templatic morphology. In Mushira Eid and John J. McCarthy, eds., *Perspectives on Arabic linguistics: papers from the Second Symposium*, pp. 1–54. Amsterdam: Benjamins.

McCarthy, John J. and Alan Prince. 1991a. Prosodic minimality. Lecture presented at University of Illinois Conference on The Organization of Phonology.

McCarthy, John J. and Alan Prince. 1991b. *Linguistics 240: Prosodic Morphology*. Lectures and handouts from 1991 LSA Linguistic Institute Course, University of California, Santa Cruz.

McCarthy, John J. and Alan Prince. 1993a. *Prosodic Morphology I: constraint interaction and satisfaction*. University of Massachusetts, Amherst, and Rutgers University, New Brunswick, NJ. RuCCS-TR-3. ROA-482.

McCarthy, John J. and Alan Prince. 1993b. Generalized Alignment. In Geert Booij and Jaap van Marle, eds., *Yearbook of Morphology 1993*, pp. 79–153. Boston: Kluwer Academic Publishers. ROA-7.

McCarthy, John J. and Alison Taub. 1992. Review of Carole Paradis and Jean-François Prunet, eds., *The special status of coronals*. *Phonology* 9, 363–70.

McClelland, James L. and Kawamoto, Alan H. 1986. Mechanisms of sentence processing: assigning roles to constituents. In David E. Rumelhart, James L. McClelland, and the PDP Research Group, eds., *Parallel Distributed Processing: explorations in the microstructure of cognition*, vol. 2: *Psychological and biological models*, ch. 19, pp. 272–325. Cambridge, MA: MIT Press/Bradford Books.

McMillan, Clayton and Paul Smolensky. 1988. Analyzing a connectionist model as a system of soft rules. In *Proceedings of the Tenth Annual Meeting of the Cognitive Science Society*, pp. 62–8. Montréal: Erlbaum.

Mester, R. Armin. 1986. *Studies in tier structure*. Doctoral dissertation, University of Massachusetts, Amherst. [1988, New York: Garland.]

Mester, R. Armin. 1991. Some remarks on Tongan stress. Ms. Linguistics Board, University of California, Santa Cruz.

Mester, R. Armin. 1992. The quantitative trochee in Latin. SRC-92-06, Syntax Research Center, University of California, Santa Cruz. [1994, *Natural Language and Linguistic Theory* 12, 1–61.]

Michelson, Karin. 1988. *A comparative study of Lake Iroquoian accent*. Dordrecht: Kluwer.

Miikkulainen, Risto and Dyer, Michael G. 1991. Natural language processing with modular PDP networks and distributed lexicon. *Cognitive Science* 15, 343–99.

Mohanan, K. P. 1991. On the bases of radical underspecification. *Natural Language and Linguistic Theory* 9, 285–325.

Mohanan, K. P. 1993. Fields of attraction in phonology. In John Goldsmith, ed., *The last phonological rule*, pp. 61–116. Chicago: University of Chicago Press.

Myers, Scott. 1987a. *Tone and the structure of words in Shona*. Doctoral dissertation, University of Massachusetts, Amherst.

Myers, Scott. 1987b. Vowel shortening in English. *Natural Language and Linguistic Theory* 5, 485–518.

Myers, Scott. 1991. Persistent rules. *Linguistic Inquiry* 22, 315–44.

Nespor, Marina and Irene Vogel. 1986. *Prosodic phonology*. Dordrecht: Foris.

Noske, Roland. 1982. Syllabification and syllable-changing rules in French. In Harry van der Hulst and Norval Smith, eds., *The structure of phonological representations. Part II*, pp. 257–310. Dordrecht: Foris.

Oehrle, Richard. 1971. Some remarks on the role of morphology in the assignment of stress. Ms. MIT, Cambridge, MA.

Paradis, Carole. 1988a. On constraints and repair strategies. *The Linguistic Review* 6, 71–97.

Paradis, Carole. 1988b. Towards a theory of constraint violations. *McGill Working Papers in Linguistics* 5, 1–44.

Paradis, Carole and Jean-François Prunet, eds. 1991. *The special status of coronals: internal and external evidence*. As *Phonetics and Phonology*, vol. 2. New York: Academic Press.

Payne, David. 1981. *The phonology and morphology of Axininca Campa*. University of Texas, Arlington, and Summer Institute of Linguistics.

Payne, David, Judith Payne, and Jorge Sánchez S. 1982. *Morfología, fonología y fonética del Ashéninca del Apurucayali (campa–arawak preandino)*. Serie Lingüística Peruana, 18. Lima: Ministerio de Educación and Instituto Lingüístico de Verano.

Perlmutter, David. 1971. *Deep and surface structure constraints in syntax*. New York: Holt, Rinehart, and Winston.

Piggott, Glyne. 1992. Satisfying the minimal word. Ms. McGill University, Montréal.

Piggott, Glyne and Raj Singh. 1985. The phonology of epenthetic segments. *Canadian Journal of Linguistics* 30, 415–53.

Pinker, Steven. 1984. *Language learnability and language development*. Cambridge, MA: Harvard University Press.

Pinker, Steven and Alan Prince. 1988. On language and connectionism: analysis of a parallel distributed processing model of language acquisition. *Cognition* 28, 73–193.

Pollack, Jordan B. 1988. Recursive auto-associative memory: devising compositional distributed representations. In *Proceedings of the Tenth Annual Meeting of the Cognitive Science Society*, pp. 33–9. Montréal: Erlbaum.

Pollack, Jordan B. 1990. Recursive distributed representation. *Artificial Intelligence* 46, 77–105.

Poser, William J. 1985. Cliticization to NP and Lexical Phonology. In Jeffrey Goldberg, Susannah MacKaye, and Michael Wescoat, eds., *Proceedings of the Fourth West Coast Conference on Formal Linguistics*, pp. 262–72. Stanford: CSLI.

Poser, William J. 1986. Invisibility. *GLOW Newsletter* 16, 63–4.

Poser, William J. 1990. Evidence for foot structure in Japanese. *Language* 66, 78–105.

Prince, Alan. 1976. 'Applying' stress. Ms. University of Massachusetts, Amherst.

Prince, Alan. 1980. A metrical theory for Estonian quantity. *Linguistic Inquiry* 11, 511–62.

Prince, Alan. 1983. Relating to the Grid. *Linguistic Inquiry* 14, 19–100.

Prince, Alan. 1984. Phonology with tiers. In Mark Aronoff and Richard T. Oehrle, eds., *Language sound structure*, pp. 234–44. Cambridge, MA: MIT Press.

Prince, Alan. 1985. Improving tree theory. In Mary Niepokuj, Mary VanClay, Vassiliki Nikiforidou, and Deborah Feder (with Claudia Brugman, Monica Macaulay, Natasha Beery, and Michele Emanatian), eds., *Proceedings of the Eleventh Annual Meeting of the Berkeley Linguistics Society: parasession on poetics, metrics, and prosody*, pp. 471–90. Berkeley: Berkeley Linguistics Society.

Prince, Alan. 1990. Quantitative consequences of rhythmic organization. In Michael Ziolkowski, Manuela Noske, and Karen Deaton, eds., *Papers from the 26th Annual Regional Meeting of the Chicago Linguistic Society*, vol. 2: *Parasession on the syllable in phonetics and phonology*, pp. 355–98. Chicago: Chicago Linguistic Society.

Prince, Alan. 1993. In defense of the number *i*: anatomy of a linear dynamical model of linguistic generalizations. Technical Report RuCCS TR-1, Rutgers Center for Cognitive Science.

Prince, Alan and Paul Smolensky. 1991a. Optimality. Talk given at Arizona Phonology Conference. University of Arizona, Tucson.

Prince, Alan and Paul Smolensky. 1991b. Notes on connectionism and Harmony Theory in linguistics. Technical Report CU-CS-533-91. Dept. of Computer Science, University of Colorado, Boulder.

Prince, Alan and Paul Smolensky. 1992. Optimality: constraint interaction in generative grammar. Revised and augmented handout from talk delivered at West Coast Conference on Formal Linguistics, February 22, UCLA.

Prince, Alan and Paul Smolensky. 1993. *Optimality Theory: constraint interaction in generative grammar*. Technical Report CU-CS-696-95. RuCCS-TR-2. [2002, as ROA-537.]

Pulleyblank, Douglas. 1983. *Tone in Lexical Phonology*. Dordrecht: Reidel.

Pyle, Charles. 1972. On eliminating BM's. In Paul M. Peranteau and Judith N. Levi, eds., *Papers from the 8th Regional Meeting, Chicago Linguistic Society*, pp. 516–32. Chicago: Chicago Linguistic Society.

Rager, John and George Berg. 1990. A connectionist model of motion and government in Chomsky's government-binding theory. *Connection Science* 2, 35–52.

Rizzi, Luigi. 1990. *Relativized Minimality*. Linguistic Inquiry Monograph 16. Cambridge, MA: MIT Press.

Rosenthall, Sam. 1994. *The phonology of vowels and glides*. Doctoral dissertation, University of Massachusetts, Amherst. ROA-126.

Rubach, Jerzy and Gert Booij. 1985. A grid theory of stress in Polish. *Lingua* 66, 281–319.

Rumelhart, David E. and James L. McClelland. 1986. On learning the past tenses of English verbs. In James L. McClelland, David E. Rumelhart, and the PDP Research Group, eds., *Parallel Distributed Processing: explorations in the microstructure of cognition*, vol. 2: *Psychological and biological models*, ch. 18, pp. 216–71. Cambridge, MA: MIT Press/Bradford Books.

Rumelhart, David E., Paul Smolensky, James L. McClelland, and Geoffrey E. Hinton. 1986. Schemata and sequential thought in PDP models. In James L. McClelland, David E. Rumelhart, and the PDP Research Group, eds., *Parallel Distributed Processing: explorations in the microstructure of cognition*, vol. 2: *Psychological and biological models*, ch. 14, pp. 7–57. Cambridge, MA: MIT Press/Bradford Books.

Samek-Lodovici, Vieri. 1992a. Universal constraints and morphological gemination: a crosslinguistic study. Ms. Brandeis University, Waltham, MA.

Samek-Lodovici, Vieri. 1992b. A unified analysis of crosslinguistic morphological gemination. In *Proceedings of CONSOLE-1*. ROA-149.

Sapir, Edward. 1930. The Southern Paiute language. *Proceedings of the American Academy of Arts and Sciences* 65, 1–296.

Schachter, Paul. 1987. Tagalog. In Bernard Comrie, ed., *The world's major languages*, ch. 47, pp. 936–58. London and Sydney: Croom Helm.

Schachter, Paul and Fe Otanes. 1972. *Tagalog reference grammar*. Berkeley: University of California Press.

Scobbie, James. 1991. *Attribute Value Phonology*. Doctoral dissertation, University of Edinburgh.

Scobbie, James. 1992. Towards Declarative Phonology. *Edinburgh Working Papers in Cognitive Science* 7, 1–26.

Selkirk, Elisabeth. 1980a. Prosodic domains in phonology: Sanskrit revisited. In Mark Aronoff and Mary-Louise Kean, eds., *Juncture*, pp. 107–29. Saratoga, CA: Anma Libri.

Selkirk, Elisabeth. 1980b. The role of prosodic categories in English word stress. *Linguistic Inquiry* 11, 563–605.

Selkirk, Elisabeth. 1981. Epenthesis and degenerate syllables in Cairene Arabic. In Hagit Borer and Joseph Aoun, eds., *Theoretical issues in the grammar of the Semitic languages: MIT Working Papers in Linguistics* 3, pp. 111–40. Cambridge, MA: Dept. of Linguistics, MIT.

Selkirk, Elisabeth. 1984. *Phonology and syntax: the relation between sound and structure*. Cambridge, MA: MIT Press.

Selkirk, Elisabeth. 1986. On derived domains in sentence phonology. *Phonology Yearbook* 3, 371–405.

Selkirk, Elisabeth. 1993. The prosodic structure of functional elements: affixes, clitics, and words. Handout of talk presented at the Signal to Syntax Conference, Brown University, Providence.

Sherer, Tim. 1994. *Prosodic phonotactics*. Doctoral dissertation, University of Massachusetts, Amherst. ROA-54.

Singh, Raj. 1987. Well-formedness conditions and phonological theory. In Wolfgang Dressler et al., eds., *Phonologica 1984*, pp. 273–85. Cambridge: Cambridge University Press.

Smolensky, Paul. 1983. Schema selection and stochastic inference in modular environments. In *Proceedings of the National Conference on Artificial Intelligence*, pp. 378–82. Washington, DC: American Association for Artificial Intelligence.

Smolensky, Paul. 1984. The mathematical role of self-consistency in parallel computation. In *Proceedings of the Sixth Annual Conference of the Cognitive Science Society*, pp. 319–25. Boulder, CO: Erlbaum.

Smolensky, Paul. 1986. Information processing in dynamical systems: foundations of Harmony Theory. In David E. Rumelhart, James L. McClelland, and the PDP Research Group, eds., *Parallel Distributed Processing: explorations in the microstructure of cognition*, vol. 1: *Foundations*, ch. 6, pp. 194–281. Cambridge, MA: MIT Press/Bradford Books.

Smolensky, Paul. 1987. On variable binding and the representation of symbolic structures in connectionist systems. Technical Report CU-CS-355-87, Dept. of Computer Science, University of Colorado, Boulder.

Smolensky, Paul. 1988. On the proper treatment of connectionism. *The Behavioral and Brain Sciences* 11, 1–74.

Smolensky, Paul. 1990. Tensor product variable binding and the representation of symbolic structures in connectionist networks. *Artificial Intelligence* 46, 159–216.

Smolensky, Paul. 1995. Constituent structure and explanation in an integrated connectionist/symbolic cognitive architecture. In Cynthia Macdonald and Graham Macdonald, eds., *The philosophy of psychology: debates on psychological explanation*, pp. 221–90. Oxford: Blackwell.

Smolensky, Paul, Géraldine Legendre, and Yoshiro Miyata. 1992. Principles for an integrated connectionist/symbolic theory of higher cognition. Technical Report CU-CS-600-92, Dept. of Computer Science, University of Colorado, Boulder.

Smolensky, Paul and Mary Riley. 1984. Harmony Theory: problem solving, parallel cognitive models, and thermal physics. Technical report 8404, Institute for Cognitive Science, University of California, San Diego.

Sommerstein, Alan H. 1974. On phonotactically motivated rules. *Journal of Linguistics* 10, 71–94.

Spring, Cari. 1990. *Implications of Axininca Campa for Prosodic Morphology and reduplication*. Doctoral dissertation, University of Arizona, Tucson.

St. John, Mark F. and James L. McClelland. 1990. Learning and applying contextual constraints in sentence comprehension. *Artificial Intelligence* 46, 217–58.

Stampe, David. 1969. The acquisition of phonetic representation. In Robert I. Binnick, Alice Davidson, Georgia M. Green, and Jerry L. Morgan, eds., *Papers from the Fifth Regional Meeting of the Chicago Linguistic Society*, pp. 433–44. Chicago: Chicago Linguistic Society.

Stampe, David. 1973. On chapter nine. In Michael Kenstowicz and Charles Kisseberth, eds., *Issues in phonological theory*, pp. 44–52. The Hague: Mouton.

Stampe, David. 1973/79. *A dissertation in Natural Phonology*. Doctoral dissertation, University of Chicago. [1979, New York: Garland Publishing.]

Steriade, Donca. 1982. *Greek prosodies and the nature of syllabification*. Doctoral dissertation, MIT, Cambridge, MA.

Steriade, Donca. 1988. Greek accent: a case for preserving structure. *Linguistic Inquiry* 19, 271–314.

Stevens, Kenneth and S. J. Keyser. 1989. Primary features and their enhancement in consonants. *Language* 65, 81–106.

Stevens, Kenneth, S. J. Keyser, and H. Kawasaki. 1986. Toward a phonetic and phonological theory of redundant features. In Joseph Perkell and Dennis Klatt, eds., *Invariance and variability in speech processes*, pp. 241–54. Hillsdale, NJ: Erlbaum.

Stolcke, Andreas. 1989. Unification as constraint satisfaction in structured connectionist networks. *Neural Computation* 1, 559–67.

Stump, Gregory. 1989. A note on Breton pluralization and the Elsewhere Condition. *Natural Language and Linguistic Theory* 7, 261–73.

Topping, Donald M. 1973. *Chamorro reference grammar*. Honolulu: University Press of Hawaii.

Touretzky, David S. 1989. Towards a connectionist phonology: the "many maps" approach to sequence manipulation. In *Proceedings of the Eleventh Annual Conference of the Cognitive Science Society*, pp. 188–95. Ann Arbor, MI: Erlbaum.

Touretzky, David S., ed. 1991. Special issue: *Connectionist approaches to language learning*. *Machine Learning* 7, 105–252.

Touretzky, David S. and Deirdre W. Wheeler. 1991. Sequence manipulation using parallel mapping networks. *Neural Computation* 3, 98–109.

Vennemann, Theo. 1972. On the theory of syllabic phonology. *Linguistische Berichte* 18, 1–18.

Visch, Ellis. 1989. A metrical theory of rhythmic stress phenomena. (*Een metrische theorie van ritmische klemtoonverschijnselen*). Dordrecht: ICG.

Voltaire. 1759. *Candide ou l'Optimisme*. Revised 1761 [for the worse, in our view]; tr. Lowell Bair as *Candide by Voltaire*, 1959. New York: Bantam Books.

Wertheimer, Max. 1923. Untersuchungen zur Lehre von der Gestalt II. *Psychologische Forschung* 4, 301–50. Translated as "Laws of organization in perceptual forms," in W. D. Ellis, ed., 1938, *A source book of Gestalt psychology*, pp. 71–88. London: Routledge and Kegan Paul.

Wheeler, Deirdre. 1981. *Aspects of a categorial theory of phonology*. Doctoral dissertation, University of Massachusetts, Amherst.

Wheeler, Deirdre. 1988. Consequences of some categorially motivated phonological assumptions. In Richard Oehrle, Emmon Bach, and Deirdre Wheeler, eds., *Categorial grammars and natural language structures*, pp. 467–88. Dordrecht: Reidel.

Wheeler, Deirdre W. and Touretzky, David S. 1993. A connectionist implementation of cognitive phonology. In John Goldsmith, ed., *The last phonological rule*, pp. 146–72. Chicago: University of Chicago Press.

Wilkinson, Karina. 1986. Syllable structure and Lardil phonology. Ms. University of Massachusetts, Amherst.

Wilkinson, Karina. 1988. Prosodic structure and Lardil phonology. *Linguistic Inquiry* 19, 325–34.

Wiltshire, Caroline. 1992. *Syllabification and rule application in Harmonic Phonology*. Doctoral dissertation, University of Chicago.

Woodbury, Anthony. 1981. *Study of the Chevak dialect of Central Yupik Eskimo*. Doctoral dissertation, University of California, Berkeley.

Wurzel, Wolfgang. 1985. On morphological naturalness. *Nordic Journal of Linguistics* 7, 145–63.

Yip, Moira. 1988. The Obligatory Contour Principle and phonological rules: a loss of identity. *Linguistic Inquiry* 19, 65–100.

Yip, Moira. 1993a. Cantonese loanword phonology and Optimality Theory. *Journal of East Asian Linguistics* 2.3, 261–93.

Yip, Moira. 1993b. Phonological constraints, optimality, and phonetic realization in Cantonese. University of Pennsylvania Colloquium.

Zec, Draga. 1988. *Sonority constraints on syllable structure*. Doctoral dissertation, Stanford University, Stanford, CA.

Zec, Draga. 1994. Coda constraints and conditions on syllable weight. Ms. Cornell University, Ithaca. [1995, Sonority constraints on syllable structure. *Phonology* 12, 85–129.]

Zoll, Cheryl. 1992a. When syllables collide: a theory of alternating quantity. Ms. Brandeis University, Waltham, MA.

Zoll, Cheryl 1992b. Remarks on the OCP. Personal communication.

Zoll, Cheryl. 1993. Ghost consonants and optimality. In Erin Duncan, Michele Hart, and Philip Spaelti, eds., *Proceedings of the Twelfth West Coast Conference on Formal Linguistics*, pp. 183–99. Stanford: Stanford Linguistics Association.

Zonneveld, Wim. 1976. Destressing in Halle's English stress rules. *Linguistic Inquiry* 7, 520–5.

Index of Constraints

Index of Languages

General Index